Learning to Compete in European Universities

Learning to Compete in European Universities

From Social Institution to Knowledge Business

Edited by

Maureen McKelvey

Professor, Industrial Management, School of Business, Economics and Law, University of Gothenburg, Sweden

and

Magnus Holmén

Associate Professor, Department of Technology Management and Economics, Chalmers University of Technology, Sweden

Edward Elgar

Cheltenham, UK • Northampton, MA, USA

Published by
Edward Elgar Publishing Limited
The Lypiatts
15 Lansdown Road
Cheltenham
Glos GL50 2JA
UK

Edward Elgar Publishing, Inc.
William Pratt House
9 Dewey Court
Northampton
Massachusetts 01060
USA

Paperback edition 2010

A catalogue record for this book
is available from the British Library

Library of Congress Control Number: 2008939765

Mixed Sources
Product group from well-managed
forests and other controlled sources
www.fsc.org Cert no. SA-COC-1565
© 1996 Forest Stewardship Council
FSC

ISBN 978 1 84844 001 2 (cased)
ISBN 978 1 84980 434 9 (paperback)

Printed and bound by MPG Books Group, UK

Contents

Figures

Tables

Contributors

Mats Benner, Associate Professor and Director, Research Policy Institute, Lund University, Sweden

Andrea Bonaccorsi, Professor of Economics and Management, Pisa University, Italy

Shiri M. Breznitz, PhD, University of Cambridge, United Kingdom

Anders Broström, PhD student, Division of Economics, Royal Institute of Technology, Sweden

Robin Cowan, Professor, UNU–MERIT, University of Maastricht, the Netherlands and Professor, BETA, Université Louis Pasteur, Strasbourg, France

William B. Cowan, Associate Professor, David R. Cheriton School of Computer Science, University of Waterloo, Canada

Enrico Deiaco, Managing Director, The Swedish Institute for Studies in Education and Research, Sweden

Maryann P. Feldman, Professor, University of North Carolina, USA

Luke Georghiou, Professor, University of Manchester, United Kingdom

Ana M. Gren, Researcher, The Swedish Institute for Studies in Education and Research, Sweden

Olof Hallonsten, PhD student, Research Policy Institute, Lund University, Sweden

Magnus Holmén, Associate Professor, Department of Technology Management and Economics, Chalmers University of Technology, Sweden

Mattias Johansson, PhD student, Center of Entrepreneurship, University of Oslo, Norway

Francesco Lissoni, Associate Professor, University of Brescia, Italy, and Deputy Director, CESPRI-Bocconi, Italy.

Daniel Ljungberg, PhD student, Department of Technology Management and Economics, Chalmers University of Technology, Sweden

Patrick Llerena, Professor, BETA, Université Louis Pasteur, Strasbourg, France

Mats Magnusson, Associate Professor, Department of Technology Management and Economics, Chalmers University of Technology, Sweden

Maureen McKelvey, Professor of Industrial Management, School of Business, Economics and Law, University of Gothenburg, Sweden

Göran Melin, Senior researcher, The Swedish Institute for Studies in Education and Research, Sweden

Bulat Sanditov, Researcher, UNU–MERIT, University of Maastricht, the Netherlands

Christian Sandström, PhD student, Department of Technology Management and Economics, Chalmers University of Technology, Sweden

Matteo Versiglioni, master student, Department of Technology Management and Economics, Chalmers University of Technology, Sweden

Preface

We wrote this book for several reasons. One is simply that we want to understand and explain more about competition and evolutionary economic processes. Our curiosity does not stop solely at the doorstep of firms. Indeed, we wanted to 'test' whether relatively controversial and vague ideas about competition in European universities can be developed, from an evolutionary and innovation perspective. Americans have of course, known about competition and specialization of universities for a very long time. But what about Europe? What is going on here; do universities increasingly behave like firms or are they changing in some other manner? Participants in the workshops, presentations and writings in the project 'Universities as Knowledge Environments of the Future' sometimes surprised us by telling us we were dead wrong or sometimes surprised us by telling us we were 'too right, mate', followed up by, they wished we weren't.

Yet another reason was that we felt that what happens at European universities now and in the near future will affect the future competitiveness of European societies. Now that is a big statement! But we have worked in, talked to researchers, and visited, universities in Australia, the USA, China, Singapore, and many European countries. Many feel that Europe might be falling behind – and yet few seem to have thought seriously about the consequences on firms and society. Or, to put it in EU and OECD language: the question of what is happening, and what can happen to universities – and to their personnel and services – seems particularly urgent to address when more and more European countries argue that they have reached the knowledge society. EU and other national governments have made the argument that despite outsourcing of production and back-office services, 'knowledge' production will remain the basis of competitiveness in these countries.

Many writers seem to assume that Europe can continue competing in 'knowledge' production. That would suggest that European universities are either doubly important – because they increasingly will be the basis of future competitiveness – or else they could become increasingly irrelevant, if Europe loses out in the global competitive game. Still, whatever the new basis of competition in the knowledge society will be like, Europe has to be part of the game. Most of the leaders of universities know this – but perhaps the stakes are far higher than public policy leaders and firm leaders have so far realized.

A final reason is that academic books like this one provide us editors – whom are active researchers, teachers and societal translators – with an opportunity to work with the larger issues and analysis, rather than the extremely specific and detailed focus of writing journal articles. Many of these chapters will be sharpened, revised, and submitted as journal articles. Still, they have to be based on scientific methods and literature to be included here. This book as a whole – and the underlying meetings and work – does provide us the opportunity to debate, discuss, provoke, confirm and ask questions about larger issues of emergent competition and strategies within universities. Finally, this type of book provides a training ground, so that younger researchers and PhD students can design studies and write in interaction with more senior researchers. They, after all, will create the future and will be the knowledge workers of the future. Thus, despite the metrification of science to journal publications and citations, a book like this offers us the chance to consider how different bits of science link together and form an understanding of a whole, which is not really possible from any of the parts.

This book resulted from the project 'Universities as Knowledge Environments of the Future', financed by SISTER (Swedish Institute for Studies in Education and Research www.sister.nu) and their owner-financiers.

Initially, many pieces were written specifically about Sweden, but then it was decided to work on this international book, which kicked-off in December 2005. Its ideas will be further developed through the EU Network of Excellence DIME, Dynamics of Institutions and Markets in Europe (www.dime-org.eu).

A special thanks to Enrico Deiaco for persistently encouraging and arguing for new ways of thinking about what universities do and how they do it. He took the initiative to this work, which involved three Swedish research teams at SISTER, RIDE-IMIT and at CIRCLE/Lund.

We wish to express our thank to all the people involved, whom have been authors, discussants, participants or reviewers. In addition, we particularly thank Peter Schilling and Olle Edqvist, both from SISTER. Peter gave many good comments and led much of the Swedish work. Olle on the other hand never stopped asking questions. Indeed, Olle has forever been challenging us to explain what we meant by competition and learning to compete. His comments prompted us to take at least some of these vague concepts, and instead explain and be more specific about if and how they apply to the university sector, which has been extremely valuable for writing the book.

We wish to thank the following foundations and institutions that financed various parts of the research project: Swedish Foundation for

Strategic Research; The Bank of Sweden Tercentenary Foundation; The Knowledge Foundation; The Swedish Foundation for International Cooperation and Higher Education; Centre of Excellence for Science and Innovation Studies (CESIS); R&D; Innovation and Dynamics Economies (RIDE) at the Chalmers University of Technology and the Institute for Management of Innovation and Technology (IMIT).

Finally, we wish to thank Daniel Ljungberg for his never-ending enthusiasm and help in finalizing the manuscript! We are much obliged!

Enrico Deiaco
Maureen McKelvey
Magnus Holmén

1. Introduction

Maureen McKelvey and Magnus Holmén

1. INTRODUCTION

This book, *Learning to Compete in European Universities: From Social Institution to Knowledge Business* will challenge the reader by asking how and why European universities are changing and learning to compete.[1] Anglo-Saxon universities, particularly in USA, UK and Australia, have been subject to, and responded to market-based competition in higher education for a long time. We will argue that Continental and Nordic universities and higher education institutes (HEI) are now facing similar pressures that are leading to structural transformation of the university sector. Thus, one of the major societal institutions in Europe is undergoing transformation, and becoming a knowledge business. Regardless of whether one believes that this increasing competition has positive or negative effects, the transformation will affect academics and students, as well as the ability of firms and nations to compete in the global knowledge society. This book provides some steps towards explaining what is going on; towards analysing how individuals, groups and organizations are responding; and towards discussing the implications for society and universities.

This book is designed to raise debates and stimulate new research agendas about this transformation of the university sector and about the underlying need to learn and develop new types of organizational forms and behaviour, as well as strategic action. Our research shows that European universities are moving from a national institution providing a public good, to a business delivering services to students and various other stakeholders.[2] In this conceptualization, universities are delivering knowledge-based services such as education, research and different types of societal interactions like commercialization of scientific results. Later chapters review relevant academic literature in relation to specific changes within universities and higher education. As a whole, this book contributes to new debates because it focuses upon new issues such as strategy, learning, diversification, and because some empirical results challenge 'accepted wisdom' about Europe.

Empirically, the evidence suggests that European universities have not yet learnt to compete globally, with the possible exception of the universities in the UK. *The Economist* (26 February 2005, p. 63) framed the debates about European universities, in comparison with American universities and those further afield. 'There used to be three near-certainties about higher education [in Europe]. It was supplied on a national basis, mostly to local students. It was government-regulated. And competition and profit were almost unknown concepts. . . . How that has changed.' *Newsweek* (August 2006) stresses instead that universities must become global, in order to compete. However, not all universities will be able to be 'globally competitive'. Indeed, globalization of research and education is only one of several strategies available for universities. Instead, we interpret the changes in a broader way that universities need to learn and change how they compete, and understand their role in relation to global collaborators and competitors.

This conceptualization of 'learning to compete' reflects the relative position of European universities, especially compared to Anglo-Saxon universities but also in relation to the rapid development of universities in India and China. This phenomenon of a new competitive regime has been visible in the USA, Australia and UK for a number of decades but is now more strongly felt within Continental and Nordic Europe. So this book addresses the formal and informal roles of universities and university staff and what they can and should do in this new selection environment. Certainly, one can argue whether these shifts necessarily move universities closer towards a more market oriented mode in a traditional economics sense but this book explores broader issues of learning, strategies, and competencies, during this period of transformation towards a more competition based mode within Europe. The argument of the book is that significant changes are underway and that these universities and higher education institutes must learn to compete – or to react to reverse the current trend towards 'knowledge based businesses' by better articulating and protecting the traditional values and contributions of universities to society.

The new competitive regime for universities in Europe and Asia depends upon the following factors: (a) Increased globalization of students, resources and faculty; (b) Changes in national public policy for education, science and innovation; and (c) Changes in business R&D strategies, which are attempting to make university research linked to firms' R&D strategies (Slaughter and Leslie, 1997; Geuna, 1999; Chesbrough, 2003; Lawton Smith, 2006). At the moment, the sense is that these economic and political changes will lead to new societal rules and institutions, which fundamentally will change higher education (Fuller, 2000; Reichert, 2006).

This view affects the present and has implications for the future. Regardless of whether colleges, universities and institutes are publicly or privately owned, they are facing new pressures within a more business-oriented environment, or what we call the new competitive regime of universities. These pressures are placing high demands on the organizations to learn to develop strategies and react. Relevant examples are numerous. They include, but are not limited to:

- Expansion from elite to mass education;
- Bologna process to reform and unify degrees in Europe;
- Reforms of research through the European Research Area;
- New national mechanisms for managing the flow of national resources to teaching and education;
- Increasing emphasis on university–industry relations, especially commercialization through patents and academic entrepreneurship.

European universities should deliver knowledge-based services. Moreover, European universities and their financiers are increasingly demanding not only that these services are performed, but also that they are excellent and address relevant societal problems, as formulated in the political and policy domains. These empirical changes demand new ways to conceptualize and explain universities as actors, where strategic processes may be driven 'top-down' through leadership and 'bottom-up' through research groups and individuals.

In this new situation, universities will have to be 'knowledge businesses' rather than 'societal institutions', and this has implications not only for the future of universities but also the 'knowledge economies'. Some organizations will never enter (or 'lose') the global race and instead find new positions and missions at the local and national levels. Clearly, the race up the ladder is already happening, because we can clearly see that many universities and colleges are already trying to position themselves globally, and to raise their standings in the rankings. National rankings and effects are also predicted.

The Americans – followed by the very top British universities – have impressive leads over Europe and the rest of the world. In 2006, for example, seven of the top ten universities in the *Financial Times* survey were American, and the other three were British. The first Continental European university was at 18th place in 2006, and it had dropped seven rankings since 2005. Another recently widely cited ranking is the Shanghai Jiao Tong University Rankings.[3] While the rankings are measured through somewhat different metrics the Chinese survey shows similar results at the national level as the *FT* survey.

European leaders in politics, science and universities have noticed the American lead and the European lag, and they are responding in different ways. European leaders in most countries are increasingly focused upon the need to compete for the top faculty, top students and staff internationally (Ramsden 1998; Neave et al. 2006). Ireland and Germany, for example, have had explicit strategies for repatriating leading scientists active elsewhere and for promoting excellence. Some countries try to focus upon more specialized niches to promote excellence. For example, the Nordic countries are focusing on large-scale and focused research environments and the benefits of regional colleges when interacting with local industry (Bauer et al., 1999; Schilling, 2005; Melander, 2006; Benner and Sörlin, 2007).

Of course, Anglo-Saxon countries moved towards a competitive model much earlier than Continental and Nordic countries. As compared to the general European picture, the United Kingdom is in some ways similar to Australia (Clark 1998, 2004; Marginson and Considine 2000). Their relatively favorable position in attracting international students, for example, could be due to an early move into a competitive regime for research funding and students, but it can also be due to less imitable aspects such as the inherent advantage of the English language. Hence, the fact that the Continental and Nordic countries are 'latecomers' raises interesting strategic issues about the extent to which these universities and countries should imitate given strategies or develop new ways of developing competencies and attracting resources. This book therefore concentrates on those countries, but will make some comparisons with the Anglo-Saxon countries.

This book differs from much of the existing literature reviewed in its various chapters as it proposes a new line of research on the strategic action and economic transformation of universities per se. Such topics are just beginning to be addressed, as demonstrated by projects at the international forefront. Several books recently published on related topics include Geuna (1999), Bonaccorsi and Daraio (2007), and Lawton Smith (2006).

The book has thirteen chapters, and the analysis is structured around four themes, namely 'Emergent Strategy', 'Differentiation and Specialization', 'Rethinking University–Industry Relations' and 'Reflections'.

Section 2 provides detailed information about each of the chapters, as each contributes to a specific theme and to the overall analysis put forward in the book. Relevant literature can be found within each chapter, which may include evolutionary economics, higher education, innovation and strategic management, innovation systems, science policy and triple helix. Some chapters also address specific topics of relevance to public policy, such as the effects of the search for excellence, new interpretations of university–industry relationships, and how universities evolve strategies to survive. This multidisciplinary approach is necessary because this book addresses a problem area that crosses several boundaries. Section 3 then goes further in discussing the four themes and also provides a comparison across chapters. This section helps explain why and how the book introduces a series of more general ideas, analytical tools and theoretical approaches by which we can analyse universities as competing within knowledge-based services. Thus, Sections 2 and 3 provide a useful 'roadmap' of the book for the reader.

2. DETAILED INFORMATION ON CHAPTERS

This section provides detailed information on the chapters. It also provides an abstract for each chapter. They are in turn organized within four horizontal themes, which represent broad ideas and research questions of relevance to this book:

1. Emergent strategy
2. Differentiation and specialization
3. Rethinking university–industry relations
4. Reflections

The first theme is 'emergent strategy', which includes Chapters 2 to 4.

Chapter 2, 'Exploring university alliances and comparable academic cooperation structures' is written by Enrico Deiaco, Ana M. Gren and Göran Melin. The main emphasis is to explore the creation of alliances and collaboration between universities. Ten major alliances are analysed in terms of motives and outcomes, with particular emphasis on the rationale of university leaders. These are mostly European cases, although several of them include partners from the USA and Asia. The chapter provides a framework for analysing the benefits and risks of this strategic option. The authors recommend that if alliances are to provide positive benefits, alliances should open up opportunities for interaction at many levels between the universities, and also facilitate large-scale research grants. This chapter thus explores an option to 'going it alone', which many European organizations are pursuing to gain excellence and resources on the global scene.

Chapter 3, 'Strategy to join the elite: merger and the 2015 agenda at the University of Manchester' is written by Luke Georghiou. Two of the UK's research universities with a shared history, the Victoria University of Manchester and UMIST, merged in October 2004 to form the country's largest university. The rationale for this merger was that world-class universities drive economic development yet the UK's world class universities

– Oxford, Cambridge, Imperial, UCL, and LSE are all in one region – the prosperous South East. There was a perceived need for a world-class university in the North of England and Manchester was the obvious base. This chapter analyses the motivations and process of the merger and reviews the strategy of the new University of Manchester as set out in its Vision Document *Manchester 2015*: 'To make the University of Manchester, already an internationally distinguished centre of research, innovation learning and scholarly inquiry, one of the leading universities in the world by 2015.' The nine-part strategy is defined in terms of key performance indicators, which are assessed in an annual planning and accountability cycle. The strategy has several distinctive features including a policy of 'iconic appointments' and a desire to make the university distinctive from other UK leaders in its social inclusivity and engagement with the community. Substantial challenges are faced in achieving these goals. Hence, this chapter focuses on how the university as an organization can introduce a major change to reach strategic goals.

Chapter 4, 'Large-scale international facilities within the organization: MAX lab within Lund University' is written by Olof Hallonsten and Mats Benner. This chapter analyses how and where specialized labs as part of international 'big science' fit within the strategic processes of universities in Sweden. Following de Solla Price's seminal book *Little Science, Big Science* (1963), many studies have focused upon characteristics of scientific endeavour becoming international, large-scale and with personal relationships as boundaries amongst the 'invisible college' of scientists. This chapter provides a detailed case study, which juxtaposes the 'big science' carried out within the MAX lab on synchrotron lights with the university strategy process of its host, Lund University, and of the peculiarities of Swedish science policy. This chapter therefore raises interesting questions about how the workings and notions of big science lie within the strategy process carried out within universities. It also addresses where the responsibilities for initiating and running large facilities should lie, when there is a broad constituency, including public, private, multiple disciplines, and national and international stakeholders. This chapter mainly focuses on the lab, as an arena within which research groups, universities and science policy-makers interact.

The second horizontal theme is 'differentiation and specialization', which includes Chapters 5 and 6.

Chapter 5, 'Division of academic labour is limited by the size of the market: strategy and differentiation of universities in doctoral education' is written by Andrea Bonaccorsi. A key notion for competition is differentiation and performance. The chapter explores the notion of differentiation of higher education institutions, from a quantitative point of view. Faced with waves of increase in participation rates (the ratio between young cohorts attending universities and young population in the same age class), universities in Western countries have progressively differentiated their structure, following a process of specialization in terms of offering profile and resource mixes used. Following Smith, Young and Stigler, the author argues that following increases in student numbers and deregulation, universities find it increasingly difficult to procure funding and high-quality space while competing on all dimensions in output space as decisions become too slow and resources are spread too thin. This necessitates a reorientation towards differentiation in their strategic profile. The chapter introduces an economic analysis of the notion of differentiation of universities and proposes a quantitative measure. The general notion of differentiation is applied to the activity of universities in doctoral education and the empirical observations are on emergent strategies, not deliberate strategic decisions. The measure is based on the availability of the large dataset created by the project Aquameth that, for the first time, has integrated census microdata on all universities in several European countries for a decade. This chapter explores these issues following an original approach, based on quantitative indicators built upon a large dataset of comparable microdata. Data refer to all universities in Finland, the Netherlands, Switzerland, the United Kingdom, Spain, and Italy. A way of developing an overall measurement of institutional differentiation is built using information theory and entropy measures. The variation of this metrics over time and across countries is observed. The chapter organizes the analysed countries into (a) institutional inertia, (b) dynamic differentiation, (c) institutional abundance, and (d) consolidated differentiation.

Chapter 6, 'Polarization of the Swedish university sector: structural characteristics and positioning' is written by Daniel Ljungberg, Mattias Johansson and Maureen McKelvey. It relates the structural characteristics of Swedish universities, to the propensity of different categories of university to attract external research funding, including industry financing. Existing literature about the ability of universities to obtain research grants in general, and to obtain industrial funding for research in particular, have focused on questions such as the quality of the research performed, the impact of informal networks in creating constructed communities, and the 'Matthew effect' for individual researchers. While these streams of literature raise interesting relevant issues about the quality and orientation of research, this chapter takes a different angle. By addressing structural characteristics, it is related to debates about the need for critical mass and excellence, not only within research groups but also within universities. These notions leads first to a categorization of the Swedish university sector, and second to the ability of the different universities to obtain external research funding. The chapter draws upon a national database of statistical material reported to the government and additional sources to test these ideas. It thus addresses the university sector in Sweden, based on time-scale data at the micro-level of specific universities.

The third horizontal theme is 'rethinking university–industry relations', which includes Chapters 7 to 10.

Chapter 7, 'The American experience in university technology transfer' is written by Maryann Feldman and Shiri Breznitz. This chapter examines the American experience with technology transfer, recounting the history of university involvement with industry in the search for additional sources of revenue. American universities have been more active in formal university tech transfer and for longer than other countries. American research universities entered a new era in 1980 with the passage of the Bayh–Dole Act. Moving beyond publication and teaching, the traditional modes of disseminating academic inventions, universities now actively manage their discoveries in a process known as technology transfer. All American research universities now have operations dedicated to securing invention disclosures from campus research and establishing intellectual property rights over them. These offices then work to license the rights to use the intellectual property, either to existing firms or encouraging the formation of new firms for this purpose. This chapter documents the formal establishment of university technology transfer offices and other entities such as arm's-length foundations to manage commercial relationships. Finally, the chapter analyses the growth in litigation over university IP ownership and licensing agreements.

Chapter 8, 'Academic patenting in Europe: evidence on France, Italy from the KEINS database' is written by Francesco Lissoni, Patrick Llerena, Maureen McKelvey, and Bulat Sanditov. It asks whether national institutions determine patenting behaviour of academics located in three different European countries. Cleaned patent data drawn from the CESPRI database on EPO patents, was gathered by the researchers, for each of the three countries over the period 1978 to 2004. We would expect differing national institutions to affect propensity to the patent. However, the results indicate that the patenting patterns are similar across the countries, and also within scientific disciplines across countries. Comparisons are made with evidence from the USA, indicating similar levels of academic patenting and firm involvement. The chapter thus focuses upon the patenting of academics at the individual level, and uses that data to describe the patenting behaviour in terms of countries and disciplines.

Chapter 9, 'The Forgotten individuals: attitudes and skills in academic commercialization in Sweden' is written by Mats Magnusson, Maureen McKelvey, and Matteo Versiglioni. It addresses whether and why individual researchers have the skills and attitudes necessary for commercialization in Sweden, and place this in relation to the services provided by the university for commercialization. The Swedish innovation system has been focused upon explicitly organizing the support structure of an individual university, and includes services such as technology transfer offices, access to patent attorneys, localities of science parks, consultancy for business plans and setting up companies, etc. Much current public policy and also the strategy documents of specific universities stress the need to build such large-scale systems. This chapter analyses commercialization and patenting, through a questionnaire to 1200 Swedish university researchers, with a 24 per cent response rate. The researchers work within six research fields, namely fluid mechanics, wood technology, biotechnology, computer science, automatic control and inorganic chemistry. The questionnaire of Swedish academics also includes research groups at different universities within these fields. All research centres financed by the strategic research grants had a mission to both develop 'high quality science' and to 'promote interaction with industry' within their field. This chapter thus turns the question from the national innovation system towards skills and attitudes of the individual researcher.

Chapter 10, 'Elite European universities and the R&D subsidiaries of MNEs' by Anders Broström, Maureen McKelvey, and Christian Sandström. It analyses why large multinational firms are willing to invest resources in long-term collaboration with leading universities. This chapter is based on interviews with the multinationals at universities in Sweden, Switzerland, and the United Kingdom. The issue of how and why multinational corporations are willing to invest in longer-term collaboration with universities relates back to the core of the 'positive' interpretation of the knowledge society for Europe – namely how to remain an attraction node for R&D. This chapter thus moves to the perspective of the firm, in their interactions with university-based researchers active in top universities in different fields.

The fourth horizontal theme is 'reflections', which includes Chapters 11 to 13.

Chapter 11, 'Running the marathon' is written by William Cowan, Robin Cowan and Patrick Llerena. It raises issues and implications about the rate of change and the unintended consequences of introducing competition mechanisms into European universities. It provides ideas and thoughts, thereby providing room for reflection at a time when university leaders are quick to proclaim they are 'competing' and economists are increasingly giving advice about productivity and efficiency. The authors argue that this is deeply problematic. In particular, the chapter differentiates between the 'university of culture' and the 'university of innovation' where too much focus on the latter may lead to dire, unintended consequences. Much recent policy making, the authors argue, is based upon a flawed view of what the university is for. The focus on competition in straightforward metrics misses the point that universities should be much more long-term in their focus. Consequently, the chapter discusses the overarching goal of the university in relation to the speed of change of this societal institution and in relation to university–industry relations.

Chapter 12, 'What does it mean conceptually that universities compete?' is written by Enrico Deiaco, Magnus Holmén and Maureen McKelvey. The modern rhetoric states that universities compete but is hardly very precise in formulating what this entails. This chapter asks what competition may mean for universities and other HEIs. It describes an evolutionary economics and innovation management perspective for understanding international trends and the responses of specific universities, but also comments upon the limits to such competition as regulated by government, laws, etc. The chapter portrays universities as knowledge-based service providers with a set of different stakeholders (students, firms, governments). From a selection perspective, the chapter analyses what type of outputs these stakeholders are interested in and what metrics there are in terms of assessing these outputs. This analysis is conducted in terms of characteristics of the university sectors in terms of value, resources and appropriation for education, research and 'innovation'. This chapter thus addresses what competition and transformation mean for universities, focusing on universities within a global sector providing knowledge-based services.

Chapter 13, 'From social institution to knowledge business' is written by Enrico Deiaco, Magnus Holmén, and Maureen McKelvey. It analyses the main results, in terms of the four horizontal themes introduced above, focusing on what we have learnt theoretically and empirically about European universities learning to compete. It concentrates on the implications for the future, of this new competitive regime, as universities, institutes of technologies and colleges move from social institutions to knowledge businesses. The future implications are presented in terms of restructuring the university sector at the macro level and in terms of strategies at the micro level. Hence, these conclusions are particularly relevant both for public policy and for decision-makers within universities, at all levels ranging from heads of research groups to vice chancellors and presidents.

3.   LEARNING TO COMPETE: THEMES AND COMPARISONS

This section provides an overview of the themes. Subsequent chapters are summarized for a detailed comparison in terms of specific issue, main level of analysing the university, which countries are included, and the main methodology and data. After this comparison, each horizontal theme is described.

The first theme is 'emergent strategy' and includes Chapters 2 to 4. The chapters can be summarized in terms of main issues, countries and data as found in Table 1.1.

'Emergent Strategy' is the horizontal theme that describes strategy as an emergent result of an on-going, interactive process from the bottom-up as well as top-down. These chapters provide empirical evidence that European universities are responding to pressures to transform. They ask different questions about emergent strategy, in the sense of how and why universities as organizations and research groups are active in creating their new positions, within institutional contexts. These chapters raise different questions about how well different organizations are able to obtain resources, students, prestige, industrial funding, etc. in relation to internal and external pressures for change.

The second theme is 'differentiation and specialization', which includes Chapters 5 to 6, which are compared and contrasted in Table 1.2.

The historical development of the universities, research institutes and higher educational system in European innovation systems has generally been tied to societal goals such as general education and welfare state ideals. In line with this, the European Union Lisbon Strategy of 2000 will rely upon science and education to boost competitiveness, sustainability and social cohesion. Despite these national and European goals, the current trend is that market-based mechanisms and different types of competition are increasingly differentiating the population of universities. These chapters provide empirical evidence and conceptual discussion that suggest that European universities are already facing significant new competitive regimes, and in particular, they identify more pronounced patterns of differentiation and niche specializations, in ways similar to Anglo-Saxon countries. Implications of these new patterns of globally competitive, nationally useful, and regional focus are discussed in relation to differentiation.

The third theme is 'rethinking university–industry relations', which includes Chapters 7 to 10, with details in Table 1.3.

This theme of 'Rethinking University–Industry' asks what is going on in the USA as well as how well Europe is doing in terms of university–industry relations, given the widespread belief that Europe greatly lags the USA. According to Dosi et al. (2006), belief in the European paradox has focused attention upon the role of the universities in commercialization, despite the fact that economic growth is generally driven by other forces. Europe supposedly faces a paradox of investing a great deal of money into R&D but

Table 1.1 *Emergent strategy theme*

	Specific issue, relevant to European universities learning to compete	Main level of analysis: interaction	Universities located in country/countries	Methodology and data
Ch.2, 'Exploring University alliances and comparable academic cooperation structures' is written by Enrico Deiaco, Ana M. Gren and Göran Melin	Explores the creation of alliances and collaboration between universities	University as an organization Interactions with global competitors	Australia, Canada, China, Denmark France, Germany, Japan, Netherlands, Singapore, Sweden, Switzerland, USA, United Kingdom	Illustrative case studies Strategy documents Evaluation studies Interviews
Ch.3, 'Strategy to Join the Elite' is written by Luke Georghiou	Examines the merger of Victoria University of Manchester and UMIST, as a strategy to become a world leading university	University as an organization Interactions with national system	United Kingdom	In-depth case study Participant observer, as researcher and university leader Strategy process, including diverse empirical material
Ch.4, 'Large-scale international facilities within the organization' is written by Olof Hallonsten and Mats Benner	Analyses how and where specialized labs as part of international 'big science' fit within the strategic processes of universities in Sweden	Research group Interactions with individuals, other research groups, and national context	Sweden	University lab at Lund University, case study

Table 1.2 Differentiation and specialization theme

	Specific issue, relevant to European universities learning to compete	Main level of analysis: interaction	Universities located in country/countries	Methodology and data
Ch.5, 'Division of academic labour is limited by the size of the market' is written by Andrea Bonaccorsi	Identifies the existence and effects of differentiation (specialization) in doctoral education, in different European countries	University as organization Interactions with national system	Finland, Italy, Netherlands, Spain, Switzerland, United Kingdom	Quantitative data Metrics of institutional differentiation Micro-based data of all universities within the national context
Ch.6, 'Polarization of the Swedish university sector' is written by Daniel Ljungberg, Mattias Johansson and Maureen McKelvey	Relates the structural characteristics of Swedish universities, to the propensity to attract external research funding, including industry financing	Universities as organizations Interactions with national context	Sweden	Quantitative data of all universities, regional colleges and HEIs Descriptive data and micro-level data at each university Indicators for many variables NU database, revised by authors

Table 1.3   Rethinking the university–industry theme

	Specific issue, relevant to European universities learning to compete	Main level of analysis: interaction	Universities located in country/countries	Methodology and data
Ch.7, 'The American experience in university technology transfer' is written by Maryann Feldman and Shiri M. Breznitz	Reassesses American experiences with technology transfer	University as organization Interactions with individuals and with national context	USA	Reviews multiple sources of data
Ch.8, 'Academic patenting in Europe' is written by Francesco Lissoni, Patrick Llerena, Maureen McKelvey, and Bulat Sanditov	Asks whether national institutions determine patenting behaviour of academics located in three different European countries, or whether disciplinary differences	Individuals Interaction with national systems	France, Italy, Sweden Some comparison with evidence from USA	EPO data All university senior researchers (professors) within the country Analysis of database results
Ch.9, 'The Forgotten Individuals' is written by Mats Magnusson, Maureen McKelvey, and, Matteo Versiglioni	Addresses whether and why individual researchers have the skills and attitudes necessary for commercialization in Sweden, and place this	Individuals Interactions with research group and with universities as organizations	Sweden	Quantitative data Survey/questionnaire sent out to researchers in fluid mechanics, wood technology, biotechnology, computer science,

14

				automatic control and inorganic chemistry
	in relation to the services provided by the university for commercialization			
Ch.10, 'Elite European universities and R&D subsidiaries of multinational enterprises' is written by Anders Broström, Maureen McKelvey and Christian Sandström	Analyses when R&D subsidiaries of multinational firms are 'customers' of the research service that universities provide, in terms of motivations and modes of collaboration	Research groups	Sweden, Switzerland, United Kingdom	Cases of multinational enterprises, with R&D subsidiaries located outside their home country Interviews Archival material

receiving little in terms of commercialization and innovation. The argument is usually that 'something is wrong with the universities' in Europe because they are not performing as 'optimally' as they could. These chapters provide insights into American technology transfer as well as questioning the existing view of European academic inventors and university–industry relations, based on novel data. They ask questions about how often researchers patent in different countries and disciplines and their attitudes towards commercialization and also investigate the reasons for firms interacting with universities. These chapters thus question 'accepted wisdom' about Europe and about the traditional policy implications of promoting patenting and start-up companies.

The final theme is 'Reflections', which includes Chapters 11 to 13, but no table is included because they are more conceptual and theoretical. This theme thus addresses the positive and negative consequences of introducing a competition-based paradigm for universities within Europe. These chapters are intended to stimulate debate and raise questions about how the identified competition and transformation is fundamentally changing the behaviour and goals of universities. These chapters thus raise questions about whether and how universities are indeed competing – despite all the rhetoric – and if so, whether and how unintended consequences arise.

We have written this book partly because we believe that EU and national policy-makers have begun to discuss the relative merits of the 'entrepreneurial university' as opposed to the 'Humboldtian university' – but without sufficiently understanding and debating the implications. Aspects of these debates are evident within this book. Some authors argue that universities are not competing, or should not compete, because they represent different values and roles in society than businesses. Other authors argue that European universities are acting as if they are competing, and therefore, in this context, it is useful to explore the limits of concepts from strategy, industrial dynamics, modularity and other fields. Such developments may help us understand why and how the conception of the 'usefulness' and 'value-added' of the European university is slowly changing from a primarily national institution serving the public good to a population of diverse actors trying to attract resources and competencies in order to grow and survive. Hence, this book should provide insight and debates about what happens now and in the future, when European universities learn to compete, as well as stimulate future research.

NOTES

1. 'University' as a concept tends to have different meanings. Some chapters in this book refer to 'higher education institution' including universities, higher educational institution, technical universities, and colleges. Some chapters refer to examples of the larger, global research universities.
2. A public good refers to a good that is non-rival and non-excludable. Non-rival means that the consumption of the good by one individual does not reduce the amount available for others. Non-excludable means that it is not possible to exclude individuals from consumption.
3. (http://feedbus.com/wikis/wikipedia.php?title=Academic_Ranking_of_World_Universities). Wikipedia has listed the methodology and critiques of some of the major international rankings.

REFERENCES

Bauer, M., B. Askling, S.G. Marton and F. Marton (1999), *Transforming Universities. Changing Patterns of Governance, Structure and Learning in Swedish Higher Education*, London: Jessica Kingsley.

Benner, M. and S. Sörlin (2007), 'Shaping strategic research: power, resources and interests in Swedish research policy', *Minerva*, **45** (1), 38–50.

Bonaccorsi, Andrea and Cinzia Daraio (2007), *Universities and Strategic Knowledge Creation*, Cheltenham, UK and Northampton, MA, USA: Edward Elgar.

Chesbrough, Henry (2003), *Open Innovation: The New Imperative for Creating and Profiting from Technology*, Boston, MA: Harvard Business School Press.

Clark, Burton (1998), *Creating Entrepreneurial Universities: Organizational Pathways of Transformation*, Oxford: Pergamon Press.

Clark, Burton (2004), *Sustaining Change in Universities: Continuities in Case Studies and Concepts*, Buckingham: Open University Press.

Dosi, G., P. Llerena and M. Sylos Labini (2006), 'The relationship between science, technologies, and their industrial exploitation: an illustration through the myths and realities of the so-called "European Paradox"', *Research Policy*, **35** (10), 1450–64.

The Economist (2005), 'Special report on universities', 26 February.

Fuller, Steve (2000), *The Governance of Science*, Buckingham: Open University Press.

Geuna, Aldo (1999), *The Economics of Knowledge Production: Funding and the Structure of University Research*, Cheltenham, UK and Northampton, MA, USA: Edward Elgar.

Lawton Smith, Helen (2006), *Universities, Innovation and the Economy*, Abingdon, UK and New York, US: Routledge.

Marginson, S. and M. Considine (2000), *The Enterprise University: Power, Governance and Reinvention in Australia*, Cambridge: Cambridge University Press.

Melander, Fredrik (2006), *Lokal forskningspolitik. Institutionell dynamik och organisatorisk omvandling vid Lunds universitet 1980–2005*, Lund, Sweden: Lund Political Studies 145, Political Science, Lund University.

Neave, G., K. Blückert and T. Nybom (eds) (2006), *The European Research University: an Historical Parenthesis?*, New York: Palgrave Macmillan.

Ramsden, Paul (1998), *Learning to Lead in Higher Education*, London: Routledge.
Reichert, Sybille (2006), *Research Strategy Development and Management at European Universities*, Brussels: EUA Publications.
Schilling, Peter (2005), 'Research as a source of strategic opportunity?', PhD thesis, Umeå Studies in Economic History, Umeå University, Sweden.
Slaughter, Sheila and Larry L. Leslie (1997), *Academic Capitalism: Politics, Policies, and the Entrepreneurial University*, Baltimore, MD and London: Johns Hopkins University Press.
Slaughter, Sheila and Gary Rhoades (2004), *Academic Capitalism and the New Economy*, Baltimore, MD and London: Johns Hopkins University Press.
de Solla Price, Derek (1963), *Big Science, Little Science*, New York: Columbia University Press.

2. Exploring university alliances and comparable academic cooperation structures

Enrico Deiaco, Ana M. Gren and Göran Melin

1. INTRODUCTION

Institutions of higher education have historically been characterized by a trend towards expansion (Trow, 2005). Although new sources of research funding are constantly appearing, there are also more players who want a share of available funds, thus creating a competitive environment for the available resources. This is an international phenomenon that is particularly evident in some national academic systems where universities lack their own sources of capital and fixed assets, and where alternative sources of funding besides the state budget funds are limited (Neave et al., 2006). The forces behind this development are familiar within the academic sector in the United States, where the phenomenon has been studied by a number of researchers who conclude that it is evident that competition is on the increase – for students, for academic staff members, as well as in terms of financing resources (Trow, 1996; Clark, 1998; Florida, 2002). Moreover, this tendency is also on the increase within the international academic arena (Castells, 1996, 1997, 1998). In Europe, the Processes of Bologna and Lisbon combined with the creation of the European Research Council, and the European Technology Platforms can be considered as signs of the ongoing changes of the structure of the academic sector. The formation of these processes will most likely strengthen the incentives for collaboration and differentiation that exists today within the European Union.

According to Harman and Meek (2002) and Georghiou and Duncan (2002), university alliances and partnerships, even mergers, are among the responses to these changes. Some of the findings conducted by these authors indicate that it is possible to imply that if mobility among students increases, and if competition for resources grows, alliances may be one way for university administrations to lower their risk of missing out on resources. Forming alliances may also provide an opportunity for universities to increase their resources by becoming more competitive, and to maintain the brands for which they are recognized. They will be able to work in traditional areas while generating new ideas and concepts, while at the same time combining strengths and resources such as the knowledge base of former competitors, as well as being able to take on new challenges and exploit new niche areas that are constantly emerging.

The purpose of this study is to explore the phenomenon and development of alliances between universities. A particular goal is to discuss the structure of selected alliances including their current status and accomplishments since their inception. In some instances, alliances have developed as a reaction that aims to follow a trend in the academic environment, marked by positive synergies and success observed in alliances composed by top universities. In other cases, alliances have formed as a response to variables such as a fierce international competitive climate in the academic sector.

In this study, we present ten academic alliances that have been established during the past decade throughout Europe, North America, and Asia. A brief background on each of the selected alliance structures is provided, drawing attention to the objectives or purpose of their establishment, and highlights some significant outcomes since their initiation. Reflections are presented based on the current outcomes of the cases analysed, with the goal to provide a discussion platform in terms of potential policy implications, as well as recommendations for further research in this subject. It is asserted through this study and the review of the literature that a number of different variables, including changes in market structures, internationalization, globalization, technology, as well as powerful international competitors are among the drivers that have forced some universities to consider new strategic choices to address current demands, and ways of positioning themselves in the future. Thus, in reviewing the different cases in this study, it has been possible to detect that in some cases the formations of alliances have been devised along with strategic decisions to create possibilities for larger academic environments, and to widen research possibilities. It has been possible to detect that there are diverse formulations for new methods in the management of higher education programmes, which include new structures in teaching and research, as well as different modes of cooperation within what once might have been considered as competing institutions.

It is possible to make a connection and suggest that alliances can be seen as a result of external pressure for change, increased competition and reduced predictability. Nevertheless, it is also feasible to consider a different view and argue that alliances can be the result of something other than mere strategic business-oriented decisions, and to question whether they are in fact in search of 'real' cooperation, or whether the fact that they are structured is merely a way to demonstrate what league of players a university can be associated with, as a means to promote their interests. It is also possible to question if creating an alliance is part of a marketing plan, possibly with the aim of recruiting students or attracting corporate funding. Plausibly, there is a range of different types of university alliances where the results of their structure are producing results that do not account for more than signed papers, while others may contain massive institutional collaboration. Nonetheless, it is clear that a response to external pressures, as well as to the potential opportunities for capitalizing from the changing context within the academic environment, is the formation of alliances, partnerships, consortiums, and other types of close forms of cooperation between universities. Thus, one of the objectives of this study is to describe the selected alliances, providing a brief account of their recent accomplishments and results within the academic environment in which they operate, and to consider whether or not the selected alliances are performing according to their stated purposes when joining forces. In addition, through the review of the literature regarding academic cooperation structures, one goal with this study is also to provide an account of the type of arrangements that might comprise the formation of an alliance, which might include a range from extremes such as voluntary cooperation agreements to merger structure types.

2. BACKGROUND TO RESEARCH ON UNIVERSITY ALLIANCES AND METHODS APPLIED

During the time of this study, it has been found that the available literature and research material in this subject matter is limited, with most of the data and literature concentrated on university mergers. Often in the literature the definitions on university and academic joint ventures and mergers are unclear, and can be labelled with different types of classifications. Kay Harman and Lynn Meek edited a special issue in *Higher Education* on academic mergers (2002), and many of the contributions in that issue touch upon circumstances of relevance to both mergers and alliances. Lang (2002) refers to a figure previously suggested by Harman (1989), which may serve as an illustration of the problem of the lack of concrete terms or definitions, or as what we can interpret as slightly 'sliding' definitions (Figure 2.1). Harman (1989) places different types of cooperation and academic joint ventures in a range in two extremes, sliding or moving between the ranges of 'Voluntary cooperation' to 'Amalgamation through merger'. Hence, what in one case one might call cooperation might, in a different case or situation it be called 'consortia'.

Learning to compete in European universities

Voluntary cooperation   Consortia   Federation   Amalgamation through merger

◄───►

Source: (Lang, 2002)

Figure 2.1   Harman's continuum of inter-institutional arrangements

> While the term 'cooperation' is often loosely used to subsume consortia, feder-
> ation, affiliation and even mergers, they are in practical fact different. An
> affiliation is not a federation. A federation is not a consortium, and so on. The
> fact, however, that the various forms of inter-institutional cooperation are
> different and far from inter-changeable does not mean that they do not occupy
> a common theoretical continuum. (Lang, 2002, p. 157)

Using the terminology presented by Harman (1989) and referred to by
Lang (2002), (for the purpose of our analysis of academic structures in this
study, and not with the purpose of presenting terminology for a lexicon of
inter-institutional cooperation), we rely on and interpret these terms in the
following manner:

- *Voluntary Cooperation*: intentional collaboration or mutual
  assisting without requiring any specific commitment from the partners.
- *Consortia*: a joint association that takes place in agreement with
  various partners, establishing terms for collaboration and joint
  efforts towards a common goal. Consortia are formal organizations
  that exist apart from the institutions that constitute their member-
  ships. These institutions are separately incorporated, and they have
  internal regulations and statues as independent organizations. They
  have a relative permanency and have a formal structure and typically
  are 'one-dimensional' in the sense that they provide only one service
  or programme (Lang, 2002).
- *Federation*: the formation of a coalition or a partnership between
  parts, with each institution retaining authority to grant degrees. In
  federations the participating institutions remain autonomous. Each
  retains its assets and it is responsible for its own management, and its
  liabilities. Its governing board remains in place, and it holds authority to make academic appointments, admissions, and offer employ-
  ments. Its faculty competes for and receives grants for research
  directly (Lang, 2002).
- *Amalgamation through merger*: the combination or fusion of two or
  more organizations, becoming a single entity.

Table 2.1   Selected alliances between universities

1. Wharton–INSEAD Alliance (USA-France)
2. Cambridge–MIT Institute (CMI) (USA-UK)
3. The SETsquared Partnership – Universities: Bath, Bristol, Southampton, Surrey (UK)
4. The White Rose University Consortium (UK)
5. The Øresund University (Sweden–Denmark)
6. Royal Institute of Technology–Chalmers (Sweden)
7. University of Miami (USA) and McGill University (Canada)
8. IDEA League (UK–The Netherlands–Switzerland–Germany)
9. Glasgow–Strathclyde Universities Strategic Alliance (Synergy) (UK)
10. The International Alliance of Research Universities (IARU) (eight countries)

3. METHODS OF ANALYSIS

In this study we consider ten academic alliances (Table 2.1) that have been established during the past decade throughout Europe, North America, and Asia. Background material on each of the selected alliances is provided, drawing attention to the original objectives, current conditions, and highlights of significant outcomes. It should be noted that each alliance is treated as a case study, and that the selection process of these was based on variables such as the described types of structures in the alliances or partnerships and geographic locations. There are a number of other alliances that have been explored; however, the lack of accessibility to data has precluded their inclusion. The selected alliances are listed in Table 2.1.

It is worth mentioning that for this study it has been useful to rely on findings from a parallel investigation and in-depth analysis of the preconditions and prerequisites for a merger or alliance between two Swedish universities: Örebro University and Mälardalen University (Broström et al., 2005). The in-depth research conducted on these universities has provided valuable information applicable to this project, by allowing the use of reference material in order to reflect upon different conditions and similarities from these experiences. In addition, we also draw on the experiences from an earlier study of the preconditions for an alliance between two Swedish technical universities: The Royal Institute of Technology in Stockholm and Chalmers University of Technology in Gothenburg (Broström et al., 2004). This Swedish alliance is included and presented among the ten cases in this study.

With these selected objects of investigation we explore and discuss the phenomenon of university alliances with respect to the following questions:

- What are some of the objectives and results that are sought after through an alliance?
- What are some potential risks that can arise from the formation of an alliance?
- Are there tangible benefits from the collaborating structures formed?

With the purpose of addressing these questions, a number of methods including semi-structured interviews have been conducted with representatives from the investigated universities. In addition, a simple questionnaire was sent to representatives of the alliances, in which they were asked to provide a ranking behind potential motives for the formation of their respective alliances. The ranking included variables for potential motives like: economies of scale, synergies, revenues, efficiency, recruitment, renewal, commercialization benefits, joint marketing of research and teaching, and stronger leadership.

The respondents were asked to rank these variables from least important (1) to most important (5). Responses to this questionnaire were not provided by all of the fundamental partners in the alliances, and some of the respondents requested that information be kept confidential. Thus, the synthesis of potential motivations for structuring of an alliance, and the summary table which we present in this study, are based on our analysis of the material obtained through public information documents. In some cases, this is also supported by information provided through the questionnaire responses and interviews conducted. It is also appropriate to mention that most interviews were conducted over the telephone, with the exception of personal interviews held with representatives from Øresund University, and from the Cambridge–MIT Institute.

Hence, relying on these information sources, as well as on the collected empirical material, a synopsis of each of the selected alliances is provided, drawing attention to the original objectives, current conditions, and highlighting significant outcomes. The information gathered has permitted us to make some reflections related to the positioning of the structure of alliances, as well as to analyse and establish a discussion of potential risks and benefits associated with the formation of alliances.

4.   ALLIANCES CONSIDERED IN THE STUDY

Wharton–INSEAD Alliance (USA–France)

An important incentive for the alliance between the already top-ranking business schools Wharton (United States), and INSEAD (France), has been to take advantage of the opportunities that internationalization offers. This alliance, which was established in 2002, renewed their commitment to continue to work together for three more years in 2004 (Wharton/INSEAD Alliance, 2007a).

This alliance has been operating successfully, indicated by the growth in the number of MBA students registered, the number of courses, joint programmes, and research projects conducted in parallel. Currently the alliance offers courses in four of their university campuses in Fontainebleau, Singapore, Philadelphia, and San Francisco. By providing access to four campuses this alliance can access multinational clients demanding global executive education, as well as open enrolment pro-grammes that allow students to choose several locations for their studies (Wharton/INSEAD Alliance, 2007a). Among some of the stated essential tools that ought to be offered by a global education system, which the alliance aims to provide, is the fact that it allows for a diverse student body working together both inside and outside the classroom. Accordingly in 2006, the enrolment for the MBA class was made up of more than 30 per cent non-United States students, which brought a different perspective into the education, which enriches the overall learning experience. In addition, an essential element for a successful international alliance and international programme is the global content in teaching materials, and faculty, which needs to be actively engaged in research that impacts on global businesses.

In aiming to reach their objectives, this alliance has been focusing heavily on research as a means of developing new business knowledge. Thus this alliance has also allowed students and faculty to capitalize and to take advantage of each of these schools' 'breadth and depth of connections'. This has also resulted in their reporting of successful student exchange pro-grammes, successful joint executive education programmes, and new col-laborations in terms of research (Wharton/INSEAD Alliance 2007b). In addition, as both INSEAD and Wharton focus on research 'as a means of developing new business knowledge', and with the aim of supporting faculty members from both schools working together on research pro-jects, and pedagogical materials this alliance recently established the Center for Global Research and Development (INSEAD/Wharton Alliance, 2007b).

Overall, both Wharton and Insead state that they are pleased with the relationship, which was launched at a difficult time given the downturn in the economy, the bursting of the dot.com bubble, and the September 11 effects, which pointed to a high risk at the time. However, according to the Wharton reports, the results have been a positive experience. This can be demonstrated by the fact that together the alliance has been able to partic-ipate in a number of significant research projects, joint education courses, as well as the growing numbers of MBA students registered in the diverse campuses. (INSEAD/Wharton Alliance, 2007a).

Cambridge–MIT Institute (CMI) (UK–USA)

From the time of its inception, the alliance between Cambridge University and the Massachusetts Institute of Technology, MIT (Cambridge–MIT Institute, CMI) has aimed at bringing together the cutting-edge expertise of both the universities to enhance entrepreneurship, productivity and competitiveness. One important point of departure for the alliance is that innovative ideas arise when researchers at leading institutions work together and exchange and develop ideas. CMI's mission is thus to 'think the unthinkable' by funding experimental research projects with direct applications in industry (Cambridge–MIT Institute, 2004). Over the past six years, these two universities have been working together to explore new ways in which universities in partnership with others might help enhance productivity, competitiveness and entrepreneurship. They state that they have developed new approaches to education, exchange and research, by 'convening' a broad range of representatives from industry, government and universities. Thus, the result from working together has led to the development of transferable capabilities in terms of educating, convening, and exchanging and sharing of ideas. 'Over 100 other academic institutions, more than 1000 companies, and a wide range of other stakeholders have participated' (Cambridge–MIT Institute, 2006b).

Accordingly, over the last six years, the Cambridge–MIT Institute has funded over 100 projects involving multiple partners at Cambridge, MIT, and beyond which have included significant activities and results within disciplines ranging from health care, transport, engineering, IT, and others. In addition, the types of projects range from the development of courses in a joint manner, such as development of new courses to support a curriculum in biological engineering, to joint urban planning and design studios. The joint urban planning and design studios aim at educating planning and architecture students at the University of Cambridge and MIT about ways in which to use space, design, transportation, and public policies to accommodate technology and development (Cambridge–MIT Institute, 2006b). In November 2006, a project that received significant attention in the media was a joint one in which a silent aircraft, aiming at quieter and more environmentally sustainable flying, took one step further as researchers from the two universities presented this revolutionary concept. The Silent Aircraft Initiative has been funded by the Cambridge–MIT Institute since 2003, as a collaboration led by professors at Cambridge University Engineering Department, and professors at the Aeronautics and

Astronautics at MIT. The project, which has a grant from CMI of £2.3 million, brings together teams involved in different aspects of aircraft design for a multidisciplinary approach. The initiative has involved 40 researchers all driven by a common cause with a very clear mission (Cambridge–MIT Institute (2006c).

Further results from the alliance include the establishment of the Cambridge–MIT Institute 'Partnership Program', which has a goal to provide opportunities to facilitate work towards building of 'meaningful and sustainable research and education partnerships related to science, technology and innovation' (Cambridge–MIT Institute, 2006a). In summary, the timeline of projects developed in partnership since their start, as presented in the document 'Working in partnership' (2006), indicates that the collaboration from these universities has been significant from the time of its inception, clearly visible from the increase in the number of exchange students, joint publications, graduates from the programme, as well as the number of joint events that have increased and which continue to grow significantly (Cambridge–MIT Institute, 2006b).

The SETsquared Partnership – Universities: Bath, Bristol, Southampton, Surrey (UK)

The SETsquared partnership is an alliance and collaboration of the universities of Bath, Bristol, Southampton and Surrey. The partnership, which was formed in 2002, supports and encourages the development of business 'spin-outs' from collaboration in university research. The partnership collaborates with industry, by providing access to university knowledge and their facilities, as well as business operations and technology transfer through services specifically aimed at high-growth potential technology start-ups from both within and outside the university setting (SetSquared Partnership, 2007).

One of the objectives of the Partnership is to invest in 'top research' which is considered an essential component that catches the interest of venture capitalist and research foundations, which are interested in university companies. For this purpose, and with the intention of gaining access to seed capital, all four SETsquared Partnership universities have agreements for accessing support for commercialization activities, seed capital finance, and ongoing strategic and financial support for spin-out companies to maximize their chances of success. Additionally, global collaboration is essential in their objectives, and for this they work with a Department of Trade and Industry's £1.5 million 'Science Bridge' grant. With this type of funding the Partnership has been able to develop a link with the University of California San Diego, and the University of

California Irvine. The aim of this has also been to identify areas of collaboration for research in the areas of bioengineering, wireless technology, and sustainable and environmental habitats (SetSquared Partnership 2007).

Furthermore, the Partnership maintains that some 170 companies have been supported by the different SETsquared Centres, and that private investors have been contributing with over £15 million. Among major achievements one may consider that their support in the development of four spinout companies since the start of 2002 has created a combined market capitalization of over £160 million. In addition, the Partnership reckons to have raised over £45 million of follow-on funding for various ventures, and in a number of trade sales (SetSquared Partnership 2007a).

The White Rose University Consortium (UK)

The White Rose University Consortium is a strategic partnership between Yorkshire's three leading research universities in Leeds, Sheffield and York. The consortium was established in 1997. The aim of the partnership is to develop the region by combining the strengths of the universities, particularly in science and technology. The means to achieve this are increased collaborative research, intensification of industrial partnerships and joint postgraduate programmes. The Consortium aims to enable the combined research strengths of the three universities to more easily attract major research projects and increase the share of private funding. The partnership also aims at a combined research power that is comparable to that of the universities of Cambridge and Oxford (White Rose University Consortium (2007)).

The Consortium does not provide funding, however it works to facilitate and support the partner universities' creativity and innovation, and to ensure that together they can secure the funding and resources they need for their research, teaching and entrepreneurial initiatives. The model has been a success. The Consortium managed to exceed its original goal of £3 million by a good margin. In 2003/04 it managed to secure funding and research projects for a value of £40 million for the White Rose universities. In June 2006, partners from the Universities of Leeds and Sheffield were awarded £4 million to undertake world-class research and provide advanced research training in Japanese and Chinese Studies as part of a government drive to strengthen Britain's specialized research capacity in the area. They established a White Rose East Asia Centre (WREAC) with the objective of creating what will be one of five new collaborative centres to diffuse the UK's understanding of emerging markets in the region, China, Japan and Eastern Europe (White Rose University Consortium, 2007a).

In addition, in May 2006, the public was expected to benefit from closer links between researchers, healthcare companies and doctors as a grant of £4.7 million was secured by a consortium of Yorkshire's universities, health trusts and global companies. The grant was provided by the Higher Education Innovation Fund (HEIF), with the goal of having a White Rose Health Innovation Partnership (WHIP), coordinated by the White Rose University Consortium, with the aim of having 'innovative partnerships' that could provide a dynamic framework for the delivery of new technologies, methodologies and practices into the medical and healthcare sector at a much faster rate than has previously been possible. When the announcement was made about partnership, three global healthcare companies – Smith & Nephew, Johnson & Johnson and B. Braun confirmed their participation in the initiative. This demonstrates the amount of interest that this type of partnership receives, as well as the potential for increasing the amount of expertise and expertise from which the partnership can benefit from toward their overall objectives (White Rose University Consortium, 2007a).

The Øresund University (Sweden–Denmark)

The Øresund University was established in 1997 as collaboration between universities in the Øresund region (Denmark and Sweden), including the major ones such as Lund University, Copenhagen University and the Technical University of Denmark. The collaboration includes other schools as well and together there are twelve universities and university colleges that participate. The idea was to create a loose association of universities, which, over time, would collaborate in research and education. The Øresund Bridge, which was being constructed around that time over the sound between Sweden and Denmark, was an important driving force. The bridge was expected to provide more opportunities for taking full advantage of what the region of the sound had to offer. In particular, student mobility would be easier and the universities could therefore make courses available across the border (Øresund University, 2007a).

There were three important reasons for creating the Øresund University: one was 'selective excellence' based on the realization that no university can excel in every area, especially not the smaller ones. An alliance with a large, combined resource base was considered as a structure that would make it possible for each of the members, in good conscience, to select the fields in which to concentrate their resources, and thereby achieve excellence (Øresund University, 2007a). The member universities are:

1. Copenhagen Business School
2. Danish University of Education

3. IT University of Copenhagen
4. Lund University
5. Malmö University
6. Roskilde University
7. Technical University of Denmark
8. The Royal Academy of Fine Arts School of Architecture, Denmark
9. The Royal School of Library and Information Science, Denmark
10. The Swedish University of Agricultural Sciences/Alnarp
11. University of Copenhagen
12. University of Kristianstad

According to the Øresund University (2007a) the collaboration between the 12 universities includes the following achievements and facts and figures:

- 140,000 students
- 10,000 researchers
- 6,500 PhD students
- 4,000 international students
- 800 international partner universities
- 8 Nobel Prizes
- 5th in Europe in scientific output.

Source: (Øresund University, 2007b)

The facts and figures presented are impressive, nevertheless, it is difficult to assess the level of collaboration that these universities have had since their inception. One tangible project that the collaboration has begun is the Øresund Study Gateway. This is an online web portal that gathers information about all the study possibilities at the 12 universities in the Øresund University consortium. This should provide the possibility of accessing more than 4000 educational programmes and courses for the students of the collaborating schools (Øresund University, 2007a).

Royal Institute of Technology – Chalmers University of Technology (Sweden)

The strategic alliance between the Royal Institute of Technology and Chalmers University of Technology in Sweden was formed in 2005 after a thorough investigation of the pro and cons of enhanced co-operation (Broström et al., 2004). The decision to form an alliance between the most prominent Swedish technical universities, and the historical rivals, was followed with great interest in the Swedish university system. Both universities conducted an independent strategic review, which disclosed an increased competitive landscape of students, researchers and cooperation with companies. The consideration of forming an alliance grew out of these strategic findings. The major opportunity envisaged with the alliance was to market the two universities to students and researchers, particularly in Asia.

The alliance has so far established several new initiatives in the development of various master programmes. However the main single event is the formation of an Asian office (together with the Karolinska Institute) in Beijing with the objective of marketing the three universities to Chinese students and to search for collaboration with Asian universities in various research fields. The alliance has led to intense collaboration and information exchange between the two technical universities, even including joint board meetings. Nevertheless, there are no joint programmes offered to date, but there appears to be continuous interest in further extending the collaboration efforts between these universities.

University of Miami (USA) and McGill University (Canada)

The University of Miami (UM) in the United States and McGill University in Canada signed a strategic alliance in 2004, with the purpose to collaborate in the fields of engineering and information technology. The objectives as presented in the announcement documents were to boost joint ventures, grant-making opportunities and faculty and student exchanges between the two universities (McGill University, 2004). As part of the faculty exchange that is expected to result from the alliance, UM and McGill University were expected to write joint proposals to international funding agencies to improve research initiatives and increase the economic impact in their respective communities. Since the announcement of this alliance, it has been difficult to find further information with regard to the level of joint efforts after 2004, and whether or not the formation has resulted in further research or further commitment, or whether this alliance has continued. Through the contact taken with the responsible parties of this alliance, the responses indicated that there appears to be some collaboration taking place; however, it has not been possible to determine whether there are current ongoing projects that can provide tangible results of their collaboration.

IDEA League (UK–Netherlands–Switzerland–Germany)

The IDEA League is a strategic alliance initiated in October 1999 between: Imperial College in London, Technische Universiteit in Delft (TU Delft),

Eidgenössische Technische Hochschule in Zürich (ETH Zürich), and Rheinisch-Westfalische Technische Hochschule in Aachen (RWTH Aachen). A Memorandum of Understanding was signed on 27 March 2006, in which the Grandes Ecoles de Paris (ParisTech) joined the IDEA League. The inclusion of this school to the alliance adds a number of collaboration initiatives including the ability to create joint master courses, the first IDEA summer school focusing on biotechnology and bioengineering applications in medicine. There are joint grant schemes for research and grant applications. The initiatives are in line with the objectives of the IDEA League, which from the time of its initiation has been committed to working with the highest international standards in both research and education. Collectively, the purpose of the alliance is to develop competitive master programmes in line with the universities' internationalization policy and in accordance with the Bologna Process.

The benefits that IDEA anticipated from the alliance included the ability to recruit international students, as well as using their collective resources to attract more public and private funding. Thus from the time of its inception, the following are some of the major achievements accomplished up to 2006:

- ParisTech (Grandes Ecoles de Paris) joined the IDEA League, signing of Memorandum of Understanding on 27 March 2006.
- First IDEA summer school: biotechnology and bioengineering Applications in Medicine, in September 2006.
- Collaboration on ethical issues: establishment of an IDEA statement on ethics, preparation of a summer school for 2007.
- Implementation of a grant scheme for research collaborations.
- Preparation of a statement on level of degrees for Bologna follow-up meeting (May 2007 in London).
- Preparation of a workshop in materials science for 2007: 'Multi-scale modelling in materials science and engineering'.
- Setting up of a joint course, for instance in applied geophysics (between Aachen, Delft and ETH).
- Agreement introducing a grant scheme for research projects for students.
- Scholarship programme launched.
- The IDEA League initiated an E-learning collaboration. The first workshop led to various joint projects, including:
  - developing a joint distant-learning programme;
  - focusing on libraries to form collaborating virtual knowledge centres;
  - sharing software tools in evaluation schemes.

In order to achieve these results and standards, the IDEA League states that it has been essential to use common quality management principles for their educational programmes (IDEA League, 2006). Furthermore, the official representatives of the IDEA League partner universities are committed in terms of making the structure work and develop, for this they hold annual meetings for evaluation and validation of the achievements of the various projects, as well as to set directives for further co-operation (Buttner, 2002).

Glasgow–Strathclyde Universities Strategic Alliance (Synergy) (UK)

The alliance between University of Glasgow and University of Strathclyde (Synergy) was established in 1998. The objectives were to establish higher levels of joint research activity, offer an improved range of teaching and learning opportunities and to enhance administrative and service functions. A number of new research and teaching activities have been initiated in areas of, for example, understanding schizophrenia, smart splints to mend tendons and several new teaching initiatives such as the Glasgow School of Law and the Glasgow School of Social Work (launched in August 2004). The expected outcomes regarding research were higher quality research and higher research income mainly through critical mass and economies of scale, enhanced interdisciplinary research and the joint marketing of research. In teaching, the main expected outcomes were in offering more attractive programmes and enhanced curricula as well on economizing on the development of new teaching initiatives (Glasgow–Strathclyde Strategic Alliance, 2004).

The universities have a combined research portfolio of over £100 million, thus the universities claim that they are major international forces in research (Glasgow–Strathclyde Strategic Alliance, 2004). Part of the claimed success by Synergy is given to the fact that since 1998, the partnership has shifted the focus of research efforts in the two universities from competition to collaboration. Accordingly, the shift provided the opportunity to enhance both institutions and to provide academic and financial benefits. Currently, it includes collaborations in teaching, some of which share resources and reduce costs, as well as others, which aim to develop new courses that neither institution could offer alone (Glasgow–Strathclyde Strategic Alliance, 2004). As Synergy has developed over the years, the benefits (as demonstrated by the large research portfolio), clearly demonstrate that the collaboration is working and can confirm that what once began as a strategic alliance in research has developed into research, teaching and into the support of essential infrastructure in areas such as library provision at the two universities (Glasgow–Strathclyde Strategic Alliance, 2004).

Although as any other universities, this alliance continues to face con-straints from reductions in government funding, those who can access opportunities can nevertheless market their research, expertise and teach-ing programmes in a global marketplace. 'Optimum success world-wide requires collaboration at local, national and international levels. It is within this context that the partnership between the two Universities is taking place' (Glasgow–Strathclyde Strategic Alliance, 2004).

The International Alliance of Research Universities (Eight countries)

The International Alliance of Research Universities (IARU) was officially created in early 2006. The members of IARU include ten of the world's leading research universities: Australian National University (ANU), ETH Zürich, National University of Singapore, Peking University, University of California, Berkeley, University of Cambridge, University of Copenhagen, University of Oxford, the University of Tokyo and Yale University. The alliance's aim is to sponsor a range of student and faculty exchange pro-grammes but also plan to go beyond traditional exchanges to introduce joint and dual degree programmes, joint research projects, and scholarly conferences. One goal established for the future, as the alliance develops, is to seek support for its research projects and to enhance collaboration in commercialization of research. Joint research projects have been discussed including topics such as global movement of people, ageing and health, food and water, energy, and security (International Alliance of Research Universities IARU, 2007a). This is a relatively new alliance thus there are no specific tangible results presented or available for evaluation. Nevertheless, the following activities are planned, encouraged and are to be supported by the Alliance: summer (northern hemisphere) internships; key conferences with encouraged participation/contribution from alliance academics; student exchange at both undergraduate and postgraduate level; develop-ment of joint/dual degree arrangements; arrangements at each university to support faculty exchange.

One current programme is through the Australian National University (ANU), which is actively involved in several IARU projects including a research theme entitled 'Global Change'. This has been stated to be the inte-grating research theme for IARU collaboration over 2005–07, which was to be explored via topics and 'led' by IARU members. For each topic, prepa-ration of discussion papers was proposed, and the first of the academic workshops for each topic were held in Europe over September to November 2006 (International Alliance of Research Universities IARU, 2007).

Furthermore, the workshop hosts had been asked to produce papers by mid-February 2007 in which outlines for specific research (and education) proposals were to be presented. Stated topics are to have been explored in a similar way to the 'Global Change and Sustainability' research topics. Finally, as this is recently established cooperation, there are a number of plans that comprise their goal in continuing the development of this international alliance, including stated interests to work jointly on benchmarking and develop shared positions on key public policy issues that are relevant globally (International Alliance of Research Universities IARU, 2007).

SYNTHESIS OF MOTIVES

In several of the case studies we found underlying motives behind forming an alliance, with establishing of an alliance philosophy regarded as essential. Some of these factors could be summarized as follows (see Table 2.2): cooperation facilitates profiling, specialization and international excellence, which enables the universities to achieve international critical mass, something that is often considered as crucial in the competition for external funding from both national research councils and global corporations. Sometimes, as with The White Rose University Consortium, the Wharton–INSEAD alliance and the Cambridge–MIT Institute, the cooperation exceeds the expectations with respect to securing more funding from the business community. However, in some cases the need for increased corporate funding is still an important element to work towards, having access to more funding from the private sector is an important prerequisite in order to increase levels of government financial support.

A number of illustrative key words and phrases appear in strategy documents and in articles that describe the new competitive landscape: 'scale', 'world class', 'restructure', 'full range of services' and 'create new centres of excellence'. The internal discussion is thus focusing on more efficient universities and perhaps, most important, universities that are more forceful and competitive in what they deliver, even if they may be more selective when doing so. The case studies show that key terminology like 'profiling', 'cooperation' and 'strategy' are no longer merely education policy rhetoric; they are a reality. We are already beginning to see the results internationally through new field formations. Often the experiences are positive ones such as in the cases presented above where tangible results in terms of high quality research conducted, courses developed, as well as amounts of capital raised for international efforts. Nevertheless, it is also difficult to separate how much of the results presented or the goals and objectives presented by the different alliances are actually tangible or achievable. Thus what is the difference between the rhetoric and reality? In some cases it is

Table 2.2 Summary of alliances' significant accomplishments

Alliance/partnership/consortium	Significant achievements
Cambridge–MIT Year established: 2000	• Establishment of the Cambridge–MIT Institute, 'Partnership Programme'. • The programme aims to provide opportunities to facilitate work towards building of 'meaningful and sustainable research and education partnerships related to science, technology and innovation' • The partnership has collaborated in over 100 joint projects and publications. (Cambridge–MIT Institute, 2006a)
Wharton–INSEAD Year established: 2002	• First co-branded Alliance programme. • Newly established Alliance Center for Global Research and Development. • Book published by the alliance: H. Gatignon and J.R. Kimberly (eds) (2004). • The alliance has collaborated in over 70 joint projects and publications (Wharton–INSEAD Alliance, 2007a)
McGill University – University of Miami Year established: 2004	• No further information material was available on this alliance, aside from the announcement of the formation of the alliance made public in 2004.
SETsquared Year established: 2002	• The flotation of four spin-out companies since the start of 2002 created a combined market capitalization of over £160 million. • The Partnership has obtained over £45 million of follow-on funding for various ventures in difficult markets and has succeeded with a number of trade sales. (SetSquared Partnership, 2007a)
The White Rose University Consortium (White Rose) Year established: 1997	• Through collaborative partnerships they exceeded their goal of £3m. • In 2003/4 financial year achieved funding and research projects worth £40m. for the White Rose universities. (The White Rose University Consortium, 2007a)

Øresund University is a consortium of twelve universities in Sweden and Denmark Year established: 1997	Through collaborative efforts the following results are presented: • 140,000 students, 10,000 researchers, 6,500 PhD students • 4,000 international students, 800 international partner universities • 8 Nobel Prizes, 5th in Europe in scientific output (Øresund University, 2007a)
IDEA League Year established: 2000	• On 27 March 2006 the Grandes Écoles de Paris (ParisTech) joined the IDEA League. • The addition of this school to the alliance includes a number of collaboration initiatives including the ability to create joint master courses • Establishment of the first IDEA summer school focusing on: biotechnology and bioengineering applications in medicine. (IDEA League, 2006)
Glasgow – Strathclyde Synergy Year established: 1998	• Combined research portfolio of over £100 million per annum. • 4,600 researchers (Glasgow – Strathclyde Strategic Alliance, 2004).
IARU 10 universities from inception. More to be considered for addition after the first 3 years Year established: 2006	Joint projects within the theme of streams of 'Global Change' research are: • Movement of people (Oxford and Berkeley) • Longevity and health (Copenhagen and Peking) • Energy, resources and environment (ETH Zurich, Tokyo and NUS) • Security (ANU and Cambridge) (International Alliance of Research Universities IARU, 2007)
Chalmers and KTH Year established: 2005	• Started initiatives for the development of various master programmes. • Formation of an Asian office (together with the Karolinska Institute) in Beijing, China. (Broström et al., 2004)

clear that there are tangible results and it is possible to state that the alliances are actually working and producing positive results. In other cases it is necessary to critically analyse their results presented.

It is also possible to state that in the analysis of these alliances, a theme recognized is that of the fields on which the universities and the business community operate. Despite the completely different backgrounds and traditions, that is, between the traditional academic vs. business environments, these appear to overlap and resemble one another. Universities and the business community will essentially remain different and continue to operate in distinct normative systems; it is a question of degree rather than type. However, since it is a process that follows a gradual change, it is possible for different universities to take different strategic positions and to lean more towards the modes of the business communities (Clark, 1998). In the cases analysed it is clear that many of the alliances and partnerships aim to capitalize on the opportunities offered of capturing larger markets and participating in the globalization economy. However, it is still clear that in many of these cases, their goals, at least as stated, are still set in terms of academic and research endeavours and with sights set on furthering scientific environments. The benefits for universities are instead the opportunities for branding, profiling, differentiation and synergies in teaching, research and cooperation. In this respect, the potential is both significant and likely to be fulfilled with a well-executed alliance.

The alliances in this study were formed over the past ten years, and interesting variables have been found that ought to be considered for further evaluation in future studies of a different nature. The positive experiences included the emergence of unexpected and new ideas as a result of the alliance. The negative experiences included problems that they had encountered in terms of underestimation of the management capacity, and the extent of resources needed to make the alliance happen. In this respect, it is possible to state that the experiences from university alliances can be similar to those in the business world. Thus, the probability of an alliance's success can be increased when organizations match each other with respect to physical, intangible and organizational resources, and where there are significant common value-systems – historically, culturally and strategically.

It is possible to state that there are different premises in terms of the structural changes in the academic sector, and with further analysis it should be feasible to find different variables in the ten alliances, however, the scope of this study limits an in-depth examination of the particular factors that have encouraged the formation of each individual alliance. Nevertheless, without examining the specific factors that may lead an alliance to form, a synthesis of potential motives behind the formation of alliances is presented in Table 2.3. The motives analysed included variables like: economies of scale, synergies, revenues, efficiency, recruitment, renewal, commercialization benefits, joint marketing of research and teaching, stronger leadership and increased international image. Table 2.3 illustrates some of the assessed important motives for the ten alliances in our study.

The table was created using responses to rankings provided by some of the alliances, for which we have included only the variables that were given the highest ranking in the responses. In the cases where we did not receive responses from all the appropriate members in the alliances, we have used our analysis of the public documents reviewed, in which statements of purpose or goals were presented. Thus the table presents some of our assessment and views of what might be potential motives behind their formation.

The motives behind the alliances appear to vary, but a common theme recognized is the need for preparation for a new international approach that emphasizes the need to reach larger markets. In addition, there is need to address issues concerning renewal, profiling, and branding of research, and educational offerings, and competition for internationally mobile students and companies. These are among demands leading to consideration of alliance type structures of cooperation.

5.   DISCUSSION

Alliances are formed and will keep being formed in the higher education sector, just as they have been formed in the business world. The benefits are likely to be opportunities for profiling and branding, combination of strengths and generation of synergies in education, research and cooperation. Therefore one important priority is the creation of a common vision for a possible alliance, defining content, the level of ambition and the connection to the overall strategic development.

Returning to the interpretation of academic cooperation structures, it is possible to state that after our analysis of the ten alliances, we consider that the arrangements elucidate variables that are found in 'federation and consortiums' type of structures. It is relevant to state that we can place the alliances analysed within the sliding scale that goes from voluntary cooperation to a merger structure. Hence, following the terminology that we referred to in the beginning of this chapter, and as presented by Harman (1989), and Lang (2002), we can interpret the term 'alliance' to explain variables from both 'consortia' and 'federation', – Figure 2.2. In our interpretation of alliances, the term refers to arrangements which after being

Table 2.3 Summary of potential motives behind the formation of ten international alliances and partnerships

Motives	Wharton–INSEAD	UM–McGill	SETsquared	CMI	White Rose	Øresund	IDEA	Chalmers–KTH	Synergy	IARU
Economies of scale			✓	✓		✓		✓	✓	✓
Synergies	✓	✓	✓	✓		✓		✓	✓	✓
Revenues	✓		✓	✓	✓	✓		✓		✓
Efficiency			✓			✓	✓		✓	
Recruitment		✓				✓	✓			
Renewal	✓	✓	✓	✓			✓	✓		✓
Commercial-ization Benefits		✓	✓	✓	✓	✓	✓			✓
Joint marketing of research and teaching	✓	✓		✓			✓	✓	✓	✓
Stronger leadership				✓						
Increased International Image	✓									✓

Figure 2.2   Adapted from Harman's continuum of inter-institutional arrangements

examined, we consider indicate that they elucidate variables that are particularly found in these two types of structures. The structure that follows an alliance seems more intensive than one would find in a 'voluntary cooperation' arrangement. And, in our analysis of the ten cases, none of the alliance structures examined go all the way to explain the variables particularly found in a merger.

It is however apparent that there is a great variety among the structures and accomplishments in the alliances, where some configurations and organizations are flexible and 'intentional' in their character, while other structures can be intensive and far-reaching, and may involve a different number of partners. Some as we have indicated, have not developed as expected, and perhaps it could be questioned whether they have been structured for marketing reasons, or whether there were specific events in the implementation processes that caused them to stagnate.

In addition, it is possible to state that there can be a number of risks and negative experiences, which might result from an alliance. There are threats and risks that arise during the inception periods and in the implementation processes. However, these risks play side by side with large opportunities such as the potential to create and establish powerful forms of cooperation to compete for international grants, research programmes, as well as for attracting corporate endowments, such as in the Cambridge–MIT, and the Wharton–Insead alliances. In relation to these factors, the analysis of the various case studies indicates that building alliances cannot be treated as yet another separate endeavour among a university's already diverse range of activities. Alliances can be considered actually as a way to deal with the lack of cohesion. The process of structuring, developing, maintaining, and expanding an alliance requires, aside from financial and human resources, constant care, new incentives, new structures and the capacity of the alliance participants to be open to the new opportunities that alliances can and often do provide. There is also much more to learn in this regard from how the business community exploits the benefits of alliances, in a manner as to minimize these risks on academic alliances.

Perhaps the most significant risk relates to 'soft' values linked to traditions, the brands and the role that each of the universities play at the national and regional levels and internally with respect to its own staff and students. These are assets that are difficult to account for and difficult to value, nevertheless it is essential to consider these variables, specifically during initial formation stages, in order to minimize the potential threat to these values. An alliance must build legitimacy based on its own merits, and in that manner gradually convince the players that it is appropriate to proceed to the next stage. This is another argument for ensuring that a number of clear strategies are defined regarding how to tackle the initial phases of an alliance. These strategies should not have problematic or irreversible consequences if the alliance, despite efforts made, runs into difficulties. Therefore, it can be preferable to begin with educational initiatives with short take-off times rather than attempting to restructure research.

One question that could be asked is whether 1+1 really equals 2 as is often assumed in the business alliance literature (Gomes-Casseres, 2002). In terms of this question, it is possible to relate it to the fact that research funding, whether it derives from a government source or a research council or a foundation, does not fall under any formal distribution policy mandate. At the same time, it is difficult to get away from the fact that such considerations are fairly common in reality. From this point of view, it may be risky for the parties in an alliance to be seen as one player. This could actually lead to them being punished for their cooperation. Therefore, in order to minimize this potential risk, an alliance ought to be formed in a strategic manner, in a way such as that it becomes a 'third player', at least initially. A third player ought to, through cooperation, be able to act as a recipient of resources without this hindering or inhibiting resource-seeking activities by the participants in the alliance.

The difficulties related to geographical distances should not be underestimated. With today's technology, contact networks can easily be extended to other places, as is exemplified by CMI and the Wharton–INSEAD alliance. However, experience from other sectors show that everyday personal contact and interactions are important, and perhaps even crucial – for the long-term success of an alliance. Thus, there needs to be a great deal of ingenuity and new forms of concrete collaboration to avoid a situation where an alliance is merely a set of general strategic decisions, or at worst a 'distribution policy'.

Perhaps one major risk is that an alliance is announced, attracts attention, is motivated by expectations for change and great improvement, but then in practice does not lead to much change at all. This, to some extent, appears to be what has happened with the Øresund University.

One uncertain factor in this respect will always be the staff and the students, i.e. the very groups that are supposed to gain from an alliance. To begin with, the students and the staff need to believe that the essential

Table 2.4   Arguments for and against an alliance

Arguments in favour:	Arguments against:
• Profiling and concentration	• Traditions, reduced autonomy
• Easier to compete for increased funding	• Regional linkages
• Greater opportunities for renewal	• Distance
• Cooperation, critical mass, competence	• Relative weakening of the influence of heads of faculties (or equivalent)
• Recruitment (international)	• More bureaucracy, slower reactions
• International cooperation	• Legal and financial administration obstacles
Opportunities:	**Threats:**
• Classic merger arguments (synergies etc.)	• Weakened identity and brand
• Easier to obtain new resources for reappraisal and restructuring	• Less chance of establishing strong alumni support
• Educational opportunities (international recruitment, masters and Ph.D.s)	• Impact on undergraduate education
• Relationship with industry and the community	• Many subjects will feel threatened (more than the number that will benefit?)
• More resources to handle intellectual property issues	• Trade union aspects

benefits of an alliance outweigh the disadvantages. It is crucial that a thorough and sensitive process is carried out to ensure maximum commitment to the changes. This is not to say that every individual will experience a change. In a situation like this, one cannot ignore the fact that there will be the usual opposition and a well thought-out strategy should be put in place for such a scenario.

Some of the potential arguments for and against an alliance are summarized in Table 2.4. This also contains perspectives on the opportunities and threats that a strategic alliance may include. Although these perspectives have not been deeply analysed, they are presented here with the intention of introducing a topic considered to deserve further discussion, and which is suggested for further development in later studies.

The possible positive and negative effects of many of the alliances will become more apparent with time. But throughout this analysis only a few cases have been found where the main motive for an alliance has been to rationalize operations according to the classic business model through extensive closures and restructuring measures. Rather, the reason behind alliances is to collaborate in order to deliver more efficient education and research programmes, especially in terms of what is offered to international students, top researchers and global corporations.

The content and level of ambition of an alliance must be related to the overall systemic effects. Experience from the business world indicates that strategic alliances must be in line with the overall visions and strategies of the players. An alliance must be seen as a means of achieving the organization's objectives rather than an end in itself. A number of unsuccessful alliances might be marked by this type of confusion. The analysis of the ten university alliances considered in this study indicate that their structures have different purposes, and are organized in different ways depending on the overall focus and the route the parties are taking.

Furthermore, among the goals presented by many of the alliances are that they are eager to become more attractive to external financing organizations and to secure more corporate funding. Several alliances have enjoyed success in this respect. It appears as if companies have welcomed their aspirations for bigger and more specialized research initiatives. The new competitive climate and the fact that industry and enterprise are becoming increasingly global, means that the challenge is to ensure that the actors have enough cutting-edge expertise and critical mass to attract both regionally-based as well as globally-active companies to support research at the universities, or conduct research in cooperation with them. High-profile research in an international perspective and a willingness to fully commit to research initiated by external players are crucial factors, and strong, interacting institutions are the lubricant.

Hence, in the same manner as in the business world, university alliances must be built from below (Gomes-Casseres 2002). We suggest the following to be some management related points to consider for the success of university alliances:

- In alliances there needs to be a strong commitment from the participating institutions and their staff, as well as strong support from the presidents.
- It is crucial to have a common vision of the alliance's future and potential benefits.
- The staff must be involved in both the planning and implementation processes. The decision processes must be open and transparent.
- The staff must be informed promptly about possible changes in positions/job descriptions. The students must also be informed about any changes in the courses and academic programmes.
- There should be a well-thought-through plan for negotiations concerning the alliance and for implementing agreements that relate to the alliance.

- Decisions regarding the name of the new alliance must be taken as quickly as possible.

It is possible to conclude that alliances are dynamic rather than static, thus it is essential for alliances to evolve over time so that the universities can get maximum benefit from their structures. They must be managed, organized and coordinated, and require participation from the highest levels of management. Experience shows that the management issues and costs must not be underestimated so that a strategic alliance will require significant leadership capacity. This may even have to limit collaboration activities with universities other than the alliance partner over a long period of time. This picture suggests that the traditional rationalization benefits are probably limited. International experience with respect to alliances supports this conclusion. Nor is there any simple or immediate way of influencing the research structure that exists in terms of cooperation in an alliance. Rather, the opportunities offered by an alliance involve increased interfaces between the universities at all levels. This is of course a process that requires delicate planning and a strong mutual understanding of each side's strengths and weaknesses. It also requires an efficient measure of mutual trust, which means that a joint declaration regarding a lasting alliance is essential, and perhaps even a prerequisite.

Research collaboration within strong areas takes time and must be preceded by careful analysis as well as strong relationships between research groups. Alliances, if organized in the right manner, can lead to a significant formal and informal growth of knowledge and knowledge transfer where 1 plus 1 equals 3, to use a common cliché for describing alliance benefits. The benefits will most likely often appear in unexpected, new and exciting collaboration processes.

ACKNOWLEDGEMENT

The authors wish to thank Sverker Sörlin for contributions in the early phase of the study, and Anders Broström for contributions, comments and advice throughout the study. Our special thanks go to Karla Anaya-Carlsson for her unwearied document research and assistance.

REFERENCES

Beerkens, H. (2004), *Global Opportunities and Institutional Embeddedness – Higher Education in Europe and Southeast Asia*, Enschede: Center for Higher Education and Policy Studies, University of Twente.

Broström, A., E. Deiaco and S. Sörlin (2004), 'Tekniska universitet på världsmarknaden? – motiv och förutsättningar för en strategisk allians mellan KTH och Chalmers', SISTER working paper **2004**, 32.

Broström, A., Deiaco E. and G. Melin (2005), 'Vägval för Örebro universitet och Mälardalens högskola. Utredning av förutsättningarna för fusion, allians eller annan samverkan', SISTER working papers **2005**, 38.

Buttner, H.G. (2002), 'Ideals of the IDEA League', paper presented at the IMHG General Conference, 16–18 September.

Cambridge–MIT Institute (2004), 'Report by the Controller and Auditor General', ordered by the House of Commons. Printed 15 April 2004, London: The Stationery Office, information from the website (www.ac.cam.uk), and an interview with Gordon Edge, member of the institute's advisory board, also available on the National Audit Office website, www.nao.gov.uk.

Castells, M. (1996, 1997, 1998), *The Information Age: Economy, Society and Culture*, vol. 1–3, Malden, MA: Blackwell.

Clark, B.R. (1998), *Creating Entrepreneurial Universities: Organizational Pathways of Transformation*, Oxford and New York: Pergamon Press.

De Meyer, A., P.T. Harker and G. Hawawini (2004), 'The globalization of business education', in H. Gatignon and J.R. Kimberly (eds), *The INSEAD–Wharton Alliance on Globalization, Strategies for Building Successful Global Business*, London: Cambridge University Press.

Florida, R.L. (2002), *The Rise of the Creative Class: And How it's Transforming Work, Leisure, Community and Everyday Life*, New York: Basic Books.

Gatignon, H. and J.R. Kimberly (eds) (2004), *The INSEAD – Wharton Alliance on Globalization, Strategies for Building Successful Global Business*, London: Cambridge University Press.

Georghiou, L. and T. Duncan (2002), 'Background report on academic mergers, research quality and other added value issues related to the scale institution arising from the merger of UMIST/Victoria University of Manchester', background report 18.09.02 (PREST).

Gomes-Casseres, B. (1996), *The Alliance Revolution: The New Shape of Business Rivalry*, Cambridge, MA: Harvard University Press.

Gomes-Casseres, B. (2002), 'Alliances (inter-firm)', in *Routledge Encyclopedia of International Political Economy*, Barry Jones (ed.), London: Routledge.

Harman, K. and V.L. Meek (2002), 'Introduction to special issue: "Merger revisited: international perspectives on mergers in higher education"', *Higher Education*, **44** (1), 1–4.

Lang, W.D. (2002), 'A lexicon of inter-institutional cooperation', *Higher Education*, **44**, 153–83.

Markusen, A. (1996), 'Sticky places in slippery space: a typology of industrial districts', *Economic Geography*, **72** (3), 293–313.

Neave, G., K. Blückert and T. Nybom (eds) (2006), T*he European Research University: An Historical Parenthesis?*, New York: Palgrave Macmillan.

Saxenian, A. (1994), *Regional Advantage: Culture and Competition in Silicon Valley and Route 128*, Cambridge, MA: Harvard University Press.

Trow, M. (1996), 'Trust, markets and accountability in higher education: a comparative perspective', *Higher Education Policy*, **9** (4), 309–24.

Trow, M. (2005), 'Reflections on the transition from elite to mass to universal access: forms and phases of higher education in modern societies since WWII', in Philip Altbach (ed.), *International Handbook of Higher Education*, Norwell, MA: Kluwer Academic Publishers.

University College London (2004), Provost's green paper: towards a vision and strategy for the future of UCL, accessed 7 August, 2008 at www.ucl.ac.uk.

Internet Sources

Cambridge–MIT Institute (2006a), 'Opportunities', accessed 12 April 2007 at www.cambridge-mit.org/opportunity/cmipp/.

Cambridge–MIT Institute (2006b), 'Working in Partnership. Cambridge University & MIT', downloaded document source, 26 March 2007 at www.cambridgemit.org/object/download/1823/doc/cmi%20brochure%20final.pdf.

Cambridge–MIT Institute (2006c), accessed 18 April 2007 at www.cambridge-mit.org/projects/.

Glasgow–Strathclyde Strategic Alliance (2004), 'Synergy: a world class partnership', accessed 29 March 2007 at www.strath.gla.ac.uk/synergy/ foreword.html.

Harman, G. (1989), 'The Dawkins reconstruction of Australian higher education', *Higher Education Policy*, **2** (2), 25–30.

IDEA League (2006), History, 19 September 2006, accessed 26 March 2007 at www.idealeague.org/about/history.

INSEAD/Wharton Alliance (2007a), 'The INSEAD Wharton Alliance', accessed 14 April 2007 at www.insead.edu/alliance/.

INSEAD/Wharton Alliance (2007b), 'List of alliance center research & development projects, accessed 26 March 2007 at www.insead.edu/alliance/faculty/research_projects.htm.

International Alliance of Research Universities IARU (2007), IARU Projects, accessed 4 April 2007 at http://info.anu.edu.au/OVC/Alliances/IARU/Projects/index.asp.

International Alliance of Research Universities IARU (2007a), IARU Prospectus, accessed 4 April 2007 at http://info.anu.edu.au/OVC/Alliances/IARU/_Files/IARU_prospectus.pdf.

McGill (2004), 'University of Miami and McGill team up', *McGill Reporter*. 9 September 2004, **37** (01), accessed 7 August, 2008 at www.mcgill.ca/reporter/37/01/miami/.

Øresund University (2007a), 'Introduction', accessed 18 April 2007 at www.uni.oresund.org/sw2006.asp.

Øresund University (2007b), 'Facts and Figures', accessed 18 April 2007 at www.uni.oresund.org/graphics/Oeresundsuniversitet/presentationer/PresentationOresundUniversityEnglish.ppt#277,2,Bild 2.

SetSquared Partnership (2007a), accessed 26 March 2007 at www.setsquaredpartnership.co.uk/about-us/.

SetSquared Partnership (2007b), accessed 4 February 2007 at www.setsquaredpartnership.co.uk/companies/.

Wharton/INSEAD Alliance (2007a), www.wharton.upenn.edu/campus/alliance/.

Wharton/INSEAD Alliance (2007b), 'Frequently Asked Questions', accessed 4 March 2007 at www.wharton.upenn.edu/campus/alliance/faqs.cfm.

White Rose University Consortium (2007a), 'The White Rose Consortium Structure', accessed 22 March 2007 at www.whiterose.ac.uk/NewsDetail.aspx?id=60 Structure.

White Rose University Consortium (2007b), 'The White Rose University Consortium History', accessed 4 April 2007 at www.whiterose.ac.uk/AboutDetail.aspx?id=2.

3. Strategy to join the elite: merger and the 2015 agenda at the University of Manchester

Luke Georghiou

INTRODUCTION

The logo of the University of Manchester incorporates a date of establishment of 1824 but this display of pedigree disguises the much more recent foundation of a new university by Royal Charter[1] on 1st October 2004. This new university, immediately the United Kingdom's largest, was formed through an effective merger of two institutions, the Victoria University of Manchester[2] (VUM) and the University of Manchester Institute of Science and Technology (UMIST). At the time the use of the term 'merger' was discouraged as the project was not principally driven by the typical merger objectives of rationalization and achieving scale. Rather the aim was to create a new institution that would drive towards a much higher position in the pantheon of world elite institutions than either of its predecessors had achieved in modern times but with a distinctive identity that did not emulate the UK's so-called Golden Triangle of Cambridge, Oxford and the leading London universities, nor the highly-endowed US Ivy League.

This chapter will examine the rationale and expectations for the most ambitious project in British higher education and track the process of change. A particular focus will be the blueprint for this transformation, known as the 2015 Agenda – a set of evolving goals and performance indicators. Progress to date and the challenges, expected and unexpected, that have surfaced will be discussed. In an ongoing project and with an insider's viewpoint there is no possibility of arriving at an objective assessment but some conclusions about the experience will nonetheless be drawn.

RATIONALE FOR A MERGER AND NEW UNIVERSITY

The history of the two universities had been one of an unusually close relationship. UMIST, which as its name implies was principally a technical university but with a large management school, had its origins in 1824 (the aforementioned establishment date) when a group of prominent local citizens established a Mechanics Institute for the education of the workforce. By 1883 it had become a Technical School but from the point of view of the relationship, a key stage came in 1905 when it acquired the status of the Faculty of Technology of the Victoria University of Manchester and hence was able to award degrees. Formal university status came in 1955 when the institution received its own charter and funding stream from the University Grants Committee (an agency which distributed core funding to universities at arm's length from the government). Nonetheless the close relationship with VUM and the joint Manchester degree persisted until 1993 when the then Vice-Chancellor Professor Bob Boucher led a move to complete independence with any cooperation to be on the basis of equal but separate institutions.

The Victoria University of Manchester was a much larger comprehensive university which had begun with a bequest from the Victorian merchant and philanthropist John Owens in 1851 and gained a Royal Charter in 1880. An illustrious history with pioneering Nobel Prize winners such as the physicist Ernest Rutherford and the economist Arthur Lewis had flattened out to a position of being a large civic university of good standing but falling behind the UK's first rank institutions.

The explanation of the merger that was to come involves both an internal and an external rationale. Exploring first the internal logic, conditions in 2001 were favourable for change. Bob Boucher, who had strongly pursued the separation agenda had unexpectedly moved back to Sheffield University from where he had come and had been replaced by a new Vice-Chancellor, Professor John Garside, an internal appointee with a different outlook. VUM's Vice-Chancellor, Sir Martin Harris, was approaching a decade in office and did not have long-term ambitions to remain in post.

Perhaps more relevantly, after the results of the 2001 Research Assessment Exercise both universities were in a mood to contemplate their futures. For UMIST it was apparent that its small size and narrow focus made it vulnerable to potential shocks, for example in the supply of science and engineering students or in the overseas student market on which it was heavily dependent. This was not a strategy of desperation; the institution was on an upward trajectory with new buildings, increased student numbers and entry into biological sciences from its traditional base in physical sciences and particularly engineering.

At VUM, while some areas such as life science were thriving, there were concerns about the long-term viability of investment-hungry physical sciences and engineering for similar reasons to those for UMIST, and a more general realization that the current model probably offered no better future than maintaining the present position. On the positive side, finances were in better shape than for most universities and the University was the most popular in the UK in terms of numbers of undergraduate applications.

The campuses were contiguous, a unique situation in the UK for two research-led universities. Despite the recent withdrawal of UMIST from a number of shared services, social connections were strong and two major joint ventures, in business and management and in materials science, showed that joint working was possible. The first of these was a federal arrangement, The Manchester Federal School of Business and Management was an umbrella that linked UMIST's Manchester School of Management (MSM) with VUM's Manchester Business School and two more specialized management-related subjects, VUM's School of Accounting and Finance and the research institute PREST. The arrangement involved a series of committees which aimed to avoid duplication and promote new teaching and research ventures. The material science departments of the two institutions were joint, sharing a building and facilities such that even in a single corridor academics of both affiliations could be found.

However, favourable the internal circumstances, the impetus came primarily from a perception of growing external pressures and challenges. Explicit attention was subsequently given to six of these:[3]

- Increasing complexity of research problems demanding broader interdisciplinary solutions and teams of critical mass with access to modern infrastructure;
- Increasing importance of the knowledge economy and the recognition of the role of universities in contributing to business and the community;
- Changing nature of course provision, with rising student fees being accompanied by greater emphasis on quality, relevance to employment and student choice;
- Globalization of higher education increasing competition for students, top quality academic staff and research funding;
- The need to modernize governance and management structures to make decision-making more streamlined and agile; and
- A recognition of limited resources for both teaching and research and increased selectivity in funding mechanisms.

A more specific external logic lay in the shape of the UK economy. Despite several years of relative prosperity, the UK is essentially a uni-nodal economy with a very strong concentration of activity in London and the South East. This is also reflected in scientific investment – in the Golden Triangle mentioned above and most public and privatized government laboratories. Other cities have lacked economic dynamism and past genera- tions of regional policy have failed to make any real impact. Present policy is people-centred with an emphasis on skills and flexibility and more recently a concept of 'Science Cities' adding a knowledge economy dimension.

Greater Manchester has been seen as the main national success case in terms of regeneration, based on a highly coordinated strategy among local authorities working with business and professional leaders. Cultural and sporting institutions (including hosting the Commonwealth Games – a sporting event second only to the Olympics – and the world-brand of Manchester United Football Club) have featured strongly in a shift from traditional industries to a service-based economy with some key high-tech establishments such as Astra Zeneca's research centre on the outskirts. However, to pursue a strategy of a sustainable transition to a knowledge- based economy the city–region would need access to a world class acade- mic institution, driving change through contributions from its research and training activities.

In the light of these challenges a Joint Working Group was established chaired by Dr John Beacham, a former ICI executive and government adviser with regional affiliations. Its remit was 'to consider various ways to develop a closer relationship between UMIST and the Victoria University of Manchester in order to build on existing strengths, with the aim of achieving world class standing in research, scholarship and teaching across a broad range of disciplines.'

When the group began, the way forward could have been one of several options considered. The *status quo* of no increased cooperation was regarded as a base case which was not acceptable in itself but would be used as a reference point against which to judge other options.[4] The other options were:

- Grassroots collaboration: separate institutions but encouraging indi- vidual academics to collaborate in research or teaching. This was seen as relatively easy to implement on a small scale but creating con- fusion and numerous ad-hoc demands on issues such as regulations when scaled up;
- Federal collaboration: provision of an overarching structure for col- laboration between separate institutions. The experience of the mate- rials and business collaborations suggested that this would have relatively high transaction cost and present a confused view to the outside world;

- Trade model: separate institutions but making identities more distinct through combination of common departments and allocation to one or other institution. It was considered that agreement on respective specialisms would be hard to achieve;
- Combined institution: a newly constituted combined university.

The preferred option of the Joint Working Group was the dissolution of the two existing universities and the creation of a single new chartered university. It was concluded that neither university was likely to achieve world-class status in all disciplines on its own or to compete realistically with the very best universities. To overcome a future of, at best, incremental growth a strategy for a step-change in performance was needed and this could only be achieved through the combined new university option. The overall aim of this process of integration would be to enhance research excellence at international level, to increase student choice through new and interdisciplinary courses and to contribute to the economic well-being of the region.

PROCESS OF CHANGE

The processes of decision and of implementation were both of necessity complicated. The internal approval timetable began in April 2002 when the governing bodies of both universities agreed to proceed to a due diligence phase. This ran until the following October and the activity was given the name Project Unity. Due diligence was undertaken through a managed structure involving over 250 staff, students and lay members with support from specialist advisers on issues such as pensions and finance. A communications infrastructure was set up to keep internal stakeholders informed; this involved open meetings, briefings and newsletters with a dedicated website. Project Unity operated in all of the key dimensions needed to design and operate a university: governance and administration; research; teaching, learning and assessment; estates; human resources; information systems; and finance.

Ambitious goals and detailed proposals were set out in each case. No policy, procedure or structure from the 'legacy institutions' was retained by default – all were designed or selected on the basis of the needs of the new university. The estates strategy was particularly demanding in financial terms, involving several new buildings and refurbishments and a better external environment, both to allow co-location and more generally to support the research and teaching mission of the new university. The strategy eventually was realized as the largest capital programme ever undertaken in the British university system and at one point was the country's second largest capital project of any kind. The dominant visual image was a forest of cranes. At this point, however, the issue was to find the finance to allow the project to go ahead.

A total cost of around £300 million was estimated, the bulk to be spent on estates. Most of this was to come from the formula allocations due to the universities from the Funding Council, from the universities' own reserves and disposal of surplus assets (in the UK it is usually the case that universities (at least the older ones) own their buildings. Specific funding was sought from the Funding Council's Strategic Development Fund (the lion's share of which went to this single project). In addition, the Office of Science and Technology – responsible for the Research Councils – provided £10 million in support of specific research projects in Photon Science and Neuroscience and a substantial contribution was made by the regional authority, the Northwest Development Agency.

For many universities a financial undertaking on this scale would be out of the question. Why then was it possible to mobilize a public investment on this scale? For the answer it is necessary to recall the arguments made above concerning the external logic for the merger. In this environment, the case for this extraordinary investment in support of a second node in the economy received a sympathetic hearing at both national and regional levels.

On the basis of the due diligence exercise the academic and overall governing bodies agreed in general to proceed in October 2002 subject to securing external funding, and with more precision in March 2003 at which time full integration was set for 1st October 2004. By July 2003 dissolution of the two universities on 30th September 2004 was agreed subject to the Charter being granted. The process was not quite as smooth as this timetable implies. Staff concerns about potential job losses had been largely allayed by a guarantee of a two-year moratorium after Foundation and that in any event there would be no compulsory redundancies, though an early retirement and voluntary severance package was available on a selective basis. At the level of the governing body of UMIST there had been some opposition to Project Unity with concerns about losing the distinctive heritage of the institution and of selling science short. Eventually the doubters were won round to secure full approval.

During the transition, the challenge was to keep both universities operating normally so as not to disrupt research and the student experience but also to initiate the structures of the new University. The adopted solution was to create a Company Limited by Guarantee (CLG), a form of not-for-profit organization, with powers derived from both governing bodies and advised by both academic governing bodies. An Interim Executive Management Team reporting to the Board of the CLG, chaired alternately by the two vice-chancellors, oversaw a programme office which in turn ran a series of projects. The new structure of the University emerged at this point with four large faculties (in three cases on the scale of medium-sized universities) and a limited number of large schools (initially 23) which would in many cases consolidate departments and disciplines. The four faculty deans, also university vice-presidents (accompanied in a matrix structure initially by four 'policy' Vice-Presidents in the areas of research, teaching and learning, innovation and knowledge transfer, and external relations), would be budget holders, along with the Registrar and Secretary. Until such time as the Deans could be appointed, Interim Faculty Leadership teams and an interim acting Dean (from another faculty) would develop the structures.

The key appointment of President and Vice-Chancellor (a new title with more international currency) was made such that the chosen candidate, Professor Alan Gilbert, would have time to shape the institution before taking operational control. In practice he was present for eight months before the inauguration as President and Vice-Chancellor designate. During this period, in his own words he had:

> several months free from the burden of day-to-day operational management in which to build a senior leadership team, develop the 'step-change' agenda in con-sultation with colleagues across the merging institutions, and design the kinds of governance and management structures that the embryonic institution would need to facilitate its ambitions. (Gilbert, 2007, pp. 182–3)

In terms of process the merger was close to being an unqualified success. At the time of writing, four years on, few staff refer to or identify with the legacy institutions except occasionally as geographic descriptions of parts of the campus. There was little or no disruption of students and courses and the new schools became quickly operational. Probably the only area of significant technical setback was with IT systems – the systems supporting finance and student services were changed simultaneously with the merger and that proved too much to digest, with frustrating delays impeding many activities and even basic services such as e-mail proving troublesome. It took some time before these problems could be resolved. For universities elsewhere contemplating mergers it is useful to summarize the success factors, though these may not be replicable. In essence these were:

- A clear strategic rationale;
- Universities similar in research standing;
- External support and resources (again with a strategic rationale);
- Internal support from staff and students (in part an outcome of a good communications strategy;

- Contiguous campuses;
- Both Vice-Chancellors retiring so no dispute about the CEO position.

For the remaining parts of this chapter the story will not be one about a process of merger but rather about the subsequent efforts to create a world-class university on a new model. However, the consequences of issues created by decisions during the merger phase will occasionally be revisited.

THE 2015 AGENDA

It is quite common for universities to project their mission statements by means of their public websites and other media. Far rarer is the presentation of an operationalized strategic plan but any visitor to the University of Manchester's website will find there a document called 'Towards Manchester 2015'. Although updated in minor ways on an annual basis, this has represented from the start the blueprint for the transformation or 'step-change' that the University is seeking to achieve. It originated as the President's pre-merger planning document and it was endorsed by a series of planning conferences in the Spring of 2004 and by the Board of the Company Limited by Guarantee, and again by the Board of the new University early in 2005 on the advice of the Senate.

The formal mission is set out in terms of a target:

> To make The University of Manchester, already an internationally distinguished centre of research, innovation, learning and scholarly inquiry, one of the leading universities in the world by 2015.

Academic, social, ethical and moral values are stated and used as a foundation for a vision that puts ten adjectives in front of the word institution and explains each of them.[5] However, the core of the document is the 2015 Agenda itself, a set of nine goals and strategies and accompanying key performance indicators (KPIs) that if achieved will constitute the 'preferred future' for the university by that date. Why nine? According to the President they reflect years of engagement in trying to challenge strong, large, research-intensive universities to take on step-change improvement.[6] The choice of nine reflected his judgement of what the cardinal goals were, though in a couple of cases they could have been conflated or separated for presentational purposes. The goals are summarized below, the first four in more detail:

Goal One – High International Standing

> *To establish The University of Manchester by 2015 as a world renowned centre of scholarship and research, able to match the leading universities in the world in attracting and retaining teachers, researchers and 'critical mass' research teams of the highest quality, and as a higher education brand synonymous with the finest international standards of academic excellence, and with pioneering, influential and exciting research and scholarship.*

In some senses this goal is an encapsulation of the rest, as an international reputation is likely to result only from improvement in other key areas. However, there are some actions in terms of positioning (working with leading partner institutions around the world), marketing and promotion and most specifically the appointment of 'iconic' scholars and research teams. An iconic scholar is defined as one whose virtuosity has been recognized in ways that provide iconic status within and beyond the international academic community. Nobel prizes are cited as the most obvious criterion and one KPI is the presence on staff of at least five Nobel Laureates (or equivalent) by 2015, at least two of whom are full-time and three such appointments being secured by 2007. The other KPI attached to this goal is clear evidence of improvement in the University's international and domestic standing as measured by reputable international higher education rankings. The selected measure is the Shanghai Jiao Tong Academic Ranking of World Universities which for all its idiosyncrasies is seen as being objectively based rather than relying on non-reproducible and methodologically obscure peer review elements as do some of its rivals.

Goal Two – World Class Research

> *To establish The University of Manchester by 2015 among the 25 strongest research universities in the world on commonly accepted criteria of research excellence and performance.*

Elite universities are typically judged by their research performance and standing. Apart from striving to create a supportive environment for research and gaining funding for research, the strategy has focused on people, with a heavy emphasis upon recruitment and retention of outstanding individuals. This particular dimension was reinforced by the new University having to encounter a major test of research standing rather earlier in its lifetime than it would have chosen, the UK Government's Research Assessment Exercise (RAE). Since 1986 the RAE has been used to allocate core funding for university research (Barker, 2007). The 2008 exercise, the last of its kind, is grading Manchester's performance over a seven-year period, hence a significant part of the period covered was pre-merger, and in terms of publications even more so. Hence, recruitment of virtuoso researchers represented the quickest strategy for improvement against this test. The longer-term project of raising further the quality of the entire research activity could only be partly fulfilled at this stage. The University has always been clear that its strategy is driven by its own agenda, not the RAE and indeed it has instituted an external review process which is probably more demanding.

The KPIs under this heading have evolved over time. The initial focus was couched in the terminology of the previous RAE, accompanied by fairly crude quantitative targets (such as the doubling of the number of postgraduate research students and postdocs by 2015). A revised approach matches quantity with quality with the current set being:

- Annual increase in the University's share of the world's high impact research publications;
- Achieving annual increases in external grant income consistent with a doubling of such income (in real terms) by 2015;
- Annual increases in total audited research expenditure (TARE) consistent with the trebling of such expenditure by 2015;
- Achieving annual increases in the number of postgraduate research students successfully completing their programme within the specified period consistent with doubling the number of completions by 2015.

This list also illustrates Manchester's main advantage. While it can be hard to compete in their own fields with some small specialized institutions, the large University can achieve a leading position on indicators which combine quality and quantity – sometimes referred to as 'research power'.

Goal Three – Exemplary Knowledge Transfer

To contribute to economic development regionally, nationally and interna-tionally, and greatly to increase opportunities for the University and its staff and students to benefit from the commercialisation and application of the knowledge, expertise and intellectual property (IP) that they develop in the University.

There was a determination from the start that the new University would take a fresh approach to what is commonly termed the Third Mission

(Larédo, 2007). An early move was to develop an IP policy which gave the most generous terms available to innovators and creators of intellectual property while putting in place an infrastructure for its effective exploitation. To overcome cultural resistance in some quarters of academic life, the principal reward system of promotion allows progression through the ranks to full professor on the basis of outstanding performance in knowledge transfer. This was an area where some national KPIs had been discredited, with examples such as counting the number of spin-off firms created taking no account of their size, profitability or sustainability. These would then be open to manipulation. The more rigorous approach adopted by Manchester has been to set annual increases of 10 per cent in the value of third-party investments in university spin-out companies and in the number and value of licence deals done with third parties. Collaboration with business takes place within the framework of overarching agreements with companies wherever possible. This reduces transaction costs by creating a ready-made and consistent framework for pricing, IP, etc. and maximizes the chance of spillovers whereby a relationship based, say, on engineering research may also lead to contracts for executive education in management studies. The KPI for this activity is that the University should increase the proportion of research grant income through industrial sponsorship from its level of 8 per cent in 2004 to 20 per cent by 2015. A remaining challenge is to find a way to consistently measure knowledge transfer of the type more open to social science academics, making a major and sustained contribution to policy and practice.

Goal Four – Excellent Teaching and Learning

To provide students with teachers, learning environments, teaching and learning infrastructure and support services equal to the best in the world.

This goal was turned into a strategy by emphasizing the need to enhance the Manchester student experience, using e-learning to enrich teaching and learning, listening to students and, in a similar way to knowledge transfer, creating clear promotion tracks based upon excellence in teaching. Key performance indicators are sustained high levels of satisfaction among key employers with the quality of Manchester graduates, as measured by properly validated employer satisfaction surveys; and annual increases each year until 2015 in the number of students enrolled on on-line programmes. The third indicator, annual improvements in student satisfaction with the quality of teaching they receive and of the learning environment they experience in Manchester, has been the source of much concern. The National Student Survey is a government-backed survey on behalf of the Funding

Councils targeted at final-year undergraduates. Manchester has not performed well in this, possibly because of the focus on research, stoked up further by the RAE.

Concern about teaching and learning has led to a multifaceted and comprehensive Review of Undergraduate Education which seeks to restore to parity of esteem with research and postgraduate training what many external stakeholders see as the core business of a university. At the core of this is a determination to achieve personalized learning, that is working in small groups with tutors and ensuring a close relationship with an academic adviser, in an era when massification of higher education and the consequent decline in the unit of resource available per student has driven universities away from this ideal.

Remaining Goals

The 2015 agenda looks outward to the community as well as to business and two goals address different aspects of this. Goal Five is that of Widening Participation by 'making Manchester the UK's most accessible research-intensive university by providing international students from economically deprived backgrounds and home students from traditionally under-represented sections of society with a supportive learning environment in an inclusive and welcoming University community'. Also in this vein is Goal Nine – More Effective Service to the Community, spelt out as 'to contribute to the development of a secure, humane, prosperous and sustainable future for human society and, beginning in its local communities in Greater Manchester, to explore opportunities to enrich the social, cultural and economic development of the communities, regions and countries in which the University works'.

Conversion of these high-level goals to practical action has centred upon two courses of action. For widening participation, the University has devoted a higher proportion of fee income than any of its peers to established merit-based bursaries and scholarships for both home and overseas students from disadvantaged backgrounds, in the latter case from selected developing countries. Community service focuses upon existing students with a flagship 'Manchester Leadership Programme' which gives students credits for voluntary work in the local community while contributing to their personal and professional development. Broader regional and community engagement also came into this part of the strategy.

The remaining three goals are more inward looking and focus upon the managerial achievements necessary to drive the other goals. Goal Eight addresses the critical topic of Internationally Competitive Resources and is stated as being 'to ensure that the University acquires the recurrent and capital resources necessary to be competitive at the highest international level.' As noted earlier, without the large endowments of its international rivals the University needs to develop income flows that give it the resource base to achieve its ambitions. Strategies include increased fee income, proceeds from knowledge transfer and a much more organized approach to fundraising than has been the case historically for British universities.

Goal Seven is Efficient, Effective Management and is embodied through efforts to achieve simple flat management structures with a minimum of hierarchy and a rational, simple committee system. Linked to this is Goal Six, Empowering Collegiality, where the key words are 'people-oriented' and 'engagement', no mean challenge in an institution of this size. KPIs are built from a staff satisfaction survey and measures of diversity in the staff profile.

Progress and challenges

Almost four years on what has been achieved and what are the major challenges facing the University? Rather than work through all the KPIs some highlights are presented here. Concerning the goal of high international standing there was an immediate beneficial effect on the position in the World University Rankings with a move from VUM's position of 78 in 2004 to 53 a year later (the scoring system favours scale). Since then progress has been upwards but incremental, reaching 48 in 2007 which places the University ninth in Europe and fifth in the UK. The challenge of breaking into the top 25 can be illustrated by Figure 3.1 which shows the average number of papers in Nature and Science in the past five years.

This shows the score of one of the factors in 2006, worth 20 per cent of the total score. At number 50, Manchester is in the midpoint of the top 100 universities shown. What is striking is the fairly flat profile of the lower half and the rapid acceleration towards and within the top 25.

In another dimension of international standing, the university is right on track. Two Nobel Prize Winners, Joseph Stiglitz and Sir John Sulston have taken on part-time positions as have two further iconic appointees, the influential Harvard political scientist Robert Putnam and the novelist Martin Amis. The benefits of iconic appointments were clearly demonstrated when an external donor almost immediately endowed the World Poverty Centre which Stiglitz chairs with a sum greater than the cost of the appointment. Perhaps more important, is the effect in attracting top class academics and students to work in the University.

Research income has been another area of spectacular growth, rising from £116 million in 2003–04 to £174 million in 2006–07. Total audited

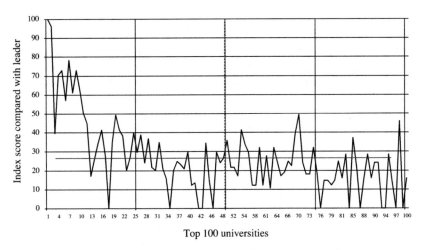

Figure 3.1   World university ranking for papers in nature and science

research expenditure, which covers all activities, has risen by almost 45 per cent in the same period, to £372 million. Knowledge transfer has shown good progress but has been typical for the sector in that successes are very lumpy – notably the flotation of a spin-off company Renovo which raised £50 million. Achievements against the KPIs are satisfactory in themselves but given the increasing weighting given to knowledge transfer by the UK government, even as a driver of other income sources, this area will need more attention in the future. One spectacular success was the securing of £25 million over five years from the supermarket giant Tesco to found an Institute for Sustainable Consumption, the largest single corporate research contract to a UK university.

The challenges have surfaced more at the level of the underpinning goals. In particular, the University faced a large operating deficit in 2006 of around £30 million (out of total expenditure of £611 million), some of which was the result of deliberate investment ahead of the RAE but which also reflected a 'structural deficit' of around £10 million attributable to the additional costs from the merger and exacerbated by the two-year moratorium on job losses. The salary bill had been driven up by higher than expected increases across the UK sector and a post-merger growth in staff numbers of some 2800 staff in 30 months. While much of this had been driven by increased research income it was clear that urgent action was needed to improve efficiency and eliminate the deficit. A combination of tighter financial management and an early-retirement/voluntary severance scheme that reduced numbers by around 630 people has drastically reduced the deficit for 2007/08 and a return to surplus is in prospect. Nonetheless, this episode has highlighted the marginal nature of higher education finance and its exposure to potential shocks. A secure financial future is only possible through continued improvements in productivity and growth of high revenue areas such as overseas students, executive education and full-cost applied research. Performance in the first two of these has been below the demanding targets set and means that redoubled efforts will be necessary in the future if the planned course is to be maintained. All of these areas are highly competitive markets in which only the best will prosper.

Part of the productivity challenge lies in a need to rebalance staff time. Success in research depends upon freeing up time without reducing the quality of the student experience. While students undoubtedly benefit from research-informed and research-led teaching, the rising fee rates have fostered a consumerist attitude which does not tolerate any hint of neglect. Solutions can only lie in increasing the efficiency of teaching, including effective use of online learning, use of graduate teaching assistants, and consolidation of uneconomic course options. The latter challenge should be easier in a large University where wide choice can be sustained through the presence of such a large number of specialisms. However, all of these measures depend upon students perceiving the kind of personalized teaching and learning environment that is being sought through the current Review and staff perceiving that excellence in this dimension of their work will be rewarded in the same way as research excellence.

Productivity also lies in administrative efficiency and here there is a careful balance to be struck between relieving academics of as much of the administrative burden as possible while not creating a large and expensive bureaucracy which drives up overheads on research and teaching. Overall, the administration is many ways a model for others. Its management of the merger was far better than is often witnessed in the private sector[7] and the main phase of the capital programme is largely complete in time and under budget.

At the time of writing seven years remain to achieve the 2015 goals. In the timescale in which reputations are built this is a rather short period. It seems likely that the attraction of that date will diminish as it approaches even if targets are being met – the middle-to-long distance always appears more inspirational – and it would not be surprising if a major renewal of the concept became necessary about midway to the present end-date. It also needs to be emphasized that there is not a fixed target at which point the status of top 25 is achieved and all can relax. The nature of the modern university and the expectations society and the economy place upon it is itself evolving. Manchester is seeking to redefine the rules for excellence, not only because the Golden Triangle and the Ivy League are clubs closed to new members but also because those institutions in their present form may themselves not be fit to meet the challenges likely to be imposed upon Western universities. While the verdict is clearly still open the hope is that the maxim of the Industrial Revolution will hold once more, 'What Manchester does today, the World does tomorrow'.

ACKNOWLEDGEMENT

This chapter is the view of an 'insider' who was involved but not at the centre of activity. It is a personal interpretation and does not represent the view of the University. I would like to thank those colleagues who provided key inputs, notably Rod Coombs, Alan Gilbert, Albert McMenemy and Alistair Ulph. Any errors or misinterpretations are entirely the author's responsibility.

NOTES

1. A Royal Charter is a means of incorporation granted by the Sovereign of the United Kingdom on the advice of the Privy Council. The UK's older universities derive their legal identity by this means, and though largely dependent upon government funding, are independent not-for-profit bodies with their own governing bodies with responsibilities similar to those of a company board.
2. This was the formal name of the predecessor institution, reflecting its Victorian foundation, but it was almost universally known by the same name as its successor, the new University of Manchester. Prior to the merger, UMIST staff and students almost universally referred to it as 'Owens' after its historic college origins.
3. List based on a table in the business plan for the merger.
4. Left unstated was the further factor that the status quo could have degenerated into unproductive local competition.
5. In detail, the statement is that as one of the world's leading universities, Manchester in 2015 will be a people-centred, research-led, innovative, learning, liberal, independent, international, inclusive and engaging institution, and finally a Manchester institution.
6. Personal communication 23 August 2007.
7. A study by the author and colleagues of the effects of industrial mergers on R&D activities of firms – the closest analogue to universities in a business merger – found that companies typically underestimated the issues involved and did not subsequently achieve the improvements in innovative performance that they expected (James et al., 1998).

REFERENCES

Barker, K. (2007), 'The UK Research Assessment Exercise: the evolution of a national research evaluation system', *Research Evaluation*, **16** (1), 3–12.
Gilbert, A. (2007), 'The Manchester merger, stretching the Golden Triangle', in H. de Burgh, A. Fazackerley and J. Black (eds), *Can the Prizes Still Glitter? The*

Future of British Universities in a Changing World, Buckingham: University of Buckingham Press.

James, A.D., Georghiou, L. and J.S. Metcalfe (1998), 'Integrating technology into merger and acquisition decision making', *Technovation*, **18** (8/9), 563–73.

Larédo, P. (2007), 'Revisiting the third mission of universities: toward a renewed categorization of university activities?', *Higher Education Policy*, **20** (4), 441–56.

4. Large-scale international facilities within the organization: MAX lab within Lund University

Olof Hallonsten and Mats Benner

1. INTRODUCTION: LARGE-SCALE RESEARCH FACILITIES AND SWEDISH RESEARCH POLICY

Small states face a policy dilemma in research: how should a country that produces 1 per cent of the total scientific output in the world, organize its research activities? Should it try to spread its resources evenly over the whole spectrum of research, to maximize its capacity to absorb results produced elsewhere? Or should it, instead, specialize in certain niches, to increase its international visibility, even at the price of 'ignorance' in many important areas? Should it try to develop its own infrastructure for expensive research fields, or should it instead maximize its participation in international research facilities?

The answer to all these questions is in many cases to try to pursue all of these strategies at the same time. There is no clear-cut small-scale/large-scale divide in research policy. Even smaller countries attempt to have a presence in highly competitive fields, and do make important contributions in them (although much of their research is repetitive and follows rather than leads the 'research frontier'). Similarly, many small countries rely on international research facilities in large-scale and cost-intensive fields, but also maintain national facilities in these areas. How, then, has Sweden managed the small states dilemma in research policy? This broad issue will be analysed by a focus on the evolution of a national research facility, MAX-lab.

The Swedish research policy system is pluralistic. The institutional setup in research policy is rather widely dispersed, that is many different policy agents have been set up to implement (but also to some extent formulate) research policy. Policy coordination, on the other hand, has been notably weaker. Sweden has no designated ministry for science. Instead, research affairs are cohabitants with education, ranging from preschool to graduate training in the same political setting. This political level is also, following the tradition of small cabinets and large administrative bodies, rather weak in its steering of the research system, mainly concentrating on the formulation of broader political goals. There have been attempts at coordinating research as a policy field, the first of which was taken back in 1962 when the governmental research committee, at the time chaired by the Prime Minister Erlander, was established. A new attempt at strengthening the 'steering core' was taken in the 1980s, when a system of three-year research bills was introduced, where all R&D policies were included in the same governmental bill. By this, coordination between policy areas was to be strengthened. A concerted effort was also expected to create political and financial space for more adventurous investments and initiatives.

After 20 years of a so-called coordinated research policy at the central level, we can conclude that policy coordination is still relatively weak and that instances of concentration around a few broadly-based goals are rare. The research policy system has also been notoriously weak in identifying (and serving) needs for large-scale initiatives, with long delays in the decision-making procedure. In some cases, the government has relied on private sources (e.g. genomics, proteomics).

The administrative system is decentralized in a similar manner. Basic research has remained the cornerstone of the national research council's mandate, while industrial innovations and other types of 'applications' have been relegated to mission-oriented agencies with a special task to fund and support applied research and academic-industrial collaboration. The research councils themselves are also strongly decentralized in their decision-making structure, and resource allocation within and between research fields are primarily determined in a collegial manner. After a funding reform in the 1990s, international collaboration has been integrated into the activities (and funding portfolio) of the research councils (and today in the Swedish Research Council), together with the funding of large-scale facilities. Priorities for national and international collaboration as well as large-scale facilities are set by a government agency as part of its budgetary considerations. Thus there is no established structure through which the government could grasp the initiative and make policy reconsiderations to initiate an effort of the size necessary to establish a large-scale research facility. As we shall see, such initiatives must have their roots elsewhere. The formation of KFI – the committee for research infrastructure at the Research Council – can though be seen as a first attempt at least on paper to create such a structure within the system.

Some numbers that are rather striking may serve as an illustration. The Ministry of Education, in whose responsibilities are included research policy overarching management of all governmentally funded research in

Sweden, employs a total of nine people whose primary agenda is focused on higher education and research. At the Swedish Research Council, an estimate of 80 full-time people works with research issues. Adding the governmental agency Vinnova, which might be considered an equally important player in the research policy field, about a hundred people are employed at governmental agencies for the task of governing the Swedish public research system. In total, the number of full-time researchers at the Swedish universities and university colleges can be estimated to around 20 000. These numbers – even though they are incomplete and represent only a rough estimate – make a clear point: the power must lie elsewhere.

Still though, universities in Sweden have relatively weak steering systems, where resources generally are earmarked for so-called research areas (*vetenskapsområden*). Universities have the possibility of redistributing resources between research areas, but often follow the ring-fenced allocations from parliament (which in themselves follow historical resource trajectories). Universities therefore tend to have limited resources – and limited legitimacy – in creating and opening new areas, and redirecting resources for new and/or cost-intensive initiatives. Therefore, such costly and well-aligned targeted efforts within the university system are critically dependent on a university management dedicated to a long-term commitment to the research area(s) concerned, in practice meaning viewing them as central to attaining the university's strategic goals. Such commitments are not always easy to make, given the competition for funds always present within the university.

The Swedish research system is decentralized and strong on breadth, continuity and incremental reforms (and with a flexible deployment of resources), but relatively weak in taking joint and demanding initiatives. When new areas emerge, it is not necessarily one agency or organization that takes the lead. The issues of who decides, who funds, who carries out the work are not easily resolved in a highly decentralized system. Sweden also has a history as a scientific player of some magnitude; i.e. there is an idea of expansion and breadth in the system. The belief that Swedish research should be all encompassing remains strong. The ideal that Sweden could have a presence in highly competitive, highly internationalized fields is vivid throughout the system – from the laboratory to parliament. At the same time, budget restrictions continue to grow, and more and more areas compete over scarce resources. Priorities are therefore seldom explicitly set, and large-scale investments can become very cumbersome for the system to manage.

A large-scale research facility – defined as a demarcated piece of experimental equipment with a total construction cost of more than hundred times the average yearly salary of the experimenter dedicated to using it – is a good example of a large-scale project of the kind discussed above.

Large-scale research facilities are typically thought of as particle accelerators and telescopes – experimental facilities with very restricted disciplinary limits which puts the obvious question of usefulness and priorities in resource allocation in focus. Facilities such as CERN (the European Laboratory for Particle Physics) or ESO (European Southern Observatory) operate at an extraordinary high cost, given that they support comparably small scientific communities. Translated to the local Swedish university case, a research facility need not be overwhelmingly huge or costly to also qualify as large-scale in this respect. Swedish universities traditionally have the task of facilitating a broad spectrum of disciplines, and the concentration of resources within the university on a large-scale research facility might in itself be considered controversial.

Increasing financial constraints, the challenge of new needs and demands, institutional change and the rearrangement of inner and outer boundaries are inevitable processes in the change of academic science. According to Ziman (1994, 2000) they are generally visible and evident throughout the whole system, and summarized under the concept of the dynamic steady state of science. This state is steady but not static in the sense that the unpredictable progress of scientific research will be forced to take place under severe resource limitations. At the same time and in close interaction thereto, institutional change and rebuilding of alliances will take place, all in all transforming the organization, management and performance of science into a new 'post-academic' reality. Science will thereby adjust to the steady state of a fixed envelope of resources simply by the loosening of previously rigid structures in new dynamic, changeable and unpredictable customs. An academic research institution need naturally not be large-scale or in any other sense stand out among others to be affected by – and become forerunners of – this change, although the most visible examples perhaps are the largest institutions. The case we are about to present as an insight to the structures and channels by which a research policy system of high ambitions but limited impact facilitates an initiative of extraordinary character might very well best be understood in the light of Ziman's PAS theories.

How does a generally weak research policy system like Sweden's handle an initiative of extraordinary character, such as MAX-lab? The question might be reformulated as to how MAX-lab as an institution manages to establish itself, develop and grow large-scale within the Swedish system. We will attempt to answer that question by closely examining the history of MAX-lab in its context of national and local interests, expansion of scientific objectives and instrumental opportunities, change of user demands and institutional response, and the continuous struggle to make do with a limited resource envelope: Where do initiatives originate? How do different levels of interest relate, and how do they collaborate? How are demands formulated, plans carried out and critical decisions taken? And how, given the weakness of the Swedish system and its institutional landscape, is a successful large-scale project undertaken?

2. MAX-LAB, A SWEDISH NATIONAL LABORATORY

Synchrotron radiation was first detected in 1947 as the unwanted waste product of particle accelerators used in high energy physics for the purpose of colliding particle beams (Blewett 1998). The light produced by an accelerated beam of electrons is not just very bright and strong, its wavelength covers the wide spectrum from infrared radiation to x-rays (which includes visible and ultraviolet light), giving synchrotron radiation extraordinary good potential as a research tool. Since the 1970s, particle accelerators has been constructed for the sole purpose of producing the light, which has led to enormous leaps in performance of the machines and vast improvements of the experimental techniques. Today, representatives from almost all disciplines within the natural sciences are frequent users of the light, and new application areas are constantly discovered and exploited. This not only makes synchrotron radiation one of the most useful experimental techniques in the natural sciences today; the continuous exploitation of new areas of usage during the past two decades has also given synchrotron radiation a status of being very promising and full of possibilities also in a future perspective.

A typical synchrotron radiation laboratory is built around a storage ring, named that way because of its main purpose, to store the accelerated electrons that produce the light. Once a certain amount of electrons are injected to the ring's vacuum chamber, they run around at a velocity near the speed of light, passing through so-called bending magnets and insertion devices, where they by changing direction in a given manner produce light.[1] The light is brought out of the ring to beamlines, where it passes a monochromator in which the preferred light with respect to wavelength and intensity is collected. Through a variety of optics devices, designed mainly to focus the beam, the light finally arrives at the experimental station (normally called end station), where the actual experiments are done. Depending on the technique, one single beamline can support several end stations.

The variables governing what kinds of experiments it is possible to conduct on a synchrotron radiation laboratory are multiple. Different experiments make use of light in different wavelengths, and every accelerator has its own technical characteristics and therefore specific possibilities regarding what kind of light can be produced. Down the stream, mono-chromators, vacuum chambers and detectors, along with a myriad of other technical particularities, decide what experiments are possible. This trivially implies the aforementioned wide variety of experimental possibilities, but it also means that beamlines to a large extent are built to be unique, also on a global level. It may not be possible for a beamline perfectly suitable for one particular lab or ring to be mounted on another ring, and if it were, it might not give anything like the same experimental performance.

Beamtime, that is, access to a running experimental station in a synchro-tron radiation laboratory, is normally given to research groups on the basis of international peer reviewed competition. The principle for granting access to beamtime is common for most synchrotron radiation laboratories throughout the world, with minor differences. In principle, anyone can apply for beamtime, regardless of disciplinary, institutional or national belonging. The applications for beamtime at a laboratory are reviewed by an external peer review committee, who have been given the task of select-ing the applications for allocation of beamtime on the basis of scientific excellence, usually meaning an assessment of the quality of the scientific case, the track record of the applicants, and the purely technical possibili-ties of conducting the experiment successfully. Beamtime is free of charge for everyone, with the only demand that the results be published. Many lab-oratories also offer industrial users the possibility to buy beamtime.

MAX-lab is a Swedish national laboratory for synchrotron radiation research, located on the northern university campus of Lund University. MAX-lab operates three storage rings with a total of about 15 beamlines,[2] and also facilitates a research programme in nuclear physics. MAX-lab is run as a so-called special entity ('*särskild verksamhet*') within the university, which means that the university is the formal employer of the staff. The operation of the facility is however the responsibility of the Swedish Research Council, which supplies an annual operational budget of about SEK 60 million. The laboratory is governed by a board, composed by two representatives from each party of interest, the university, the research council and the user association, and an independent chairman. The board appoints the director and the committees. Beamtime at MAX-lab is granted through applications that are reviewed once every year by the Program Advisory Committee (PAC). Formally, no considerations other than those regarding scientific excellence are made when beamtime is allocated. In practice, there are exceptions to this, which we will come back to later. MAX-lab is mainly an academic institution. Not only does it function more or less exactly as any department within the university structure; manage-ment and operation of the laboratory has a stamp of academia. The machine group, responsible for running the storage ring, consists mainly of the same people as the university department for accelerator physics, headed by Professor Mikael Eriksson. The coordinator for the synchrotron radiation activity is also professor of synchrotron light instrumentation, Ralf Nyholm. The close ties and the near collaboration between the laboratory and its host university, manifested partly by this coordination of academic activities and laboratory operation is regarded an important link between the cultural belonging of the user community and the management of the lab. To some extent, these matters are manifestations of the healthy relationship with the host university. In the latest Swedish Research Council's Review of the Swedish National Facilities, this is strongly emphasized: 'The university sees facilitating world class research at MAX-lab as part of its fundamental research profile. One could hardly ask for a more positive relationship between a laboratory and its host university.' (Vetenskapsrådet 2002).

The definition of large-scale research facility used in the beginning of this chapter, namely that a facility is large-scale when its complete setup of experimental equipment has a total construction cost of more than hundred times the yearly salary of the average user, is indeed applicable on MAX-lab. It might be appropriate to point out here that not having used the term Big Science so far is deliberate. Big Science is a concept to which is attached a great deal of ambiguity, partly due to a transit of the term from scientific to popular culture and thereby from the vocabulary of analysts of scientific practice and policy to the language of all and everyone, which points at its 'linguistic attractiveness' and 'analytical intractability' (Capshew and Rader 1992). The terms large-scale and small-scale facilities, on the other hand, are easily defined as above and not loaded with rhetoric power. They might therefore very well be used to highlight important and interesting characteristics at the core of the synchrotron radiation facility, perhaps especially MAX-lab.

The synchrotron light source laboratory is a large-scale facility for small-scale research. Most experiments conducted at MAX-lab are done by groups of less than five people, undertaking research projects funded and organized in an ordinary academic manner. Nothing distinguishes a group doing experiments at MAX-lab from its counterparts in the home institution not using synchrotron radiation, of course apart from the fact that they happen to be travelling to Lund from time to time. This combination of small-scale and large-scale might seem trivial, but two things related to this are important to remember for the following. First, a large-scale facility supporting a great number of small-scale scientific projects from a wide range of disciplines can be built and developed step-by-step, growing gradually from small to large as new user groups are continuously added. This might actually counteract the fact that policy formulation, coordination and implementation needs to be strong in order to make it happen. Second, the representation of a wide variety of scientific disciplines among the user community might prevent disputes over distribution of funds and asymmetric research investments. This would in turn ease the overall process of establishing consensus around decisions and gain policy stability in a dispersed system. Let us keep in mind these corollaries of the above large-scale/small-scale conceptual reflection when we now start the account of the history of MAX-lab.

2.1   The Offspring of Particles and Politics

Against the background of synchrotron radiation-based research being the originally unwanted child of particle physics, it is somewhat ironic that the first steps towards MAX-lab was taken in the outcome of a rather distressing debate over Swedish involvement in the upgraded joint European particle physics laboratory CERN II. At the beginning of the 1960s CERN – located in Geneva and once upon a time the first European intergovernmental collaboration after World War II – found itself in the midst of the 'energy race' between the scientific efforts of the two superpowers of the time. At the time, an upgrade of the laboratory (which meant the construction of a larger accelerator) was deemed necessary (Krige 1996), but the effort was initially regarded as too big for the existing organization and inter-state collaboration and was therefore treated as a second, independent research programme and laboratory.[3] For Sweden as well as many other countries, this led to the first real science policy debate over CERN, containing the arguments well-known nowadays, of utility, purpose and domestic resource scarcity. The eventual decision – that Sweden should join the so-called CERN II – was based mainly on considerations of Swedish scientific 'reputation' in Europe and pressure on the highest Swedish foreign policy level (Hadenius 1972, see also Widmalm 1993).

At the same time, accelerator physicists in Lund had been constructing their own accelerator for nuclear and particle physics experiments. This accelerator, called LUSY (Lund University Synchrotron), was of a comparably reasonable size, measuring only a few metres in diameter, and had its home at the department of physics in Lund. As a result of the rather significant Swedish science policy decision to join the 'new' CERN collaboration – and thereby concentrating the financial efforts on particle physics research on the laboratory abroad – LUSY's financial support from the Swedish Atomic Research Council (Atomforskningsrådet) was discontinued, with the effect of the closing down of the whole project. The surrounding research group, who had anticipated the coming end of LUSY and therefore had extended their activities to cover other areas and conducting experiments on other accelerator laboratories abroad, took the opportunity to plan a new accelerator project based in Lund, with new and complementary performance and scientific opportunities. A combination of scientific and engineering talent and vision, great support from the rector and central administration of the university and the research council's request for the group in Lund to reformulate their research programme, gave rise to the MAX concept. The council, as well as Lund University, acted with vigilance, and positively, so the plans could continue. During the rest of the 1970s, the MAX accelerator was built piece by piece, with no overarching financial support but with the aid of several smaller budgetary contributions continuously granted the MAX project group. By the end of the decade the accelerator in itself, 'the naked MAX', was financed, but the group was lacking money for experimental equipment for nuclear physics research. Some lively ambassadors of a new experimental technique under the name of synchrotron radiation came to their aid.

Towards the end of the 1970s, when the problem of financing the MAX accelerator project was almost solved, the planned research activities of the project were still entirely focused on nuclear physics. It is possible to elaborate on the thought that the research council, having agreed to fund the ring itself but not the intended research programmes, had a rather ambivalent attitude towards the MAX project. This is not to be treated exclusively as a historical oddity, but rather as an illustration of the contrasts between the general science policy approach towards well-known nuclear and particle physics accelerator projects and the coming synchrotron light research programmes. Undoubtedly though, the inclusion of synchrotron light in the MAX project caused a clear shift in the attitude from the Swedish research councils.

Ideas had already been drafted in the mid-1970s that the MAX accelerator could be used for producing synchrotron light, and through the initiatives of a few visionary people, proposals for funding of a 'National Synchrotron Light Source' were submitted to the research council, with the clear intention of expanding the purposes of MAX to include the production of synchrotron radiation. Although according to Forkman (2000) people in central positions in the Swedish research councils regarded synchrotron light a 'high risk project' (a fact that we will have reason to get back to later), key persons with experience of the growing interest of synchrotron radiation based research in the United States raised positive voices for the idea early on, and with the growing support from both the MAX group and related research groups in Linköping, Gothenburg and Uppsala, the work group appointed by the research council to enquire about the possibilities of expanding the MAX project to include synchrotron light soon stated its support for the project. It is highly appropriate to question the possibilities of survival for the accelerator and nuclear physics programme if not the idea had been raised to devote the MAX project partly to synchrotron light. It is also somewhat significant to the story of MAX-lab that the eventual main purpose of the laboratory – to function as a national research facility providing synchrotron light to experimenters – was not included in the original plans for the laboratory. Making ends meet with funding and organization of the laboratory and research programme seems to have been an everlasting series of obstacles to overcome, but the MAX group continued to work on the accelerator, seemingly unaffected by matters of money. In 1979, the MAX accelerator was inaugurated, still located in the experimental hall where once LUSY had been running. A few years later, MAX was moved to a larger building, so that space could be given to beamlines and end stations.

During the following years, the potentials of synchrotron radiation seemed to become evident to both policy-makers and scientists at most levels of the research system in which MAX found itself. Once it was established as a synchrotron light source project, MAX's potential as a large national scientific resource was recognized by central Lund University officials. In 1981, the board of the university laid down the statutes for MAX-lab, in which it was clearly formulated that the laboratory was a common facility for Swedish science, and that international researchers also should be granted access to the laboratory. Already at this point, before MAX-lab got its status as National Laboratory, an organization was established that ensured close contacts with both the research council at national level and the host university locally. MAX-lab gained its real entrance at national policy level in the government's budget proposition of 1982. There, the wide potential of synchrotron radiation was acknowledged, and MAX-lab was mentioned as a possible 'unique' piece of research infrastructure for both Sweden and the Nordic region as a whole. The government granted the project a financial contribution to cover expenses related to the national use of the facility, 'as a first step'. In the same paragraph the governmental ambition to establish MAX-lab as a national research resource is stated. When MAX I was inaugurated in 1987, it had the status of a Swedish National Laboratory (Forkman 2000).

2.2   Home-made accelerator, home-made organization

It is important to remember here the means by which the original storage ring MAX I came into being. It is widely recognized that MAX I was a 'home-made' accelerator. [4] This trial and error work mode of the MAX group when building the accelerator had its part to play in the success story. 'Home-made' accelerator refers primarily to the technical design. MAX I was built piece by piece and under severe budget constraints, which meant that the accelerator group, lead by 'the Wizard' Mikael Eriksson, never really knew whether the project they were devoting years of their lives to would ever be finished. The construction of a piece of comparably large-scale research infrastructure under such conditions is not only a rare exception but also a fascinating story. It does also play an important part in the eventual success of MAX-lab, not least in the narrow and purely technical sense that it forced the accelerator group to design and construct its machines at the cutting edge of both technical and financial effectiveness. Rather unnoticed, in the shadow of the larger players in the field, extraordinary technical solutions have been developed at MAX-lab. Some would claim that neither MAX II nor MAX III would ever have come into being if it weren't for the innovative skills of the machine group, skills that – it is claimed – can only be learned when one is forced by a limit of financial resources. But shortage of funds and the amazing technical innovativeness of the machine group also had its obvious effects on the organization surrounding the accelerators. This has lead to the evolving of a complex, diversified and rather fluid organization of MAX-lab. In contrast to other laboratories of comparable size, MAX-lab is to a large extent organizationally dependent on informal and decentralized decision-making processes.

As already mentioned, the experimental stations at a synchrotron light source are separate entities with technical specialties of their own. A complete beamline with experimental station is normally just as costly as an accelerator ring to build, which makes the whole laboratory a kind of assemblage of very specific and costly separate entities. In effect this means that no complete experimental setup at MAX-lab has ever been fully financed from the start. Although the research council(s) and the Wallenberg Foundation together incur most of the financing and all initiatives are coordinated centrally at MAX-lab, every project has been organized and funded on its own; the three storage rings, the injector, and the total of about 15 beamlines. The operation budget of MAX-lab has never had the scope for planning, designing and building beamlines. Instead all of the beamlines and experimental stations have been completely constructed by external groups in collaboration with MAX-lab staff. In some cases even the continuous maintenance and administration of beamlines has been 'outsourced' to the groups involved in design and construction.

This way of financing a National Laboratory and large-scale research facility is an immediate consequence of the pluralistic and dispersed Swedish research policy system. It has always been the articulated policy of the Swedish research council(s) that experimental equipment at MAX-lab for the most part should be financed separate from the annual operational budget provided by the council. As an example, the operating costs of MAX-lab 1998–2002 were SEK 83.6 million including funds not only from the research council(s) but also from private foundations and companies, while funding of scientific equipment at MAX-lab, in other words funds applied for either by MAX-lab as an organization, in-house MAX-lab scientists and other staff, or external groups of researchers with ties to the laboratory, amounted to SEK 171.6 million in the same period (Vetenskapsrådet 2002). A beamline project at MAX-lab has its typical origin in initiatives among the various informal networks of user groups and communities. Such initiatives are developed and refined into concrete proposals through the informal and formal management structures at the laboratory. The importance of the informal mechanisms in this process is stressed by the fact that the real origin of the initiatives, along with the original reasons for appointing a certain external group of researchers to the design and development of the instruments, are nearly impossible to trace. In the words of the managers, administrators and committee members of MAX-lab, as well as the researchers, initiatives of this kind just 'happen'.

This has two peculiar organizational dimensions. First, the separation of funds for the facility in the categories 'operational costs' and 'funding of scientific equipment' marks a principally decentralizing function, reinforcing the small-scale/large-scale divide and thereby – as we would argue – making the facility possible at all for the stakeholders to handle. This is because of the previously mentioned weakness of the Swedish research policy system, in which the scientific community as a whole and in the specific fields covered by MAX-lab, the host institution (Lund University) and the formally responsible governmental agency namely the Swedish Research Council all are situated. Second, the division of funding channels also gives rise to decentralization in the internal organization of MAX-lab. Through different formal or informal agreements, specific research groups are given rather significant responsibilities for parts of the scientific instrumentation in the lab. The design, construction, commissioning and continuous maintenance of scientific instrumentation of the kind at MAX-lab are heavily demanding activities, and there is simply no way MAX-lab could put up either the money or all the skilled personnel required. One reason was that the operational budget of the lab was not sufficiently large to finance expensive scientific instruments and equipment. Therefore the responsibility for experimental stations, from the writing of the application for funds in the design phase down to user support and technical maintenance when the equipment has been taken into usage, has been to a large extent given to external groups. Applications for funds for experimental instrumentation can be written by any group and submitted to the Research Council's special body for 'expensive equipment' ('*dyrbar utrustning*'). The choice of the lab as to which projects to support in the referral process – and thereby what experimental equipment the lab chooses – is done by the Program Advisory Committee on behalf of the board. This way, initiatives always come from the users, but the final decision what instrumentation to build is divided between MAX-lab and the Research Council.

To compensate for the money and time certain external groups are devoting to instrument development at MAX-lab, they are given special privileges in the beamtime allocation process. At two beamlines, so-called PRTs (Participating Research Teams) have been established as the model for this. The normal peer review procedure of beamtime allocation in the Program Advisory Committee (PAC) is then short-circuited and the PRTs are given a specific amount of the scheduled beamtime to allocate to experimenters within and outside the PRT on their own account. At one of the beamlines in question, I511, the PRT is given 75 per cent of the scheduled beamtime, and they are required to use at least 25 of this 75 per cent for so-called collaborations, where they invite external groups to use the beamline. At the other one, I311, 50 per cent is given to the PRT and 25 is required to go to collaborations. Even though only two of the beamlines at MAX-lab have so called PRT arrangements, all of them have come into being with the help of people and money external to MAX-lab. At beamlines not equipped with a PRT, the Program Advisory Committee is supposed to take into account the work done by external groups when beamtime is allocated, though of course only after the scientific merits of the applications have been judged. The routines and procedures by which arrangements of this kind are done are not always crystal clear. No formal regulations exist for the Program Advisory Committee to rely on when allocating beamtime on the basis of external groups' investments on the beamlines. The contracts between the MAX-lab management and the PRTs are either outdated or non-existent, and in fact not all members of PRTs know exactly what is stated in those contracts. These are unmistakable examples of the informal organizational structure developed at MAX-lab. Many agreements are made on the basis of informal relations and trust and many responsibilities are carried out on the basis of personal devotion or the day-to-day recognition of immediate needs. This comparable lack of organizational structure is probably at least partly the result of MAX-lab being a thoroughly academic project, a small-scale initiative that has grown evolutionary through the years, as opportunities has been given or coincidences have concurred. Some involvement of traditional academic organizational features can be detected, such as the existence of an 'Old Boys Network' that makes the establishment of formal agreements and writing of contracts unnecessary, and a general 'Barter Economy' of which the above described arrangements on beamlines with no PRT is a good example.

The system has strong advantages. The 'outsourcing' of beamline planning and construction – in some cases even operation – is the extreme of an important planning strategy used by most large-scale laboratories in the world. Scientific planning and development of instrumentation – on the short-term as well as long-term – need always be done in close proximity to the existing and potential users. Often the experimental techniques and sophisticated specialties of instrumentation demand not only continuous collaboration with advisory committees of experts but also active involvement of the users. Most laboratories have learned this, and initiatives are often summoned at conferences, further developed at special meetings with potential users and sometimes even the temporary engagement of researchers in the construction phase on site. The direct 'outsourcing' of instrument development through the agreements with certain external research groups means in practice that the users build their instruments themselves. This can be seen as strengthening of the already important small-scale/large-scale divide, but it is also a method of ensuring scientific excellence or usefulness. Formulated in a rhetorical question, what better expertise in instrument development are to be found than the ones that will use the instrument? The aforementioned Review of the Swedish National Facilities acknowledges this: 'MAX-lab gained a very high reputation worldwide for its foresight by careful planning the radiation sources, the beamlines and the instrumentation together with highly competent user groups' (Vetenskapsrådet 2002).

2.3   EXPANSION AND GROWTH

MAX I opened for experiments in 1987. Ten years later, in 1997, the 1.5 GeV storage ring MAX II opened, marking a major upgrade of the laboratory making possible the expansion of the areas of research to eventually include structural chemistry, biology, medicine and pharmaceutical sciences. Such research is done with the use of light of a shorter wavelength, so-called hard x-rays, which for technical reasons it isn't possible to produce with the MAX I ring. The opinions differ among the key persons in the MAX-lab history whether it was at all recognized during the planning and design phase of MAX II that the ring could be used also for producing hard x-rays. What is clear though is that the MAX II initiative didn't primarily build on the ambition to expand the scientific possibilities to new disciplines but rather on the will to unleash a more powerful scientific resource to the existing user communities. In the written motivation for the grant, the Natural Sciences Research Council (NFR) mentions only the disciplines atom physics, molecular physics and condensed matter physics among the disciplines supposed to benefit from the construction of MAX II (Forkman 2000).[5]

But powerful it was. Two important things made MAX II large-scale as opposed to its predecessor MAX I. First, it was an aligned effort, a coordinated initiative from a purposeful group of machine constructors, instrument developers and forefront researchers. This meant that it got attention and became an 'issue' in the whole of the Swedish research policy system, from university department level up to research council or even ministry. Second, it did indeed expand the scientific opportunities at MAX-lab, which increased the number of stakeholders and made the project engage a larger number of discussants. The debate that followed must be seen in this context. In a short-term and hands-on perspective, the question arising was of course concerned with the financing of the facility as such, but also the amount of money eventually granted to the construction of the ring did not amount to more than about SEK 60 million in today's prices. The real pledge, made by the council particularly in that they commit to make funds available for scientific instrumentation and running costs,[6] and by the Swedish scientific community in general, in that they agree to add MAX-lab to the envelope of natural science research projects of national interest, is a far greater one. Some influential biology and chemistry representatives in the council opposed, primarily with the argument that MAX II was a physics laboratory with possible areas of expansion in other natural science disciplines, but far too much of a gamble given that the real scientific opportunities for biology and medicine weren't sufficiently investigated. Arguments were also put forward that a project of this size would kill other initiatives for a long time ahead, initiatives that were not necessarily scientifically competing but for which no financial resources would be left if the commitment to MAX II was to be made. It is said that the eventual success of the project within the council, which lead to the government decision in January 1991, was the work of a few dedicated individuals who managed to convince the council of the project's importance for the broader Swedish scientific community. It is not at all a rash conclusion that the real leap for MAX-lab onto the national scientific stage was taken through MAX II. Things did evolve one after another and MAX II is not even at present date equipped with end stations to make full use of its potential.[7] As mentioned earlier though, the decision taken by first and foremost the council, but also the various actors in the decentralized and informal Swedish research policy system in the early 1990s to give MAX-lab its full support, was a long-term and large-scale commitment. Expansion of scientific opportunities means expansion of the user community, and most important is perhaps the development of beamlines and end stations for structural chemistry, biology and medicine. Voices have been heard

claiming that the 21st century is the 'century of biology', and one of the ini-
tiators of the structural biology beamlines at MAX-lab, Professor Anders
Liljas at Lund University, calls MAX-lab 'Our Hubble Space Telescope'.
Regardless of the rhetorical attractiveness of such statements, MAX-lab as
a whole has only gained from the broadening of its scientific base, especially
when taking into account that industrial firms have been engaged in the laboratory as a direct consequence of the expansion to pharmaceutical applications. With the widening of the scientific base, MAX-lab has grown in
importance for the whole of the Swedish scientific community.

2.4   EXTENSIVE INVOLVEMENT OF USERS

MAX-lab was initially a small-scale university laboratory and the MAX I
ring was originally planned and designed to support only a marginally
larger user community than the one already found within the department
of nuclear physics at Lund University. Hence including synchrotron light
in the plans for MAX-lab meant not only a technical revision of the laboratory but also a complete change of perspective in terms of flexibility and
outreach. At the time, synchrotron radiation was a relatively new experimental tool, and it is reasonable to claim that no immediate user community was to be found within Lund University. Instead, would-be user groups
from other Swedish universities responded to the MAX-lab plans and
became associated with the laboratory early on. This was especially the case
for Uppsala.

Professor Kai Siegbahn at Uppsala University had won the 1981 Nobel
Prize for Physics 'for his contribution to the development of high-resolution electron spectroscopy' (Nobel Foundation 2006), immediately turning
Uppsala into the 'capital of spectroscopy' and making possible the extension of the experimental groups at Uppsala University Department of
Physics. Even though it is said that Professor Siegbahn himself initially kept
a very sceptical attitude towards synchrotron light and MAX-lab,[8] other
groups identified the possibilities of developing the technique further with
the help of synchrotron light. The largest MAX-lab user group subsequently established itself in Uppsala during the years of construction of the
first MAX I beamlines, and took part in the planning, building and commissioning of instruments from the beginning. Also smaller groups in
Linköping and Gothenburg joined in the preparations. In this early history
of MAX-lab, two things are especially important to note. First the fact that
these groups were exclusively physicists, and second that the users came
from elsewhere in the country, particularly Uppsala (and to a small extent
from abroad).

Generally, one can say that MAX-lab was a designated physics laboratory before the opening of MAX II. Not only was the lab initially planned and designed to be a nuclear physics lab, the first beamlines and experimental stations were built by and for physicists. In comparison with MAX-lab and its users today, this meant that the early user community was both very small and relatively homogenous, not only with respect to academic discipline but also work mode. The later development of the MAX II ring and the beamlines for structural chemistry, macromolecular crystallography and the like, has broadened the user base significantly in numbers, but has also meant that the laboratory as experimental site has become heterogeneous and multifaceted with respect to the everyday work of the experimenters. Broadly, nowadays two distinct groups of users populate the laboratory. The first type generally consists of surface physicists, condensed matter physicists, or atom physicists. One of the main distinguishing characteristics of most physicists using synchrotron light for experiments is that they tend to be scheduled in longer blocks of beamtime, sometimes up to three weeks and seldom or never shorter than one week. Most physicist MAX-lab users call their own laboratory work 'experiments' and in general they need to maintain a solid base of knowledge regarding the whole laboratory's technical system, from the vacuum tube, the magnets and the insertion devices down to the monochromator, the optics and the experimental chamber at their own station. Even though it is claimed to be decreasing, the general interest in instrument development and design and construction of beamlines and experimental stations is high among these users. Both of these features have to do with the dynamic and generic nature of the physics experiments done with synchrotron light. The quality of the output data of the experiments is decided by a large number of factors, all of which must be known and corrected by modification of different pieces of the equipment on site. In the words of one experimenter, a beamline and experimental station is 'like an old car. . .everything is not always working perfect'. It is crucial for these researchers to know the experiment and the instrument well enough to be able to identify inaccuracies in the output data and judge whether it is caused by insufficient quality of their measured sample or the technical system of the instrument. For these reasons, physicists often work in close collaboration with technical support staff at the beamlines and in-house scientists.

In contrast to the typical physics users are the crystallographers. These users have a usual beamtime block of one or two days and their work is generally of a routine character, meaning that the experiment in itself is standardized and often involves very little if any technical modification and optimization of the equipment. The common way to refer to work of this kind in the laboratory is not as 'experiments' but 'measurements', a terminology also used among the researchers themselves. Determination of a protein structure by hard x-ray light from a synchrotron is a procedure with a critical phase, not in the direct use of the light but in the preparation of a crystal to measure. Preparation is always done in the home laboratory, and the work at the synchrotron radiation laboratory is the standard procedure of mounting a crystal at the experimental station and collecting the data. It is the quality of the crystal and not possible inaccuracies of the instrumental setup that decides whether a measurement is successful. Therefore the demand for deeper knowledge or understanding of the inner secrets of the accelerator is very low. Exceptions do of course exist, but crystallographers are in general satisfied as long as the light is on, and they care very little about the possible reasons for beam loss. If possible, these users would probably be happy to let someone else do their measurements at the synchrotron. The fascinating concept of remote control measurements, developed among others at the ESRF (European Synchrotron Radiation Facility) in Grenoble, France, has been introduced to meet exactly these demands; users can send their crystals by mail to the synchrotron and hand them over to in-house personnel to do the actual work. They themselves only need to monitor the procedure over the Internet.

As mentioned earlier, the original user community at MAX-lab consisted solely of physicists. The small size and informal character of the organization made these original users very influential on the institution and organization. Even though the clear ambition is to keep disciplinary variety in all committees, in the board and the staff, MAX-lab is to a large extent still run by physicists, and mainly physicists from the original small group of MAX-lab enthusiasts. In pure numbers of users, there is nowadays only a slight domination of physicists in the laboratory. For the academic year 2004–2005, the total number of registered synchrotron radiation users was 572, of which 281 (approx. 49 per cent) were physicists, 126 (approx. 22 per cent) chemists, and 165 (approx. 29 per cent) had life sciences affiliations.[9] Here is important to point out that the category described above as 'physicists' corresponds fairly well to the group termed 'physicists' in the user statistics. Although the numerical domination of physicists in the lab is diminishing, it is clear that the physicists in most cases still are the most influential user group. This is of course due to physicists generally spending more time in the laboratory and interacting more with in-house scientists, technicians and administrative staff. These users are also to a larger extent involved in lab questions over injections, beamtime schedules, organization of maintenance tasks and the like, since these are matters often directly or indirectly affecting the scientific performance of their experiments. Generally speaking, the overall relationship between the visiting physicists and the laboratory is thus of a rather different kind than the one between life science or chemistry users and the laboratory. Exceptions are of course normal and variations great. All in all, these differences in user-laboratory relationships that build on the general work mode differences between user groups, has meant that the physicists still enjoy a dominant position in the laboratory. This is not to say at all that physicists or members of a particular branch of physics have privileges over other user communities in any of the formal processes by which the continuous MAX-lab scientific mission is carried out. The main point is that the differences between disciplines and user communities are also valid and evident when it comes to the organizational development of the lab. The ongoing process of extending the scientific base to cover other areas and disciplines continues to place new demands on the organization, as new users with a sometimes radically different experimental work mode and atypical relationship to the instruments are to be served. One immediate consequence is the 'loyalty' of the users. During the academic years of 2003/04 and 2004/05 the structural biology beamline I911 at MAX-lab experienced severe technical problems, which both decreased the number of beamtime shifts granted to users and of course had negative impact on some users' experiments. This lead to a measurable decrease in applications for the coming years, indicating that the crystallography users react quickly to bad machine performance and take their experiments elsewhere, which is confirmed by MAX-lab staff. The often self-chosen lack of interest in the technical performance of the ring, the beamline and the end station equipment is thus coupled with a lack of patience with operational instability and technical problems. Nothing of the like has happened at physics beamlines. This example is put forward primarily to point out the possible challenges that meet the laboratory when new user groups from other disciplines, with different habits and demands, are to be served and supported. Perhaps the scientific disciplines shouldn't be given too much emphasis in this respect; there is always a problematic dimension of ascribing certain characteristics or common behavioural patterns to disciplinary or sub-disciplinary groups. The differences in work mode, interaction and relationship to the laboratory put forward in the above are not claimed to be valid for any other representatives of the mentioned disciplines but only the groups under study here. Elevating the groups of physicists that once built MAX-lab to this level of importance is only an attempt to put further emphasis on the existence of a very strong and important academic culture of MAX-lab, a culture with continuously growing demands put on it to communicate and collaborate with representatives of several other academic and non-academic cultures. Industrial usage has begun at MAX-lab but hasn't so far become a large enough portion of the activities for general conclusions to be drawn, but the extension of user communities in new disciplinary directions has had highly visible effects that serve well to symbolize the challenges an academic culture can meet when its areas of interest are broadened.

It would have been reasonable to assume that at least part of the reason for Lund University committing to hosting the MAX-lab project was the possibilities for existing university departments or research groups benefiting from the establishment of a synchrotron radiation source at the university campus. Strangely enough, this was not at all the case: although potential users of course existed, their number was not at all large and their interest has been described as moderate by Forkman (2000) and others. The real potential user community was to be found in Uppsala, where Nobel laureate Kai Siegbahn led the progress in high-resolution electron spectroscopy. The physics department in Uppsala quickly became an important external hub of synchrotron radiation users, and has continued to function as important external collaborative institution for MAX-lab ever since.[10] Most interesting is perhaps not the over-representation of Uppsala physicists but the initial under-representation of Lund physicists. It is realistic to ask the question how an initiative like MAX-lab could earn its support from the central university administration and the faculties without being a project with clear advantage for Lund to pursue. The answer and one key to the history of MAX-lab might be that the actual case – MAX-lab initially not giving advantages to specific areas with already strong positions within the university – made it easier for the university to handle the initiative. In the large university structure, competing interests from researchers from different disciplines are probably easier convinced to give their support to a project that is not favouring one or a few of them.

2.5   OUTLOOK

MAX-lab have developed evolutionary from a small-scale nuclear physics project well within the frames of an ordinary university department to a national facility with a mission to serve the whole of the Swedish natural science community and a great portion of international users. We have pointed before at the fact that synchrotron light sources are flexible laboratories also in the purely technical sense; instruments may be substituted, new areas of application may be added and the scientific user base extended. This has been the case with MAX-lab, and still is. The ambitions of the in-house staff, the committees and the directorate to constantly look for new improvements and developments of the scientific possibilities of the facility – at every level – might best be understood by the metaphor used by MAX-lab's present director, Professor Nils

Mårtensson, that MAX-lab in itself ought to be seen as 'a giant research project'. The ambition and determination to constantly reach for a new development or optimization is vivid within MAX-lab, and is largely due to the academic nature of the laboratory. Therefore, new projects continuously get drafted.

At present time, the largest scientific project ever in Sweden is planned at MAX-lab, namely the new ring MAX IV with surrounding laboratory. MAX IV is at the same time an overwhelmingly great leap and a natural next step in the development of MAX-lab. The user community has grown continuously since its opening, and it is judged to have a potential of expanding for many years to come. MAX IV is more than an upgrade of the existing facility, it is by and large a completely new project and – should it be realized – the ultimate commitment of Sweden to become one of the leading European countries in synchrotron radiation. On the policy level therefore MAX IV is an overwhelmingly large project, especially given the premises. On the scientific level however, it is only the natural next step. The gradual evolving of leading expertise in accelerator physics and synchrotron radiation instrumentation, along with the piecemeal establishment of front-end scientific research in the related field places the demand for upgrade and expansion. The synchrotron radiation user community have kept and managed the initiative during the whole history of MAX-lab. The fact that the very same user community now has its focus on MAX IV makes the project an inevitable consequence of history.

At the same time, MAX-lab operates within the dynamic steady state. Along with expansion and upgrades comes the broadening of areas to cover, the extension of existing alliances and the establishments of new ones, and not least the rearrangement of institutional practices. Nobody would disagree on that MAX-lab so far has been a success story, given the constant resource scarcity. In the words of the Research Council's review panel, MAX-lab 'provide remarkable scientific output' in proportion to its operating budget (Vetenskapsrådet 2002). Some things that have evolved as results of the resource scarcity are also important to keep when MAX IV is established, such as this effectiveness and the generally excellent ability to stimulate and facilitate initiatives from the grass roots of the user community. The fluid and informal organizational structure and the barter-economy-like shortcircuiting of the peer review system through the PRTs and the informal agreements are though, entirely inappropriate for a larger laboratory establishment. The real challenge for the management of the laboratory is the walk on the tightrope between the transformation to a more appropriate laboratory organization and the keeping of the healthy climate of commitment and spirit.

3. CONCLUSION: MAX-LAB AS A MICROCOSM OF THE SWEDISH RESEARCH SYSTEM

The evolution of synchrotron-light-based research, and in particular its widening circle of applications and the ensuing demands for a different scale and scope of synchrotron light facilities, highlight both the opportunities and limitations of the Swedish research strategy. MAX-lab emerged as a result of a combination of piecemeal solutions, bottom-up approaches, local initiatives and a do-it-yourself strategy, and decentralization. It was never anticipated that a facility like the MAX-lab of today would emerge. It was a local initiative that grew in an evolutionary manner, eventually gaining a broad constituency. Therefore, we might coin the phrase 'MAX-lab the laboratory that was never intended to be'. The key conclusion here is the highlighting of the inability of the system to anticipate the eventual outcome of the project. It was not until results showed, and the internal scientific reputation of MAX-lab was fairly well established, that policy-makers to a greater extent realized its success and its potential. Synchrotron light is a rather new experimental resource for the natural sciences, and in Sweden synchrotron light is synonymous with MAX-lab. The politics around the laboratory and the development and facilitating of initiatives has lain within the university structure, on different levels and locations, during the whole of the MAX-lab history.

Parallel with MAX-lab's growth as a laboratory, new disciplines have gradually associated themselves with synchrotron light and the original user communities has expanded and strengthened themselves. But the key is in acknowledging that the importance lies exactly with the users. Being the laboratory that was never intended to be, MAX-lab is also the laboratory that should never have survived. The fact that the laboratory not only has survived but also made it to significant size and importance in a national perspective is most of all due to the user-involvement. A few dedicated and visionary individuals developed the ideas and the plans, and a few dedicated and visionary individuals made the plans pass through the council. The support from Lund University and the forging of the national facility and academic institution link at the university level helped retain the original academic spirit helped by the close proximity to the user groups during expansion.

That MAX-lab has maintained its thoroughly academic character despite being a designated national research facility since the late 1980s has made the maintenance of the laboratory strongly dependent on a system of informal coordination, underfunded flexibility and heroic efforts from small groups of committed staff. This combination successfully took MAX-lab into the third generation of synchrotron light facilities in the mid-1990s, and still manages to keep the facility on a fairly competitive international position. This has, among other things, gained MAX-lab its great reputation, both domestically and internationally.

It is ironic that a laboratory that was never intended to be and that should never have survived has managed to take hold of and developed scientific opportunities that were never anticipated but whose promising future was grasped only by a few enthusiasts. After all, MAX-lab is the only Swedish National Laboratory of its size. Today, MAX-lab is a vital part of the strategic goals of Lund University. It is also viewed among the most important strategic assets for Swedish research. Against the background of this chapter, it is thought not only possible but perhaps also necessary to argue that the ways by which MAX-lab of today has come into being – what might be called the ideal collection of coincidences, opportunities and small-scale initiatives – is the only possible way in which large-scale research facilities can be established in Sweden.

But the story does not end here. The MAX IV project is under consideration and preparation, and the MAX-lab organization has realized the challenges built in the project. Our material indicates that several of the issues that are confronting the Swedish research system (growing internationalization, needs for prioritization, new relations with the private sector, reorganization of universities, etc.) are present in the case of MAX-lab. Its history – and its future – is the history and the future of Swedish research.

NOTES

1. A storage ring is never really a ring, but rather a polygon. The bending magnets are located in the angles of the polygon and the insertion devices (so-called '*wigglers*' and '*undulators*') at the straight stretches. When the electron beam is bended by a magnet, it looses energy that is emitted in the form of synchrotron light. Wigglers and undulators are collections of a large number of different magnets that bend the electron beam back and forth several times and thereby cause energy loss and light production. With wigglers and undulators it is possible to produce light of a greater focus and intensity. Normally only one beamline is set up per bending magnet or insertion device, making the total beamlines possible for a ring to support exactly twice the number of angles in the polygon (Margaritondo 2002).
2. Counting the beamlines at MAX-lab can be done in different ways, depending on what one chooses to name an individual beamline or end station. The number 15 is therefore an average with the reservation to give or take three.
3. Even the location of the new laboratory was under discussion, despite the site of the existing CERN lab in Geneva. In Sweden as in most other member countries, discussions took place on whether to apply for hosting the lab. However, it was eventually decided that the laboratory should be located at the same site as the original one.
4. And is. MAX I is still running, supporting both the nuclear physics research programme of MAX-lab and producing synchrotron light for experiments.
5. The council furthermore states that 'MAX II in a highly favorable manner complements the Swedish commitment to research with x-rays at ESRF in Grenoble' (Forkman 2000).

   As opposed to MAX II, ESRF (European Synchrotron Radiation Facility), a joint European facility, was already on the drawing board and intended to cover a wide wavelength spectrum and serve a broad community of users also from chemistry, biology and medicine.
6. Which indeed is not a bargain. The money needed for beamlines and experimental stations, including day-to-day operation, maintenance and occasional upgrades has so far amounted to more than twenty times (average) the grant for the 'naked' accelerator (Vetenskapsrådet 2002).
7. This is said with the reservation that the 'full potential' of MAX II is not easily grasped, and the step-by-step construction and commissioning of scientific instrumentation at MAX-lab is still ongoing, due partly to the fact that new areas of application are continuously discovered and investigated.
8. It is said that Professor Kai Siegbahn regarded MAX-lab a rival institution to his own. Later, when results started to arrive, he is said to have grasped the possibilities of synchrotron light and become a great supporter.
9. These numbers are not absolutely accurate, and the disciplinary borders are somewhat fuzzy. The numbers are based on the user's own registration; every user is supposed to log in to the computer network and submit name, home institution, beamline used, beamtime period, supervisor of the experiment and discipline. There are no real restrictions on this – some users neglect to register but are granted access anyway, they are therefore not included in the statistics. Also the disciplinary division between physics, chemistry and life sciences is not exact: users may choose their own disciplinary affiliation during registration, between these three broader areas.
10. Three of perhaps the most important positions within the MAX-lab organizational structure were until recently held by Uppsala professors: the director of the laboratory Prof Nils Mårtensson, the chairman of the Scientific Advisory Committee (SAC) Prof Joseph Nordgren, and the chairman of the Program Advisory Committee (PAC) Prof Börje Johansson. Forty-one individual users from the Department of Physics, Uppsala University visited MAX-lab in the academic year 2004–05.

REFERENCES

Blewett, John P. (1998), 'Synchrotron radiation – early history', *Journal of Synchrotron Radiation*, **5**, 135–9.

Capshew, J.H. and K.A. Rader (1992), 'Big Science: price to the present', *Osiris*, 2nd series, **7**, 3–25.

Forkman, Bengt (2000), *Och det blev Ljus: Hur MAX-lab kom till, växte upp och blev stort*, Lund: Lund University.

Hadenius, A. (1972), *Sweden and CERN II – the Research Policy Debate 1964–1971*, FEK report 3, Stockholm: Committee on Research Economics (FEK).

Krige, J. (ed.) (1996), *History of CERN*, vol. III, Amsterdam: Elsevier.

Margaritondo, Giorgio (2002), *Elements of Synchrotron Light for Biology, Chemistry and Medical Research*, Oxford: Oxford University Press.

Nobel Foundation (2006), *The Nobel Prize in Physics 1981*, Electronic, accessed 30 November 2006 at http://nobelprize.org/nobel_prizes/physics/laureates/1981.

Vetenskapsrådet (international review of the Swedish National Facilities) (2002), *Review of the Swedish National Facilities 2002*, Stockholm: Swedish Research Council. (Vetenskapsrådets Rapportserie 6)

Widmalm, S. (1993), 'Big Science in a small country: Sweden and CERN II', in S. Lindqvist (ed.), *Center on the Periphery: Historical Aspects of Swedish 20th-Century Physics*, Canton, MA: Watson Publishing International, pp. 107–40.

Ziman, John (1994), *Prometheus Bound: Science in a Dynamic Steady State*, Cambridge: Cambridge University Press.
Ziman, John (2000), *Real Science: What it is, and What it Means*, Cambridge: Cambridge University Press.

INTERVIEWS

Andersen, Jesper N., Professor of Synchrotron Radiation Physics, Lund University, Senior Researcher beamline I311, MAX-lab. Lund, 11 October 2006.
Cerenius, Yngve, Beamline Manager I711, MAX-lab. Lund, 10 October 2006.
Eriksson, Mikael, Professor of Accelerator Physics, Lund University, Operation Manager and Deputy Director, MAX-lab. Lund, 17 March 2006 and 28 March 2007.
Fahlman, Mats, Associate Professor, Department of Physics and Measurement Technology, Linköping University, Chairman of the Association of MAX-lab Users (FASM), Linköping, 24 August 2006 and on telephone, 3 October 2006.
Flodström, Anders, Vice-chancellor Royal Institute of Technology, Stockholm, former coordinator for synchrotron radiation research, MAX-lab, former member of the board of the Swedish Natural Research Council, Stockholm, 22 March 2007.
Gidefeldt, Lars, former research secretary, Swedish Natural Science Council (1977–2000), member of the MAX-lab board 1991–94, Stockholm, 16 November 2006.
Honeth, Peter, former Head of Administration, Lund University, Lund, 9 June 2006.
Johansson, Börje, Professor, Department of Physics, Uppsala University, Chairman of the MAX-lab Program Advisory Committee. Member of the ESRF review committee, Uppsala, 12 October 2006.
Johansson, Leif I, Professor, Department of Physics and Measurement Technology, Linköping University, Lund, 16 May 2006 and Linköping, 25 August 2006.
Liljas, Anders, Professor Emeritus of Molecular Biophysics, Lund University, Lund, 10 November 2006.
Lindau, Ingolf, Professor of Synchrotron Radiation Physics, Lund University, former director of MAX-lab (1990–97), Senior researcher at SSRL, Stanford, Lund, 29 January 2007.
Mårtensson, Nils, Professor of Surface Physics, Uppsala University, Director of MAX-lab (since 1997), Lund, 29 March 2006 and 7 November 2006.
Nordgren, Joseph, Professor of Atomic Physics, Uppsala University, former chairman of MAX-lab Scientific Advisory Committee (1990–2006), Uppsala, 13 October 2006.
Nyholm, Ralf, Professor of Synchrotron Radiation Instrumentation, Lund University, Coordinator for Synchrotron Radiation Research, MAX-lab, Lund, 9 March 2006 and 4 October 2006.
Skogö, Ingemar, Chairman of the Board, MAX-lab, Lund, 31 August 2006.
Sörensen, Stacey, Professor, Department of Physics, Lund University, Lund, 3 October 2006.
Uhrberg, Roger, Professor, Department of Physics and Measurement Technology, Linköping University, Linköping, 25 August 2006.
Ursby, Thomas, Beamline Manager, beamline I911, MAX-lab, Lund, 20 October 2006.

5. Division of academic labour is limited by the size of the market. Strategy and differentiation of European universities in doctoral education

Andrea Bonaccorsi

1. INTRODUCTION

The economics of universities is a very young field, originated by a surge of interest for institutions producing and diffusing knowledge. [1] While there is a large literature on the economics of higher education, examining mainly the investment decision of individuals in their human capital, the analysis of universities as knowledge production units has traditionally been done in a very application-oriented context. Only more recently has economic theory been attracted by a number of interesting empirical problems and puzzles with large policy implications.

This chapter is a contribution to the literature developed with an empirical goal. We will introduce an economic analysis of the notion of differentiation of universities and propose a quantitative measure. The general notion of differentiation is applied to the activity of universities in doctoral education. The measure is based on the availability of the large dataset created by the project Aquameth that, for the first time, has integrated census microdata on all universities in several European countries for a decade.

2. THE UNIVERSITY AS A PRODUCTION UNIT

From an economic point of view, universities can be examined as production units. Universities produce highly heterogeneous outputs in at least three areas: education (student education; production of degrees at undergraduate, master and doctoral level; professional training), research (publications; patents; scientific know-how and practices; scientific instrumentation) and contribution to economic growth and social problems (spinoff creation; participation in social debates; scientific expertise for societal problems; contribution to standard setting; advisory role to policy-making; creation of networks). In order to produce these outputs, universities use heterogeneous inputs represented by personnel (academic staff, non-academic staff), capital (laboratories, libraries, classrooms), or financial resources (funding). Therefore university production can be characterized as multi-input multi-output. However, in contrast to multiproduct firms largely examined in economic theory, universities do not have market signals to drive their production decisions. In fact, if examined from the point of view of economic analysis, university production can be characterized as follows. Some of the characterizations apply to universities in general, others to European ones in particular, due to historical and cultural factors.[2] We articulate these characterizations with respect to the production process (points 1–4), the productivity of individual members (items 5–7), and the organizational setting (items 8–10).

First, university production is subject to strong positive complementarity effects in inputs. To teach physics a university needs a professor of physics, but also a laboratory, materials, consumables and other inputs. To do research in plant physiology it needs researchers, but also seeds and a greenhouse. These inputs are difficult to substitute among themselves: having a larger greenhouse but less researchers does not produce the same research output. The internal relations between these various inputs are unlikely to be represented by the continuous marginal rates of substitution assumed in conventional theory of production. For some inputs, university production comes closer to Leontief fixed coefficients, so that it falls to zero if a given input is not present, or not present at a given level. In general, the overall production function toolbox seems deeply inadequate for careful representation of the activity of universities. Little is known, however, on the precise nature of internal relations between inputs.

Second, university production is also subject to positive and negative complementarity effects in outputs. Positive complementarity arises, for example, between education and research, because teaching to university students allows the identification of talented young students and promising future researchers, as well as permits to conduct laboratory experiments at lower cost, or exposes new research ideas to a larger audience of critical subjects, and the like. The Humboldtian model of most European universities is largely based on this effect. Another case of positive complementarity takes place between basic research and industrial research in several technical and scientific fields, because being exposed to frontier application problems from industry may foster creative ideas of fundamental value. But at the same time there are also negative complementarity, or substitution effects (trade-offs). For example, education and research may be positive complement up to a certain point, but beyond a given level of teaching load the time left for research may diminish significantly.[3] Or the time allocated to contract research may in fact be subtracted from fundamental research. Or even the constraints on publication accepted as part of dealing with industrial partners may reduce the publication output.[4] In principle, both negative and positive effects may be in place. The fact that there are no market prices to guide these allocation decisions, however, makes it difficult to formulate general propositions.

Third, university production takes place under uncertainty. A given combination of inputs may produce a vector of outputs only in probability. This is particularly true for research, whose final value is indeterminate at the beginning, and in general is uncertain and delayed. A deterministic representation is inappropriate.

Fourth, as already mentioned, most outputs of universities are not subject to market prices. Although the functioning of market or market-like mechanisms in higher education has been the subject of intense debate (Texeira et al., 2004), it is accepted that market prices do not capture the opportunity costs of universities.

All this means that decision-makers cannot base their production decisions following the rules of optimal mix in multi-product production. The resolution of the complex trade-offs illustrated above cannot be done via optimality calculations.

For example, the literature on economic analysis of basic research (Salter and Martin, 2001; Nelson, 1986) has made clear that the direct product of research (i.e. publications) is only part of the total production of knowledge, most of which resides in skill, competencies and know-how embedded in researchers. This knowledge is not diffused by means of open science, but is accessed mainly by students and postgraduate students in laboratory practice and in technical expertise. Although there is a large productive activity, there is no way to measure this type of knowledge via the price system. Even more complicated, sometimes outputs are also inputs and vice versa. For example, doctoral students can be considered an output of postgraduate education, but in most cases they are also active inputs to the research activity. Publications are research outputs, but they also enter as inputs to further research, so that production takes a cumulative nature, possibly subject to positive feedbacks. Funding is an input to the research activity, but since part of the funding is allocated in proportion to publications, receiving research funds can be considered also an output of the activity. It is easy to see that these features are not found in conventional market production.

This also means that there is no way to summarize the multidimensional activity of universities into a single metrics, unless a weight system is adopted. In the absence of a price system, any weight scheme is not value-free, but reflects, often implicitly, value judgements. There are therefore methodological reasons to reject the claim that international rankings of universities simply reflect reality (Zitt and Filliatreau, 2006). Ranking is a legitimate activity, but is never value-free.

Fifth, the individual productivity of academic personnel in research activity is not distributed normally, but in a highly asymmetric way (Stephan, 1996). This means that productive scientists are not marginally better than their colleagues, but very much more so. A large number of important organizational problems follow from this stylized fact.

Sixth, individual productivity in research activity declines with age, a phenomenon sometimes called life cycle (Levin and Stephan, 1991; Bonaccorsi and Daraio, 2003). Quite a large number of academic personnel stop being active in publications at some point in their career, while still being active in teaching.

Seventh, significant agency problems are at work. From the organizational point of view, university personnel are a professional category. Professions are ruled by codes of conduct, self-regulation and autonomy, not by hierarchical supervision. Professionals do not accept organizational fiat, but must be left free to accomplish their duties. Because of the professional nature of academic work, and also the uncertainty of research, it is impossible for administrators to monitor every aspect of academic activity. This creates classical contractual problems of observability of effort and enforceability of obligations. The accepted solution is one in which activities that are easier to observe, such as teaching, are regulated by a contract defined on inputs (e.g. a given number of hours of courses per year), while activities that are more difficult to observe, such as research, are regulated by contracts on outputs (e.g. the academic promotion is assigned only if a certain number of articles have been published in certain journals, irrespective of the effort actually put in place).[5]

Eighth, universities are dual hierarchy organizations, in the sense that the administrative chain of command is separated from the academic one. The former is usually much less powerful than the latter. In turn, academic power for recruitment and promotions may be located mainly internally to the individual university (as it happens mainly in Anglo-Saxon model) or externally to the academic community (as it is more often the case in Continental Europe). In the former case the internal faculty has strong collective power on recruitment and promotions, and can implement consistent institutional rules in the long run; in the latter case academic disciplinary circles, mainly at national level, make decisions autonomously and ask universities to accept. This is an important element of the overall governance of universities (Amaral et al., 2002; Del Favero, 2003). Related to this organizational feature to some extent, the balance between the chains of command may be designed differently. The so-called collegiate model, typical of European universities, concentrates almost all power in the academic body, usually with processes of shared decision-making. The presidential model, which is adopted in the United States, creates a strong counterbalance to the academic power, with a powerful Board of Trustees chaired by an authoritative President.[6]

Ninth, academic personnel are motivated by economic incentives, but also by intrinsic satisfaction. This is an interesting aspect of university production that deserves more attention. Although the importance of economic incentives cannot be denied, a consistent literature shows how researchers receive intrinsic satisfaction from their own work, very much like artists and creative people, as well as give considerable importance to non-pecuniary incentives, such as esteem, reputation, visibility and the like. Managing economic and non-economic incentives together, keeping into account their interplay, is one of the difficulties of university management.

Finally, universities do not have financial endowments and cannot borrow money, at least in the European context. In contrast to other production units, they find it difficult to fund their activities on the financial market. Partly because of uncertainty of activities, partly because of the value of their assets is mostly in human capital, universities do not receive credit unless it is backed by government guarantee or by an endowment (which is typical of Anglo-Saxon universities but virtually absent in Continental ones). This means that, irrespective of decisions made on inputs and outputs, universities are cash-constrained by government policies (Neave and van Vught, 1994; Geuna 2001; Geuna and Martin, 2003). The structure and administrative regulation of funding has profound influences on the way in which universities are managed. In particular, the overall institutional framework at national level and the model of governance shape the way in which they can operate.

3.   STRATEGY, DIFFERENTIATION AND POSITIONING OF UNIVERSITIES IN THE EUROPEAN CONTEXT

From this characterization a number of conceptual implications can be drawn. Let us start from the notion of strategy. At a very general level, a strategy is a consistent course of behaviour adopted by an agent, in response to an environment that includes opponents. Following the strategy the agent must have some manoeuvring over (partially irreversible) resources to be deployed. To be credible for opponents, a strategy must involve some costs: if changing the strategy has no cost, then the strategy has no commitment and hence no value. This broad definition can be applied to market agents as well as non-market ones. It does not imply a private model of universities, nor does it naively import concepts from the field of management to the public sector.

Is it possible to talk of strategy with respect to universities? What would be the content of a university strategy? Who would be in charge of defining and implementing such a strategy?

While these questions are routine in the US context, they sound strange and somewhat provocative in the European one. The collegiate model, in fact, implies that universities do *not* have a strategy, i.e. a course of action at top level that, more or less stringently, places constraints on actions of organizational units of lower level. In this perspective universities should remain loosely coupled systems (Weick, 1976), without a strategy. Following the stylized characterization of university production outlined above, in fact, one could say that a strategy should include:

- A long-term vision of the desired mix of output to be offered, with respect to the three main dimensions of education, research, and third mission and their internal aspects;
- A clear positioning with respect to other universities;
- A plan to deploy production inputs in a way consistent with the mix of outputs;
- A governance model that assigns organizational responsibility for the implementation of the strategy;
- A communication plan to socialize all members to the organization.

It is easy to see how distant this concept is from the practical life of universities in most European countries.

Still, we believe that the notion of strategy is a necessary step in the institutional evolution of universities in Europe. Universities have been granted autonomy by a wave of legislative reforms in the 1980s and 1990s. These reforms deeply changed the contract between universities and the state largely illustrated by the literature in higher education (Henkel and Little, 1999; Jongbloed et al. 1999). The old contract, mainly developed after the Second World War, guaranteed universities funding to manage the explosive growth of student participation and relatively abundant funding for research, against a centralized control by the ministerial bureaucracy on crucial resources. These were mainly the allocation of funding and of chairs. According to the old contract, universities had to bargain on an individual basis with the political power in order to receive more resources; in parallel, scientific academia negotiated the rate of expansion for their disciplines. With several national variations, this governance model has been fully in place until the late 1970s.

The new contract is the result of the implementation of the notion of *autonomy*. Universities received financial and administrative autonomy from the law, meaning that they had the responsibility to draw up the budget, for which they would receive funds from central government, and are not permitted to incur into losses. In some countries, autonomy extended to the power to select and recruit personnel.

The movement towards autonomy marked a change in the relations between government and universities: from a command mode to a steering mode. The governments still exert strong influence, for example in dictating scientific and technological priorities in research (although the allocation of funding by disciplines change slowly), but do not determine financial and resource decisions of universities.

Still, the autonomy experiment is radically inadequate to manage the challenges of the end of the 20th century and beyond. In fact, autonomy as dictated by these reforms suffers from strong limitations.

To start with, it does not extend fully to the selection, recruitment and promotion of academic staff. In most Continental Europe countries the legal status of academicians is a public one and the government retains a strong role in procedures for admission to the role. Within legally enforced rules, the government delegates the decision to the peer evaluation of the scientific community, with a variety of elective rules (Musselin, 2004; 2005). Unfortunately, there is no balance between the autonomous decisions of scientific communities and the strategic orientation of universities. Universities cannot autonomously select academic staff, nor can they make a strategic choice within lists of candidates selected by scientific communities. The power of universities in selecting staff is, in practice, very limited.

In addition, although universities have financial autonomy, they have limited discretionary power. On the funding side, the level of student fees is dictated by the law or administrative rule, while the share of funding coming from private sources (contract research, but also non-profit foundations and donations) is kept at a minimum due to lack of fiscal incentives and bureaucratic obstacles.

On the expenditure side, the cost of academic staff, that is the overwhelming portion of the budget, is often influenced by centralized negotiations with trade unions, on which universities have no power. Government money still funds universities on principles of marginal cost, or additional funding, wrongly considering all capital equipment and overhead as covered by block ministerial funding.

Finally, and more important, autonomy is deeply limited by the prevailing governance model. This model reflects the power of academic personnel but articulates it at all levels of decision using inefficient elective rules, giving in practice power of veto to the status quo. Critically, there is not a countervailing power to balance the dominance of academic power. This is an important institutional difference between the European model and the US one. In the US model, the Board of Trustees, representing funders, external coalitions and stakeholders, elects a President who is not necessarily a member of the academia. The President is in a powerful position vis-à-vis academia and is usually the catalyser of university strategy. Charismatic Presidents can often radically change the competitive positioning and long-term success of universities, as it is witnessed by a number of autobiographic and historical accounts. Nothing similar is found in European universities. Here a strategy can only emerge from internal consensus of the academic faculty, without any external counterbalance. The role of funders as legitimate sources of strategy is extremely limited. No pressure is placed on academicians to develop a strategy whatsoever.

The institutional framework of autonomy, as experienced in the last two decades by European universities, is deeply inadequate to meet the new challenges. Consider the following factors:

- The job market for academic talent is now largely globalized, not only with brain drain towards the USA, but also with Asian countries attracting European junior faculty (Avveduto, 2005);
- The mobility of undergraduate students has increased significantly, particularly from large emerging countries and from middle-income countries (Trembley, 2002);
- The market for postgraduate education is also subject to a massive process of internationalization, with PhD programmes actively competing worldwide for mobile students (Moguerou, 2005);
- The emergence of the knowledge society means that a new wave of social demand for education is arriving, in addition to mass participation rates of young people, requiring customized content and sophisticated delivery and training methods (De Weert, 1999; European Commission, 2003, 2005);
- Large multinationals source knowledge worldwide and locate their R&D facilities close to top-class research locations, placing universities in competition for funding and collaboration;
- The proportion of research funding channelled by governments and intermediaries through contract research or project funding, hence on a competitive basis, is increasing (Laredo 2007).

These factors mean that universities find it increasingly difficult to procure funding and high quality staff and to compete in the output space at the same time for students, graduate students, services to society, basic research and contract research. Trying to compete on all dimensions of performance at the same time and with the same level of effort is too risky. Decisions become too slow, resources too thin. Even more important, competing along all dimensions makes the university less credible and attractive for potential inputs, such as new faculty or new sources of funding. Talented staff and generous donors have high opportunity costs: European universities are only one among many alternatives.

European universities, for historical reasons, have been asked to perform well along *all* dimensions of performance, without considering possible trade-offs. The governance model is historically designed to balance all aspects of activity, from mass education to excellence in research to compliance with society's needs.

The key to address these new challenges is a drastic orientation towards differentiation in the strategic profile.

By differentiation we do not mean a legislative action that creates *categories* of universities, nor a discrimination based on formal administrative criteria. Quite to the contrary, the strategic choice of the desired mix of outputs and of the levels of performance associated to each of them should be left to individual universities. Universities should accept that it is not possible to excel along all dimensions. Attracting master students in search of a professional qualification and access to good prospects for a job cannot be done at top class world level while also trying to compete in PhD education. Even at lower levels of performance, there is benefit from giving up some activities, or keeping them at the minimum required by the institutional framework, and trying to compete more actively on the others.

Note that this does not imply the dismissal of the traditional Humboldtian model of European universities, but rather its renewal and qualification in a changed landscape. Large and generalist universities should try to maintain a broad spectrum of educational activities and also to excel in research, fostering *internal* specialization and division of labour: but in order to do so they will have to develop new professional roles and to select those research areas in which to compete on a world basis. Smaller and/or specialist universities should consider a stronger institutional or *external* specialization, by limiting their scope of activities. All universities should identify their position in the output space by making selective decisions along the dimensions of activity. We identify the following dimensions:

1. Education: undergraduate, Master and professional education, PhD education, lifelong learning;

2. Research: fundamental research, contract research;
3. Third mission: industrial research, patenting, entrepreneurship, consultancy;
4. Discipline: number of disciplines covered (generalist vs specialist), type of disciplines;
5. Size of the market: world class, international attractiveness, national, regional, or local attraction.

The notion of strategic differentiation implies that universities should define a vector of outputs with a clear view of the structure of the competitive landscape, the size of the reference market, and the internal areas of strength.

This conclusion can also be seen as the application of the fundamental principle, discovered by Adam Smith and formalized by Young and subsequently by Stigler, that division of labour is limited by the size of the market. When markets grow in size, perhaps due to the elimination of barriers, then it becomes more convenient to specialize and to increase the division of labour. In applying Smith's theorem, of course, we keep in mind the difference between market and non-market activities; however, we insist that it gives an important insight on the evolution of academic institutions.

When 'markets' (in all senses) for both inputs and outputs of universities were mainly national or local, there was a large place for undifferentiated universities, in which all activities could reach a reasonable quality at the same time. Differentiation was not needed; indeed, it was considered a threat. Historically, the public goal of offering all students a similar level of education irrespective of the place of origin dictated a policy orientation to avoid any differentiation.[7]

Now virtually all markets for inputs and outputs are, or are becoming rapidly, international in size. In the international competition there is much benefit in taking a specialized profile, leaving to other, perhaps more dedicated universities, non-strategic activities.

As it happens in strategic management, the definition of a strategy would require some notion of positioning. A strategy can be thought as the definition of a position in a multidimensional output space, backed by consistent and adequate resources and inputs. Inevitably, the choice of a strategy depends on the consideration of the position occupied by competitors in the same space.

Therefore the emergence of the theme of strategy for European universities will generate a demand for tools that support the definition and visualization of the relative positioning in the multidimensional space of outputs.

4. DEFINING DIFFERENTIATION OF UNIVERSITIES

Notwithstanding these powerful arguments, it can be said that the institutional framework of Continental Europe is not conducive to differentiation of universities. Not only the historical tradition of the Humboldtian university, but also the funding mechanisms, the formula-based allocation rules, the governance model and the overall legal framework reinforce the lack of differentiation. While this claim is largely accepted in the literature, there has been no attempt to measure it in quantitative terms. This chapter offers a demonstration on just one variable, i.e. PhD intensity. On the one hand, it is a highly informative variable on the strategic positioning of European universities. On the other, it is a first methodological effort to explore the potential of diversity and differentiation measures applied to microdata. In this section we therefore give an account of the overall research programme on differentiation, of which a demonstration will be given in subsequent sections.

We first develop a model of strategy in the output space (Bonaccorsi and Daraio, 2007b). We consider three dimensions of output (education, research and third mission) and we develop measures for each of them. These measures should capture the strategic orientation of universities, as visible in decisions to allocate resources, or to establish an offer profile for various categories of users, or to actively search for sources of finds.

Measures of strategic orientation must therefore conform to the following requirements:

- Observability (the underlying metrics must be explicit and transparent);
- Comparability (the meaning of the variable must be the same for all universities in the sample);
- Stability (there must not be large unexplained variability over time);
- Leverage (there must be some degree of freedom for the actors at university level in influencing the value of the variable);
- Absence of ambiguity (the meaning of a variation in the variable must be explicit).

We map directly the strategic measures on observable variables. We are aware of the complexity of the notion of strategy from the point of view of social research, that suggests building structural models in order to capture latent variables. However, the meaning of the variables we are going to use is explicit and the notion of strategy we adopted does not call for latent variables.

The condition of leverage is particularly important, although difficult to demonstrate. Take as an example the teaching load. If we observe a university in which there are many teachers per student, does it mean that it has a strategic orientation towards undergraduate education, offering better educational services and care, or rather that it does not attract enough students? Since universities are not economic agents in equilibrium, we cannot assume any optimality in the use of resources.

It is clear that answering this question would require qualitative analysis. In order to address this methodological issue on the basis of available information we will follow several approaches. One is to normalize data against the national average. This may reduce some noise in data, although the final interpretation would require comparing the national average with other countries. Another approach is to interpret several variables together. If the teaching load alone is ambiguous, it may take a specific meaning when associated to, for example, cost per student, or the number of different curricula offered to students.

Still a more powerful approach, not pursued in this chapter, is to compute efficiency scores for each university and then interpret the strategy variables in the light of these scores. If for example we find a university with a large ratio of academic staff to students (low teaching load) but a poor efficiency score, we may conclude that it could increase the number of students without increasing the inputs, that is, it does not exhibit strategy but inefficiency. The combined use of efficiency scores and strategic variables is a novel methodology that will be the object of future papers.

We also make no claim about deliberateness of strategy. As it is well known, it is very difficult to ascribe a strategy to an organization without a programme of checking and cross-validation of information. We know nothing about the internal decision processes of the units under analysis (apart some quite general remarks) and cannot say whether an observed pattern of behaviour corresponds to a deliberate strategy or not. We only observe emergent strategies, not deliberate ones (Mintzberg, 1979).

Having made these methodological remarks, let us turn to the data available. They come from a pioneering project, called Aquameth, that has collected data on all individual universities in 11 European countries (United Kingdom, Spain, Italy, Switzerland, Portugal, Norway, France, Germany, Netherlands, Hungary, Finland), whose first results are published in Bonaccorsi and Daraio (2007b). The book also contains a full-length analysis of legislative reforms and government policies in six countries in the sample.

Data come from administrative sources, not statistical offices, and are census data. With a few missing data point in some years of the time series, and some complete lack of data for a few variables, time series of most data are available for the period 1994–2004. The list of variables is presented in Table 5.1.

Table 5.1   The Aquameth dataset

Area	Categories
General Information	• Year of foundation • City, province, region (NUTS) • Number and type of faculties/schools/disciplines covered • Governance (public, private) • Type (university, technical college) • Other relevant historical information
Revenues	• Total revenues of the university • General budget of the university (in federal countries divided between national and regional appropriations) • Tuition and fees • Grants and contracts, if possible divided between government, international, private and private non-profit • Other revenues
Expenditure	• Total expenditures (excluding investments and capital costs) • Personnel expenditures, if possible divided between personnel categories • Other expenditures
Personnel	• Total staff (FTE or headcount) • Professors • Other academic staff • Technical and administrative staff
Education production	• Number of undergraduate students • Number of undergraduate degrees • Number of PhD students • Number of PhD degrees
Research and technology production	• ISI publications • Technological production indicators

Based on the Aquameth dataset we can build a number of indicators of strategy of universities and then of positioning and overall differentiation:

1. Education
    1.1 Undergraduate teaching load (number of undergraduate students/ total academic staff)
    1.2 Master teaching load (number of master students/total academic staff)

    1.3   Cost per student (total expenditure/number of (undergraduate + master students))

    1.4   Teaching diversification load (number of curricula total academic staff) (only for a few countries)

2.   Research

    2.1   PhD intensity (number of PhD students/number of undergraduate students)

    2.2   Research intensity (number of international publications/total academic staff)

    2.3   Cost of publications (total expenditure/number of international publications)

3.   Third mission

    3.1.   Private funding (private funding/total funding)

4.   Funding structure

    4.1   Non-government funding (student fees + private funding/total funding)

    4.2   Government funding (government funding/total funding).

We interpret these variables as follows. Assuming for the time being that efficiency is not an issue (which of course is not true at all), we will say that universities that exhibit low teaching loads, high cost per student, and high diversification loads are strategically oriented towards education. They try to offer a diversified range of courses while keeping the number of students per teacher under control. They also spend a lot of money per student. Following the discussion above, it is still possible that these variables, taken individually, are ambiguous, but taken together they should give a clear picture.

In the same direction, but with less ambiguity, we will say that universities that exhibit high PhD intensity and high research intensity are strategically oriented towards research. The intensity indicator is particularly powerful, as we shall see. The meaning of cost per publication is perhaps more ambiguous. Again, its meaning could be disentangled by normalizing against the national average, and above all by combining the information with the analysis of efficiency score.

Finally, we have available only a very crude and imperfect measure of third mission production, i.e. the share of private funding on the university budget. This variable is subject to difficult comparability issues, because in some countries (e.g. Spain) it includes public funding of research awarded through project funding, in others (e.g. the United Kingdom) it includes a large share of donations and grants from non-profit foundations, not recorded elsewhere, while in other countries it represents mainly the amount of contract research coming from industry. The only solution we have here is to normalize data against the national average and interpret the ratio as an orientation towards a more or less proactive role with respect to private support.

These three categories define strategy in terms of outputs. The final category includes two complementary variables, describing the share of total budget coming from the government and the share coming from the two largest and most important non-government sources. These are interpreted as indicators of the degree of autonomy in the formation of the budget, when normalized against the national average.

Other data are available in the Aquameth database (for example, disciplines covered, or subject mix), but not for all countries. They are not considered in this chapter.

5.   MEASURING DIFFERENTIATION

With these variables available we build up a measure of overall differentiation of the university system. This measure is an aggregate property that takes into account the entire distribution of values of these variables.

We first build up measures of differentiation, referring to the literature on diversity or variety in economics (Saviotti, 1996; Frenken, 2006). There are two main types of measures of diversity or differentiation, i.e. entropy measures and distance measures. The entropy measure is applied when discrete events are considered. [8] Let e_i stand for an event that occurs with probability p_i. Then:

$$h(p_i) = \log (1/ p_i)$$

is the information content associated to that event. Considering n events with probabilities adding to 1, the entropy measure is defined as:

$$H = \sum_{i=1}^{n} p_i \log(1/ p_i)$$

The entropy measure is zero if one event has probability one, and is maximum at $\log n$ when all events are equiprobable.

In order to apply entropy measures to the population of universities we would need nominal or categorical variables corresponding to the events. This is not possible, because the classification of European universities is a controversial issue, which is itself the object of current research. There is no such thing as the Carnegie Mellon Classification in the USA, validated at institutional level and updated periodically (McCormack, 2004). Under these conditions, any effort to define discrete variables would be somewhat arbitrary. Future research work is under way to use our data as an input to a new classification exercise.

We then turn to distance measures which can be applied to continuous variables. They do not require an ex ante classification to be used. These measures have never been applied to universities in Europe due to the lack of microdata collected on a comparable basis. The Aquameth project provides the first opportunity to experiment diversity measures on continuous variables.

There are several possible applications of distance measures. In this chapter we will follow the simplest definition, i.e. unweighted Euclidean distance. We compute the Euclidean distance between each university and all other universities in the same country, compute the square of distance and sum these squared distances across all universities (SSD, sum of squared distances). Formally:

$$\text{SSD} = \sum_{i=1}^{n}\sum_{j=1}^{n}(w_i - w_j / \hat{w})^2$$

where w is the value of the variable under analysis and $\hat{w}$ is the mean value. As a preliminary step, we compute SSD for one variable (PhD intensity), leaving to future work, the integration of all the available variables into a synthetic measure. For simplicity we sum all distances in the matrix, even though the resulting sum duplicates values along the diagonal (the matrix includes the distance between i and j but also between j and i).

The SSD clearly increases with the size of the sample. We present data for each country with no normalization in order to study the dynamics over time in a more intuitive way. In order to make the measure comparable across countries we divide SSD by the square of the number of universities in each country.

$$\text{MSSD} = (1 / n^2)\sum_{i=1}^{n}\sum_{j=1}^{n}(w_i - w_j / \hat{w})^2$$

The mean sum of squared distances tells us the average diversity or differentiation content for each cell of the distance matrix.

The sum of squared Euclidean distances is a rough measure, because it assumes that all distances have the same weight, so that the Euclidean space is homogeneous. This assumption can be appropriate when dealing with one variable, as in our case. When we aggregate into one single measure distances across several variables, this assumption may be less appropriate.

If we deal with more than one variable and have any reason to depart from this assumption, the Mahalanobis measure could be applied. In this case the distances are weighted by the inverse of the variance–covariance matrix of the variables, so that if two variables are strongly correlated, the respective distances weigh less.[9]

The more general measure of diversity is Weitzman's measure (Weitzman, 1992). Let Z stand for a non-empty set, its diversity can be represented by a recursive function as follows:

$$V(Z) = \max_{x \in Z} \ (V(Z \mid x) + d(Z \mid x, \ x))$$

In practice we should recursively pick a unit x out of the set Z, leaving the set $Z|x$, compute all the distances between x and the units of the remaining set $Z|x$, and choose the smallest distance. Repeating it for all x in Z and choosing the maximum value gives the required measure. Weitzman's definition includes all kind of distance measures, not only Euclidean. Although this measure has a number of desirable properties, it is computationally expensive since the number of recursions is exponential in the number of units. For this practical reason it is not used in this chapter, but will be the object of a future dedicated effort.

A final remark on limitations of our measure. We apply SSD and MSSD measures to PhD intensity. This is a ratio variable, i.e. the ratio between the number of PhD students and the number of undergraduate students of a university. The mean value of this distribution is unweighted, i.e. a small university with 2 per cent PhD students has the same weight than a huge one with the same PhD intensity. The resulting mean does not necessarily reflect the national ratio of PhD students over undergraduate students. Consequently, all Euclidean distances normalized by the mean value do not reflect the distribution of individual students across institutions. This is because we are more interested in structural and strategic characteristics of universities, not in the quantity of students at national level. This latter data can be easily retrieved from official sources. Weighted distances could be computed in future work.

6. NATIONAL PATTERNS OF DIFFERENTIATION IN PHD EDUCATION

In this section we discuss the pattern of institutional differentiation of universities that refer to PhD education. While using just a single variable, we get an impressive clear picture of differences across European countries and of the role of policy options.

PhD education is a highly challenging activity, that requires dedicated effort in teaching and supervision and adequate facilities. It is strongly complementary to research, so that it is a legitimate question whether PhD students amount as outputs of the university production, like undergraduate students, or are more likely to be an input, like researchers.

In European countries, the number of PhD students depends on government grants allocated to universities, more rarely on student fees paid privately. However, the number of grants a university can receive is a function of the attractiveness of the doctoral education, since positions must be filled.

Universities can manage PhD education with a variety of approaches. At one extreme, they may build dedicated structures, such as a graduate school, international PhD programmes, and the like. At the other extreme, there may be small courses spread across all departments. In a more or less related way, doctoral programmes may be attractive on an international basis, receiving lots of applications, or may just be designed for local students.

The way in which doctoral education is organized is at the heart of the debate on the future of European universities. In fact, it is well known that in most Continental countries (such as France, Germany or Italy) doctoral education has been traditionally organized on a local basis, with limited competition between applicants and with supervisors that overlap with tutors in undergraduate education. For example, in the French system, before the Reform in 1992, made compulsory in 1999, doctoral grants were directly transferred from the Ministry to the directors of master programmes, who in general selected the brightest students in their courses (Dahan, 2007; Mangematin and Robin, 2003; Mangematin, 2000). No competition was organized with external applicants. In the German system the PhD supervisor is still called 'father', to emphasize a long-term relation. More generally, the degree of competition before application, during the first and second-year courses, before submission of the thesis proposal and in the defence of the final dissertation is much less severe than in Anglo-Saxon countries.[10] There is not an explicit goal of attracting students from all the national domain, even less from abroad. Doctoral courses are usually taught in national languages, not in English. Consequently, the organization of doctoral education is compatible with the profile of almost all existing universities, irrespective of their research quality. Small doctoral courses can easily survive alongside mass undergraduate education. On the other hand, it is unlikely that these courses will become attractive for international applicants. Universities that adopt a strategy of attracting doctoral students must have dedicated resources, courses in the English language and appropriate facilities.

We believe the PhD intensity measure captures all significant aspects of the strategy towards PhD education. If the number of PhD students is very low with respect to undergraduate students, it is likely that the strategic orientation of universities will be more tilted towards satisfying the much larger mass of students, asking for time-consuming teaching, counselling and practical activities, rather than dedicating efforts to a small group of graduate people. If this is the case, it is unlikely the university will be able, as a norm, to organize truly international PhD programmes, that require not only an international faculty, but also strong organizational capabilities and international reputation. Due to the increasing mobility of PhD candidates, the attractiveness of a programme depends strictly on the consolidated reputation of the faculty and the quality of the education.

Universities with a larger than average PhD intensity, on the contrary, are more likely to have dedicated structures, motivated faculty, and more international orientation. Our analytical issue is to examine to what extent the institutional landscape is differentiated with respect to doctoral education. This is reflected not only in a large range in the intensity value between specialized and underspecialized universities, but also in the density distribution. For a national system to be differentiated we sought several universities specializing in doctoral education, not a single outlier. (Also for this reason we eliminated one outlier in UK and one in Italy, namely universities that do not offer undergraduate courses on a regular basis.)

The analysis proceeds in two steps. First, we discuss the evolution in time of the PhD intensity and of the differentiation index (SSD) for each country individually, trying to give an account of their relationship. Second, we compare countries using MSSD and derive comparative implications.

In general data cover a decade, a sufficiently long period to draw conclusions. Time series are not always strictly comparable, since for some countries data start later (e.g. the United Kingdom) and have less observations (e.g. Italy). We select from the Aquameth dataset those countries for which data are complete over at least three years.

(a) PhD intensity

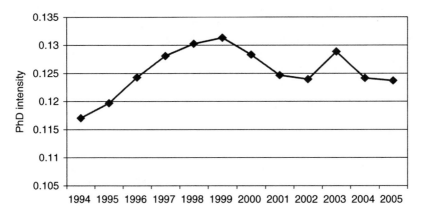

(b) Differentiation in PhD intensity

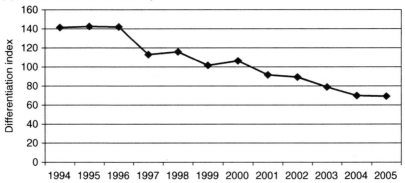

Figure 5.1   Mean value and differentiation in PhD intensity of Finnish universities, 1994–2005

Finland

Finland is one of the European countries with the largest investment in R&D and higher education. The university sector comprises 20 institutions. PhD intensity stood between 11 and 13 per cent for most of the decade under consideration, a remarkably high level. With some fluctuations, PhD intensity increased by one percentage point over the decade (Figure 5.1a). During the same period the differentiation index halved, from a non normalized value of 140 to around 70 (Figure 5.1b).

This interesting dynamic is due to the convergence around the mean value of those universities that at the start of the period had lower intensity. It has not been driven by universities increasing PhD intensity far beyond the mean value, which is already very large. At the same time it is likely that government policy did not push those universities below the mean value to despecialize further into doctoral education. Quite the contrary, they moved up towards the mean, reducing the overall differentiation.

Faced with this evidence, an intriguing question is whether pushing all institutions to pursue doctoral education with similar effort levels is an effective and efficient policy.

The Netherlands

It is interesting to compare the case of Finland with the experience of the Netherlands, another small country with strong R&D investment and orientation. The population considered is 13 universities, excluding institutions for vocational training.

Here the PhD intensity is far lower but increased significantly in both absolute and relative terms, from slightly more than 3 per cent in 1994 to 4.7 per cent a decade later (Figure 5.2a).

In this country the differentiation index witnessed a spectacular increase, from a value of 50 in 1994 to 141 in 2004, doubling in the first three years (1994–97). This effect is due to a small group of universities adopting a rapid and aggressive strategy for doctoral education and almost doubling the PhD intensity over the decade (Figure 5.2b). The PhD intensity value increased in the period 1994–2004 from 5.44 per cent to 11.28 per cent for the Technical University of Eindhoven, from 4.92 per cent to 7.81 per cent for Twente and from 5.49 per cent to 10.06 per cent for Wageningen University.

These are remarkable achievements in an institutional landscape that has steered the university system with a well designed and balanced funding mechanism.

As explained by Jongbloed (2004), in fact, in the Netherlands' funding formula performance elements such as master's diplomas and PhD degrees are driving the allocation of resources. Looking at research funds alone, around one third is currently based on performance. Highly competitive and prestigious Research Council funds represent around 11 per cent of research funding. Contracts for research represent a quarter of research funds and have shown the largest increase in recent times. Summing up performance-based formula funding and competitive allocations, the result is that almost 60 per cent of the total university research funding is performance-based. This funding system has offered the strongest incentives to individual universities to specialize in their strongest activities and to differentiate.

(a) PhD intensity

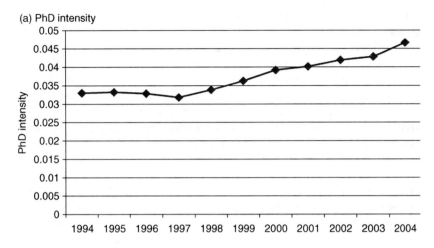

(b) Differentiation in PhD intensity

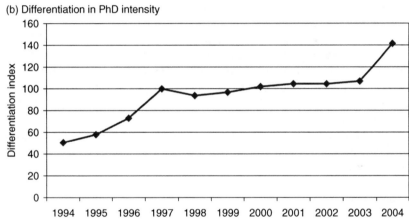

Figure 5.2   Mean value and differentiation in PhD intensity of Dutch universities, 1994–2004

Switzerland

Let us consider another small country, with 12 universities. Switzerland has a historical tradition of large funding of universities and high costs per student (Filippini and Lepori, 2007). Universities are funded at cantonal and Federal level. Graduate education is a large part of the higher education system since many professions require continuing education after the degree. Also, many doctoral students are permitted to work during their PhD. With these details in mind, it is still remarkable that the mean PhD intensity was 15.7 per cent in 1994 and increased to 17.4 per cent in 2003 (Figure 5.3a).

The differentiation index had a mixed dynamic, from a value of 52 in 1994 to a peak of 67 two years later, then a decline down to 39 at the end of the period. Over the entire period there was a moderate decline (Figure 5.3b).

This is in contrast with the sharp decline experienced by Finland and the impressive increase of Netherlands. In fact, this dynamic is the result of contrasting strategic paths of Swiss universities. Obviously, in a small system the overall differentiation index may be influenced by a few entities. In 1994 the three universities most oriented towards doctoral education were St Gallen (intensity 34.6 per cent), ETHZ (21.9 per cent) and Basel (19.0 per cent), with the Federal School of Lausanne (EPFL) at a relatively modest 14.1 per cent. St Gallen was at more than twice the national mean, contributing greatly to the differentiation index. At that time the newly created University of Lugano (USI, Università della Svizzera Italiana) had no doctoral students, again contributing to differentiation.

Nine years later, three universities have exceeded 26 per cent intensity (Basel, ETHZ, but also an impressive EPFL at 26.1 per cent), while St Gallen collapsed at 20.5 per cent. At the same time USI gained 6.7 per cent doctoral intensity. Therefore the overall differentiation increased due to the best performers moving well beyond the country mean, but also decreased because St Gallen and USI converged to the mean, from the top and the bottom of the distribution, respectively.

The institutional system of Switzerland has permitted a few universities to accelerate their involvement into doctoral education, with remarkable results.

United Kingdom

The British case is a complex one, with 116 institutions coming from different historical traditions, particularly with respect to doctoral education (Crespi, 2007; Geuna and Crespi, 2006).

Being a large country, a PhD intensity of more than 15 per cent in 1996 (16.1 per cent) is a major achievement, largely based on attraction of foreign students and dedicated institutions. Data suggest that intensity increased up to 21.6 per cent in the year 2000 and then declined slightly, then fell to 13.8 per cent in 2003 (Figure 5.4a).

Differentiation witnessed a sharp U-shaped dynamic, from a very large value of 7860 in 1996, to a low of 4220 in 2000, then to a new record of almost 9000 in 2003 (Figure 5.4b).

Keeping in mind the starting level is important. In 1996 United Kingdom was by far the more differentiated university system in our

(a) PhD intensity

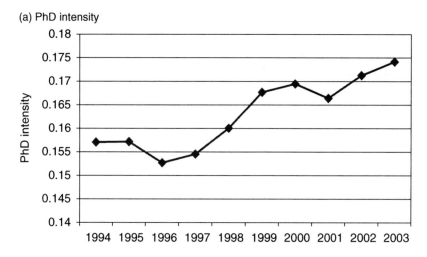

(b) Differentiation in PhD intensity

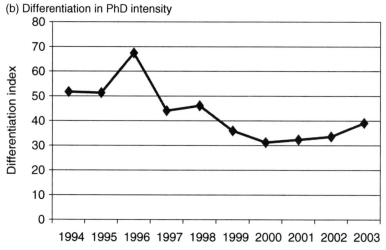

Figure 5.3   Mean value and differentiation in PhD intensity of Swiss universities, 1994–2003

sample, particularly with respect to the other two large countries, Spain and Italy. Keeping the differentiation high in a large country means having clear policies that permit, or even encourage, universities to depart rapidly and massively from the mean value, managing mass education without making universities similar to each other (Wagner, 2006). Due to the race for research funding, however, some universities, particularly those that were transformed from polytechnics, started in the late 1990s

(a) PhD intensity

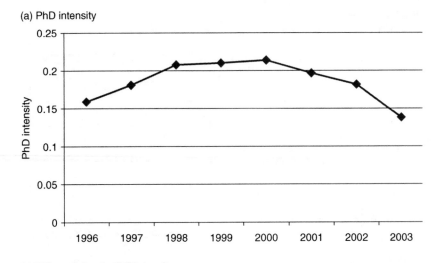

(b) Differentiation in PhD intensity

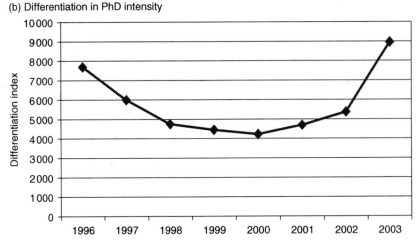

Figure 5.4   Mean value and differentiation in PhD intensity of British
universities, 1996–2003

to invest in postgraduate education. This has increased the mean PhD
intensity, but correspondingly decreased the differentiation. The sharp
increase in differentiation in 2003 is to be understood in the light of UK
government policies. From inspecting individual data it seems that many
universities whose PhD intensity was close to the mean value decreased
significantly, perhaps as an effect of selection in government funding. This
was due to the operation of funding based on the Research Assessment

Exercise and the strong orientation towards performance funding in research.

Our data are able to track nicely, changes occurring in the policy orientation and to describe the adaptation processes that follow.

Spain

In Spain, PhD intensity increased one percentage point, from 3.7 per cent to 4.8 per cent due to an increased investment from the government (Garcia-Aracil, 2007) (Figure 5.5a).

This occurred with almost no change in differentiation, with the exception of a isolated peak in 1997 and an increase in the final year (Figure 5.5b). In fact, there are few institutions dedicated to doctoral education and these witnessed an increase in PhD intensity, but not an impressive one. In 1994 three universities lead the PhD intensity ranking: Alcala at 9.36 per cent, Autonoma de Barcelona at 9.2 per cent and Autonoma de Madrid at 8.7 per cent. The latter are strategically oriented towards doctoral education. All of them increased in 2002, but only marginally, at 12.8 per cent, 9.8 per cent and 11.8 per cent respectively, nothing similar to the jump experienced by leading universities in Netherlands or Switzerland. Therefore they did not contribute at all to an overall increase in the differentiation index.

A positive contribution came from two other universities, that were not ranked high at the start of the period. One is Complutense, that moved from 5.5 per cent to 11.9 per cent, and another one was a newly created one, Pompeu Fabra, that jumped from 3.5 per cent to 10.5 per cent. Quite a remarkable success, but perhaps not enough to mobilize the entire institutional system in Spain.

Italy

The Italian system is a large one (79 universities in the period) characterized by an extremely low involvement into doctoral education. PhD intensity increased in the period from 1.3 per cent to 1.8 per cent, a reasonable increase in relative terms but negligible in absolute terms and with respect to similar countries (Figure 5.6a). For the sake of precision, our data do not include the small universities dedicated to excellent undergraduate education and to doctoral studies, such as Scuola Normale Superiore, SISSA and Scuola Superiore Sant'Anna, since official data are not available for the years covered. In these schools doctoral students make up a large proportion. These would not change the mean value dramatically, but would contribute somewhat to the differentiation index.

(a) PhD intensity

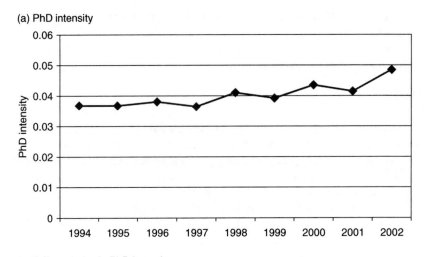

(b) Differentiation in PhD intensity

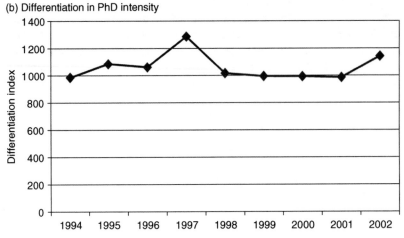

*Figure 5.5   Mean value and differentiation in PhD intensity of Spanish
universities, 1994–2002*

Italy is also the only large country in which differentiation declined
almost monotonically and in a short period, only four years (despite an
increase in the final year) (Figure 5.6b). Most of the differentiation comes
from universities, some of which created in the last decade or after 2000,
dedicated to undergraduate studies. Even research-oriented universities,
such as Milan, Padua, Bologna or Pisa have PhD intensity lower than 3
per cent.

(a) PhD intensity

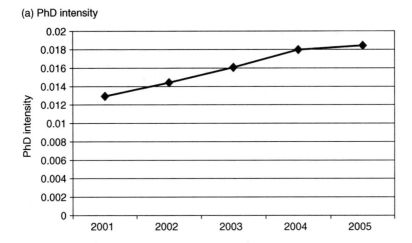

(b) Differentiation in PhD intensity

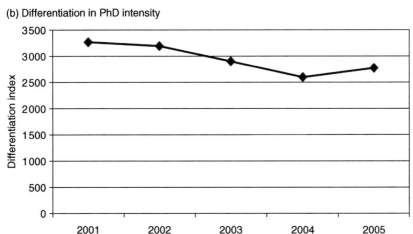

Figure 5.6   Mean value and differentiation in PhD intensity of Italian universities, 2001–05

7.   A QUANTITATIVE COMPARATIVE ANALYSIS OF DIFFERENTIATION IN PHD EDUCATION

Comparative analysis is a necessary step in the study of higher education, due to the intrinsic differences across countries and the complexities associated with historical patterns of growth. It is no surprise that the literature is fairly well divided into quantitative studies, more or less based on

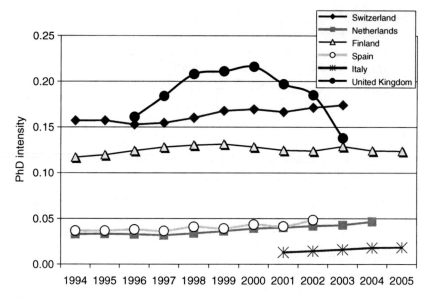

Figure 5.7   Comparative analysis of PhD intensity, all countries,
*   1994–2005*

national data (e.g. efficiency analysis) and qualitative studies, often with a comparative flavour.

The construction of large datasets based on microdata opens a new perspective. Comparative analysis could be carried out on comparable data and using the same metrics, leading to much more rigorous conclusions. Quantitative analyses could be complemented by historical, legislative and institutional arguments.

In order to compare the six countries under analysis, we built a new indicator called MSSD (mean sum of squared distances) by dividing the overall index by the square of the number of universities in the country. In fact, the number of distances computed in SSD grows with the square of the number of units, counting all distances twice. The results are shown in Figure 5.7 and 5.8.

Figure 5.7 shows that there are three groups of countries with respect to the level of the PhD intensity ratio: Switzerland, Finland and United Kingdom over 10 per cent, Netherlands and Spain between 3 and 5 per cent, and Italy at 1–2 per cent. The ranking is almost invariant over time.

With respect to growth, the intensity increases significantly in Switzerland, Netherlands, Spain, and less vigorously in Italy, while is stable in Finland and has a inverted U-shaped dynamic in UK.

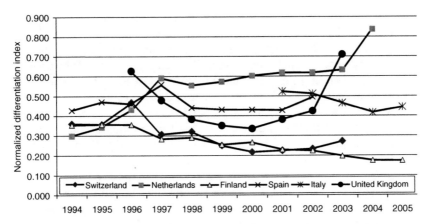

Figure 5.8   Comparative analysis of the differentiation index in PhD intensity, all countries, 1994–2005

With respect to patterns of institutional differentiation, Figure 5.8 gives several important insights.

Larger countries are in general more differentiated, as is evident for UK, Italy and Spain. It is possible to identify four patterns of change in differentiation:

1. *Institutional inertia* (Spain, Italy): there are very few universities above the country mean, a large number of universities close to the mean, leading to an institutional landscape of very limited differentiation and few incentives for universities wishing to grow rapidly in PhD education. Ordinary universities are overwhelmed by the growth in demand for undergraduate education and do not allocate strategic resources to PhDs. Competitiveness in international market for PhDs is limited. Government efforts to create or support dedicated institutions (e.g. Pompeu Fabra in Spain, excellence schools in Italy) are worthwhile but too weak to change the institutional inertia;

2. *Dynamic differentiation* (Netherlands): in a context of growth of importance of doctoral education, government policy is coupled by academic entrepreneurship to create, in a few years, dedicated and vibrant universities, that are also able to attract students from abroad;

3. *Institutional abundance* (Finland): in small and rich countries, universities do not have incentives to differentiate too much from each other. The government provides resources for a strong involvement in doctoral courses and offers incentives to students to pursue further

education after the degree. Growth in doctoral education is then managed by all universities roughly at the same pace;

4. *Consolidated differentiation* (United Kingdom): in this system there is a sharp institutionally embedded differentiation across universities, with a very large range between universities close to the model of teaching university (having a small number of doctoral students, if any) and world-class graduate schools. In particular, there is a solid group of research-oriented large universities that have an international strategy to attract doctoral students from all over the world. From this starting point, variations in both numerator and denominator of the differentiation index may induce wild variation in the overall measure. In particular, since there is probably an upper bound to the intensity measure, the most likely dynamic is one of slow increase in universities below the average, leading to a reduction in differentiation. This does not change at all, however, the overall institutional picture. In a sense, it would be sensible to ask whether there is excess differentiation in the system.

Using this categorization, we would place Switzerland mid-way between (2) and (3). In fact, in the Swiss system, incentives to differentiation do exist and a few entrepreneurial universities have grown rapidly (e.g. EPFL). This pattern is similar to the Dutch dynamic differentiation. However, this is not reflected in the differentiation index, that declines, because in small countries the overall index is more sensitive to small changes. In the case of Switzerland, these come from the sharp decline of St Gallen and the rapid rise of USI, both factors leading to less differentiation inasmuch as they converge towards the mean. In addition, the Swiss system, like the Finnish one, provides all universities large resources, perhaps making the pressure for differentiation less stringent.

8.   CONCLUSIONS

This chapter has for the first time addressed the important issue of institutional differentiation of higher education in Europe providing a quantitative measurement. Using the new Aquameth dataset it is possible to provide a rigorous assessment of the dynamics of universities, as well as of the impact of national policies.

The main message from the chapter is that differentiation is a strategic imperative for universities in the new global knowledge landscape. With scientific and technological opportunities growing at a faster pace, particularly in new emerging fields, both inputs and outputs of universities are subject to increasing competition at the international level. When the size of the market increases, division of labour becomes more convenient, and with division of labour comes specialization, increasing returns, and differentiation from others.

This is totally new for many national systems. Many governments are totally unprepared to manage this change.

We have chosen a particular profile of university activity, where it is crucial to compete internationally, i.e. doctoral education. This is clearly only part of the overall picture, but one that is strategically important. We have provided evidence of sharp differences in the way in which national institutional settings support (or hamper) universities in their move towards strategic positioning and differentiation. The policy implications of our analysis are clear: give more real autonomy to universities, help them to position themselves where they can do their best, allocate resources not on an equal basis but on the basis of best opportunities.

The chapter is part of a larger research programme. Several lines of further research can be considered. One is to extend the analysis of differentiation to other indicators made possible by the Aquameth dataset and come up with a synthetic measure, combining into a model, the multi-dimensional production activity of universities in education, research, and third mission. Another line is to develop new measures of distance (e.g. Mahalanobis) or fully compute the Weitzman's measure of diversity. Given the axiomatic properties of this measure, it would provide an information-ally compact but rich representation.

Furthermore, it would be interesting to track the changes in the institutional landscape at national level, for example in legislative reforms and government policies, in parallel to the evolution of measures. This would strengthen the policy implications of the analysis and provide a solid background for policy decisions.

NOTES

1. The chapter was developed under the Aquameth project, supported by the Network of Excellence PRIME, 6th Framework Programme. The overall project would not have been in existence without the work of Cinzia Daraio. A first draft was presented to the Aquameth meeting held in Brighton, September 2007. The comments of Cinzia Daraio, Ben Jongbloed, Aldo Geuna, Tarmo Rati, Leopold Simar are gratefully acknowledged. I am also indebted with Alessandro Daraio for assistance in data management and with the Italian Ministry of Research for financial support (FIRB-IRIS).
2. For an introduction to comparative institutional analysis of universities see Clark (1983), Kyvik and Skovdin (2003), Kyvik (2004), McCormick (2004), Jongbloed et al. (2005).
3. There is a large literature on the relation between research and teaching in universities: see for example Graves et al. (1982); Cohn et al. (1989); Braxton (1996); Clark (1997);

Vidal and Quintanilla (2000). More recently the issue has been examined in the light of the theory of delegation and screening: Dewatripont et al. (2002); Gautier and Wauthy (2004).

4. The issue of trade-off between open science and various forms of contractual research, patenting, and third mission activities is at the core of a active debate. See, for example, Balconi and Laboranti (2006) and Boumadhi and Carayol (2005) for case studies of individual universities (Pavia and Strasbourg, respectively), and Baldini et al. (2004), Calderini and Franzoni (2004) and Patrucco (2006) for large-scale analyses. Connolly (1997) and Payne (2001) raise the question of substitution in research funding. A large literature has in particular addressed the effects of policies oriented towards commercialization of research on the US university system: e.g. Henderson et al. (1998), Thursby and Thursby (2000), Jaffe and Lerner (2004); Mowery et al. (2004).

    We provided a re-assessment of this issue in Bonaccorsi et al. (2006) and Bonaccorsi et al. (2007a).

5. Economic analysts have long been attracted by the academic labour market: see, for example, McPherson and Winston (1983); Carmichael (1988); Siow (1995); Ehrenberg (2003).

6. For some accounts of the presidential model see Birnbaum (1992); Balderston (1995); Slaughter and Leslie (1997), Bowen and Shapiro (1998); Clark (1998); Freeland (2001); Thelin (2004).

7. The comparative analysis of institutional history across countries suggests a number of explanations. On the notion of research university, for example, see Geiger (1993); Graham and Diamond (1997).

8. The notion of entropy applied to information was first introduced by Shannon (1948) and then developed by Theil (1967). The idea is that the information content is larger when it states that an event occurred, whose a priori probability was small. Therefore a measure of information must be decreasing in probability. If all events are equally likely to occur, the entropy is maximum. If the entropy measure is defined as a base 2 logarithm it can be interpreted as the information content in terms of bit, or binary variables.

9. Mahalanobis distance is particularly appropriate in matching pair exercises, in which the goal is to minimize the distance between units to be compared but the variables whose distances are computed may be linked to each other. See an application to propensity score methods for the evaluation of public incentives to R&D in Merito et al. (2008).

10. Compare these features with a description of the US doctoral system: 'Doctoral education, particularly in the sciences, is perhaps the most efficient competitive market in higher education. Each winter a limited number of students with the requisite qualifications apply to those science and engineering departments that they would most like to attend and that would be most likely to accept them. The applicants are well informed about the training they seek, and they are highly mobile as well. Each department is a small, autonomous producer, and the departments in each subject area collectively form a national market. Except for pricing, doctoral education approaches the requirements for perfect competition. The key feature of this market is that both applicants and departments vary in quality in ways that are fully understood by both parties: applicants and departments can therefore be ranked according to desirability. Thus, a dual competition takes place – departments seek to attract the most preferred students and students seek places at the most preferred departments in their field. This situation produces a *queuing* process of allocation. Top departments choose, and are chosen by, the best students; departments in the next tier do the same with the remaining students; and so on down the list. However, this market is highly competitive and the terms of competition fairly delimited' (Geiger, 2004, pp. 163–4). Although with different national trajectories, many Nordic universities (particularly in Netherlands, Denmark, Sweden) have been following the Anglo-Saxon model, at least in doctoral education.

REFERENCES

Amaral, A., G.A. Jones and B. Karseth (eds) (2002), *Governing Higher Education: National Perspectives on Institutional Governance*, Dordrecht, the Netherlands: Kluwer Academic Publishers.

Avveduto, S. (2005), 'International mobility of scientists and engineers: a study on brain drain and obstacles to mobility', in T. Gabaldon, H. Horta, D.M. Meyer and J.B. Pereira-Leal (eds), *Career Path and Mobility of Researchers in Europe*, Gottingen, Germany: Cuvillier Verlag.

Balconi, M. and A. Laboranti (2006), 'University–industry interactions in applied research: the case of microelectronics', *Research Policy*, Triple Helix Special Issue, **35** (10), 1616–30.

Balderston, F.E. (1995), *Managing Today's University: Strategies for Viability, Change and Excellence*, San Francisco: Jossey-Bass.

Baldini, N., R. Grimaldi and M. Sobrero (2006), 'Institutional changes and the commercialization of academic knowledge. A study of Italian universities patenting activities between 1965 and 2002', *Research Policy*, **35** (4), 518–32.

Birnbaum, R. (1992), *How Academic Leadership Works: Understanding Success and Failure in the College Presidency*, San Francisco: Jossey-Bass.

Bonaccorsi, A. and C. Daraio (2003), 'Age effects in scientific productivity: the case of the Italian National Research Council (CNR)', *Scientometrics*, **74** (1) (January), 15–37.

Bonaccorsi, Andrea and Cinzia Daraio (eds) (2007a), *Universities and Strategic Knowledge Creation. Specialization and Performance in Europe*, Cheltenham, UK and Northampton, MA, USA: Edward Elgar.

Bonaccorsi, A. and C. Daraio (2007b), 'Theoretical perspectives on university strategy', in A. Bonaccorsi and C. Daraio (eds), *Universities and Strategic Knowledge Creation. Specialization and Performance in Europe*, Cheltenham, UK and Northampton, MA, USA: Edward Elgar.

Bonaccorsi, A. and C. Daraio (2008), 'The differentiation of the strategic profile of higher education institutions. New positioning indicators based on microdata', *Scientometrics*, **74** (1).

Bonaccorsi, A., C. Daraio and L. Simar (2006), 'Size, scope and trade-off in the productivity of universities: an application of robust nonparametric methods to Italian data', *Scientometrics*, **66** (2), 389–410.

Bonaccorsi, A., C. Daraio and A. Geuna (2007a), 'Who is complementing public funding of academic research? Different sources with different strategies', paper presented to the Atlanta Conference on *Science, Technology and Innovation Policy* 2007, 19–20 October.

Bonaccorsi, A., C. Daraio, B. Lepori and S. Slipersaeter (2007b), 'Indicators on individual higher education institutions. Addressing data problems and comparability issues', *Research Evaluation*, **16** (2), 66–78.

Boumahdi, R. and N. Carayol (2005), 'Public and private funding of academic laboratories: crowding out evidence from a large European research university', *mimeo*, BETA, Universitè de Strasbourg.

Bowen, W.G. and H.T. Shapiro (1998), *Universities and Their Leadership*, Princeton, NJ: Princeton University Press.

Braxton, J.M. (1996), 'Contrasting perspectives on the relationship between teaching and research', *New Directions for Institutional Research*, **90**, 5–15.

Calderini, M. and C. Franzoni (2004), 'Is academic patenting detrimental to high quality research? An empirical analysis of the relationship between scientific careers and patent applications'. CESPRI working paper no. 162, Milan, Università L. Bocconi.

Carmichael, H.L. (1988), 'Incentives in academics: why is there tenure?', *Journal of Political Economy*, **96** (3), 453–72.

Clark, B.R. (1983), *The Higher Education System: Academic Organization in Crossnational Perspective*, Berkeley, CA: University of California Press.

Clark, B.R. (1997), 'The modern integration of research activities with teaching and learning', *Journal of Higher Education*, **68** (3), 241–55.

Clark, B.R. (1998), *Creating Entrepreneurial Universities. Organizational Pathways of Transformation*, New York: Pergamon Press.

Cohn, E., S. Rhine and M. Santos (1989), 'Institutions of higher education as multiproduct firms: Economies of scale and scope', *Review of Economics and Statistics*, **71** (2), 284–90.

Connolly, L.S. (1997), 'Does external funding of academic research crowd out institutional support?', *Journal of Public Economics*, **64**, 389–406.

Crespi, G. (2007), 'The UK knowledge production function', in A. Bonaccorsi and C. Daraio (eds), *Universities and Strategic Knowledge Creation. Specialization and Performance in Europe*, Cheltenham, UK and Northampton, MA, USA: Edward Elgar, pp. 306–46.

Crespi, G. and A. Geuna (2006), 'The productivity of UK universities', SPRU working paper no. 147.

Dahan, A. (2007), 'Supervision and schizophrenia. Professional identity of PhD supervisors and the mission of students professionalization', Université Marne-la-Valleè LATTS working paper.

De Weert, E. (1999), 'Contours of the emergent knowledge society: theoretical debate and implications for higher education research', *Higher Education*, **38**, 49–69.

Del Favero, M. (2003), 'Faculty–administrator relationships as integral to high-performing governance systems', *American Behavioral Scientist*, **46** (7), 902–22.

Dewatripont, M., F. Thys-Clement and L. Wilkin (eds) (2002), *European Universities: Change and Convergence?*, Brussels: Editions de l'Université de Bruxelles.

Ehrenberg R.G. (2003), 'Studying ourselves: the academic labor market', *Journal of Labor Economics*, **21** (2), 267–88.

Ehrenberg R.G. (2004), 'Econometric studies of higher education', *Journal of Econometrics*, **121**, 19–37.

European Commission (2003), *The Role of Universities in the Europe of Knowledge*, COM (2003) 58, Final.

European Commission (2005), *Mobilising the Brainpower of Europe: Enabling Universities to Make their Full Contribution to the Lisbon Strategy*, Brussels, 20 April 2005, COM (2005) 152 Final, accessed at http://ec.europa.eu/education/policies/2010/doc/comuniv2005_en.pdf.

Filippini, M. and B. Lepori (2007), 'Cost structure, economies of capacity utilization and scope in Swiss higher education institutions', in A. Bonaccorsi and C. Daraio (eds), *Universities and Strategic Knowledge Creation. Specialization and Performance in Europe*, Cheltenham, UK and Northampton, MA, USA: Edward Elgar, pp. 272–305.

Freeland, R.M. (2001), 'Academic change and presidential leadership', in P.G. Altbach, P.J. Gumport and B.B. Johnston (eds), *In Defense of American Higher Education*, Baltimore, MD: Johns Hopkins University Press, pp. 227–48.

Frenken Koen (2006), *Innovation, Evolution and Complexity Theory*, Cheltenham, UK and Northampton MA, USA: Edward Elgar.

Garcia-Aracil, A. (2007), 'Expansion and reorganization in the Spanish higher education system', in A. Bonaccorsi C. Daraio (eds), *Universities and Strategic Knowledge Creation. Specialization and Performance in Europe*, Cheltenham, UK and Northampton, MA, USA: Edward Elgar Publishing.

Gautier, A. and X. Wauthy (2004), 'Teaching versus research: a multi-tasking approach to multi-department universities', CORE working paper.

Geiger, Roger L. (1993), *Research and Relevant Knowledge: American Research Universities since World War II*, New York: Oxford University Press.

Geiger, R.L. (2004), 'Market coordination of higher education: the United States', in P. Teixeira, B. Jongbloed, D. Dill and A. Amaral (eds), *Markets in Higher Education: Rhetoric or Reality?*, Dordrecht, the Netherlands: Kluwer Publishers, pp. 161–84.

Geuna, A. (2001), 'The changing rationale for European university research funding: are there negative unintended consequences?', *Journal of Economic Issues*, **35** (3), 607–32.

Geuna, A. and G. Crepsi (2006), 'The productivity of UK universities', SPRU electronic working papers series no. 147.

Geuna, A. and B. Martin (2003), 'University research evaluation and funding: an international comparison', *Minerva*, **41**, 277–304.

Graham, H.D. and N. Diamond (1997), *The Rise of American Research Universities. Elites and Challenges in the Postwar Era*, Baltimore, MD: Johns Hopkins University Press.

Graves, P.E., J.R. Marchand and R. Thompson (1982), 'Economics departmental rankings: research incentives, constraints and efficiency', *American Economic Review*, **72** (5), 1131–41.

Henderson, R., A.B. Jaffe and M. Trajtenberg M. (1998), 'Universities as a source of commercial technology. A detailed analysis of university patenting 1965–1988'. *Review of Economics and Statistics*, **80**, 109–27.

Henkel, M. and B. Little (eds) (1999), *Changing Relationships Between Higher Education and the State*, London: Jessica Kingsley Publishers.

Jaffe, Adam B. and Josh Lerner (2004), *Innovation and its Discontents: How our Broken Patent System is Endangering Innovation and Progress and What to Do About It*, Princeton, NJ: Princeton University Press.

Jongbloed, B. (2004), 'Funding higher education: options, trade-offs and dilemmas', paper for Fulbright Brainstorms 2004 – New Trends in Higher Education.

Jongbloed, B., P. Maassen and G. Neave (eds) (1999), *From the Eye of the Storm. Higher Education's Changing Institution*, Dordrecht, the Netherlands: Kluwer Academic Publishers.

Jongbloed, B., B. Lepori, C. Salerno and S. Slipersaeter (2005), 'European higher education institutions: building a typology of research', CHINC report, IPTS, Seville.

Kyvik, S. (2004), 'Structural changes in higher education systems in Western Europe', *Higher Education in Europe*, **29** (3), 393–409.

Kyvik, S. and O.J. Skovdin (2003), 'Research in the non-university higher education sector – tensions and dilemmas', *Higher Education* **45**, 203–22.

Laredo, P. (2007), 'Revisiting the third mission of universities: toward a renewed categorization of university activities?', *Higher Education Policy*, **20**, 441–56.

Levin, S. and P.E. Stephan (1991), 'Research productivity over the life cycle. Evidence for academic scientists', *American Economic Review*, **81** (1), 114–32.

Mangematin, V. (2000), 'PhD job market: professional trajectories and incentives during the PhD', *Research Policy*, **29** (6), 741–56.

Mangematin, V. and S. Robin (2003), 'The double face of PhD students: the example of life sciences in France', *Science and Public Policy*, **30** (6), 405–14.

McCormick, A.C. (2004), 'The 2005 revision of the Carnegie Classification System', presentation to the Washington Higher Education Secretariat, Washington D.C., 8 June 2004, accessed at www.carnegiefoundation. org/ Classification/future.htm.

McPherson, M.S. and G.C. Winston (1983), 'The economics of academic tenure: a relational perspective', *Journal of Economic Behavior and Organization*, **4** (2–3), 163–84.

Merito, M., S. Giannangeli and A. Bonaccorsi (forthcoming), 'Do incentives to industrial R&D enhance research productivity and firm growth? Evidence from the Italian case', *International Journal of Technology Management*.

Mintzberg, Henry (1979), *The Structuring of Organizations: A Synthesis of the Research*, Englewood Cliffs, NJ: Prentice-Hall.

Moguerou, P. (2005), 'Brain drain or brain circulation. What we know and what we would like to know', European Institute working paper, Florence, presented to the Workshop on Universities in the Knowledge Society, June 2005.

Mowery, D.C., R.R. Nelson, B.N. Sampat and A.A. Ziedonis (2004), *Ivory Tower and Industrial Innovation: University–Industry Technology Transfer Before and After the Bayh–Dole Act*, Stanford, CA: Stanford University Press.

Musselin, C. (2004), 'Towards a European academic labor market? some lessons drawn from empirical studies on academic mobility', *Higher Education*, **48**, 55–78.

Musselin, C. (2005), *Le marché des universitaires. France, Allemagne, Etats-Unis*, Paris: Presses de la Fondation National des Sciences Politiques.

Neave, G. and F.A. van Vught (1994), *Government and Higher Education Relationships across Three Continents*, Oxford: Pergamon Press.

Nelson, R.R. (1986), 'Institutions supporting technical advance in industry', *American Economic Review*, **76**, 186–9.

Patrucco, P.P. (2006), 'The production of scientific knowledge in Italy: evidence from theoretical, applied and technical sciences', IUE working papers series, European Forum, RSCAS WP, 2006/12, accessed at www.iue.it/RSCAS/ Publications.

Payne, A. (2001), 'Measuring the effect of federal research funding on private donations at research universities: is federal research funding more than a substitute for private donations?', *International Tax and Public Finance*, **8**, 731–51.

Salter A. and B. Martin (2001), 'The economic benefits of publicly funded basic research: a critical review', *Research Policy*, **30** (3), 509–32.

Saviotti, P.P. (1996), *Technological Evolution, Variety and the Economy*, Cheltenham, UK and Brookfield, USA: Edward Elgar.

Shannon, C.E. (1948), 'A mathematical theory of communication', *Bell System Technical Journal*, **27**, 379–423 and 623–56.

Siow, A. (1995), 'The organization of the market for professors', Department of Economics and Institute for Policy Analysis working paper 95/01, University of Toronto.

Slaughter, Sheila and Larry L. Leslie (1997), *Academic Capitalism. Politics, Policies, and the Entrepreneurial University*, Baltimore, MD: Johns Hopkins University Press.

Stephan, P.E. (1996), 'The economics of science', *Journal of Economic Literature*, **34**, 1199–235.

Stephan, P. E. and G. Levin (1996), 'The critical importance of careers in collaborative scientific research', *Revue d'économie Industrielle*, 79/97 45–61.

Texeira, P., B. Jongbloed, D. Dill and A. Amaral (eds) (2004), *Markets in Higher Education. Rethoric or Reality?*, Dordrecht, the Netherlands: Kluwer.

Theil, H. (1967), *Economics and Information Theory*, Amsterdam: North Holland.

Thelin, J.R. (2004), *A History of American Higher Education*, Baltimore, MD: Johns Hopkins University Press.

Thursby, J.G. and M.C. Thursby (2000), 'Who is selling the Ivory Tower? Sources of growth in university licensing', NBER working paper no. 7718.

Tremblay, K. (2002), 'Student mobility between and towards OECD countries in 2001: a comparative analysis', in OECD, *International Mobility of the Highly Skilled*, Paris: OECD, pp. 39–67.

Vidal, J. and M.A. Quintanilla (2000), 'The teaching and research relationships within institutional evaluation', *Higher Education*, **40**, 221–9.

Vincent-Lancrin, S. (2006), 'What is changing in academic research? Trends and futures scenarios', *European Journal of Education*, **41** (2) 169–202.

Wagner, L. (2006), 'Expanding higher education. The British experience', in Samuel Neaman Institute (eds), *Transition to Mass Higher Education Systems. International Comparisons and Perspectives*, proceeding of the international conference, Haifa: S. Neaman Press.

Weick, K.E. (1976), 'Educational organizations as loosely coupled systems', *Administrative Science Quarterly*, **21** (1), 1–19.

Weitzmann, M.L. (1992), 'On diversity', *Quarterly Journal of Economics*, **107**, 363–406.

Zitt, M. and G. Filliatreau (2006), 'Big is (made) beautiful – some comments about the Shanghai Ranking of world-class universities', in Jan Sadlack and Nian Cai Liu (eds), *The World-Class University and Ranking: Aiming beyond Status*, Shanghai: UNESCO–CEPES/Cluj University Press, Romania; Institute of Higher Education, *JiaoTong University*, pp. 141–60.

6. Polarization of the Swedish university sector: structural characteristics and positioning

Daniel Ljungberg, Mattias Johansson and Maureen McKelvey

1. INTRODUCTION

European universities are facing major transitions, including increasing numbers of students, decreasing research funding per faculty and new types of commitments to society (Chapter 13, this book; Lawton Smith, 2006). A number of societal debates are ongoing, such as how universities can obtain external research funding and why some are relatively more successful at it than others. Due to major changes in public policy in the 1990s and high quality micro-level data, Sweden provides an interesting case of transition, new entrants and dynamic competition within the university sector. This chapter provides empirical data about a polarization of the Swedish university sector, as well as tentative explanations of which structural characteristics of individual universities help explain their positioning and access to resources for research. The 'university sector' is here defined as the total population of organizations providing both research and higher education within an economy. This population of higher education institutes (HEIs) include university colleges, institutes of technology and universities.

In contrast to the USA, where such tendencies have been visible for many years, European countries have only since the early 1980s begun to introduce more competitive mechanisms for resource allocation within the university sector (Geuna 2001; Vincent-Lacrin, 2006). Literature about Europe shows a diversity of the overall university population, in regards to certain structural characteristics, which enhance polarization into winners and losers in this new competitive regime (Geuna, 1998, 1999).

This chapter can be put in this context of changing conditions for academia. Like much of Europe, Swedish universities are moving from being state-regulated institutions providing a public good towards a more Anglo-

Saxon model, where universities more explicitly compete for resources. Major changes in Swedish research policy during the 1970s, then again in the 1990s, led to the starting-up of new colleges and universities, explicitly designed to stimulate regional economic growth and teaching, as well as to become new research centres (Sörlin and Törnqvist, 2000; Schilling, 2005). More recently, national debates and public policy initiatives have turned attention to the importance of critical mass and quality in research as well as how to design the external research funding system to become more competitive (see for example, Brändström, 2007). This chapter contributes to these debates. First, by describing structural characteristics such as size and 'R&D intensity' of the population of Swedish universities and colleges. Second, by focusing on whether these characteristics affect the success of specific universities in obtaining external research grants. There are few existing studies asking whether colleges and universities with specific characteristics tend to receive above average research funding from councils, foundations and firms. External research grants here include research money from research councils, foundations and the like as well as from companies located in Sweden and abroad. This chapter thereby analyses whether the relative success at obtaining external research funding can be related to specific structural characteristics, namely density of research personnel, research productivity as well as size and research intensity.

Our research questions arise because the whole issue of whether structural characteristics of universities tend to influence the ability to obtain external funding becomes interesting when the individual organizations face a new, competitive regime. Hence, this study is exploratory, even if comprehensive in examining the total population of universities and colleges in Sweden.

The first research question is a descriptive one, intended to investigate the potential existence of a diverse Swedish university population and thereby to improve classifications.

1. *What are the positions of specific Swedish universities according to their structural characteristics?*

Hence, the first research question is to categorize individual Swedish universities based on the identified characteristics, as well as to map the overall population of actors in the Swedish university sector.

The second research question is an analytical one, dealing with positive and negative effects of characteristics on obtaining external research resources.

2. *What are the positive and negative impacts of structural characteristics, relative to external research funding?*

Our study thus contributes to the emerging understanding of European universities, as found in Geuna (1999) and in Bonaccorsi and Daraio (2007). Section 2 provides an overview of relevant literature on European universities and structural characteristics in university–industry relations. Section 3 presents the research design and methodology. Section 4 presents the descriptive results, which shows the polarization of the Swedish higher education sector in terms of structural characteristics and section 5 provides analysis in terms of whether the ability to attract external research funding is related to this polarization. Section 6 presents the conclusions and implications.

2.   THEORETICAL OVERVIEW

Existing literature about the ability of universities to obtain research grants in general and to obtain industrial funding for research in particular have often focused on explanatory factors such as the quality of the research performed, the impact of informal networks and the 'Matthew effect' for individual researchers.[1] While some of this literature is reviewed below, this chapter also brings in relevant literature for analysing the relative position and specialization of specific organizations, within the overall university sector.

2.1   European Context and Sweden

European universities are in many ways a regulated sector, tightly coupled to public policy objectives and government financing and therefore often dependent upon national governments. Within Europe, government funding is still the largest overall source of income for university-based research (Geuna, 2001; Vincent-Lancrin, 2006). European public policy has been modified in recent decades and increasingly stresses the usefulness of science to society and for competitiveness through innovation. At the end of the 20th century, Europe began to move away from the post-World War II dominant paradigm, with its linear model of innovation, which stressed basic science as the main driver. This move has in some aspects been towards a model of applied research as a mechanism to create national wealth (e.g. Geuna, 2001; Lawton Smith, 2006).

At the same time, a decrease in the relative share of government funding has taken place in the European countries, leading to an increase in the share of external funding (Geuna, 2001; Vincent-Lancrin, 2006).[2] This suggests that governments are moving from 'automatic' flows of financing for universities, towards competitive research funding and thereby universities have to compete more amongst themselves. Hence, a transition in funding is underway, giving us cause to focus on external funding.

Despite the current focus on the economic impact of universities, we should remember that firms do not seem particularly keen on directly financing research activities at the universities. As Geuna (2001) points out, the proportion of university research that is financed by industry is low everywhere, usually less than 10 per cent. OECD figures show that the average of industry-funded higher education expenditure on R&D (HERD) in the EU-25 in 2001 was 6.7 per cent. This is slightly higher than in USA the same year and substantially higher than in Japan (Dosi et al., 2006). Sweden is similar to the rest of Europe, with approximately 6 per cent of the university research funding provided by Swedish and foreign firms in 2006 (SNAHE, 2007).

In the light of the ongoing changes, Geuna (1998, 1999) points to a polarization of the European university sector, in regards to a number of structural characteristics, into two main clusters. On the one hand, there are the pre-WW II (research) universities, which generally are large organizations with high research productivity and research orientation. These universities attract the majority of the research resources. On the other hand, there are the post-WW II (education) universities, which are mostly small in size and low in research productivity and orientation

By 1910, Sweden already had the universities of Lund, Uppsala, Gothenburg and Stockholm, as well as one specialized in medical subjects (Karolinska Institute), two specialized in engineering and technical subjects (Royal Institute of Technology and Chalmers University of Technology) and a private university specialized in business and economics (Stockholm School of Economics). Then, during the 1960s and 1970s, the first regional colleges were founded as filials of existing universities. The filials were placed in the next tier of cities such as Linköping, mainly for reasons of regional politics. The main task of these colleges was considered to be to attract more of the 'reserve of talent' into higher education, in order to provide the regional industry with workers. Later on, many of these organizations expanded and also became independent.[3]

In the 1990s, Sweden underwent major changes in research policy. The underlying mechanisms included a recession accompanied by a new belief in universities as driving economic growth. More recently, these public policy initiatives have led to debates about whether commercialization and academic entrepreneurship are effective or not within the Swedish context (Henrekson and Rosenberg, 2001; Granberg and Jacobsson, 2006).

For this chapter, one of the most interesting outcomes of the 1990 reform was that new regional university colleges were started not only for education of undergraduates but also for research and training of PhD students.

Since 1997, all universities and university colleges are given research funding from the government, which was not the case before. Another outcome was a shift in Swedish science policy towards competitive research funding, but also towards explicit initiatives to stimulate high quality research at these new university colleges. This more competitive environment and restructuring of public authorities were also facilitated by the introduction of new public research foundations. They were based on the so-called wager earners' funds and these research foundations were intended to stimulate strategic research and to enhance co-operation and interaction with industry (Schilling, 2005).

Although these reforms led to more HEIs conducting research, the overall Swedish public research funding was not enlarged, but rather spread out more thinly amongst more actors. Similar to the general trend in Europe, there has been a decrease in the relative share of government funding in Sweden. The share of general university funds, or block funding, has decreased since the early 1980s and the share of all government funding since the early 1990s (Heyman and Lundberg, 2002; Hällsten and Sandström, 2002; Vincent-Lacrin, 2006). This empirical fact, together with the mentioned policy changes, indicates that in Sweden, as in Europe, we can observe an increasing importance of external research funding and a more competitive environment regarding it. This has given rise to some public debates, such as the difficulties of conducting high-quality research in this 'boot-strapped' environment and the need for 'critical mass' and the necessary size of research groups in order to be able to conduct 'good research' (Benner and Sörlin, forthcoming).

From this, we draw a first assumption:

The Swedish university sector should display a polarization amongst HEIs in terms of size, R&D orientation and R&D productivity, as well as the ability to attract (external) research funding, similar to the rest of Europe.

2.2   Structural Characteristics Influencing University–Industry Interaction

The traditional rationale for government financing of universities, science and basic research are often attributed to an economic view of the contributions of research institutes to society (e.g. Bush, 1945). In other words, universities have a particular role, because science and education have been seen as public goods. As such, the university provides public goods in terms especially of education, research and commercialization to deliver what are now called externalities, general-purpose technologies and knowledge spillovers. These benefits are seen to promote societal development, solve societal problems and stimulate economic growth.

Universities are known to impact on society more broadly. Studies have been made on the impact of university research and science on economic growth (e.g. Salter and Martin, 2001) and on the different mechanisms and channels for knowledge transfer, across different industries (e.g. Cohen et al., 2002). Salter and Martin (2001) identify six major mechanisms for diffusion of university research to industry: increasing the stock of useful knowledge; educating skilled graduates; developing new scientific instrumentation/methodologies; shaping networks and stimulating social interaction; enhancing the capacity for scientific and technological problem-solving; and creating new firms. Similar lists can be found in many other references. Cohen et al. (2002) show that the key channels for university research to impact on industry are publications, public conferences and meetings, consulting and informal information exchange. However, recent debates have swung to stress that universities should more directly contribute to economic growth (Salter and Martin, 2001). The literature has exploded on topics such as academic entrepreneurship, commercialization of research results and university–industry interaction. For example, *Research Policy* published 43 articles using one or more of the words 'academic entrepreneurship', 'commercialization' and 'university–industry' in abstract, title or/and keywords in 2000–05 (authors' search). The majority of these studies use patents, licences and start-up companies as the empirical data, to demonstrate how universities influence society.

One topic of debate has been what quality of university research is required to stimulate university–industry interactions. Using biotechnology in the USA, Zucker and Darby (1996) put forth the 'star scientist' hypothesis, showing that prominent scientists were also prominent commercializers of science. Assuming that eminence is rewarded under a competitive funding regime, one might expect that the researchers and fields with the most external research funding to also be most active in activities such as patenting and start-up companies.

Some papers have examined the importance of having high quality of science, from the perspective of firms and different industries. Mansfield (1995) surveyed industrial technology managers in the USA, finding that the university research perceived as most important was often directly related to the quality of the faculty in relevant departments and to the size of R&D expenditures in relevant fields. High-quality science thus seems to attract more industrial interaction with universities, so that again, we would expect that high levels of quality, and hence external research funding (from any source) should be correlated with high measures of university–industry interaction.

However, this does not mean that lower quality or lower prestige universities do not interact with firms. Mansfield (1995) also found that in several industries, the relationship between faculty rating and their contribution to industrial innovation was very weak. Hence, in some industries and research fields, many modestly ranked departments play as large a role as some of the most highly ranked departments. Similarly, in the UK, it was found that the research quality of the departments did not impact on the probability to engage in various mechanisms to interact with firms (D'Este and Patel, 2007). One explanation could be that less prestigious departments may be more willing to focus on firms' immediate problems, rather than on long-term research (Mansfield and Lee, 1996). If the latter is correct, then the researchers and universities which are not performing at the absolute top of research should be able to substitute research grants for external funding.

Other literature focuses upon firms, using a rich description of structural characteristics such as the size, age and R&D intensity of those firms, in order to help explain why these firms interact with universities. It appears that firm size is positively related to interactions (e.g. Beise and Stahl, 1999; Laursen and Salter, 2004), but not to contract or collaborative research (e.g. Cohen et al., 2002; Santoro and Chakrabarti, 2002; Schartinger et al., 2002). R&D intensity, measured as R&D expenditures over sales and number of scientists in a firm, has been found to be positively related to interaction (e.g. Laursen and Salter 2004), but not be related to contract or joint research specifically (e.g. Mohnen and Hoareau, 2003). Several studies have found that intensity and types of interactions differ between industries, where industries ranked as most prone to interact with universities include pharmaceuticals, semiconductors and other manufacturing industries (e.g. Klevorick et al., 1995; Cohen et al., 2002). The age of firms is found in some studies to be related to interaction, but this is not as well researched and the results are somewhat inconclusive (Meyer-Krahmer and Schmoch, 1998; Schartinger et al., 2001; Laursen and Salter, 2004).

While the industrial side is well researched, however, literature deals less with the structural characteristics of individual universities and of populations of universities. To the extent structural characteristics are studied, they usually refer more to the university support structure for handling patenting and spin-off activities.

There are, nonetheless, a few studies specifically concerned with universities' structural characteristics and industry interaction. Schartinger et al. (2001) found that department size had a significantly positive impact on industry interaction in Austria. They also attempted to capture the effects of departments' R&D intensity on interaction, but they found no significant impact on interaction in general. Similarly to industry differences for firms, some research suggests that the intensity and type of interaction vary among research orientations and scientific fields (see, for example, Meyer-Krahmer and Schmoch, 1998; Schartinger et al., 2002).

We propose to apply the structural characteristics found to influence firms' propensity to interact with academia also on universities engaging in such and other external, relationships. We do so due to a perceived lack of such studies in the current literature. From this and the earlier discussion, we draw our second assumption:

> *HEIs in Sweden that are larger, more R&D intensive and with a higher research productivity should display a higher propensity to obtain external research funding in general, and industry funding in particular, as well as a higher relative importance of such funding, relative to others.*

3.   RESEARCH DESIGN

In the following section, we present the method and data used for this study.

3.1   Data and Methods

The method used here is primarily descriptive, using quantitative data to explore the research questions identified above. Since the first descriptive question addresses the categorization of the university sector, the use of factor- or cluster-analysis could be appropriate. However, the range of data and number of observations is rather limited, mainly due to the small number of HEIs located in Sweden and so we have concentrated on a descriptive analysis.

The data for the analysis is to a large extent drawn from a Swedish national database on universities. The database is run by the Swedish National Agency for Higher Education and uses data that the agency collects directly from all Swedish HEIs as well as from other sources, on a yearly basis.

The database contains data on students, personnel and finances, such as different sources of funding. This data is obtained at the university level and can be broken down on different research subjects at the respective HEI when it comes to personnel data but not for funding.[4]

This chapter uses the averages over the period 2001–05 for all the variables analysed except publications where we use the average for 2001–04. The main reason for this is that 2001 represents a break in the reporting of some of the data-series making it hard to combine data from the recent years with data from before. Moreover, the average over the period is used as in particular, the amount of grants and funding can vary considerably from year to year for reasons that may have to do with reporting routines rather than representing actual changes in data.

Table 6.1   Summarizing the variables, metrics and data collection

	Metric	Specific information	Source
Competitive (external) research funding	Research funding	All research funding except general university funds and internal funds (in absolute number or per researcher)	NU
Funding for undergraduate education	Income from undergraduate education	All income, including from Masters	NU
Size	Research personnel	Number, in FTE, of research assistants, research students, lecturers, other researching personnel and professors	NU
Research intensity	Research orientation	Students per professor	NU
Age	Foundation year		University web sites, annual reports
Density	Research personnel	Number, in FTE, of research personnel broken down per research subject	NU
Research productivity (Quality)	Publications	Normalized number of publications per researcher in a HEI	SCI, SSCI

To complement and check data in the NU-database we have used other sources of data, such as the websites and annual reports of respective HEIs, to obtain data on, for example, the age of the institutions. Publications were gathered from the Science Citation Index (SCI) and the Social Science Citation Index (SSCI).

3.2   Variables and Metrics

Based on the literature review and research questions, we have identified a series of variables as relevant to the analysis namely external research funding (of different types), size, research intensity, age, density of researchers and productivity (of science). For each, we have identified a metric where data can be gathered. The variables include all scientific, engineering, humanities and social science disciplines. Table 6.1 summarizes the variables and metrics and includes details of the specific information gathered and the sources. Each variable and metric is discussed in turn below.

External research funding

We take a broad definition of external research funding, but only including funding for which universities and research groups have to compete. This excludes general university funds (i.e. block funding and similar) and internal funds. In the analysis, we compare different types of external funding to income generated from undergraduate (including masters) education. Thereby, we can differentiate universities that access resources through research from those that access resources through education.

To make a more detailed analysis, external research funding is broken down into eight categories, seven of which have been used for the Swedish situation in previous literature (Sandström, 1997; Hällsten and Sandström, 2002). Earlier examination of the NU-database has suggested that it is difficult to differentiate between the grants and contract research obtained from Swedish and foreign firms (Hällsten and Sandström, 2002). In response to this problem the two categories were merged into one, representing industry-funded research.

The categories for external research resources used are:

- *Research councils* (RC): the Swedish Research Council (Vetenskapsrådet)
- *New foundations* (NF): Comprising all public foundations, such as the Knowledge Foundation (KK-stiftelsen) and the Foundation for Strategic Research (SSF).
- *Foundations* (F): Private or semi-public foundations, such as the Wallenberg Foundation, the Bank of Sweden Tercentenary Foundation (Riksbankens Jubileumsfond) and the Swedish Cancer Society. University foundations are not included, since theirs are considered to be internal funds.
- *Government institutions & EU* (G & EU): Funding from the government through institutions such as VINNOVA, local authorities, county councils and the EU.
- *Industry* (I): contract research and grants from Swedish and foreign firms.
- *Contract research (non-industry)* (CR): Contract research from all different financers, except from industry.
- *Other external funding* (O): grants from Swedish and foreign non-profit organizations, as well as 'other' incomes.

The other data has to do with metrics applied to the structural characteristics of universities and HEIs.

As an indicator for *university size*, we primarily use number of research personnel, since number of employees is commonly used to denote firm size (e.g. Cohen et al., 2002; Laursen and Salter, 2004) as well as occasionally university size (Schartinger et al., 2001). In the Swedish database, personnel categories do not easily distinguish those employees who are researching from those who are only teaching. Moreover, in Sweden, PhD students are usually university employees, actually undertaking much of the research. This chapter includes professors (chair, full), senior lecturers (e.g. associate professors), research assistants (e.g. post-docs, junior lecturers), Other researching and teaching personnel and PhD students. As a complement to this, research income and expenses is used in the first general overview of the university sector. We will also use the size in education in terms of number of students and income from undergraduate education to contrast against size in research.

In studies of firms, *R&D intensity* is usually measured in terms of R&D expenditure over sales (e.g. Mohnen and Hoareau, 2003). However, due to the nature of the university 'business' and the data available, a corresponding metric cannot be used directly. Instead, we propose that R&D intensity can be seen as research intensity or research orientation.

Our argument is based on the main businesses of the universities. Universities can be seen as having two main tasks, namely education and research (See Chapter 13, this volume). Therefore it seems feasible to construct indicators that measure the relation between these two tasks, in order to capture research intensity. Geuna (1999) uses researchers per student as an indicator, the rationale being that the higher the indicator is the higher 'the propensity of the institution to carry out research'. Hence, the detailed level of data on personnel per research field may be used to classify the universities and the university colleges in terms of being more or less science-based. Thus, what is measured here is the intensity of research as compared to education, or in other words the level of research orientation. Rather than research personnel (which is a broad category), we focus on chair professors (full professors), as they can be claimed to play a central role in research activities. Since our analysis is descriptive in nature, we use students per professor, in order to get a more easily comparable indicator of research orientation.

Age is used here mainly as a complementary variable. It is not included in the NU-database but founding year was obtained from other sources. The age in the Swedish university sector is rather skewed, ranging from a couple of very old institutions to most being fairly young. Here, the variable is mostly useful in developing categories.

Density refers to high number of researchers within specific research subjects and can also be seen as an indicator of specialization. The density of research personnel in the different research subjects reveals to some extent the intensity of the research conducted at a particular university. Here we study the share of research subjects with more than a certain number of researchers active in them. This relates to the debates about 'critical mass' and overall research intensity.

A common indicator of *quality* has been publications. A more cautious way to handle this indicator is to call it *scientific productivity* instead of quality, as has been done by, for example, Geuna (1999). Rather than analysing total publications (which would demonstrate overall research output), we here analyse publications per researcher. Therefore publications are normalized per author, so that a paper with, for example, three authors from the same HEI is counted as one paper for that institution. Each author is assigned a share of the paper. The numbers are then aggregated on the university level and averaged per HEI, by dividing by the total number of researchers at that HEI.

4. DESCRIPTIVE CHARACTERISTICS OF THE SWEDISH UNIVERSITIES

This section focuses on the relative position of individual organizations in the Swedish university sector, as defined in the first research question and the first assumption drawn from literature.

4.1 Overview Of The Swedish University Sector

This chapter uses the term 'university sector' broadly, yet there are differences amongst the HEIs. In Sweden, university status relates to the so-called 'right' to examine research students in all science areas; i.e. within medicine, natural sciences, humanistic and social sciences and technical sciences.[5] University colleges on the other hand can only examine research students within scientific areas that they are specifically granted. As of 2007, the Swedish higher education sector consists in total of 14 universities and 22 state-controlled university colleges. In addition, there are three private HEIs with the right to examine research students (Chalmers UT, Jonkoping UC and Stockholm SE). We are here interested in the HEIs performing research in a wider sense and therefore we do not study the colleges devoted to arts, pedagogy and the like. This leaves us with 30 Swedish HEIs. Our first research question is related to which characteristics are useful to define categories, as well as to position specific HEIs within these classifications. First we take a broad overview of the population in terms of age and size in research and education. Table 6.2 presents the 30 chosen

Table 6.2 Overview of the Swedish HEIs, 2005

HEI	Year of est.	Students	Professors	PhDs	Income Education	Income Research	Research expenditure
Lund U	1666	26 884	572	1 196	1 713 812	3 282 072	3 295 967
Uppsala U	1477	21 852	472	1 117	1 350 335	2 761 855	2 758 065
Karolinska I	1810	5 603	308	568	813 718	3 021 736	2 990 967
Göteborg U	1891	25 823	433	582	1 781 269	2 441 777	2 439 510
Umeå U	1965	16 904	243	565	1 383 975	1 574 108	1 574 562
Stockholm U	1904	23 126	351	719	1 047 940	1 698 178	1 707 119
Royal IT	1826	12 443	242	772	978 333	1 703 328	1 710 099
Linköping U	1970	18 041	264	685	1 260 338	1 253 291	1 232 334
SLU	1977	3 418	190	388	475 486	1 607 385	1 559 843
Chalmers UT	1829	8 554	150	585	741 257	1 371 704	1 389 577
Luleå UT	1971	8 082	89	287	617 696	566 903	561 674
Malmö UC	1998	10 241	40	77	805 768	130 274	141 400
Örebro U	1965	9 483	56	139	576 416	250 354	250 615
MittUniversity	1993	8 202	37	130	514 433	279 391	261 199
Karlstad U	1977	8 183	45	113	505 667	262 048	264 364
Växjö U	1977	7 414	42	130	479 971	207 686	206 275
Mälardalen UC	1977	8 725	41	91	573 213	131 545	130 118
Kalmar UC	1977	6 023	32	72	463 024	126 690	133 909
Södertörn UC	1995	6 382	34	89	268 519	217 454	228 996
Jönköping U	1977	6 634	31	74	426 416	138 744	130 594
Gävle UC	1977	6 102	23	15	357 934	97 182	99 869
Borås UC	1977	5 002	19	43	374 544	56 316	62 610
Blekinge IT	1989	3 320	22	55	261 725	106 761	107 493

Dalarna UC	1977	5 125	16	30	335 252	66 521	67 258
Stockholm SE	1909	1 390	32	35	88 450	152 820	222 255
Halmstad UC	1983	5 398	21	28	280 325	72 962	71 906
Kristianstad UC	1977	5 239	14	13	319 100	42 803	47 986
Skövde UC	1977	4 183	12	55	266 662	45 314	52 815
Väst UC	1990	4 056	5	20	268 672	38 652	43 592
Gotland UC	1998	2 252	8	4	129 870	23 322	19 395

Swedish HEIs, ranked according to their aggregated absolute size in these variables in 2005.[6]

The table can be interpreted as reflecting Swedish science and educational policy in the 19th and 20th centuries, especially the waves of HEI establishment in the 1970s and the 1990s. It indicates a clear size and age distribution, running the range from Lund University (LU) to Gotland College (HG). Generally speaking, the oldest organizations are also the largest, as indicated in terms of researchers and undergraduate students. Still, two of the HEIs started in the 1990s have grown larger than ones started in the 1970s, particularly Mitt University (MiU) and Malmö H (MaH). These two lie close to two of the major metropolitan areas and population centres, Stockholm–Uppsala and Malmö–Lund respectively.

However, the size–age distribution has three noticeable exceptions, especially in terms of undergraduate students. Two, namely Karolinska Institute (KI) and the Swedish University of Agricultural Sciences (SLU), have considerably fewer students than other organizations of their size in research. The third exception is Malmö, which has a rather high share of students relative to its research effort.

Hence, this first overview of the university sector suggests that most Swedish HEIs can be divided into larger-older and smaller-younger categories.

4.2   Relative Orientation Towards Education or Research

To go further with our classification, we explore variables to identify HEIs' relative orientation towards either education or research, defined in terms of relative efforts. To some extent, the age–size variable will be discussed below.

Note that orientation here simply refers to relative emphasis on one of the two activities at the organization and it does not show their relative 'share of market' within Sweden as a whole.

Figure 6.1 relates the overall size in terms of number of researchers, on the x-axis, to the research intensity related to education, in form of students per professor, on the y-axis. The different HEIs are labelled in the figure with the national so-called university code.

Figure 6.1 is striking, in that the data reveal two quite distinct groups of Swedish HEIs. The universities in the first group have a large number of researchers as well as high relative orientation towards research, in terms of students per professor. These ten institutions each have more than 1000 researchers. Their overall low numbers of students per professor indicates an orientation less directly dependent on education and with more room for research. These HEIs all have university status and seven of them are

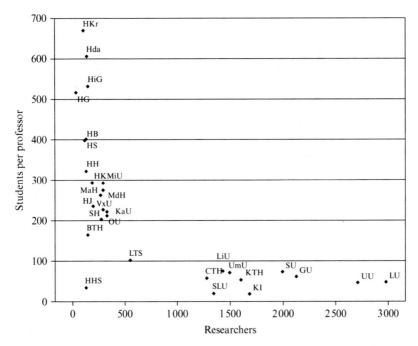

Note: *One extreme case, Väst UC (HV), has been left out in order to make the figure clearer.

Figure 6.1   Research orientation,* average 2001–06

the oldest in Sweden.[7] The remaining three of these ten universities were founded about 1970 and they represent the largest of the younger universities.

As noted in Tables 6.2 and 6.4, however, these have large absolute numbers of students and educational financing, so they combine research and teaching. The group will further on be referred to as the 'Larger (and older) Research and Teaching Intensive' universities. They are grouped along the x axis and they are (from right to left on this axis): Lund University (LU), Uppsala University (UU), Gothenburg University (GU), Stockholm University (SU), Karolinska Institute (KI), Royal Institute of Technology (KTH), Umeå University (UmU), Linköping University (LiU), the Swedish University of Agricultural Sciences (SLU), and Chalmers University of Technology (CTH).

Looking back, we can identify a few more detailed differences within this first group. One is that the age is generally, but not always, related to size. Chalmers is the exception here, in that it is relatively old compared to the population but it is also the smallest in this first group. The three younger universities in the group are all somewhat smaller than the older ones. Finally, of the three younger universities, one of them has almost the lowest student to professor ratio (SLU) whereas the other two have the highest student professor ratio in the group (Linköping U and Umeå U).

The second group has the inverse characteristics, differing on both dimensions from the first group. They have lower numbers of researchers, as well as many more students per professor. The group is composed of younger organizations, which are also smaller, as defined in terms of research. These are all regional HEIs, with the oldest founded in 1965 and the youngest founded in 1998. As can be seen in the figure, most HEIs in this group have less than 300 researchers. These HEIs distinguish themselves not only by being smaller, but also by having significantly more students per professor than the universities in the first group. In fact, almost all of them have more than 200 students per professor, which is more than twice as much as in the first group. This group will be referred to as the 'Smaller (and younger) Education Dependent' HEIs. They are grouped along the y-axis of Figure 6.1 and they are (descending order on that axis): Kristianstad (HKr), Dalarna (Hda), Gotland (HG), Gävle (HiG), Skövde (HS), Borås (HB), Halmstad (HH), MittUniversity (MiU), Malmö (MaH), Kalmar (HK), Mälardalen (MdH), Jönköping (HJ), Växjö University (VxU), Karlstad University (KaU), Södertörn (SH), Örebro University (ÖU) and Blekinge (BTH).

One organization, within this second group, has been left out in Figure 6.1, because it is an outlier when it comes to this specific characteristic. Väst (HV) is the second smallest HEI, even more specialized in education than the others, having a student per chair professor ratio that is extremely high (2301 students per professor).

One organization, Luleå UT, in some aspects lies close to the second group but also shares some characteristics of the first group. Luleå is considerably larger than the HEIs in the second group but also much smaller than most organizations in the first group. It also has a research orientation closer to those found in the first group. One interpretation is therefore that Luleå may be moving between the two groups. One organization does not follow the general pattern. Stockholm School of Economics (HHS) has one of the lowest students per professor ratio, but it combines its specialization in research with a small size. Moreover, it is among the oldest universities in the country but also private. They have obviously evolved, or chosen, a combination of research and teaching which differs significantly from the other Swedish organizations.

4.3 Density in Research Subjects

To pursue the idea of research intensity further, our next step is to identify whether the organizations have different numbers of research subjects in which they are active as well as whether they have different density of professors and researchers across research subjects, self-declared to the government.[8] In many ways, the idea of 'density' can be related to the issue of 'critical mass', in other words, do universities have many or few researchers and professors within each specific subject?

Table 6.3 presents the Swedish HEIs according to the two suggested groups, defined above, and according to density within groups. This table shows how many researchers and professors, respectively, are employed at each declared research subject within that organization. For example, Lund has more than one researcher in 63 of their research subjects and more than 50 researchers in 23 of their research subjects.

The first column in Table 6.3 suggests the total number of research subjects, per organization (the number of research subjects represented by one or more full-time equivalent researcher(s)). A first reflection is that the regional universities and colleges are present in almost as many research subjects as the larger and older HEIs. Hence, if one only looks at the column with active (declared) research subjects, it appears that all Swedish HEIs are quite similar. No striking diversity between the two groups is visible in this regard.

However, looking across the other columns, a rather striking difference is shown. This difference in density across research subjects grows the more researchers and professors you set as the minimum, as can be seen moving from left to right in Table 6.3. The 'Larger Research and Teaching Intensive' universities have a high density across research subjects, such that they are represented in most research subjects by at least 20 researchers, and in many subjects also with at least 50 people. In contrast, the 'Smaller Education Dependent' HEIs have few research subjects represented by more than 20 people, and with few exceptions no subjects with more than 50. In fact, in most cases a large share of the research subjects in these HEIs are represented by less than five people. Hence, major differences between the first and second group also hold for this characteristic.

Interestingly, while a substantial share of research subjects in the universities in the first group have more than five professors, a surprisingly small share at the smaller regional institutions in the second group have even one. For example, Dalarna UC has 38 declared research subjects, but only seven subjects with at least one professor. Similar results are shown for the other HEIs in this second group.

*Table 6.3   Number of research subjects comprising more than a specific
number of researchers and professors, average 2001–2006*

HEI	Researchers					Professors	
	>1	>5	>10	>20	>50	>1	>5
Larger research and teaching intensive							
Lund U	63	54	48	40	23	60	34
Uppsala U	54	50	44	33	17	52	26
Göteborg U	54	49	40	31	14	49	24
Stockholm U	50	39	33	28	11	45	22
Karolinska I	12	11	11	10	10	11	10
Royal IT	23	17	15	13	12	18	13
Umeå U	59	45	36	25	6	43	17
Linköping U	58	44	34	25	7	45	17
SLU	15	13	11	10	10	12	10
Chalmers UT	19	16	14	13	10	15	12
Smaller Education Dependent HEIs							
Karlstad U	36	21	13	4	0	21	0
Örebro U	34	22	14	3	0	22	0
MittUniversity	38	21	11	3	0	17	0
Växjö U	31	17	13	3	0	18	1
Malmö UC	37	16	6	3	1	13	2
Södertörn UC	24	14	8	4	1	14	1
Mälardalen UC	32	17	9	3	0	15	1
Jönköping UC	30	10	6	2	0	14	0
Kalmar UC	36	11	4	2	0	12	1
Gävle UC	29	13	3	0	0	9	0
Blekinge IT	19	7	3	1	1	8	1
Dalarna UC	38	10	1	0	0	7	0
Halmstad UC	28	11	1	1	0	10	1
Skövde UC	23	6	3	1	0	6	0
Borås UC	27	8	2	1	0	9	0
Kristianstad UC	24	7	1	1	0	6	0
Väst UC	24	6	1	0	0	2	0
Gotland UC	10	2	0	0	0	2	0
Luleå UT	26	13	10	8	5	15	6
Stockholm SE	6	4	3	2	1	5	2

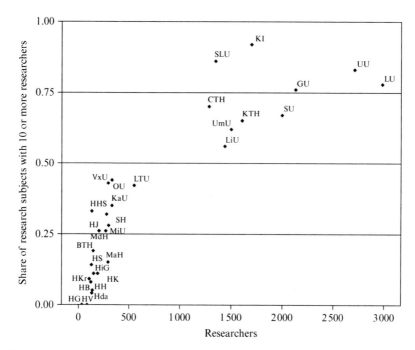

Figure 6.2   Density across research subjects, average 2001–06

This result about the density of researchers and professors, across declared research subjects, is quite provocative in the Swedish context, given the declared public policy objective of developing research at the smaller, younger HEIs. Therefore, we decided to identify more systematic differences to distinguish organizations and groups. Looking across the Swedish university sector, we made a calculation of the absolute average of researcher per research subject. From this, ten researchers per subject were chosen as a reasonable benchmark to compare the density in research subjects in the different HEIs. Figure 6.2 plots, for each organization, the share of research subjects with more than ten researchers against the total number of researchers.

The figure confirms the usefulness of discussing 'Larger Research and Teaching Intensive' and 'Smaller Education Dependent' also for density of researchers across subjects.

Figure 6.2 shows that the ten universities above identified as the first group have a significantly higher share of research subjects comprising more than ten researchers, than do those in the second group. More specifically, the organizations in the first group have ten or more researchers in more than half of their research subjects. The HEIs in the

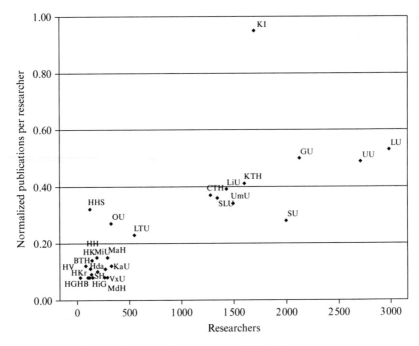

Figure 6.3   Research productivity, average 2001–06

second group, on the other hand, have less than half of the research subjects comprising more than ten researchers and in most cases substantially
less.

The same organizations are 'outliers' here as well. Looking at Figure 6.2,
Stockholm SE lies rather close to the second group, although having a
higher density relative to size. However, when studying Table 6.3, one can
see that the higher the number of researcher you set as the minimum, the
more SSE aligns with the ones in the first group. This also holds true for the
density of professors in general. Luleå UT also shares these characteristics
with this first group, but not as pronounced as SSE.

4.4   Research Productivity

We wish to check whether the HEIs in the Swedish university sector also
differ when it comes to research productivity. Figure 6.3 places the research
productivity, in terms of normalized publications per researcher, against
size, in terms of total number of researchers.

Figure 6.3 further confirms that there are clear differences between the
two groups previously suggested, in that the data reveal a relationship

between the size of research effort and research productivity. Plotting this relationship shows a clear tendency for researchers who are active at organizations with large numbers of researchers on average also publishing more papers. In other words, they have a higher research productivity as measured in output per researcher.

The 'Larger Research and Teaching Intensive' universities, all have, with the exception of Stockholm U, more than 0.3 publications per researcher and year. For the 'Smaller Education Dependent' group, the publication rate is substantially lower. In fact, all the HEIs identified as belonging to the second group are all rather similar regarding publication rate, ranging between 0.08 and 0.15 publications per researcher. Figure 6.3 demonstrates, in other words, a rather wide gap in publication rate between the first and the second group – that is, the larger universities have not only a higher research output but also higher research productivity.

For this variable as well, there are some nuances and outliers within the two groups and between the groups. Within the 'Larger Research and Teaching Intensive' group, Karolinska I has by far the largest publication rate in the first group, which may be expected since they specialize in medical research with many publication opportunities. Within the 'Smaller Education Dependent' group, the outlier is Örebro, with substantially higher publication rate. With 0.27 publications per researcher, it is by far the most research productive in the second group, being not far from Stockholm U in the first group. Finally, as before, Stockholm SE differentiates itself, by having a high number of publications relative to its size and Luleå UT ends up in between the two groups.

All in all, this overview of descriptive data of the Swedish university sector clearly supports the idea of polarization, as outlined in the first assumption stated in section 2.

5.   EXTERNAL RESEARCH FUNDING

We now turn to the impacts of structural characteristics on the level of external research funding. An overview of the external research funding is presented in Table 6.4, so that the total external research funding is displayed alongside income from undergraduate education, for the Swedish HEIs. The table also shows the external research funding per researcher and the ratio between income from education and external research funding. The table is ordered according to the two groups identified above and the total amount of external research funding received.

The HEIS that attract the largest amount of external research funding (> SEK 500 million) are the ten 'Larger Research and Teaching Intensive'

Table 6.4   *External research funding and income from undergraduate education, average 2001–06*

HEI	External research	Funding/ researcher	Education	Education Research
Karolinska I	1 514 115	892	754 475	0.50
Lund U	1 465 017	491	1 648 200	1.13
Uppsala U	1 151 363	424	1 249 355	1.09
Göteborg U	1 050 701	477	1 643 561	1.56
Royal IT	1 007 505	628	928 021	0.92
Chalmers UT	932 178	729	700 439	0.75
Stockholm U	620 613	311	1 010 096	1.63
SLU	616 715	460	507 850	0.82
Umeå U	561 873	375	1 219 809	2.17
Linköping U	554 584	387	1 205 926	2.17
Södertörn UC	199 954	731	251 062	1.26
MittUniver-sity	132 612	453	511 988	3.86
Karlstad U	97 235	295	491 642	5.06
Örebro U	76 390	233	549 419	7.19
Mälardalen UC	65 701	246	535 220	8.15
Växjö U	59 277	204	428 017	7.22
Malmö UC	58 912	205	724 515	12.30
Jönköping UC	55 160	265	383 865	6.96
Kalmar UC	47 583	252	439 061	9.23
Blekinge IT	37 955	270	251 989	6.64
Gävle UC	35 561	247	349 178	9.82
Halmstad UC	32 727	250	272 259	8.32
Dalarna UC	29 459	221	340 532	11.56
Väst UC	22 039	267	255 622	11.60
Borås	19 423	165	349 679	18.00
Skövde	19 198	158	246 960	12.86
Kristianstad	13 379	128	305 012	22.80
Gotland	7 344	255	117 936	16.06
Luleå UT	290 511	530	595 780	2.05
Stockholm SE	97 269	769	70 163	0.72
Total	*10 872 352*		*18 337 631*	*1.69*

universities. These universities, making up one third of the population, comprise approximately 87 per cent of the total external research funding and 60 per cent of income from education and also approximately 80 per cent of all researchers. The smaller, regional, HEIs in the 'Smaller Education Dependent' group on average attract less than SEK 200 million each.[9]

Studying external research funding relative to size, the pattern remains largely the same. Most of the HEIs in the second group have a substantially lower funding per researcher than those in the first group.

Looking at the ratio between income from undergraduate education and external research funding reveals a large difference. The 'Larger Research and Teaching Intensive' universities, together with the two 'outliers', all have a rather low ratio, generally receiving not more than double the sum from education than from research. The 'Smaller Education Dependent' HEIs on the contrary have substantially higher ratios.

5.1   RCA Analysis

In order to say something about the relative role of different sources of external research funding, we calculate a variable that reveals the importance of a particular funding source for a university relative to the importance for the whole population (so-called RCA – revealed comparative advantage). In Table 6.5, the RCA for the HEIs of the seven categories of external funding and of the income from undergraduate education are displayed. The RCAs which are more than one, can be said to be funding sources that are more important to the specific organization than to the overall population of HEIs studied here, in other words, a dependence above average. In order to make the patterns clearer, these RCAs are highlighted with grey. The table is ordered first, according to the two groups identified and second, according to the absolute amount of external research funding received.

Looking at the universities categorized as the 'Larger Research and Teaching Intensive' group reveals that these are the HEIs with low relative dependence on education, in terms of income. Instead, several of the external funding sources display high importance for all these universities. The HEIs categorized in the second group on the other hand all show a high reliance on income from education, while low or no reliance on most external funding sources.[10] These were identified earlier as being more oriented toward education, which supports this RCA pattern.

Only the universities in the 'Larger Research and Teaching Intensive' group, together with the two 'outliers', Stockholm SE and Luleå, show a high dependence on industry funding. Stockholm SE is close to the first

Table 6.5　RCA of external research funding and income from undergraduate education, average 2001–06

HEI	RC	NF	F	G & EU	O	CR	I	E
Karolinska I	1.59	0.92	1.95	1.01	3.06	1.57	3.09	0.53
Lund U	1.69	1.03	1.20	1.24	1.41	0.60	1.00	0.84
Uppsala U	1.97	1.12	1.80	0.93	0.80	1.29	1.51	0.83
Göteborg U	1.09	0.62	1.10	0.91	1.34	1.52	0.83	0.97
Royal IT	1.41	1.6	0.98	1.76	0.71	0.47	1.84	0.76
Chalmers UT	1.36	2.08	0.60	1.45	2.26	0.85	1.41	0.68
Stockholm U	1.71	0.36	1.10	1.27	0.50	1.02	0.43	0.99
SLU	0.35	1.54	0.20	2.38	1.64	2.01	0.68	0.72
Umeå U	0.95	0.29	0.86	0.92	0.61	1.97	0.45	1.09
Linköping U	0.93	0.99	0.54	0.97	0.46	1.18	0.65	1.09
Södertörn UC	0.29	7.97	0.13	0.95	0.11	0.38	0.00	0.88
MittUniversity	0.07	0.99	0.04	0.98	0.33	0.11	0.49	1.27
Karlstad U	0.18	0.82	0.05	0.46	0.28	1.36	0.30	1.33
Örebro U	0.25	0.72	0.19	0.45	0.06	0.36	0.12	1.40
Mälardalens U	0.08	0.63	0.02	0.42	0.13	0.21	0.38	1.42
Växjö U	0.08	0.35	0.04	0.33	0.23	1.66	0.12	1.40
Malmö UC	0.16	0.28	0.01	0.27	0.12	0.30	0.16	1.47
Jönköping U	0.06	0.28	0.06	0.33	0.35	0.82	0.47	1.40
Kalmar UC	0.18	0.53	0.00	0.25	0.52	0.05	0.13	1.44
Blekinge IT	0.04	1.10	0.00	0.47	0.41	0.24	0.06	1.38
Gävle UC	0.03	0.40	0.06	0.44	0.08	0.32	0.17	1.45
Halmstad UC	0.04	0.95	0.01	0.34	0.15	0.23	0.31	1.42
Dalarna UC	0.02	0.49	0.00	0.31	0.00	0.15	0.45	1.47
Väst UC	0.01	0.71	0.00	0.27	0.23	0.00	0.08	1.47
Borås UC	0.02	0.37	0.00	0.15	0.29	0.05	0.04	1.51
Skövde UC	0.01	0.86	0.04	0.21	0.14	0.06	0.12	1.47
Kristianstad UC	0.09	0.31	0.03	0.10	0.05	0.23	0.04	1.53
Gotland UC	0.06	0.31	0.02	0.15	0.42	0.00	0.00	1.49
Luleå UT	0.29	0.45	0.01	1.22	0.66	1.28	1.69	1.07
Stockholm SE	0.39	0.09	1.56	0.66	2.94	1.86	4.73	0.66

Source:　National Science Foundation 2005

category, showing low relative dependence on education and, for example, a very high dependence on industry funding. Luleå, previously seeming to be in the middle of the two categories, shows a low dependence on education.

6. DISCUSSION AND CONCLUSION

This chapter used existing literature about European universities and university–industry interactions, in order to identify specific structural characteristics to position individual HEIs within, and to analyse, the Swedish university sector. The starting point of the chapter was to examine whether the data would support the assumption that the Swedish university population is highly diverse, or polarized, as for other European countries. The results showed that examining size (and age), density of researchers across subjects, research orientation and productivity of the HEIs in the Swedish university sector divides the population into two distinct categories as well as two reoccurring outliers. This chapter was explorative, and did not test hypotheses, despite the comprehensive data.

Overall, our results support the idea of polarization in the Swedish university sector. They thereby resemble the findings by Geuna (1999) for other European countries. Size of research effort and age are important characteristics, even if we can also identify younger universities that have, or are currently trying, to move from the second to the first group. The positions in the polarization are dynamic and relative, not fixed, so that at least outliers in terms of structural characteristics may move between groups. Polarization is visible in many of the variables for structural characteristics of this sector. The data show that we can distinguish universities and university colleges on basis of how specialized they are in terms of education or research. The Swedish HEIs can be divided according to the degree of research intensity, in terms of relative orientation towards research or education. The results show that the 'Larger Research and Teaching Intensive' universities overall have a substantially lower number of students per professor, than the regional smaller HEIs. This indicates that the former have more room to conduct research, in relation to teaching and are therefore said to be more research oriented.

It should be noted that the 'Larger Research and Teaching Intensive' universities actually do the bulk of teaching in Sweden, educating approximately 60 per cent of all students, although being significantly fewer in number than the HEIs in the other group. Even so, the 'Smaller Education Dependent' HEIs receive a high percentage of their total funding from their smaller numbers of students. Hence, as seen, Sweden lacks a clear division of labour between providers of education and of research with advanced teaching.

The proposed polarization between the two groups is also clear in terms of research personnel and output measures. Generally, smaller universities and university colleges report quite a large number of research subjects relative to their size. In fact, by and large, these smaller HEIs report a quantity of research subjects equal to those in the first group. Hence, a quick glance at the Swedish universities would suggest a low degree of diversity. However, this diversity is not supported by the figures on actual numbers of researchers or by examining density of researchers across research subjects. The 'Larger Research and Teaching Intensive' universities have many researchers. Hence, they can concentrate employees – and thereby presumably, research activities – within a broader set of research subjects. They have more people and a higher density across subjects. In contrast, the 'Smaller Education Dependent' HEIs do the opposite. They declare many subjects but do not have many researchers. So they can be said to have a quite wide range of research subjects, and hence, of the depth that they do have, we should expect it to be in very specific research questions. In a surprisingly high proportion of research subjects, the HEIs in the second group are represented by less than five people and no professors. The figures suggest that most of the research subjects in these HEIs are fairly empty, lacking to some extent a 'critical mass'. Thus, maybe not surprisingly, only the largest universities are able to simultaneously uphold diversity, density and size. However, the four organizations that specialize in engineering, medicine or economics and management are able to combine a medium or even smaller size with high density within specific topics. Hence, an alternative for the smaller, diversified universities might be to focus upon specializations, to gain critical mass. Future research could further explore whether, and what, trade-offs exist between specialization and diversity in terms of research, education and the linkages between research and education. For example, business schools need a variety of subjects, in order to be accredited as educational providers, and yet to reach scientific excellence, they may have to choose between specialization and diversification. Similar arguments may be developed and applied to understand why the Swedish university sector includes both large, diversified universities as well as institutes dedicated to specific fields. Furthermore, the figures suggest that organizations that are older, larger and have a higher density of researchers per subject tend also to publish more papers per researcher, i.e. have a higher research productivity. These results further confirm our empirical picture of the polarization within the Swedish university sector. The causality is not specified, but given the much lower ratio of students to professors and greater number of external research funding, we can suggest that these researchers can spend time doing research, rather than teaching and also support larger, stimulating environments to interact over research issues.

Our results also bring this idea of polarization into the specific issue of external research funding, obtained in competitive situations. The same structural characteristics seem to matter in this regard. These results support the clear differences amongst the two groups. The first group, 'Larger Research and Teaching Intensive', comprising the larger universities, is 'high-performing' in regards to obtaining competitive external research funding, both in absolute numbers and in relative importance as compared to income from education. The second group, consisting of the smaller HEIs, can be viewed as 'low-performing' in this regard.

What is more, our results point to the larger HEIs with the most research funding and highest research productivity also attracting more industry funding and having a higher relative reliance on this funding compared to other sources of external research funding. In this regard, we do not see any immediate evidence that supports the idea that the 'Smaller Education Dependent' HEIs change their foci of research, in order to attract industrial funding. This is what would be expected, following the suggestion that financially weaker HEIs rely more on funding from industry (e.g. Geuna, 1999), but is not visible in Sweden.

This result is a bit surprising in the Swedish context. As noted in the literature review, Swedish policy has had explicit goals to stimulate regional economic growth and to allow regional HEIs to address the needs of local companies. Moreover, certain financiers such as some of the new foundations are explicitly dedicated to developing research – and especially 'needs-driven', industrially relevant research – at these regional HEIs.

What then are the explanations behind this apparent polarization of the Swedish university sector? On the overall European level, it has been suggested that the polarization to some extent stems from a reinforcement of the so-called Matthew effect (Merton, 1968). This may be due to the increased competitiveness regarding research funding (Geuna, 1999).

The original formulation of the Matthew effect adhered to the reward system of science and was largely an attempt to explain the disproportionate credit awarded already acknowledged researchers. Later on, Merton and his followers come to generalize it by proposing the existence of self-reinforcing processes, usually denoted as 'cumulative advantage', driving both scientific productivity and recognition.[11] The studies on the subject primarily keep on the level of the individual scientist but also deal briefly with the institutional side. Centres or universities of proven scientific excellence through this effect are allocated larger resources, such as research funding, and attract more talented researchers, in a cumulative fashion. Good scientists usually affiliate with institutions of historically proven excellence, which are more likely to have the resources necessary for high-end research. This leads to a higher quality on the institutional level and associated higher research productivity in terms of publications. In its turn, more research resources as well as high-quality researchers are attracted.

This cumulative advantage would in the long run lead to a stratification of research institutions – a self-reinforcing cycle that would be hard for new small actors to break. When the resource allocation becomes more competitive in nature, this will likely concentrate the research resources more at the 'high-quality' universities and thus further increase the impact of the Matthew effect.

Another, quite close, explanation, also adhering to the logic behind the Matthew effect, can be discussed in terms of the fundamental difference in starting conditions for the HEIs in the two different groups. Strategic management discusses positioning and relative competencies and this may be relevant in future research about the 'competitive advantage' of certain actors within a national university industry sector. In Sweden, most of the younger regional HEIs are quite new to the research game and so far have been unable to perform at the same level as 'incumbents', when it comes to research productivity (to some extent indicating quality), 'critical mass' in research subjects and the ability to attract external research funding. The older traditional universities have naturally had a longer time to build up recognition of research excellence, as well as financial and other research resources. This lead would naturally be additionally reinforced in the potential presence of 'cumulative advantages'. On the other hand, the HEIs in the 'Smaller Education Dependent' group in this respect have had less time to make their mark, explaining their relatively lower ability to attract external research funding. This is despite dedicated funding to build competencies in the smaller regional HEIs. Our results show the aggregate figures, but ad-hoc insights suggest that HEIs can build significant research competencies within niche areas. Research about strategic management, niches and development of competences are thus highly relevant to future studies of Sweden and other European countries.

From this perspective, one wonders about the future of specific organizations within the Swedish university sector. We believe that the smaller regional HEIs will find it increasingly hard to keep up their present diversity in research. In light of an increased focus on research assessments in Sweden (as proposed in, for example, Brändström, 2007), we suspect that several of these HEIs in due time will be forced to reduce the numbers of research subjects, because of lack of quality and 'critical mass'.[12]

Related to this, an interesting debate would be about specialization in research for the smaller younger HEIs. We know from studies of firms and industries that division of labour lie at the heart of productive progress (Smith, 1812; Young, 1928). Smith further states that the level of division of labour is dependent on the extent of the market, in that it is limited by the amount of products produced. This argument was later extended to the industry level by Young (1928). He suggests that the extent of the market is in its turn dependent on the level of division of labour, in that the volume of production defines the market. In effect this means that the division of labour builds the foundation for further specialization, making productivity change progressive and cumulative. At present, with a widened market with more organizations conducting research and more competitive resource allocation, why should this not apply also to the world of academic research? It is not far-fetched to think that smaller younger HEIs that narrow their research focus and perhaps also try to occupy a research niche would more easily be able to accumulate talent, gain critical mass and increase reputation. This change in behaviour may be underlying the broader trends analysed here. Hence, by specializing their research smaller HEIs would be able to build up a competitive advantage.

ACKNOWLEDGEMENT

Research for this chapter has been supported primarily by Sister (www.sister.nu), in a collaborative project about Swedish universities as knowledge environments for the future. The researchers have been part of the RIDE research network (www.chalmers.se/ride). We are grateful for comments from many individuals involved in the Sister workshops and the DRUID summer 2007 conference. This chapter has in previous paper versions been referred to as 'Does structure matter for science?: The Matthew effect in the Swedish university sector'.

NOTES

1. Merton (1968) describes the Matthew effect as a cumulative advantage operating in science, so that researchers with recognition, rewards and 'visibility' of scientific contributions tend to receive more additional recognition and resources, than researchers lacking them but making comparable contributions to science.
2. According to OECD classification, there are two categories of government funding: general university funds (GUF), i.e. 'block funding'/general grants, and direct government funds (DGF), such as contract research funding and earmarked funds (see, for example, Geuna, 2001).
3. Where not otherwise stated, this presentation draws upon the book *Knowledge for Prosperity* by Sörlin and Törnqvist (2000), authors' translation (original title: *Kunskap för välstånd*).
4. 'Research subject' refers to the lowest level of division of research in the Swedish system (four-digit level), authors' translation (Swedish: 'Forskningsämne'). There are approximately 254 research subjects (4-digit), 55 'research subject groups' (3-digit) and 12 'research areas' (2-digit). Note that due to the constraints of the database some of the smallest research subjects are grouped together in the calculation.
5. Science areas are a classification used for the government authorities' resource allocation for research and research education. To be granted a 'science area' gives the right to

examine research students within that particular area, authors' translation (Swedish: 'Vetenskapsområde').

6. For more detailed results, see the previous version in the DRUID Working Paper series (Ljungberg et al., 2008).
7. Stockholm SE is the only institution being more than 100 years old that does not show up in this group.
8. The Swedish HEIs must report their own activities within different research subjects to the Swedish government and this reporting may influence future funding. Thus, 'active' here refers to those research subjects that the specific HEI has reported.
9. Södertörn stands out in the group receiving close to SEK 200 million in external research funding, while the rest attract substantially less. The lion's share of this funding comes from the Foundation of Baltic and East European Studies (Östersjöstiftelsen) – a foundation more or less entirely focused on funding Södertörn. For the period studied, Södertörn has received SEK 130 million on average every year from this foundation. Contrasting this sum to the rest of the funding for the university makes it clear that this skews the total relation for this HEI, and thus also their relative position in this table – giving Södertörn one of the highest levels of funding in relation to size.
10. For some of these HEIs in the second group, one or two funding sources, limited mainly to new foundations and contract research, in addition to education, show some relative dependence. This can to a large extent be attributed to policy efforts, such as regional politics, manifesting itself in, for example, funding from certain foundations. For example, the Knowledge Foundation has as main objective to support the smaller regional HEIs, to stimulate university–industry interaction. The high reliance on new foundations for Södertörn is due to dependence on the Foundation of Baltic and East European Studies as a funding source, as explained earlier.
11. See, for example, Cole and Cole (1973) and Zuckerman (1977). For a review and references see, for example, Allison et al. (1982) and Merton (1988). For a review of 'cumulative advantage' in terms of economic analysis see, for example, David (1994).
12. Recently an investigation of economics education found that 17 of 23 HEIs applying to join the new Swedish economics programme, all smaller and regional, lacked in research quality within the subject(s) and were therefore denied entry to the programme (HSV, 2007).

REFERENCES

Allison, P.D., J.S. Long and T.K. Krauze (1982), 'Cumulative advantage and inequality in science', *American Sociological Review*, **47** (5), 615–25.

Beise, M. and H. Stahl (1999), 'Public research and industrial innovations in Germany', *Research Policy*, **28**, 397–422.

Benner, M. and S. Sörlin (eds) (2008), *Forska lagom och vara världsbäst. Sverige inför forskningens globala strukturomvandling, [Modest research ambitions but best in the world: Sweden's place in the global structural transformation of research]*, Stockholm: SNS förlaget.

Bonaccorsi, A. and C. Daraio (eds) (2007), *Universities and Strategic Knowledge Creation: Specialization and Performance in Europe*, Cheltenham, UK and Northampton, MA, USA: Edward Elgar.

Brändström, D. (2007), 'Resurser för Kvalitet' ['Resources for quality'], Slutbetänkande av Resursutredningen SOU 2007, 81, in Swedish.

Bush, V. (1945), *Science and the Endless Frontier*, Washington DC: National Science Foundation.

Cohen, W.M., R.R. Nelson and J.P. Walsh (2002), 'Links and impacts: the influence of public research on industrial R&D', *Management Science*, **48** (1), 1–23.

Cole, J.R. and S. Cole (1973), *Social Stratification in Science*, Chicago, IL: University of Chicago Press.

David, P.A. (1994), 'Positive feedbacks and research productivity in science: reopening another black box', in Ove Granstrand (ed.), *Economics of Technology*, North Holland, Amsterdam and London: Elsevier, pp. 65–85.

D'Este, P. and P. Patel (2007), 'University–industry linkages in the UK: what are the factors underlying the variety of interactions with industry?', *Research Policy*, **36** (9), 1295–313.

Dosi, G., P. Llerena and M. Sylos Labini (2006), 'The relationship between science, technologies, and their industrial exploitation: an illustration through the myths and realities of the so-called "European Paradox"', *Research Policy*, **35** (10), 1450–64.

Geuna, A. (1998), 'The internationalisation of European universities: a return to medieval roots', *Minerva*, **36** (3), 253–70.

Geuna, A. (1999), *The Economics of Knowledge Production: Funding and the Structure of University Research*, Cheltenham, UK and Northampton, MA, USA: Edward Elgar.

Geuna, A. (2001), 'The changing rationale for European university research funding: are there negative unintended consequences?', *Journal of Economic Issues*, **35** (3), 607–32.

Granberg, A. and S. Jacobsson (2006), 'Myths or reality – a scrutiny of dominant beliefs in the Swedish science policy debate', *Science and Public Policy*, **33** (5), 321–40.

Hällsten, M. and U. Sandström (2002), 'Det Förändrade Forskningslandskapet' [The changed research landscape], *Regionoch trafikplanekontorets rapportserie*, PM 8 in Swedish.

Henrekson, M. and N. Rosenberg (2001), 'Designing efficient institutions for science-based entrepreneurship: lesson from the US and Sweden', *Journal of Technology Transfer*, **26**, 207–31.

Heyman, U. and E. Lundberg (2002), 'Finansiering av Svensk Grundforskning' [Funding of Swedish basic research], *Vetenskapsrådet*, Swedish Research Council report no. 2002: 4, in Swedish.

HSV (2007), 'Examensrättsprövning för Civilekonomexamen' [Scrutiny of the right to exam economists], report 2007, 48 R in Swedish.

Klevorick, A.K., R.C. Levin, R.R. Nelson and S.G. Winter (1995), 'On the sources and significance of interindustry differences in technological opportunities', *Research Policy*, **24**, 185–205.

Laursen, K. and A.J. Salter (2004), 'Searching low and high: what types of firms use universities as a source of innovation?', *Research Policy*, **33**, 1201–15.

Lawton Smith, H. (2006), *Universities, Innovation and the Economy*, London, UK and New York: Routledge.

Ljungberg, D., M. Johansson and M. McKelvey (2008), 'Polarization of the Swedish university sector: structural characteristics and positioning', DRUID working paper series.

Mansfield, E. (1995), 'Academic research underlying industrial innovations: sources, characteristics, and financing', *Review of Economic Statistics*, **77** (1), 55–65.

Mansfield, E. and J.Y. Lee (1996), 'The modern university: contributor to industrial innovation and recipient of industrial R&D support', *Research Policy*, **25**, 1047–58.

Merton, Robert K. (1968), 'The Matthew effect in science: the reward and communication systems are considered', *Science*, **159**, 56–63.

Merton, Robert K. (1988), 'The Matthew effect in science, II: cumulative advantage and the symbolism of intellectual property', *Isis*, **79** (4), 606–23.

Meyer-Krahmer, F. and U. Schmoch (1998), 'Science-based technologies: university–industry interaction in four fields', *Research Policy*, **27**, 835–51.

Mohnen, P. and C. Hoareau (2003), 'What type of enterprise forges close links with universities and government labs? Evidence from Cis 2', *Managerial & Decision Economics*, **24** (2/3), 133–46.

Salter, A.J. and B.R. Martin (2001), 'The economic benefits of publicly funded basic research: a critical review', *Research Policy*, **30**, 509–32.

Sandström, U. (1997), 'Forskningsstyrning och Anslagspolitik: Studier i FoU-handläggning' [Research governance and grant politics: studies of R&D handling], research council report no. 1996: 2, in Swedish.

Santoro, M.D. and A.K. Chakrabarti (2002), 'Firm size and technology centrality in industry–university interactions', Research *Policy*, **31**, 1163–80.

Schartinger, D., A. Schibany and H. Gassler (2001), 'Interactive relations between universities and firms: empirical evidence for Austria', *Journal of Technology Transfer*, **26** (3), 255–68.

Schartinger, D., C. Rammer, M.M. Fischer and J. Fröhlich (2002), 'Knowledge interactions between universities and industry in Austria: sectoral patterns and determinants', *Research Policy*, **31**, 303–28.

Schilling, Peter (2005), 'Research as a source of strategic opportunity?: re-thinking research policy developments in the late 20th century', PhD thesis, Umeå University.

Smith, Adam (1776), *An Inquiry into the Nature and Causes of the Wealth of Nations*, reprinted 1812, London: Ward, Lock and Tyler.

SNAHE (2007), *Universitet & Högskolor: Högskoleverkets Årsapport 2007* [Universities & University Colleges Annual Report 2007], The Swedish National Agency for Higher Education's annual report 2007: 33, in Swedish.

Sörlin, S. and G. Törnqvist (2000), *Kunskap för Välstånd: Universiteten och Omvandlingen av Sverige* [Knowledge for Prosperity: The Universities and Transformation of Sweden], Stockholm: Studieförb. Näringsliv och samhälle.

Vincent-Lancrin, S. (2006), 'What is changing in academic research? Trends and future scenarios', *European Journal of Education*, **41** (2), 169–202.

Young, A.A. (1928), 'Increasing returns and economic progress', *Economic Journal*, **38**, 527–42.

Zucker, L.G. and M.R. Darby (1996), 'Star scientists and institutional transformation: patterns of invention and innovation in the formation of the biotechnology industry', *Proceedings of the National Academy of Science of the United States of America*, **93** (12 November), 709–16.

Zuckerman, H. (1977), *Scientific Elite*, New York: Free Press.

7. The American experience in university technology transfer

Maryann P. Feldman and Shiri M. Breznitz

American research universities entered a new era in 1980 with the passage of the Bayh–Dole Act. Moving beyond publication and teaching, the traditional modes of disseminating academic inventions, universities now actively manage their discoveries in a process known as technology transfer. All American research universities now have operations dedicated to securing invention disclosures from campus research and establishing intellectual property rights over them. These offices then work to license the rights to use the intellectual property, either to existing firms or encouraging the formation of new firms for this purpose. When places around the world attempt to emulate American competitiveness and technology-based economic growth, the US Bayh–Dole Act and the system of university technology transfer is one of the first policy changes considered.

This chapter examines the American experience in university technology transfer with the intention of increasing understanding of how the system currently functions. Despite the conventional wisdom, American universities have had limited success generating licensing revenue, however, technology transfer assumes new importance as institutions looking to align themselves with economic development.

Critics are concerned about the erosion of traditional academic norms and values (Slaughter and Leslie, 1997; Press and Washburn, 2000). Proponents cite the successful commercialization and social benefits of new products and processes to benefit humanity (Association of University Technology Managers, 2007). Certainly, the socially optimal long-term goal is to promote the use and diffusion of academic discoveries while preserving the potential for long-run growth enabled by unfettered inquiry and objective research.

The system is evolving as technology transfer offices in the US experiment with new business models, forms of organization and technology transfer mechanisms. It is an interesting time to study both the transformation of universities towards increased commercial relevance and direct technology transfer. Moreover, due to the success of certain American universities' technology transfer offices the American university model became an inspiration to other universities around the world. Hence, this chapter provides information on the development of the US technology transfer model. We highlight some of the important contextual factors that define the American higher education system and the process of commercializing academic discoveries. The next section provides the historical context for understanding American higher education and its orientation towards industrial outreach. The third section analyses the development of technology transfer offices in the USA. Starting with the Wisconsin Alumni Research Foundation in 1925, TTO's establishment became widespread after the passage of the Bayh–Dole Act of 1980. Section 4 reviews the different technology transfer mechanisms of sponsored research, invention disclosures, patents, licences, spinoffs, science parks, and incubators. Importantly, we conclude that while some mechanisms of the US technology transfer system produce positive results that are easily adoptable, the modification process should take into consideration the specific environment and history of the adopting university and its region, as well as the characteristics and available resources.

THE HISTORY OF AMERICAN UNIVERSITY TECHNOLOGY TRANSFER

The US system of higher education is characterized by great institutional diversity, constructed from a myriad of colleges and universities that vary by size, specialization and range of degree offered. American universities are chartered as either public or private institutions. Strong and elite private institutions of higher education are unique to the US among developed countries and reflect early attempts to build educational capacity.

Most of the private institutions had early religious affiliations. Many of them have large endowments due to special provisions in the US tax code that provide incentives for private philanthropy to institutions of higher education. For example, the endowment at Harvard University, the oldest American institution of higher education is currently valued at $35 billion (Strout, 2007). Private universities are not subject to the same government regulation and oversight that govern public institutions and it is easier for private universities to start new programmes and experiment with new initiatives.

On the other hand, public universities are state universities founded and operated by state government entities. These are a direct result of the 1862 Morrill Land-Grant Act, which gave each eligible state 30 000 acres of federal land to establish educational institutions. Public universities in the

USA have been carrying the lion's share of higher education in terms of students and research output. By mandate, public institutions have the full range of academic departments and expertise.

What all American institutions have in common is a strong relationship with industry (Geiger, 1988). At the time that the nation was industrializing, the United States reformed its higher education system along the German model of the nineteenth century. At the time, German institutions were the prominent scientific institutions where the majority of American academics received their education. The German model used to combine academic research with commercial relevance.[1] The formal use of universities for economic development needs began in the United States with the enactment of the Morrill Acts of 1862 and 1890 (Rahm et al., 2000).

The first Morrill Act provided grants in the form of federal lands to each state for the establishment of a public institution to fulfill the Act's provisions of teaching agriculture and engineering to a broad segment of the population. The emphasis was on higher education that was practical and had direct relevance to economic activity. This guaranteed that each state had a least one university. These colleges, known as the land-grant institutions, were the first higher education institutions in the United States constructed with a concept of technology transfer as a public good. Thus, technology transfer became grounded as part of the American university system.

The land-grant colleges have become the cornerstone of the US model of encouraging technology transfer. With the extension service component that required the dissemination of academic research, added through the Smith–Lever Act of 1914, the land-grant colleges and universities generated a system in which the collaboration of three partners (science, local government, and industry) was not only highly acceptable but also encouraged. This is the origins of what is now described as the triple helix (Etzkowitz, 1995).

Beginning with agriculture, the system was easily adapted to other types of outreach activity such as manufacturing extension and active technology transfer to local firms. Service to industry, a specific objective for land-grant institutions, reflects the type of more intense interaction with industry and the promotion of local economic development through assistance to existing firms. Structural economic change arguably has changed the focus of this outreach from solely focusing on agriculture to other industrial sectors.

However, until the twentieth century, American universities had limited technology capability and were of small size, thus restricting their commercialization efforts (Geiger, 1986). In the beginning of the twentieth century, science started to play a greater role in US industry. This was the result of two major changes: the emergence of professional engineering schools and the emergence of industrial research labs. Throughout World War I, universities collaborated with industry on R&D projects sponsored by the government. At that time, US scientists were involved in the building of new weapons, which laid the foundation for future science–federal government relations. In World War II the cooperation of universities and industry took another form when the government used research contracts and established entire research centres. Examples for such centres are the Manhattan project centres, which developed the atomic bomb. Throughout the war, R&D collaborations predominated and major reports describing those collaborations, such as the Vannevar Bush report and the President Science and Public Policy report on the contribution of science to the nation, were published (Rahm et al., 2000).

The result was the creation of the National Science Foundation in 1950 'to promote the progress of science; to advance the national health, prosperity, and welfare; to secure the national defense' (National Science Foundation, 2005a). During the Cold War, there was an increase in military R&D government investment in response to the perceived loss of technological prominence with the Soviet launch of Sputnik. In 1958, the National Aeronautics and Space Administration was formed through Congressional legislation with the dedicated purpose of researching flight technology (Rahm et al., 2000). Markusen (1991) argues that the federal government's spending on military R&D during that period was an important factor in the development of the high-tech and biotech industries in the United States. As can be seen in Figure 7.1, over the years, the federal government became the largest supporter of academic R&D, and currently provides 63 per cent of the total funding base (National Science Foundation, 2005b). The National Institutes of Health (NIH), within the department of Health and Human Services, is the largest funder of US universities' science and engineering spending, funding 55 per cent of federal R&D expenditures. Other agencies include the Department of Defense 9 per cent, the Department of Energy 4 per cent, National Aeronautics and Space Administration 4 per cent, National Science Foundation 12 per cent, as well as the Department of Agriculture 3 per cent.

However, in the 1980s the relationship between industry and universities took on new urgency. The decline in the US industrial growth rate in the 1970s and the strength of international competition created a debate over the government's investments in R&D, and industry's ability to commercialize this research. While US science was acknowledged as superior, this was not translated into economic growth. Calls for stronger links between universities and industry in order to improve competitiveness resulted in legislation during the 1980s, to involve universities in applied research with

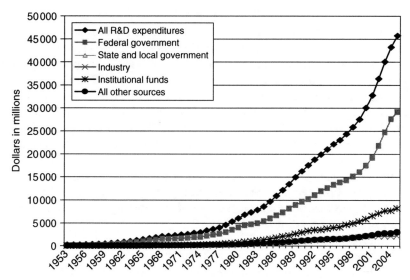

Source: National Science Foundation 2005

Figure 7.1   US universities by sources of R&D funding. The federal
            government is the largest contributor of US universities'
            funding.

direct impact on the US industrial growth rate. One of these acts was the
Bayh–Dole Act of 1980, which gave universities intellectual property rights
over federally funded discoveries:

> It is the policy and objective of the Congress to use the patent system to promote
> the utilization of inventions arising from federally supported research or devel-
> opment; to encourage maximum participation of small business firms in federally
> supported research and development efforts; to promote collaboration between
> commercial concerns and non-profit organizations, including universities; to
> ensure that inventions made by non-profit organizations and small business firms
> are used in a manner to promote free competition and enterprise without unduly
> encumbering future research and discovery; to promote the commercialization
> and public availability of inventions made in the United States by United States
> industry and labor; to ensure that the Government obtains sufficient rights in fed-
> erally supported inventions to meet the needs of the Government and protect the
> public against non-use or unreasonable use of inventions; and to minimize the
> costs of administering policies in this area. (The objectives of the Bayh–Dole Act,
> Cornell University Law Department, 2005)

Prior to Bayh–Dole, scientists and universities could petition the government funding agencies for IP rights. The Act provided universities with a

standardized process, which encouraged them to license their technology and held them accountable for achieving results. The result was a large increase in university patenting, technology licensing and revenues.

According to Mowery and Sampat (2001b) however, this growth cannot be fully attributed to the Bayh–Dole Act. During the 1970s, there was an increase in university patenting related to national incentives. One of the major changes in the United States was the shift of national R&D funding priorities towards public–private partnerships. Industry took the lead 'and became the major provider of R&D funds while continuing to be the major performer of R&D activities' (Rahm et al., 2000, p. 20). At the same time, universities increased their share of basic research from less than 2 per cent in 1953 to 12 per cent in 1996. This funding came from the federal government and universities took on the role of conducting basic research and then acting as a conduit to industry.

Although supporting the Bayh–Dole Act, Litan et al. (2007) argue that with the attempt to ease the process of commercializing academic research, new administrative and bureaucratic steps were added through the creation of the technology transfer office. Accordingly, the authors claim that many technology transfer offices have become 'bottlenecks rather than facilitators of innovation dissemination' (Litan et al., 2007, p. 3). However, this statement ignores the heterogeneity in technology transfer offices, reflecting different missions, different reporting relationships and most important, widely different resources (Bercovitz et al., 2001). Hence, not all technology transfer offices are necessarily bureaucratic and some are even essential in the process of disseminating academic ideas to the private market and commercializing technology (Breznitz et al., 2008).

While reviewing the historical background of the American university technology transfer system, it is clear that historical events and specific legislative acts shaped the way universities, industry, and the US government view technology dissemination. Importantly, these factors are not easily transferred to other countries or regions. Next we examine the operation of technology transfer offices, followed by a description of the technology transfer mechanisms.

TECHNOLOGY TRANSFER OFFICES

Although all universities gained greater intellectual property rights under the Bayh–Dole Act, there is diversity in the timing of the establishment of dedicated technology transfer offices (TTOs). The oldest dedicated technology transfer operation, the Wisconsin Alumni Research Foundation (WARF), was founded in 1925 and provides an illustrative example. In

1923, Harry Steenbock, a professor at the University of Wisconsin, invented a process for using ultraviolet radiation to add vitamin D to milk and other foods. The discovery had scientific significance as it virtually eliminated rickets, a crippling childhood disease. It also had economic significance for Wisconsin's dairy industry. Steenbock patented his invention independently and worked with companies and the dairy industry association to commercialize the invention. The university refused to be involved. To aid these efforts, Professor Steenbock created, with the help of several alumni, the Wisconsin Alumni Research Foundation (WARF). WARF's principal objectives were to seek patents to protect inventions made by university scientists and to promote the public benefit of these inventions through licensing agreements with companies. WARF filed patents and licensed them out, paying the university via an annual grant (Apple, 1989). WARF was so successful in achieving public dissemination and returning substantial revenues to the university that it became the *de facto* model for other universities.

Other universities have established technology transfer offices as early as 1935, starting with the University of Iowa, followed by MIT (1940), the Kansas State University Research Foundation (1942), and the University of California system (1950) not far behind. Notably all of these early institutions were public land-grant universities as might be expected given their public service mission.

The pace of TTO founding accelerated after the 1980 passage of the Bayh–Dole Act. Figure 7.2 presents the number of university offices by establishment date to track the diffusion of dedicated technology transfer offices. In general, two factors are associated with early establishment of technology transfer: the presence of a medical school and the status of the university as a land-grant institution. It is no accident that the presence of a medical school would hasten the establishment of a TTO; most commercially valuable university intellectual property arises from biomedical research (Mowery et al., 1999). By 2004, virtually all American research universities had established dedicated technology transfer offices. Increasingly, four-year colleges and technical schools inside the USA are creating technology offices, with the expectation that they will be able to patent inventions and license them to industry. This marks a fundamental shift in mission for these institutions, which have primarily focused on education. It remains to be seen what affect these efforts will have. However, institutions and places that do not have research universities have little choice if they wish to participate in knowledge-based economic growth.

Technology transfer operations are housed in newly created administrative units within universities. A variety of names including 'tech transfer', 'technology licensing' or 'business development' are used, depending on the

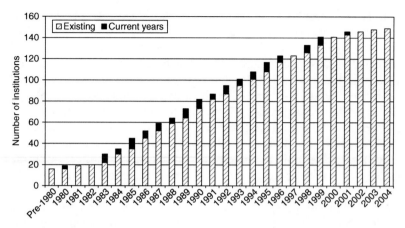

Note: N = 151 Universities

Source: AUTM Licensing Annual Surveys

Figure 7.2   Growth in the establishment of technology transfer offices after
Bayh–Dole

specific focus of the operation. Whatever the organizational form,
these offices have responsibility for keeping track of inventions made by
university-employed researchers, preparing patent applications, and negotiating licensing agreements with firms for the use of university-owned
intellectual property. Often, these operations are augmented with other
supporting functions such as research administration business incubators,
science parks and venture funds. There is great experimentation among
universities as they seek to implement active technology transfer.

Notably, there is also vast differentiation between technology transfer
offices that reflect history and culture. In the past, many state universities
were restricted by statute from engaging directly in any commercial activity, such as receiving fees, royalties, or stock in a company in exchange for
the use of university-held patents. Consequently, these universities have
established independent technology transfer organizations, called foundations, to engage in such transactions.

American universities are engaged in an ongoing search for the best way
to organize technology transfer operations. Bercovitz et al. (2001) identify
three structural features associated with effectiveness in performing the
technology transfer function. One such feature is the TTO's ability to coordinate its activities with those of several other administrative units, such as
sponsored research, corporate giving, and industrial liaison. Another is its
ability to receive, interpret, synthesize, and disseminate information both

within and outside the university. The final key feature is an effective alignment of incentives between and among the TTO, faculty, and other administrative units. These findings suggest that the performance of the TTO can only be assessed within its broader organizational setting within the university.

THE MECHANISMS OF AMERICAN UNIVERSITY TECHNOLOGY TRANSFER

Universities use a variety of mechanisms to transfer technology to industry. Each mechanism offers trade-offs in terms of achieving the university's objectives. Because technology transfer is a relatively new activity for universities, there has been experimentation in the use of these mechanisms and the terms of the agreements made with industry. Formal mechanisms include sponsored research agreements with industry, inventions disclosures, patents, licences of university intellectual property to firms, and the formation of spin-off companies. Informal mechanisms, such as industry hiring of students, faculty consulting, and knowledge trading among friendship networks also contribute to technology transfer, but do not fall under the auspices of the TTO. Each of these mechanisms will be discussed in turn.

Sponsored Research

Research is the process that creates knowledge and ideas that form the basis for university intellectual property. In 2006, an estimated $49 billion was spent on sponsored research and development (R&D) projects at US academic institutions, a growth of 86 per cent from $26.3 billion that was spent in 1998 (National Science Foundation, 2007). Through the National Science Foundation (NSF) and mission agencies, such as the National Institutes of Health (NIH), the federal government is the largest source of funding (63 per cent) for university-based research (National Science Foundation, 2007). Federal funds usually support basic research, which is conducted without concern for practical use but is instead oriented to fundamental understanding and discovery.

As we can see from Figure 7.3, companies and other industrial organizations also sponsor university research projects. Industry support of academic research has grown from less than $264 million in 1980 to $1.9 billion in 1998, and $2.4 billion in 2006 (National Science Foundation, 2007). There is great diversity among universities in the receipt of industrial research funding. Those schools most favoured by these sponsors, such as

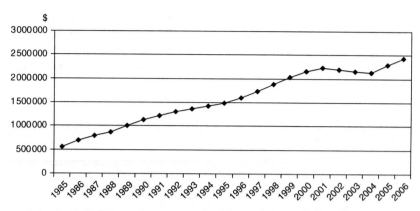

Source: National Science Foundation (2007)

Figure 7.3   R&D expenditures at universities and colleges funded by industry

Duke University, receive 20 per cent of their total R&D funding from industry (Foundation, 2005). The average industrial funding for all universities is about 5 per cent (National Science Foundation, 2007). This figure has declined in recent years from 7 per cent in 2001, with concerns that American companies are outsourcing to foreign universities (National Science Foundation, 2007, Testimony of Susan B. Butts, 2007, Thursby and Thursby, 2006).

Sponsored research with companies specifies ownership of the resulting intellectual property involves a quid pro quo relationship. The university gains financial resources, while the contracting firm gains research results and access to university scientists. Industry-sponsored research is typically more applied in nature than federally-funded research and, thus, closer to practical application and realization of commercial potential. A research agreement between a university and industrial sponsors will specify the distribution of any intellectual property that results from the project. In addition, the agreement will differentiate between the background knowledge created within the university (and which may derive from a variety of different funding sources) and the foreground knowledge created by the new project. The industrial sponsor will typically retain ownership of intellectual property resulting from the sponsored research or will have the right to review such property with the first option to license.

Again, firm strategy and market characteristics shape such agreements (Bercovitz and Feldman, 2007b). If the technology is broad-based and involves network externalities, the sponsor may choose to let the university retain ownership and license the technology on a non-exclusive basis to other companies. If the company does not take ownership, if there is ambiguity about ownership due the difficulty of disaggregating funding sources or if federal funding is involved, then an invention disclosure will be filed and the formal process of technology transfer begins.

University–industry collaboration can take place in the process of investigating a joint interest of a company and an academic laboratory. Some universities provide the latest results of research in specific fields through a research consortium, for which companies pay to participate. Companies pay an annual fee in order to receive access to seminars and papers on the most current research relevant in their fields (Sharon, 1994). Such is the case of the MIT Consortia, where companies support research at MIT by 'joining with other companies to fund ambitious, industry-changing projects in areas of mutual interest' (MIT Industrial Liaison Program, 2007). In some cases, faculty members provide consulting services to companies on particular research projects; sit on the board of directors and on scientific boards of companies (Casper and Karmanos, 2003).

Invention Disclosures

While attention focuses on outcomes such as the dollar amount of licensing revenues and the number of new companies, the entire technology transfer process in American universities is predicated on the filing of invention disclosures. All of the subsequent measures of the university's progress toward this new organizational initiative depend on individual faculty disclosing their research results (Bercovitz and Feldman, 2007b). At face value, the decision to disclose research results should be straightforward.

First, increased technology transfer activity has become an articulated goal of the university administration and is espoused as a strategic initiative. Royalty-sharing incentives have been adopted and technology transfer offices have been organized to actively encourage faculty participation. Second, disclosing research results to the technology transfer office is a stipulation of federal research grants, which constitute the largest source of university research funding. Faculty may be driven to disclose in order to remain in compliance with, and thus eligible for, future government grants. Third, the costs associated with disclosing an invention are negligible, and forms are readily available online. Fourth, any idea may be disclosed, as there are no objective standards that faculty discoveries are required to meet to warrant filing an invention disclosure with the technology transfer office (Jensen et al., 2003).[2] Indeed, technology transfer managers actively try to encourage faculty to disclose all ideas that may qualify as inventions, since the number of faculty disclosures is one criterion used to evaluate

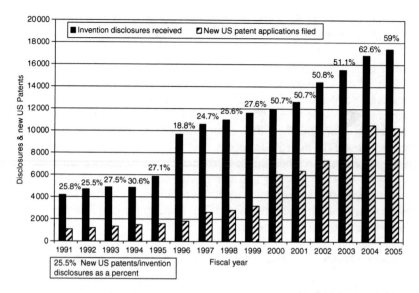

Figure 7.4   Disclosures received and new US patents filed, AUTM, 2007

technology transfer office performance. Mowery et al. (1999) note that about 20 per cent of disclosures were patented after six years, indicating that greater scrutiny accompanies the post-disclosure stage of the technology transfer process (see Figure 7.4).

Thursby et al. (2001) argue that invention disclosures represent only a subset of university research with commercial potential. And, Thursby and Thursby (2003) discuss reasons why faculty would choose not to disclose research results. First, it is claimed that faculty may not disclose because they are unwilling to spend time on the applied R&D required to interest businesses in licensing the invention. This is perhaps countered by the trend toward patenting basic scientific results from projects like the human genome which, though basic, may have immediate commercial potential. Second, faculty may not disclose because they are unwilling to risk publication delays, which may be required to allow prospective licensees to initiate the patenting process. Bercovitz and Feldman (2007b) argue that this is more a perceptual problem than reality as there are strategies to accommodate both interests. A reason many faculty members may not disclose is because they believe that commercial activity is not an appropriate activity for an academic. This view represents an older norm of open academic science (Bercovitz and Feldman, 2007a).

There is an additional concern that faculty may behave opportunistically, bypassing the technology transfer process and not disclosing inventions in order to commercialize them without university involvement. Owen-Smith and Powell (2001) suggest that incentives favour disclosure in the life sciences, as licensing of biomedical patents is a demonstrated way for faculty to earn economic returns and protect academic freedom for follow-on research. Of course, faculty participation will be influenced by the perceptions of the competence and capabilities of the university technology transfer office (Colyvas et al., 2002). These perceptions, in turn, are shaped by institutional history and environments. Once an invention disclosure is filed, the university technology transfer office evaluates the discovery to determine if there is commercial potential. The office then chooses whether to file a provisional or a full patent. The following section provides an explanation on patenting at US universities.

Patents

According to the United States Patent and Trademark Office, patents are

> The grant of a property right to the inventor, issued by the United States Patent and Trademark Office. Generally, the term of a new patent is 20 years from the date on which the application for the patent was filed in the United States or, in special cases, from the date an earlier related application was filed, subject to the payment of maintenance fees. U.S. patent grants are effective only within the United States, U.S. territories, and U.S. possessions. (United States Patent and Trademark Office, 2007)

In the early twentieth century, not wishing to compromise their commitment to open science, universities were not as keen to patent and license their technologies (Sampat, 2006). Thus, there was experimentation with a centralized system called the American Research Corporation (Mowery and Sampat, 2001a). Other universities, such as MIT, Princeton, and Columbia signed contracts with the Research Corporation to manage its patent portfolio.[3] Others, such as Harvard, Johns Hopkins, Penn, and Chicago, while adopting patent policies developed other policies discouraging faculty from patenting.

The 1960s and 1970s saw major changes to US universities patent policies, resulting in direct university patent management. First, due to reduction in revenues the research corporation, which managed many of the universities' patents, encouraged universities to manage their own patent portfolio, a step that later resulted in its own demise (Mowery and Sampat, 2001a). Second, the rise in federal support for biomedical research resulted in the creation of microbiology as an academic field. However, universities found it difficult to negotiate patents with the funding federal agencies. These concerns provided the basis for universities' support of the US Bayh–Dole Act of 1980.

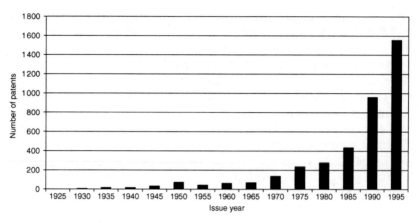

Source: Sampat, 2006

Figure 7.5   Growth of patents issued before and after Bayh–Dole.

As can be seen from Figure 7.5, after Bayh–Dole, there was a large
increase in university patenting, technology transfer, and commercialization. In 1980 less than 400 patents were issued to research universities, this
number grew to a little above 400 patents in 1985. However in 1995, this
number almost reached 1600 patents while in 2005, 10 270 patents were
issued. According to Mowery and Sampat (2001b) however, this growth
was not solely the result of the Bayh–Dole Act. During the 1970s, they
argue, there was an increase in university patenting, related to national
incentives, which was accelerated by the Bayh–Dole Act and would have
continued without its induction (Mowery and Sampat, 2001b). One of the
main benefits resulting from Bayh–Dole was a federal policy that equally
allowed all universities to own their patents without worry of political
changes. However, from studies of Bayh–Dole and its impact on the
American university systems a new debate is rising. Bayh–Dole was created
to allow the public use of university research; however it is not clear
whether American universities are patenting technology or science
(Sampat, 2006).

Since the 1980s there has been a broad trend towards vertical disintegra-
tion and a pro-patent shift of the US courts. Starting in 1982, two adjust-
ments by Congress to the patent process and change in the process of
appeal of patent cases as well as changes to the fees of the US patent office,
resulted in 'an alarming growth in legal wrangling over patents' (Jaffe and
Lerner, 2004, p. 2). The authors warn us that while the patent process was
simplified many patents are issued to trivial and not innovative ideas, such
as how to 'swing on a swing' at a playground. Moreover, these changes have

overturned the main reason for patents, to bring innovation to the market. Thus, many products are not developed and consumers have less access to products due to legal issues. Fear of a lawsuit and legal proceedings has changed the innovation process for both individuals and firms. The result is patent guarantee to firms with the best lawyers and not necessarily with the best inventions (Jaffe and Lerner, 2004). Starting in 1995, practitioners began filing provisional patents. These are patents that can be applied for a twelve-month basis. There is no need for a full description and the fees are lower than a non-provisional patent (Gunderman and Hammond, 2007). After twelve months a non-provisional patent must be applied for. Many offices will not incur additional expenses on converting provisional to full patents if there is no interest from industry.

Licences

Licences are contractual agreements that provide firms with rights to use intellectual property. The number of licences executed by TTOs has grown rapidly from a mere handful in 1970 to 936 in 1991 to 4932 in 2004. In return for the use of university intellectual property, the licensee will typically provide an up-front payment at the time of signing the agreement and make periodic payments at certain milestones, such as when regulatory or technical hurdles are cleared. In addition, licensing agreements typically include provisions for royalty payments, calculated as a percentage of product sales, which become a steady revenue stream when the product reaches the commercial market. Technology transfer offices typically have great latitude and flexibility in negotiating these agreements (Mowery et al., 1999).

The typical licensing agreement has changed significantly over time. Initially, most university licences were granted on an exclusive basis to one company. This approach limited the potential number of transactions and the amount of potential revenue. Universities are now more likely to negotiate licences that are calibrated to certain applications or specific geographic markets. There is also significant variation in licensing agreements with respect to royalty rates, duration, and future option rights (Raider, 1998; Barnes et al., 1997). Certainly, more research is warranted to understand how these contracts are negotiated and which partner, the university or the corporation, exerts the greatest bargaining power and under what circumstances.

As we can see from Figure 7.6, the distribution of licensing revenues is highly skewed, with a few big commercial successes generating large returns for a small number of universities. For example, the cancer fighting drug Taxol, which is based on intellectual property owned by Florida State

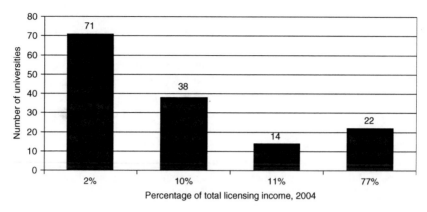

Source: AUTM Reports, 2007

Figure 7.6 Highly skewed distribution of licensing revenues

University, has worldwide annual sales worth $1.2 billion and yielded some
$60 million in licensing revenue in 2000 (Zacks, 2000). Successes like
Cohen-Boyer, Taxol, Gatorade (University of Florida), cisplatin and car-
boplatin (Michigan State), and fax technology (Iowa State) are well-
known, but they are exceptional. Most university technology transfer
operations do not break even. Their licensing revenues are not sufficient to
cover administrative costs and the costs of filing and maintaining patents.
In 2004, 22 out of 145 universities generated 77 per cent of all American
universities' licensing income.

American universities continue to experiment with the licensing process.
One example of such experimentation is the practice of taking an equity
interest in the licensing company in lieu of traditional licensing fees
(Feldman et al., 2002). This practice originated with cash-starved start-up
firms that had little other than an ownership stake to offer, but it is now used
in a variety of situations to streamline the negotiation process and align the
interests of the university and the industrial partner. If the company suc-
ceeds, the university stands to make a larger financial gain than might be
expected from a traditional agreement. Another experiment involves the
monetization of licensing royalties. In Yale University's agreement with
Royalty Pharma (Blumenstyk, 2001), for instance, the university sold the
stream of future royalties from its intellectual property in exchange for a
lump-sum, up-front payment. This transaction allowed Yale to build several
new laboratory buildings and also eliminated the problem of what might
happen when a significant stream of revenue came to an end. Such experiments aim to improve the financial rewards from technology transfer and
illustrate a commitment to learning on the part of technology transfer offices.

Link and Siegel (2005) found that higher share of royalties enhances technology licensing and argue that 'Universities that seek to enhance licensing should allocate a higher share of royalties to faculty member' (Link and Siegel, 2005, p. 179). Royalties are the sum of money paid to the proprietor or licensor of intellectual property (IP) rights for the benefits derived, or sought to be derived, by the user (the licensee) through the exercise of such rights. In the case of universities, royalties refer to the payments the university and inventors receive from the licensing or equity of a university patent. According to the authors, changes in faculty incentives change their behaviour, hence resulting in more inventions being licensed out to existing companies. The authors strengthen this point by their finding that it is full and associate professors that do most of the invention disclosures and patenting. Accordingly they claim that the creation of policies which will encourage and protect junior faculty will increase universities patents and licences (Link and Siegel, 2005).

There is some evidence, however, that licensing has not been an entirely satisfactory mechanism from industry's perspective. In a survey of industry licensing executives, Thursby and Thursby (2000) found that 66 per cent (199 business units out of a total of 300) had not licensed intellectual property from universities. The reasons given included the feeling that university research is generally at too early a stage of development (49 per cent); that universities rarely engage in research in a related line of business (37.4 per cent); that universities refuse to transfer ownership to companies (31 per cent); that universities have policies regarding delay of publication that are too strict (20 per cent); and that faculty cooperation for further development of the technology would be too difficult to obtain (16 per cent).[4] These results suggest that there may be some additional evolution in licensing agreements or in the organization of technology transfer operations.

University-based Spin-offs

Spin-offs are an increasingly important means of commercializing university research. Given the difficulty of evaluating the economic potential of university intellectual property, the researchers who made the relevant discovery may be in the best position to carry the work forward toward commercialization. Life-cycle models suggest that scientists invest heavily in human capital early in their careers to build reputations and establish positions of primacy in their fields of expertise (Levin and Stephan, 1991). In the later stages of their careers, they are more likely to seek an economic return on this investment. Starting a company may serve the purpose of realizing that return. It also allows the founders to appropriate the value of the intellectual property they created while at the university and to accelerate progress on their research agenda by providing access to additional funding. The potential financial rewards of starting a company coupled with tightening university budgets and competition for the relatively fixed pool of public funding create incentives for scientists to engage in entrepreneurial activity (Powell and Owen-Smith, 1998).

Di Gregorio and Shane (2003) found that there is an inverse correlation between the percentage of an inventor's royalties and the number of university spin-outs each year. Furthermore, Shane claims that allocating a lower share of royalties to inventors promotes spin-out capability (Shane, 2004). Thus, an allocation of fewer royalties to inventors will reduce the number of licences and promote the creation of spin-offs. According to Shane, the reason for the inverse relationships in royalty share and spin-out formation is based on the allocation of royalties at the university. The higher the royalty share of the inventor, the higher the opportunity costs of the inventor to spin off a company; therefore, the lower his or her incentives to do so:

> As a result, the greater is the inventor's share of royalties from licensing a technology, the more incentive the inventor has to license his or her technology to a third party because the opportunity cost of starting a firm to exploit the invention goes up with the inventor's share of licensing income. (Shane, 2004, p. 75)

Di Gregorio and Shane also identified another policy influence: that universities willing to take equity for patenting and licensing expenses have a start-up rate higher than universities that refused equity. In his (2004) book, *Academic Entrepreneurship*, Shane summarizes university policies and their influence on university spinouts. In addition to the reasons mentioned above, he stresses the importance of universities allowing exclusive licensing, offering leave of absence, permitting the use of university resources, allocating a lower share of royalties to inventors, and providing access to pre-seed stage capital (Shane, 2004).

The Association of University Technology Managers (AUTM) is the main source of data on university-based spin-off companies. AUTM defines a university spin-off as a firm formed around a university licence of intellectual property. This definition is not the only one that may be employed. Two caveats are worth mentioning in this context. First, many more spin-offs are likely to be formed by individuals with some association with the university other than the licensing of intellectual property. Thus, the AUTM numbers may understate the impact of universities on entrepreneurship. However, there is a countervailing influence. Discussions with university technology transfer officials reveal that they are under pressure to report as many spin-offs as they can in order to compare well with other

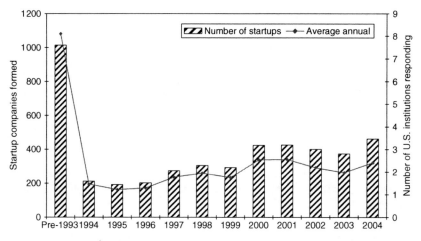

Source: AUTM Annual Surveys

Figure 7.7   University spinouts per year, 1993–2004

universities in the AUTM reports and other benchmarking activities. These anecdotes suggest that universities may not strictly adhere to the AUTM definition in their reporting.

With these caveats in mind, Figure 7.7 reports AUTM numbers of university-based spin-off firms. In 1999, there were 275 firms of this type, an average of about two companies per university. The average, however, is somewhat deceptive. The distribution of spin-offs among universities is highly skewed. The majority of universities report no spin-offs. At the high end of the range is a university that produced 19 companies in 1999. In addition, it should be noted that the total number of spin-off companies reported has increased simply because the number of universities actively involved in technology transfer has increased.

Universities are now investing their own funds in start-up companies as well. For example, Vanderbilt University established a $10 million Chancellor Fund to invest in university spin-offs. There are concerns about the feasibility of these investments, as witnessed by Boston University's financing of its start-up firm, Seragen, which absorbed $120 million of BU's money between 1987 and 1997. The company was not successful. The failure is not a surprise; only about 5 per cent of venture capital-backed firms are very successful, and another 30 per cent are moderately successful. In this case, the university only recovered a fraction of its investment, raising concerns about its fiduciary responsibility and objectivity. There is great potential in these relationships for conflict of interest and the threat of a fundamental re-ordering of university priorities.

Science Parks and Incubators

There are several additional ways for industry to sponsor university research. Some universities created collaborative research centres where some companies pay an annual fee to be part of research consortia that provide the latest results in different technological fields. Science parks and university incubators allow companies a direct and simple way to collaborate with universities. A university science park is built in a short distance to, with funding or land from universities, for example, University Park at MIT, in Cambridge, Massachusetts, where the university leased the land to a real estate development company that constructed a science park (Breznitz, 2000). As defined by the international association of science parks:

> A Science Park is an organization managed by specialized professionals, whose main aim is to increase the wealth of its community by promoting the culture of innovation and the competitiveness of its associated businesses and knowledge-based institutions. To enable these goals to be met, a Science Park stimulates and manages the flow of knowledge and technology amongst universities, R&D institutions, companies and markets; it facilitates the creation and growth of innovation-based companies through incubation and spin-off processes; and provides other value-added services together with high quality space and facilities. (IASP International Board, 6 February 2002)

The purpose of the park is to provide companies proximity to university research labs.

Incubators on the other hand are usually smaller spaces, sometimes within a university (as in the case of the University of Cambridge) and sometime in close proximity to a university but managed by developers. As defined by Investorwords.com, an incubator is defined as:

> A company or facility designed to foster entrepreneurship and help startup companies, usually technology-related, to grow through the use of shared resources, management expertise, and intellectual capital. (Investorwords.com, 2006)

Especially important for start-ups, incubators provide low rent and joint services such as conference rooms and administrative services. Incubators allow start-up companies to develop while keeping a close connection to a university laboratory. The move from a university laboratory to become a commercial firm and/or locating in a close proximity to a university provides stability and options for university–industry collaborations (Massey et al., 1992; Rothaermel and Thursby, 2005).

REFLECTIVE CONCLUSIONS

Technology transfer has become an important part of the operation of American research universities. Nelson (2001) worries that the increased emphasis on intellectual property will interfere with the norms of open science and adversely limit the role of universities in the US system of innovation. These are important questions to ask in light of the aggressive moves that this chapter has described. The process may be viewed as an experiment and practices have not yet solidified and reached a steady state. Scholars are only beginning to understand the impact of experiments in the commercialization of academic research on the broader national system of innovation (Feldman and Owens, 2007; Feldman and Schipper, 2007). The success of technology transfer in the USA are only part of the story and masks the great diversity in organizational motives, strategies and incentives at the various institutions. Many institutions do not yet make money licensing technology and those institutions that are profitable typically licensing royalties average two to four per cent of the universities' research budget (Nelsen, 2003).

The same questions are also worth thinking about at the regional level as universities are asked to become engines of local economic development. Universities have demonstrated great adaptability in fulfilling their commitment to active technology transfer. Their attempts to spin off new companies satisfy an increased expectation that they be engaged in local economic development and demonstrate their relevance. Yet universities add more to their local economies than the metrics of technology transfer capture. And there are certainly many different models for assessing how universities interact with and enrich their local economies. Thus, as long as the emphasis in technology transfer focuses on metric, sceptics may question if university programmes aimed to encourage entrepreneurship and local economic growth may be the best use of state and university resources. Perhaps the examples provided by WARF, Stanford, and MIT have established an unrealistic standard against which American research universities are currently being judged. As we have shown in this chapter, universities' contributions go beyond patents and licences. The potential new technology, sense of community, and economic growth, are critical in today's global economy and should not be limited by metrics. The most important role of universities may still be the education of students and the generation of new ideas. Even so, the United States has entered a new era in technology transfer and in the process has become a model that the rest of the world is trying to emulate. However, we must take into consideration that the US model of technology transfer has been influenced by specific historical factors on both the national and regional levels. Adaptation of this model must be modified to fit the specific regional and universities' characteristics.

Policies such as the Morrill Land-Grant Act followed by the Smith–Lever Act of 1914, created a system of higher education with a concept of technology transfer as a public good in which collaboration with industry was encouraged. Thus, technology transfer became grounded as part of the American university system. These strong ties in the USA between universities, government and industry can be viewed through the use of science in both world wars and the formation of the National Science Foundation in 1950. It is commonly viewed that the federal government's spending on military R&D during that period was an important factor in the development of the high-tech and biotech industries in the United States.

Nevertheless, there were calls for stronger links between universities and industry to improve competitiveness in the 1980s. The result was the Bayh–Dole Act of 1980, which gave universities intellectual property rights over federally funded discoveries: a result of the continuous government support of university research can be viewed through university research sources of funding. While some schools such as Duke University, receive 20 per cent of their total R&D funding from industry, on average, industry still funds only 5 per cent of university research. However, the federal government is still the largest source of funding (63 per cent) for university-based research (National Science Foundation, 2007). Contributing to the unique development and support of university technology transfer in the USA are specific state legislation and funding, as well as particular university mechanisms.

While many of the US technology transfer models are easily adapted, imitation is not necessarily the answer. Countries have different higher education systems. For example, the German and French systems divide their research between government research laboratories and universities. Thus, the incentives to disseminate research to the private market are unique and will not be transparent in patents and licences. However, it does not mean that these systems are not making economic contributions to their countries. While focusing on patents, licences, and spinouts is easy to measure, it has been shown to be only one of the ways in which universities impact on their economy. Examining the case of Cambridge, UK starting in the early 1980s, many high technology firms developed out of the University of Cambridge. However, intensive research has show, it was not the university's policies or actions that created the 'Cambridge Phenomenon', but the unique regional incentives and local social networks (Segal Quince Wicksteed, 1985, 2000; Garnsey and Hefferman, 2005; Breznitz, 2007).

This chapter has demonstrated that virtually all American research universities actively participate in technology transfer and have accepted the new mantle of promoting local economic development, specifically through the promotion of entrepreneurial start-up firms. In addition, a variety of new mechanisms to put licences into circulation are being used and used more creatively. Certainly, only time and additional research will reveal the long-term effects of these changes on the American system of innovation.

NOTES

1. Today, the German system is divided between application oriented universities (Fraunhofer), universities that focus on basic research (The Max Planck Institute), and shorter-term educational programmes (polytechnics). These changes resulted in lower competitiveness due to reliance on industry and regional agencies funding (Etzkowitz et al., 2000)
2. Jensen, et al. (2003) titled a paper 'The disclosure and licensing of university inventions: doing the best we can with the s**t we get to work with' – which is taken from an interview with a technology transfer administrator who was bemoaning differential quality of faculty disclosures.
3. 'Research Corporation was founded in 1912. Its operations are governed within the guidelines of a "private operating foundation," which means that it may perform activities related to science advancement in addition to funding others to carry on such activities. For many years Research Corporation did maintain an invention administration program for academic inventors and their institutions, in 1987 Research Corporation's invention administration program became the genesis for Research Corporation Technologies (RCT), a wholly independent company whose business is technology transfer' (Research Corporation, 2007).
4. Twenty-eight percent of the respondents indicated some other difficulty such as 'general attitude is poor,' 'complexity of deal and . . . weird expectations,' 'too cumbersome' and 'high licensing fees' (Thursby and Thursby, 2000).

REFERENCES

Apple, R.D. (1989), 'Patenting university research: Harry Steenbock and the Wisconsin Alumni Research Foundation', *ISIS*, **80**, 375–94.
Association of University Technology Managers (2007), 'Building a Stronger Economy: Profiles of 25 Companies Rooted in Academic Research', Technology Transfer Works: 100 Innovations from Academic Research to Real-World Application', Better World Report series.
Barnes, M., D.C. Mowery and A.A. Ziedonis (1997), 'The geographic reach of market and nonmarket channels of technology transfer: comparing citations and licenses of university patents', conference paper prepared for the Academy of Management annual meeting, Boston, MA.
Bercovitz, J. and M. Feldman (2008), 'Academic entrepreneurs: organizational change at the individual level', *Organization Science*, **19** (1), 69–89.
Bercovitz, J. and M. Feldman (2007b), 'Fishing upstream: firm innovation strategy and university research alliances', *Research Policy* **36**, 930–48.
Bercovitz, J., M. Feldman, I. Feller and R. Burton (2001), 'Organizational structure as a determinant of academic patent and licensing behavior: an exploratory study

of Duke, Johns Hopkins, and Pennsylvania State universities', *Journal of Technology Transfer* **26**, 21–35.

Blumenstyk, G. (2001), 'Turning patent royalties into a sure thing', *Chronicle of Higher Education*, 5 October.

Breznitz, S.M. (2000), 'The geography of industrial districts: why does the biotechnology industry in Massachusetts cluster in Cambridge?', master's thesis, University of Massachusetts, Lowell.

Breznitz, Shiri M. (2007), 'What's wrong with technology transfer model adaptation?',

Breznitz, Shiri M., Rory P. O'Shea and Thomas J Allen (2008), 'University commercialization strategies in the development of regional bioclusters', *Journal of Product Innovation Management*, **25** (3), 129–42.

Casper, S. and A. Karmanos (2003), 'Commercializing science in Europe: the Cambridge biotechnology cluster', *European Planning Studies* **11**, 805–22.

Colyvas, J., M. Crow, A. Gelijns, R. Mazzoleni, R. R. Nelson, N. Rosenberg and B. N. Sampat (2002), 'How do university inventions get into practice?, *Management Science*, **48** (1), 61–72.

Di Gregorio, D. and Shane, S. (2003), 'Why do some universities generate more start-ups than others?', *Research Policy*, **32**: 209–27.

Etzkowitz, H. (1995), 'The triple helix–university–industry–government relations: a laboratory for knowledge based economic development', *EASST Review*. **14**, 9–14.

Etzkowitz, H., A. Webster, C. Gebhardt and B.R.C. Terra (2000), 'The future of the university and the university of the future: evolution of ivory tower to entrepreneurial paradigm', *Research Policy*, **29** (2), 313–30.

Feldman, M. and R. Owens (2007), 'Bringing science to life: introduction to the special issue', *Journal of Technology Transfer*, **32**, 127–30.

Feldman, M. and H. Schipper (2007), 'Bringing science to life: an overview of countries outside of North America', *Journal of Technology Transfer*, **32**, 297–302.

Feldman, M.P., I. Feller, J.E.L. Bercovitz and R.M. Burton (2002), 'Equity and the technology transfer strategies of American research universities', *Management ScienceI*, **48**, 105–21.

Garnsey, E. and P. Hefferman (2005), 'High-technology clustering through spin-out and attraction: the Cambridge case', *Regional Studies*, **39** (8), 1127–44.

Geiger, R.L. (1986), *To Advance Knowledge: The Growth of American Research Universities, 1900–1940*, New York: Oxford University Press.

Geiger, R.L. (1988), 'Milking the sacred cow: research and the quest for useful knowledge in the American university since 1920', *Science, Technology, & Human Values*, **13**, 332–48.

Gunderman, R.D. and J.M. Hammond (2007), 'File now, pay later', *IEEE Spectrum*, **44** (6), 77–8.

IASP International Board (2002), 'About science and technology parks – definitions', accessed 6 February at www.iasp.ws.

Investorwords.com (2006), '*Definition*', accessed 8 April, 2008 at www.investorwords.com/2418/incubator.html.

Jaffe, Adam B. and Josh Lerner (2004), *Innovation and its Discontents: How Our Broken Patent System is Endangering Innovation and Progress, and What To Do About It*, Princeton, NJ: Princeton University Press.

Jensen, R.A., J.G. Thursby and M.C. Thursby (2003), 'Disclosure and licensing of university inventions: "The best we can do with the s**t we get to work with"', *International Journal of Industrial Organization*, **21**, 1271–300.

Levin, S.G. and P.E. Stephan (1991), 'Research productivity over the life cycle: evidence for academic scientists', *American Economic Review*, **81**, 114–32.

Link, A. and D. Siegel (2005), 'Generating science-based growth: an econometric analysis of the impact of organizational incentives on university–industry technology transfer', *European Journal of Finance*, **11**, 169–81.

Litan, R.E., L. Mitchell and E.J. Reedy (2007), 'Commercializing university innovations: alternative approaches', NBER working paper JEL no. 018.

Markusen, Ann R. (1991), *The Rise of the Gunbelt: The Military Remapping of Industrial America*, New York: Oxford University Press.

Massey, Doreen, Paul Quintas and David Wield (1992), *High-Tech Fantasies: Science Parks in Society, Science and Space*, London and New York: Routledge.

MIT Industial Liaison Program (2007), *Consortia*, accessed November at http://ilp-www.mit.edu.

Mowery, D.C. and B.N. Sampat (2001a), 'Patenting and licensing university inventions: lessons from the history of the research corporation', *Industrial & Corporate Change*, **10**, 317–55.

Mowery, D.C. and B.N. Sampat (2001b), 'University patents and patent policy debates in the USA, 1925–1980', *Industrial & Corporate Change* **10**, 781–814.

Mowery, D., R.R. Rosenberg, B.N. Sampat and A.A. Ziedonis (1999), 'The effects of the Bayh–Dole Act on U.S. university research and technology transfer', in L.M Branscomb, F. Kodoma and R.L. Florida (eds), *Industrializing Knowledge: University–Industry Linkages in Japan and the United States*, Cambridge, MA: MIT Press.

National Science Foundation (2005), 'Table 31: R&D expenditures at universities and colleges, by source of funds FY 2005'. accessed September at http://www.nsf.gov/statistics.

National Science Foundation (2005a), National Science Foundation Website, accessed September at www.nsf.gov.

National Science Foundation (2005b), 'R&D expenditures at universities and colleges, by source of funds FY 1953–2005', accessed September at www.nsf.gov.

National Science Foundation (2007), 'Info brief: universities report stalled growth in deferal R&D funding in FY 2006', accessed November at www.nsf.gov.

National Science Foundation (2007), 'US R&D expenditures 2006', accessed November at www.nsf.gov/statistics/infbrief/nsf07317/.

Nelsen, Lita (2003), 'The role of university technology transfer operations in assuring access to medicines and vaccines in developing countries', *Yale Journal of Health, Policy, Law and Ethics*, **III** (2), 301–8.

Nelson, R.R. (2001), 'Observations on the post-Bayh–Dole rise of patenting at American universities', *Journal of Technology Transfer*, **26** (1–2), 13–19.

Owen-Smith, J. and W.W. Powell (2001), 'To patent or not: faculty decisions and institutional success in academic patenting', *Journal of Technology Transfer*, **26**, 99–114.

Powell, W.W. and J. Owen-Smith (1998), 'Universities and the market for intellectual property in the life sciences', *Journal of Policy Analysis and Management*, **17**, 227–53.

Press, E. and J. Washburn (2000), *The Kept University*, Boston, MA: Atlantic Monthly Group.

Rahm, Diane, John Kirkland and Barry Bozeman (2000), *University–Industry R&D Collaboration in the United States, the United Kingdom, and Japan*, Dordrecht, the Netherlands: Kluwer Academic Publishers.

Raider, H. (1998), 'Repeated exchange and evidence of trust in the substance contract', working paper, Columbia University.

Research Corporation (2007), 'About us', accessed at www.rescorp.org.

Rothaermel, F.T. and M.C. Thursby (2005), 'University-incubator firm knowledge flows: assessing their impact on incubator firm performance', *Research Policy*, 34, 305–20.

Sampat, B.N. (2006), 'Patenting and US academic research in the 20th century: the world before and after Bayh–Dole', *Research Policy*, 35, 772–89.

Segal Quince Wicksteed (1985), *The Cambridge Phenomenon: The Growth of High Technology Industry in a University Town*, 3rd edn 1990, Cambridge: Segal Quince Wicksteed.

Segal Quince Wicksteed (2000), *The Cambridge Phenomenon Revisited*, Histon: Segal Quince Wicksteed.

Shane, Scott (2004), *Academic Entrepreneurship: University Spinoffs and Wealth Creation,* Cheltenham, UK and Northampton, MA, USA: Edward Elgar.

Sharon, A. (1994), 'Fostering technology transfer through industry–university cooperation: a practitioner's view at MIT', *Empirica*, 21, 285–296.

Slaughter Sheila and Larry L. Leslie (1997), *Academic Capitalism: Politics, Policies and the Entrepreneurial University*, Baltimore, MD: Johns Hopkins University Press.

Strout, E. (2007), 'Harvard's endowment grows to $34.9-billion', *Chronicle of Higher Education*, 54, p. A38.

Thursby, J.G. and M.C. Thursby (2000), 'Industry perspectives on licensing university technologies: sources and problems', *Journal of the Association of University Technology Managers*, 12, 9–23.

Thursby, J.G. and M.C. Thursby (2003), 'Intellectual property: enhanced: 'University licensing and the Bayh–Dole Act', *Science*, 301, 1052.

Thursby, Jerry G. and Marie C. Thursby (2006), *Here or There? A Survey of Factors in Multinational R&D Location*, report to the Government–University–Industry Research Roundtable (GUIRR), Washington D.C: National Academies Press.

Thursby, J.G., R. Jensen and M.C. Thursby (2001), 'Objectives, characteristics and outcomes of university licensing: a survey of major U.S. universities', *Journal of Technology Transfer*, 26, 59–72.

US House of Representatives (2007), 'Testimony of Susan B. Butts, Senior Director, External Science and Technology Programs, The Dow Chemical Company, before the Subcommittee on Technology and Innovation Committee on Science and Technology U.S. House of Representatives, Bayh–Dole – The Next 25 Years', accessed at http://209.85.165.104/search?q=cache:_oXKKmzF31MJ:gop.science.house.gov/hearings/ets07/July%252017/Butts.pdf+Susan+Butts+July+17+testimony+to+Congress&hl=en&ct=clnk&cd=1&gl=us&client=firefox-a.

US Patent and Trademark Office (2007), *General Information Concerning Patents*, Washington, DC: US Patent and Trademark Office.

Zacks, R. (2000), 'The TR university research scorecard', accessed at www.techreview.com/articles/july00/zacks.htm

8. Academic patenting in Europe: evidence on France, Italy and Sweden from the KEINS database

Francesco Lissoni, Patrick Llerena, Maureen McKelvey and Bulat Sanditov

1. INTRODUCTION

This chapter reports key statistics from the KEINS database, which shed new light on the patenting activity of universities and their staff in France, Italy, and Sweden. Created by the authors, along with Ingrid Schild of Umeå University, the KEINS database allows the first cross-country comparison of university patenting patterns in Europe.

The KEINS database covers inventions produced by academic scientists in active service around 2004–05 in the three countries considered, for which a patent application has been filed at EPO. In particular, it contains both the applications submitted by universities (university-owned patents) and the applications submitted by companies, individuals or governmental and non-profit organizations, as a result of various contractual arrangements between such organizations and the scientists, their universities, and other public or private sponsors (university-invented patents). For sake of clarity, we will speak of 'university patenting' when referring to university-owned patents, and to 'academic patenting' when referring to both university-owned and university-invented patents. We will always refer to patent applications (upon which almost all of our statistics are based) either in full or, for sake of brevity, simply as patents, and refer to 'granted patents' explicitly, when needed.

The key intuition behind the KEINS data collection effort is that, due to institutional differences, academic patents in Europe are much less likely to be owned by universities than in the USA. These institutional differences concern both the autonomy of universities, the control they exercise over their academic staff, and the legal norms on the assignment of intellectual property rights (IPR) over academic research results; they make European universities much less likely than US ones to own the patents over their scientists' inventions, either because of lower incentives to patent or because of less control over their scientists' activities. This does not mean that European academic scientists do not contribute effectively to the inventive activity taking place in their countries, as one could gather by looking only at the statistics on university-owned patents.

The data provided and discussed in this chapter will show that the extent of academic scientists' contribution to national patenting in France, Italy, and Sweden is quite similar to that found for the USA by other authors. Similarities also exist in the technological contents of academic patenting. What differ are the ownership regimes: in contrast to the USA, where universities own the majority of academic patents, Europe witnesses the dominance of business companies, which own no less than 60 percent of academic patents. In France, and to a lesser extent in Italy, a sizeable share of academic patents is also owned by large governmental research organizations, a result which reflects the importance of these actors within their national public research systems.

These results provide an interesting contrast to common perceptions of European academic research as lagging behind the USA one in terms of contribution to technological advancement, a perception that has shaped many recent changes in legislation and governmental policies not only in the three countries considered here, but all over Europe.

In the remainder of the chapter, we first discuss existing attitudes towards academic patenting in Europe, and argue that they are based on poor data, and poor data collection methodology (section 2). Then we move on to describe the KEINS database, first the methodology upon which it is based (section 3) and then the evidence it provides (section 4). Finally, we discuss the policy implications of our evidence, as well as our plans for future research based upon the KEINS database.

2.   ACADEMIC PATENTING IN EUROPE AND THE USA

Academic patenting is an important part of the larger phenomenon of university–industry technology transfer. In particular, patents are a key tool for protecting innovation in a number of science-based technologies, such as chemicals, pharmaceuticals, biotech, and many fields of electronics. Academic scientists contribute to these technologies both indirectly, by widening the science base, and directly, by producing inventions susceptible to industrial application, and therefore protected by patents.

In recent years, many European countries, and the EU, have introduced several legislative changes and policy initiatives aimed at pushing universities to take more patents out of their research, due to perceived problems in Europe *vis-à-vis* the USA with respect to technology transfer via patenting.

These initiatives have been based on little or no data, beyond cursory looks at the large number of patent applications filed by US universities, as opposed to the very low numbers coming from European universities.

Recent research, however, suggests that comparing Europe and the USA on the basis of university-owned patents may be misleading, due to differences between inventorship and ownership of patents.

2.1 A Perceived Patenting Gap, and the Remedies to it

Since the mid-twentieth century, the number of USPTO patents applied for by US universities has increased dramatically, even more than the total number of USPTO patent applications. As a result, the weight of US universities' patents over total domestic patents has increased from less than 1.5 percent in 1975 to almost 2.5 percent in 1988 (Henderson et al., 1998); or, even considering only the leading institutions (the so-called research universities), from 0.3 percent in 1963 to nearly 4 percent in 1999 (Mowery and Sampat, 2005).

This growth has appeared to gain strength after the introduction of the Bayh–Dole Act and to have benefited from the general strengthening of patent protection, as well as from generous funding of academic biomedical research (Mowery et al., 2004).[1] Over the same years, many US companies in science-based industries (often born as university spin-offs) have multiplied and grown rapidly, while many European large hi-tech companies have opened research facilities near US campuses, or acquired US universities' technologies and start-ups. Although never proved, a connection seemed to many to exist between the explosion of university patenting and the hi-tech boom of the 1990s.

By contrast, university patenting in Europe looks like a limited phenomenon. It is a well-known fact that no European academic institution holds as large a patent portfolio as MIT or Stanford, and that many European universities do not own patents at all (OECD, 2003).

This contrast between the USA and Europe has often been interpreted in the light of the general view of the existence of a 'European Paradox', according to which European countries have a strong science base, but also many problems in translating scientific advances into commercially viable new technologies (EC, 2003 1995; Dosi et al., 2006). In this view, universities contribute to the European Paradox by disregarding or mismanaging technology transfer activities. Thus, the scarcity of university patents is seen both a signal of a technology transfer deficit and a problem to be addressed through legislation. Examples of recent legislative initiatives by

European countries in the direction of encouraging patenting abound. Many of them revolve around the so-called 'professor's privilege' or *Hochschullehrerprivileg*, a long-standing norm of the German patent law that allowed academic scientists to retain IPRs over the results of research paid for by their universities (as opposed to R&D employees of business companies and public labs, whose research results belong by default to their employers). Based upon the intuition that universities would be better positioned to exploit their IPRs than individual professors (and therefore would have higher incentives to patent), German legislators abolished the professor's privilege in 2001, and were quickly followed by their Austrian colleagues in 2002. In 2000, Denmark had already abolished the privilege as part of a comprehensive Act on Inventions at Public Research Institutions. It aimed precisely at increasing university patenting. In the same years, Sweden considered its abolition, too (PVA-MV, 2003).

In 2001, Italian legislators *introduced* the professor's privilege, on the basis of the opposite intuition that individual scientists may have a greater incentive to patent than the university that employ them.

In addition, initiatives to increase academic scientists' awareness of IPR issues have been regularly launched throughout Europe since the mid-1990s. Sweden opened the way in 1994, along with the creation of a number of 'Technology Bridging Foundations' (Goldfarb and Henrekson, 2003). This was followed by multiple public policy initiatives to encourage academic patenting and university supporting institutions, with a recent example being the Swedish Agency for Innovation Systems (VINNOVA) programme on developing competencies of universities as key actors[2].

As for Italy, Baldini et al. (2006) describe how universities were encouraged by government to adopt explicit IPR policies throughout the 1990s. For France, Gallochat (2003) mentions IPR awareness campaigns as part of new legislation aimed at improving the commercialization of university-invented technologies, of which the Innovation Act of 1999 (also known as Loi Allégre) is a cornerstone. Other contributors to the OECD (2003) report on university patenting mention similar initiatives in other European countries.

2.2   Is the Patenting Gap Really There?

All these initiatives to stimulate patenting by universities and university staff, however, were based on scattered or no data at all. Most information on university patenting came either from surveys submitted to university technology liaison offices or from cursory looks at the identity of patent assignees. These methodologies for data collection ignore the specific institutional features of European universities.

In countries where the professor's privilege had a long-standing tradition, individual academic scientists disposed freely of their IPRs, so that we can expect many patents to be applied for in the scientists' names, or in the name of the business companies with which the scientists entertained consultancy or research cooperation links.

More generally, and also in countries where the privilege never existed, most European universities have for long lacked the autonomy and administrative skills typical of their US counterparts (See Ben-David (1977) and Clark (1993)). They traditionally resisted being involved in their professors' patenting activities, and took the shortcut of allowing scientists engaged in cooperative or contract research with various business companies or PROs to sign blanket agreements that left all IPRs in the hands of professors and their research partners.

The wave of IPR-related reform initiatives we mentioned above is too recent to have radically changed these attitudes. In addition, these initiatives have been directed only at the surface of the phenomenon (the universities' technology transfer strategies), and not at the core issue of universities' autonomy. In many continental Europe countries (such as France and Italy) professors are civil servants, whose careers, teaching loads, research opportunities, and wages depend much more on ministerial rules applied at the national level than on universities' local strategies and management decisions. Similarly, universities rely much more on funding from the national government than on self-financing of any kind; in addition, such funding comes mainly in the form of block grants, rather than through competitive bids for mission-oriented financing (Geuna, 1999). As a result, academic scientists have little incentives to disclose their inventions to their universities' administrations, and the universities' administrations lack the incentives to chase for disclosures. Although, in principle, professors–civil servants could be forced by governments to disclose their inventions and even dedicate their time to develop them, this can be hardly done in practice, due to the physical and cognitive distance that separate the individual scientist from any ministerial bureaucracy in charge of controlling/promoting technology transfer.

Finally, in countries with a public research system dominated by large public laboratories and governmental agencies (such as France and, until a few years ago, Italy), the latter used to retain control over the IPRs on the academic research they funded. Scanning any list of French patent assignees, one can spot many occurrences of CNRS (the National Centre of Scientific Research) or INSERM (the National Institute of Health and Medical Research), whose many laboratories are often placed inside universities and rely on the contribution of academic scientists. As for Italy, one can find many patents owned by CNR (the Italian equivalent of CNRS) and ENEA (the National Agency for Energy and Environment).

These considerations suggests that a large part of academic patents in Europe may simply escape the most commonly available statistics, which classify the origin of the patent according to the identity of the grantees or applicants, rather than of the inventors. If this is true, traditional comparisons with the USA may be proved to be misleading, insofar they exaggerate the scarcity of academic patents in Europe.

Following this clue, Meyer (2003) for Finland, Balconi et al. (2004) for Italy, and Iversen et al. (2007) for Norway have reclassified patents by inventor, and matched the inventor's names with available datasets on university faculties. They found out that in all three countries a significant percentage of the business companies' patents originate from academic inventors. CNR and VTT (the two most prominent PROs of Italy and Finland, respectively) also hold many patents signed by academic inventors. Overall 3 percent of EPO patents in Italy and 8 percent in Finland cover academic inventions (almost 10 percent in Norway, including non-academic PROs' inventions). Applications of the same name-matching methodology to individual universities in Belgium and France have led to similar results (Saragossi and van Pottelsberghe, 2003; Azagra-Caro and Llerena, 2003). Surveys of this literature have been produced by Geuna and Nesta (2006) and Verspagen (2006).[3]

Most recently, US researchers have also attempted to measure university-invented patents as opposed to university-owned ones. In a paper aimed at evaluating the impact of patenting on academic scientists' productivity, Fabrizio and DiMinin (2005) examine a sample of 150 'academic inventors' active in 1975–95, and find that, of 250 patents applied for in 1995, around 20 percent were assigned to business companies, while the remaining were almost all assigned to universities (a negligible number were assigned to the individual inventors). For a much larger sample of 2900 US academic inventors, Thursby et al. (2007) find a similar distribution: 62.6 percent of patents assigned to universities and no-profit organizations, 26.0 percent to business companies, 5.6 percent to individual inventors, 4.0 percent co-assigned to a university and a business company, and 1.7 percent held by a governmental sponsor. In this case, data span from 1993 to 2004, and no trend in the proportion between university-invented and university-owned patents is visible.

These figures suggest that academic patents, invented but not owned by universities, are not a peculiar feature of European countries, as they exist also in the USA. However, these same figures suggest that the proportion of university-invented patents over total academic patents may be higher in Europe than in the USA. For example, Balconi et al. (2004) found that over

60 percent of Italian academic patents were in the hands of industry, almost three times the share calculated for the USA.

In what follows we extend the methodology pioneered by Balconi et al. (2004) to France and Sweden, and update the Italian data; this same methodology can and will be extended soon to other European countries, such as the Netherlands and the UK. At the same time, we show that differences in university ownership of academic patents exist not only between the USA and Europe, but also across the three European countries considered here, and that they are largely explained by institutional differences across the university and science systems.

3. THE KEINS DATABASE

The KEINS database originates from the EP-INV database produced by CESPRI-Università Bocconi, which contains all EPO applications, reclassified by applicant and inventor; and from three lists of university professors of all ranks (from assistant to full professors), one for each of the above mentioned countries (PROFLISTs). Academic inventors have been identified by matching names and surnames of inventors in the EP-INV database with those in the PROFLISTs, and by checking by e-mail and by phone the identity of the matches, in order to exclude homonyms.

3.1 The EP-INV Database

The EP-INV dataset is part of the broader EP-CESPRI database, which provides information on patents applied for at the European Patent Office (EPO), from 1978 to January 2005. The EP-CESPRI database is based upon applications published on a regular basis by the *Espacenet Bulletin* and is updated yearly; presently, it contains over 1 500 000 patent applications. Data relevant for this chapter fall into three broad categories:

1. *Patent data*, such as the patent's publication, its priority date, and technological class (IPC 12-digit).
2. *Applicant data*, such as a unique code assigned by CESPRI to each applicant after cleaning the applicant's name, plus the applicant name and address.
3. *Inventor data*: such as name, surname, address and a unique code (CODINV) assigned by CESPRI to all inventors found to be same person (see below).

The creation of information in category 3 followed three steps, which Lissoni et al. (2006) describe in detail, and we summarize as follows:

- First, the standardization of names and addresses (in order to assign a unique code to all inventors with the same name, surname, and address);
- Second, the calculation of 'similarity scores' for pairs of inventors with the same name and surname, but different addresses;
- Third, the identification (by country) of a threshold value for the similarity score, over which two inventors in a pair are considered the same individual, and assigned the same unique code CODINV.

3.2   National PROFLISTs

Parallel to the creation of the EP-INV database we proceeded to the collection of biographical information on academic scientists in the three countries of interest. The collection effort was directed at medicine, the natural sciences and engineering.

Each PROFLIST comes with highly idiosyncratic disciplinary classification systems (in the case of Sweden we have indeed two classification systems, which overlap only partially, and are not exhaustive of the professors' list). For the purposes of the KEINS project we produced an 18-entry disciplinary classification, loosely based on the French classification system, to which each national classification can be converted (see Lissoni et al., 2006). Similarly, each PROFLIST comes with a different classification system for academic ranks, and it may or may not include non-tenured staff.

Three partner teams were involved at this stage of the KEINS project: CESPRI, BETA and CHALMERS. CESPRI produced the Italian PROFLIST, starting from data already published in Balconi et al. (2004). Those data were based on the complete list of all Italian university professors (assistant, associate, full) active in 2000, provided by the Italian Ministry of Education. A new list, updated to 2004, was obtained from the Ministry. Professors in the two lists did not come with a common code, so CESPRI matched them in the 2000 and 2004 lists by surname, first name, and the date of birth.[4]

BETA compiled a French PROFLIST also based upon ministerial records and similar to the Italian one. The French PROFLIST, however, is the result of separate records for the medical and nonmedical disciplines (only scientific and technical ones). It also refers to tenured academic staff, ranked either as '*maitre à conference*' or '*professeur*' active in 2005.

Swedish academic personnel are not civil servants, so no list of university professors could be obtained from the Swedish Ministry of Education. Ingrid Schild (Department of Sociology, Umea University) took upon herself the task of collecting lists of personnel from as many Swedish academic institutions as possible, and to work with CESPRI in order to standardize and integrate them. Lissoni et al. (2006) provide an inventory of all Swedish universities, pointing out those that contribute or not to the Swedish PROFLIST. Most of the non-contributing ones do not host scientific or technical faculties, and hence the list is quite comparable to the French and Italian one, for the purposes of our research.

A major drawback of the Swedish PROFLIST is that many universities provided lists of personnel that included both tenured and non-tenured staff, and in a few cases even technical and administrative staff. We decided to remove from the original lists the administrative and technical staff, but decided to keep the academic, non-tenured staff, for the main reason that it was not always easy to tell them apart from their tenured colleagues. As for the latter, they come classified according to four positions: professor (full or chair professor), senior lecturer (*'lektorate'*), associate professor (*'docent'*), and junior lecturer or assistant professor (*'forsk lektorate'*). However, individual universities' lists may include some idiosyncratic variations, reflecting either linguistic or organizational specificities.

As a result, we will often refer to all academic personnel in the three countries as professors, by which we mean both professors and lecturers, as well as both tenured and not-tenured positions. This will be done for sake of simplicity and in order to stress that our statistics do not refer to PhD students or post-doc researchers.

3.3   From the EP-INV to the KEINS Database: Inventor–Professor Matching

The identification of academic inventors was pursued in two steps. We first matched inventors from the EP-INV database with professors in the national PROFLISTs, by name and surname, and then sent e-mails and/or made phone calls to the resulting matched professors to ask for confirmation of their inventor status.

Whenever the matched inventor was found to be designated on at least one patent application by either a university, a public research organization, or a non-profit institution – known for sponsoring academic research – we concluded that the professor–inventor match was a sound one (i.e. not a case of a homonym) and could be retained as a 'true' academic inventor, with no need of e-mail or phone confirmation.

For example, in the case of French non-medical professors, prior inspection of the patent applicant's identity allowed the confirmation of 1116 academic inventors and 164 academic co-inventors, for a total of 1148 matches. The remaining 3025 professor–inventor matches had to be checked by contacting the relevant individuals through e-mail or phone.

This in turn required first obtaining the e-mail address or phone number of the professors.[5]

While for Italy and Sweden we managed to check up to 90 percent of professor–inventor matches, the large number observations for France forced us to limit our check only to the professor–inventor pairs whose latest patent was filed after 1993; this was done in order to maximize our chances that the inventors would still be active and reachable. As a consequence, cross-country comparisons based on the KEINS database are most meaningful when based only on patent applications filed after 1993, and on inventors still active after that year.

Table 8.1 report the populations of patent applications, inventors, and professors in the three countries considered, both for the entire period considered (1978–2004) and for the interval over which French data, and related comparisons, are more reliable (1994–2004).

4.   RESULTS

4.1   Academic Scientists' Patenting Activity

Table 8.2 reports estimates of academic patenting intensity in the three countries, as measured by the ratio between academic inventors and university professors active around 2004, in the natural sciences and engineering. The third and fourth column report respectively the number and the percentage of professors who were confirmed to be inventors; the fifth and sixth columns report analogous figures for the professors that did not deny being inventors, that is those that confirmed and those that were either unreachable or refused to answer our questions. In other words, the third and fourth columns provide a lower bound estimate of academic inventorship, while the fifth and sixth give an upper one.

'Confirmed' academic inventors professors amount to over 4 percent of tenured academic personnel in Sweden, where e-mail and phone contacts allowed us to check almost all the professor–inventor matches based upon names and surnames. The same figure for Italy (where e-mail and phone investigations were also very successful) and France is slightly less than 4 percent.

However, French data certainly underestimates the true figure, because the inventor–professor positive matches were so many (and the information provided by universities' website so poor) that we found it impossible to check all matches. So, we decided to concentrate on checking matches that involved more recent patents, and contacted only the professors which our data suggested had signed at least one patent application filed after 1993.

Table 8.1   EPO patent applications, inventors, and professors in France, Italy, and Sweden

	Patents[a] (1978–2004)	Patents[a] (1994–2004)	Inventors[a] (1978–2004)	Inventors[a] (1994–2004)	Professors[b] (active in 2004)
France	114052	53285	98035	51804	32006
Italy	51487	27446	37692	23029	32886
Sweden	29148	15361	25660	14807	12175

Sources: [a] EPO-Cespri database; [b] Ministerial records (France and Italy); own elaborations on universities' records (Sweden)

Table 8.2   Academic inventors in France, Italy, and Sweden

	Professors (n) [a]	Academic inventors (n) [b]	Academic inventors including (% of professors) [b]	Academic inventors, including unchecked (n) [c]	Academic inventors, including uncheck. (% of professors)[c]
France	32006	1228	3.84	1859	5.81
Italy	32886	1268	3.86	1313	3.99
Sweden	12175	503	4.13	530	4.35

Notes:
(a) Professors active in 2004 (Italy, Sweden) or 2005 (France). Professors are defined here as: Assistant, Associate, and Full Professors (Italy); Maitre a conference and Professor (France); forsk lektorate, docent, lektorate and full professor (Sweden).
(b) Data from checked professor–inventor matches (professors confirmed to be the inventors)
(c) All records, checked and unchecked (excl. records for which professors denied being the inventors)

As a result, the gap between the lower and upper estimate of academic inventorship for France is much higher than that for the other two countries (the upper-bound estimate is over 5 percent); this is especially true for patenting activity before 1994 and suggests that international comparisons involving France are reliable only after that year.

From now on we will consider figures based only upon 'confirmed' academic inventors. As shown in Figure 8.1, these academic inventors are responsible for over 2600 patent applications in France, 2100 in Italy, and 1200 in Sweden. Figure 8.1 also shows how figures for France are much higher for the 1994–2002 time interval, over which the KEINS database for France, as said above, is much more reliable.

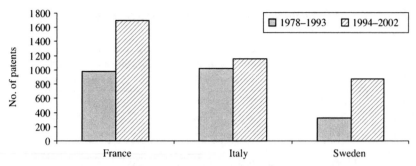

Note: * Academic scientists active in 2004 (further restrictions for France)

Figure 8.1   Academic patent applications, by country, 1978–2002

Table 8.3a shows that in disciplines traditionally close to technological applications, the share of academic inventors may be quite high. In Italy and France, 11 percent and 9 percent of university professors of chemical sciences hold at least one patent application, while figures for engineering and biological science are over 5 percent and 4 percent respectively. Figures for Sweden are similar, although less reliable, due to the absence of a proper disciplinary classification for a large number of academic scientists in our PROFLIST.

The distribution of academic inventors across disciplines also confirm the importance of chemical and biological sciences (especially for organic chemistry, life sciences, and, to a lesser extent, chemical and biological pharmacology), along with engineering and medical sciences (especially for electronic engineering and medical life sciences; Table 8.3b). The distributions of inventors are remarkably similar across countries, the only two notable exceptions being the lower weight of chemical sciences in Sweden (16 percent vs. 27–28 percent in France and Italy) and of the medical sciences in Italy (17 percent vs. 20–23 percent in France and Sweden). The first exception may be explained by the limited importance of chemical firms in Sweden, relatively to France and Italy; the second by a mere classification problem, a relatively large portion of Italian research in the life sciences being conducted in biology departments rather than medical ones.

The distribution of academic patents across disciplines closely reflects that of academic inventors, with both the chemical sciences and engineering collecting around 28 percent of academic patents across the three countries, followed by the biological sciences (17 percent) and the physical sciences (5 percent). This parallel also holds at a finer level of classification and depends upon the fact that the probability of being an academic inventor varies greatly across disciplines, but the average number of patents per

Table 8.3a   Academic inventors as percentage of total professors*, by discipline

Disciplines	Sweden	Italy	France	All
n.a.	3.6	–	–	3.5
Agricultural & veterinary	3.9	1.8	n.a.	2.1
Biological sciences	8.1	4.2	4.2	4.5
Chemical sciences	10.2	10.8	8.6	9.7
Earth sciences	0.0	0.3	0.1	0.2
Engineering	4.5	5.5	5.1	5.2
Math and info science	0.9	1.6	0.6	0.7
Medical sciences	4.3	1.9	4.0	2.8
Physical sciences	5.6	2.7	2.4	2.8
All disciplines	4.2	3.9	3.9	4.0

Note: * Professors active in 2004 (Italy, Sweden) or 2005 (France)

Table 8.3b   Academic inventors*, percentage distribution by discipline

Disciplines	Sweden	Italy	France	All
Agricultural & veterinary	3.7	2.9	0	1.7
Biological sciences	18.3	17.2	18.6	18.0
Pharmacology & pharmacol. biology	7.9	4.1	5.3	5.0
Life sciences (biological disciplines)	4.7	12.0	10.7	10.6
Biological disciplines (others)	5.7	1.2	2.7	2.4
Chemical sciences	15.8	27.7	26.7	26.0
Chemistry (theoretical)	10.2	8.0	4.0	6.5
Organic & Industrial Chemistry	5.7	12.5	19	14.7
Pharmaceutical chemistry	n.a.	7.2	3.6	4.8
Earth sciences	0.0	0.3	0.1	0.2
Engineering	30.0	28.8	26.2	27.8
Mechanical & Civil engineering	6.3	4.7	2.8	4.1
Information & Electronic engineering	16.8	15.1	17.7	16.5
Chemical engineering; Energy	6.9	9	5.6	7.3
Maths and information science	1.9	0.9	2.8	1.9
Medical sciences	22.5	16.8	20.1	18.9
Life sciences (medical)	8.6	7.4	10.5	8.9
Medical disciplines (other)	13.9	9.4	9.6	9.9
Physical sciences	7.6	5.4	5.5	5.7
All disciplines	**100**	**100**	**100**	**100**

Notes: * Professors active in 2004 (Italy, Sweden) or 2005 (France).
The disciplinary affiliation for 192 (38,1%) out of 503 Swedish academic inventors is unavailable, so the latter were not included.

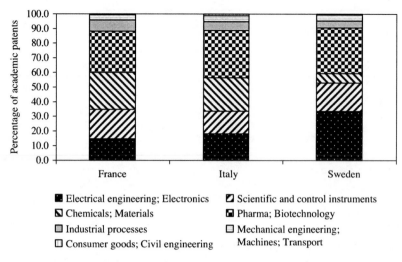

Electrical engineering; Electronics

Chemicals; Materials

Industrial processes

Consumer goods; Civil engineering

Scientific and control instruments

Pharma; Biotechnology

Mechanical engineering; Machines; Transport

Note: * Academic scientists active in 2004 (Italy, Sweden) or 2005 (France)

Source: OST (2004, p. 153)

Figure 8.2   Technological distribution of academic patent applications, by country, 1994–2002

academic inventor is the same across disciplines (in between 1 and 1.5 patents per person).

The disciplines that produce the largest number of academic patents provide inputs to a number of technologies with a strong academic science basis, such as pharmaceuticals and biotech, electronic engineering and chemical technologies, so it does not come out as a surprise that academic patents are heavily concentrated in those technologies. Based upon the DT-7 reclassification of IPC codes proposed by the Observatoire des Sciences et des Techniques, Figure 8.2 shows that over 30 percent of applications are for pharmaceutical and biotechnological patents, while around 15 percent are in the field of scientific and control instruments. In France and Italy, the second most important technological filed is that of chemicals and materials, while in Sweden this position is taken by electrical engineering and electronics.

Being based on the inventing activity of professors who were still active around 2004/05, the KEINS database is very likely to underestimate academic patenting in less recent years, particularly before 1994 (when many French patents by still-active professors are also likely to be missing). Figure 8.3a, however, illustrates a very robust growth of academic patenting and, more interestingly, a change in the technological distribution of

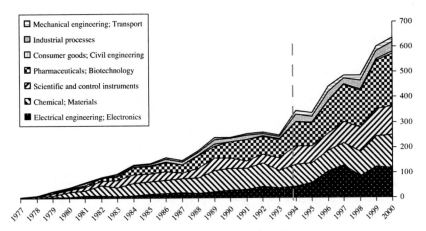

Mechanical engineering; Transport

Industrial processes

Consumer goods; Civil engineering

Pharmaceuticals; Biotechnology

Scientific and control instruments

Chemical; Materials

Electrical engineering; Electronics

Note: * Academic scientists active in 2004 (further restrictions for France)
Technologies defined as in DT-7/OST patent reclassification

Source: OST, (2004, p. 513)

*Figure 8.3a   Academic patent applications from France, Italy and Sweden,
by technology and year*

academic patents over time: older patents are dominated by scientific and control instruments and, to a lesser extent, by chemicals and materials. More recent ones, on the contrary, are increasingly concentrated in the pharmaceutical and biotechnological classes.

This pattern is very similar to the one observed for US university patents by Mowery and Sampat (2005) and reported in Figure 8.3b, which suggests that academic inventors on both sides of the Atlantic contribute to similar technologies.[6]

At a greater level of detail, Figure 8.4 shows the distribution of academic patents across a few selected DT-30 technological classes also proposed by the Observatoire des Sciences et des Techniques, between 1985 and 2000. We notice the increasing weight of biotech patents, the steady share of around 12 percent for pharmaceutical/cosmetic patents, and the decline of organic chemistry (which is the most important of all chemical-related classes). We also notice the growth of the telecommunication patent share; and the importance of scientific instruments.

4.2   Who Owns the Academic Patents?

Figure 8.5 shows that KEINS academic patents represented 2 percent of total domestic EPO patent applications of France, Italy, and Sweden in

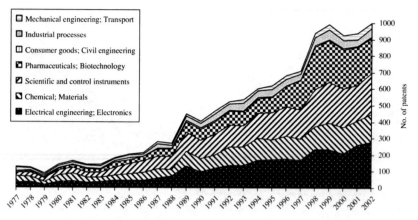

Source: adapted from Mowery and Sampat (2005)

Figure 8.3b   *University-owned patent applications from USA, by technology and year*

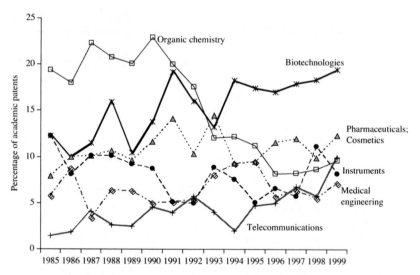

Note: DT-30/OST patent reclassification

Source: OST (2004, p. 513)

Figure 8.4   *Academic patent applications from France, Italy and Sweden, 1985–99, detail of most relevant classes*

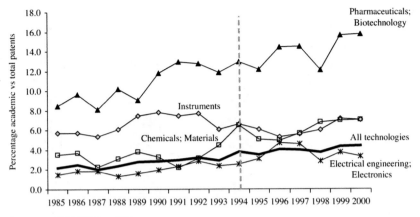

Source: OST (2004, p. 513)

Figure 8.5 *Academic patents as percentage of all patents by domestic inventors, 1985–99, detail of most relevant classes*

1985, and around 4 percent of applications in 2000. Figures for pharmaceutical and biotechnology patents are, respectively, at 8 percent and 16 percent. The weight of academic patents is also quite high in chemicals & materials and instruments.

Figure 8.6 compares the ownership distribution of academic patents in France, Italy and Sweden with that in the USA, as from sample calculations by Thursby et al., 2007. In order to make US and KEINS data comparable, we restrict the latter to just granted patents.

Well over 60 percent of academic patent applications in France are owned by business companies, which also own almost 74 percent of Italian academic patents and 82 percent of Swedish ones; in contrast, business companies own only 24 percent of US academic patents. Conversely, universities in our three European countries own a very small share of academic patents: around 8 percent in France and Italy and less than 4 percent of Swedish ones, well below the 69 percent share in the hands of US universities.

This is clearly the result of the specific institutional features of the various national research and innovation systems. One of these features has to do with the heavy weight, in France and (to a lesser extent) in Italy, of large public research organizations such as the French CNRS and INSERM, and the Italian CNR. In both countries, these PROs administer a large share of R&D funds, which they spend directly within their own laboratories rather than in universities; and even when they engage in collaborative research with academics or fund the latter's projects, there is no law

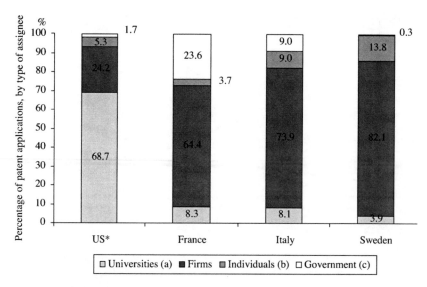

Notes: * US patent/inventor pair data from Thursby et al. (2006)
(a)   US data include no-profit organizations (4.2% of tot obs); all data include co-assigned
        patents
(b)   US data include "unassigned"
(c)   European data include public laboratories
(Missing observations: 58, all for Italy)

*Figure 8.6   Ownership of academic patents by domestic inventors in
                France, Italy, Sweden, and the USA; 1994–2001 (granted
                patents only)*

such as the Bayh–Dole Act to compel them to leave the IPRs over the
research results to their academic partners. As a result, around 24 percent
of French patents are in the PROs' hands (9 percent in Italy).

More importantly, in all of the three European countries considered,
university administrations have much less control over professors' IPRs
than in the USA. In Sweden, where the professor's privilege is still standing, academic scientists often patent in their own name, as witnessed by the
14 percent share of patents assigned to individuals. There is also reason to
believe that, in all countries, several business companies holding one or a
few academic patents have been set up by the academic inventors themselves with the explicit purpose of handling their IPRs.

In Italy and France, professors are first and foremost civil servants,
employed and overseen by the central government; invention disclosure
obligations towards their universities were introduced very recently and
remain unclear, and in any case not paying any respect to them bears little

consequences for the professors' careers. As a result, French and especially Italian professors have been so far relatively free to dispose of the IPRs over their research results (things may have changed recently, due to the emphasis on university patenting coming from central governments themselves; we will come back to it below). At the same time, French and Italian universities used to have so little autonomy from the central government that they never developed any strategy for autonomous fund-raising, let alone any skill in handling IPR matters; until the recent wave of pro-patent legislation, they were happy with leaving all IPRs either in the professors' hands or in the hands of any business company sponsoring or contracting out research with them.

Table 8.4 lists the top assignees of university patents. We notice the prominent position, in France, of both CNRS and INSERM, mirrored in Italy by the role of CNR.

Both in Italy and in France, large state-controlled companies (such as ST-Microelectronics, ENI, France Telecom, and Tales) hold a very large number of academic patents. Large multinational companies located in the country are important in Sweden, too, witness the role of Ericsson and ABB. Notice that among the top patent holders of Sweden we also find an individual professor, with 11 patents. In all of the three countries, we find only one university among the top patent holders (the country-largest universities of Rome-La Sapienza and Paris 6, and Karolinska Institute in Stockholm).[7]

Ownership patterns of academic patents seem to depend also on the disciplinary affiliation of the inventors (and therefore also on the technological contents of the patents). Thursby et al. (2007) find that biotech patents are more likely to be held by universities than electronic ones, which in turn have a higher probability to be held by business companies. We find that this is also the case for our three countries: Figure 8.7 reports combined data for France, Italy and Sweden, in the four most 'academic-intensive' technologies. It shows that business companies own almost 80 percent of academic patents in electronics and electrical engineering, but just a little more than 58 percent of those in pharmaceuticals and biotechnology (where both universities and government hold record shares of 14 percent and 20 percent, respectively). It is worth noting that academic patents in instruments also see a lower-than-average share of business ownership, and the record share of individual ownership (over 9 percent).

Table 8.5 provides a few more details, as it breaks down the four technologies examined so far into 17 smaller classes. The role played by non-business entities (universities, government and individuals) in biotechnology emerges here even more clearly, alongside with the special role of government in nuclear technologies (as one may expect, due to the political sensitivity of the issue).

Table 8.4   Applicants of more than 10 academic patents, 1978–2001 by country

Applicant	Patents (*n*)	Main technological classes
France		
CNRS	220	Biotechnology, Medical engineering
INSERM	99	Biotechnology, Organic chemistry
Total	72	Macromolecular chemistry, Thermal Processes, Basic chemistry
France Telecom	55	Telecommunications
Cea	52	Surfaces, Coating, Materials, Metallurgy
Thales	45	Instruments, Telecommunications, Electrical engineering
Rhodia	40	Macromolecular Chemistry, Materials, Metallurgy, Organic chemistry
Université Paris 6	42	Biotechnology
Adir & Co.	38	Organic chemistry
Institut Pasteur	38	Biotechnology, Organic chemistry
Institut Français du Petrol	32	General Processes
Aventis	29	Pharmaceuticals, Cosmetics, Biotechnology
Alcatel	26	Telecommunications, Electrical engineering, Audiovisuals, Analysis/Control & Measures
Inra	18	Biotechnology
Assistance Publique	17	Biotechnology
Institut Curie	11	Biotechnology
Italy		
ST-Microelectronics	143	Electronic – Electricity
CNR	111	Chemistry – Materials
ENI	97	Chemistry – Materials
Sigma-Tau	67	Chemistry – Materials
Ausimont	51	Chemistry – Materials
Telecom Italia Gruppo	33	Instruments
MIUR	26	Chemistry – Materials
Fidia Gruppo	21	Pharmaceuticals – Biotechnology
ARS Holding	19	Pharmaceuticals – Biotechnology
Optical Technologies	19	Electronic – Electricity
Procter & Gamble	18	Chemistry – Materials
Montedison Gruppo	18	Chemistry – Materials

Applicant	Patents (*n*)	Main technological classes
Università la Sapienza, Rome	18	Pharmaceuticals – Biotechnology
Pharmacia & UpJohn	17	Chemistry – Materials
Sweden		
ABB	151	Electrical Machinery And Apparatus
Ericsson	114	Telecommunications
Pharmacia & UpJohn	75	Pharmaceuticals, Cosmetics
AstraZeneca	40	Pharmaceuticals, Cosmetics
Telia	27	IT
Siemens	25	Medical technology
Karolinska Institute	19	Biotech.
A & Science Invest	17	Pharmaceuticals, Cosmetics
Sandvik	16	Materials, Metallurgy
Kvaerner Pulping	13	Materials processing
Landegren, Ulf	11	Biotechnology

This evidence may have one or a combination of the following explanations. The first explanation refers to how academic research is funded. We observe that the closer a technology is to basic science, the more likely it is that the research programmes are supported by public funds; as a consequence, universities and PROs are in a better position to claim the intellectual property rights over the resulting inventions. Nuclear technology clearly provides the best example, but so does the field of control/measure/analysis instruments, where one can expect many inventions to be the serendipitous results of research programmes addressing fundamental research questions. Notice also the 10 percent difference in the business share of biotechnology vs. pharmaceutical patents, the former being more often the result of public funded fundamental research, the latter more likely to be the outcome of applied research contracts with private partners.

The second explanation is based on the observation that the economic value of a patent depends on its grantee's exploitation strategies. It may be that universities have little interest in holding patents in complex technologies such as all those in the electronics and electrical fields, whose products result from the combination of a myriad of hardware and software components. While one single patent may be enough to cover a blockbuster drug or an instrument, a new telecommunication device or electronic

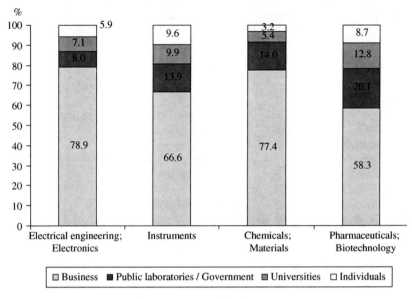

Note: Missing observations: 74

Figure 8.7   Ownership of academic patents, selected technologies, 1994–2001

apparel can be obtained only by assembling many bits and pieces, some of which may be covered by the assembler's patent portfolio, but many more may not. In this case, patents are most valuable as bargaining chips in cross-licensing agreements signed by producers who want to mutually avoid the risk of infringement when it comes to production. But since no university will enter production by itself, it may be wiser to leave the patents in some private sponsor's hands, or to quickly find some business partners willing to buy a national patent the university may have registered, and pay for its European extension.

Finally, the share of university-owned academic patent may depend on national IPR legislation for universities: as explained in section 2, in all of the three countries considered in this chapter, governments have recently encouraged universities to engage in technology transfer, and in patenting in particular. Figure 8.8 seems to suggest that these policies may have pushed universities to claim the property of a large share of academic patents (notice how such share is increasing in all of the three countries). However, it does not seem that the main 'property shift' has occurred from business companies to universities. In France and Italy, the growth of the share of university patents has gone hand in hand with both an increase in

Table 8.5   *Ownership of academic patents, for selected technologies, 1994–2001*

	Business	PROs; Government	Universities	Individuals	
Electrical engineering, Electronics					
Electrical engineering	78.1	7.1	7.1	7.6	100
Audiovisual technology	74.0	6.0	**12.0**	8.0	100
Telecommunications	88.9	3.0	3.5	4.5	100
Information technology	73.6	**12.8**	8.0	5.6	100
Semiconductors	69.4	**18.1**	8.3	4.2	100
Instruments					
Optics	78.3	9.4	6.6	5.7	100
Control/Measures/ Analysis	63.1	**17.0**	**13.1**	6.7	100
Medical engineering	69.4	7.4	7.4	**15.7**	100
Nuclear technology	37.9	**48.3**	**10.3**	3.4	100
Chemicals, Materials					
Organic chemistry	78.8	**12.5**	6.6	2.2	100
Macromolecular chemistry	82.5	9.6	4.8	3.0	100
Basic chemistry	70.3	**15.6**	7.8	6.3	100
Surface technology	70.8	**20.8**	4.2	4.2	100
Materials; Metallurgy	73.4	**20.2**	2.1	4.3	100
Pharmaceutical, Biotechnology					
Biotechnologies	52.2	**26.8**	**14.4**	6.5	100
Pharmaceuticals; Cosmetics	67.3	**10.4**	**10.6**	**11.6**	100
Agricultural and food products	66.7	9.1	9.1	**15.2**	100

Note: Numbers in bold are the technologies with non-business shares higher than 10%

the business companies' share, and a substantial decrease of the share of PROs and other governmental institutions, which may be explained by the gradual loss of centrality of largest PROs such as CNRS and CNR in the public research systems of the two countries.[8]

In Sweden, the (more limited) increase of the universities' share is correlated with a drop of individual ownership, from 30 percent in the early 1980s to 10 percent in 2000, a value that is very close to that for France and Italy. At the same time, the growth in the business share has been much

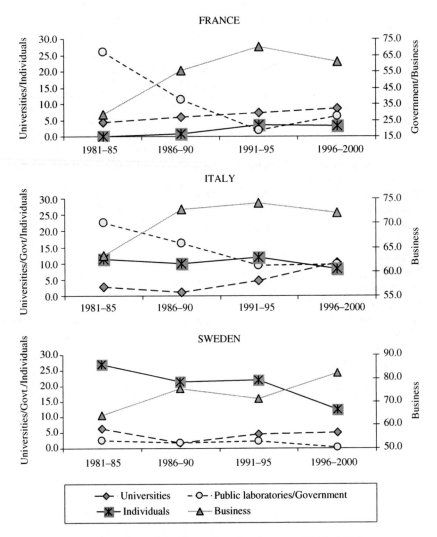

Figure 8.8   Ownership of academic patents, by year, 1981–2001

more robust than the one witnessed in the other countries. One possible explanation for this trend is the increasing diffusion of 'double appointments', by which a scientist's position in the university is subsidized by a business company, whose research the scientist is expected to contribute to.

Measuring the relative importance of these three explanations goes beyond the scope of this chapter, as it requires combining the KEINS data

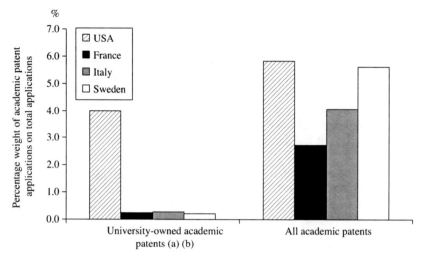

Notes:
(a) US university-owned patents include non-profit organizations (4.2% of total observations); all data include co-assigned patents (source: Thursby et al., 2006)
(b) Estimate of weight of university-owned patents in 1999, from Mowery and Sampat (2006)

Figure 8.9   Weight of academic patents on total patents by domestic inventors, by country and type of ownership (1994–2001, granted patents only)

with information on universities' source of funding, by nature of the funds (public vs. business) and field of destination.

4.3   Academic Patents in USA and Europe: A Reassessment

The different ownership distribution of academic patents in Europe and the USA may explain why, for long, it has been common to underestimate the contribution of European academic scientists to technology transfer through patenting.

In Figure 8.9, we compare the share of domestic patents held by universities (university-owned patents) with the total share of domestic patents of academic origin (university-owned plus university-invented patents), for France, Italy and Sweden. We also make the same comparison for the USA, based upon data from Thursby et al. (2007) and Mowery and Sampat (2005). We limit our calculations to years between 1994 and 2001, in order to make the USA–Europe comparison possible (Thursby's data are for 1993–2000, while our data for France before 1993 are not entirely reliable).

As with Figure 8.6, we focus only on granted patents for comparability purposes.

We notice that French, Italian, and Swedish university-owned granted patents are less than 1 percent of total domestic patents, while, in the same countries, academic granted patents are respectively around 3 percent, 4 percent and almost 6 percent. In contrast, when moving from university-owned to academic patents, US estimates move from 4 percent to almost 6 percent. What appears a huge USA–Europe gap in terms of university patents, turns out to be a more limited gap between the USA and France and Italy on one side, and no gap at all between the USA and Sweden.

Notice that our calculations for the USA are pretty rough, based as they are on a readjustment of Mowery's and Sampat's (2005) estimates for 1999 in the light of evidence coming from an altogether different source, such as the paper by Thursby et al. (2007). What we aim at is simply to give a hint of the different order of magnitude of the USA–Europe comparison one is compelled to think of, once the KEINS methodology is adopted as the proper one for measuring academic patenting.

5.   CONCLUSIONS

The key piece of evidence produced in this chapter can be summarized as follows: universities in France, Italy and Sweden do not contribute much less than their US counterparts to their nations' patenting activity; rather, they are less likely to reclaim the property of the patents they produce.

One reason for this lower propensity has certainly to do with the different IPR arrangements that regulate the relationship between funding agencies (such as the CNR in Italy and the CNRS in France). Whereas the Bayh–Dole Act allows US universities that received funds from the National Institutes of Health or the National Science Foundation to retain the IPRs over the related research results, the same does not apply to Italy and France, where CNR and CNRS (or INSERM) still control those IPRs. Similarly, the existence of the professor privilege explains the role of individual academic patent holders in Sweden.

However, most differences between the USA and the European countries considered here depend on patents owned not by public agencies, but by business companies. These do not depend upon IPR legislation, but on the institutional profile of the national academic systems, and possibly on the national specificities of the relationship between university and industry.

With respect to the institutional profile, it is interesting to notice that both Lach and Shankerman (2003) and Thursby et al. (2007) find that US public universities have more difficulties than private ones to retain IPRs over their scientists' inventions.

US private universities are free to exercise a much greater control over their scientists, both when they recruit them and later on, at the time of negotiating or re-negotiating their contractual arrangements. Therefore, they can impose somewhat tight duties or provide generous incentives to disclose inventions. They also have a long history of active fund-raising, both through commercial activities (Bok, 2003), and intellectual assets management (Mowery and Sampat, 2001).

Conversely, US public universities are less free to set proper economic incentives for their professors in order to encourage invention disclosure, and less able to profit from their patent portfolios and to provide their academic inventors with royalty shares.

By extension, it may be that European universities, all of them public, experience difficulties similar to those of US state institutions, constrained as they are by governmental regulations concerning the remunerations and duties of their academic staff.

Moreover, most public universities in continental Europe have no tradition of self-financing, let alone any possibility of entering into the details of the labour contract they sign with their scientists. They also lack the autonomy enjoyed by large US state universities, such as the University of California and many Midwestern institutions, which are not controlled directly by the central (federal) government, but are under the supervision of boards where representatives of the state sit along with other local stakeholders. US state universities recruit their scientists on the labour market, indeed the very same labour market where private ones operate. In France and Italy, by contrast, academic scientists' careers are entirely regulated by the central government, with little room for independent mobility across universities and wage bargaining. In addition, the administrative staff of universities is entirely composed of civil servants, whose task consists much more in exercising control on behalf of the Ministry of Education, than in helping the universities to raise and manage their own funds. In Sweden, universities are primarily public, with the exception of the foundation-run Stockholm School of Economics, Chalmers University of Technology, and Jönköping University. Both public and foundation universities can recruit their scientists and make independent decisions, but at the same time, both types of universities are subject to extensive regulation and legislation. After the mid-1990s reforms, universities are responsible for their budgets and strategies. Hence, Sweden represents a classic European case, which has made some reforms, inspired from the USA.

As for the role of university–industry relationships, we may speculate that some of our results depend on the nature of research contracts and collaboration agreements signed by universities and business firms. It is also possible that contracts and agreements in the USA refer to more fundamental research than their equivalents in Europe, and thus generate broader patents. Broad patents may be more valuable to universities, to the extent that they may be exploited through licensing-for-royalties, rather than through cross-licensing for production purposes. Our future research plans include investigating these explanations, as well as measuring the value of academic patents (compared to non-academic ones), and evaluating the relationship between individual scientists' patenting and publishing activities.

One policy conclusion we may draw from the data presented in the chapter, and the explanations we provided for them, is that too much of recent policies for technology transfer have been inspired by the wrong presumption that European universities do not contribute enough to the production of patentable technology. The new questions inspiring policy ought to be: Why do European universities not retain the IPRs over their scientists' inventions? Does this phenomenon depend on their relationship with industry and/or with their own academic staff?

In order to provide answers to these questions one should look into the research activities from which the patents whose existence we have uncovered come from: do they originate from research projects, whose results the universities prefer to leave in business partners' hands, possibly in exchange of a lump sum reward? Or do they originate from academic scientists' consultancy to business firms, which escape university administrations' control? How well do these arrangements promote technology transfer? Are they economically viable for universities?

In conclusion, the more we dig into the data, the more we will be forced to recognize that the observed patterns of university patenting in Europe depend much more on the institutional features of academic research and careers, than on the success or failure of IPR reform and technology transfer policies.

ACKNOWLEDGEMENTS

This chapter is also being published in *Research Evaluation* in June 2008; as they have open copyrights, held by authors, all authors also agreed to publish it as this book chapter. The KEINS database and the present papers are part of the KEINS project on 'Knowledge-based entrepreneurship: innovation, networks and systems' sponsored by the European Commission (contract no. CT2-CT-2004-506022). Besides the authors, many other people contributed to the database: Julien Penin and Muge Ozman (BETA-Université Louis Pasteur) for the French section; Ingrid

Schild and Cecilia Yttergren (Umeå University) for the Swedish section; Antonio Della Malva and Christian 'Troubleshooter' Catalini (CESPRI-Bocconi); GianPaolo Ziletti, Samuela Bellini, Riccardo Cropelli, Roberto Giusto and Massimiliano Perini (University of Brescia). The original data on patents and inventors at the basis of the KEINS database come from the EP-CESPRI database, which is also the result of a collective effort: Stefano Breschi, Fabio Montobbio, Lorenzo Cassi, and Gianluca Tarasconi are among those who have most contributed to it. Participants to the KEINS workshops held at the Universidade Técnica de Lisboa in October and at the Max Planck Institut in Jena provided useful comments to successive drafts of the chapter, which also benefited from discussions at the UNI-KNOW/RIDE workshop 'Universities as Knowledge Environments of the Future' (Chalmers University, Göteborg, 11–12 December 2006), and at occasional seminars at the Eindhoven Centre for Innovation Studies and at the Faculty of Engineering of University of Bergamo. Bhaven Sampat kindly provided us with the necessary data for Figure 8.3b. Two anonymous referees also provided useful suggestions for improving an early draft. Responsibility for errors and omissions remains with the authors.

NOTES

1. Introduced in 1980, the Bayh–Dole Act is a piece of legislation which granted to universities all IPRs over federally funded research, including the right to grant exclusive licenses over patents (see Mowery and Sampat, 2005, and references therein).
2. See: http://www.vinnova.se/In-English/Activities/Commercialisation-/The-Key-Actors-Programme/.
3. Attempts to measure the number of academic patents in Germany have relied on the thinner tactic of looking for the academic title 'Professor' in the inventor's field of patent applications. According to this kind of calculation Schmiemann and Durvy (2003) suggest that 5 percent of German patents at EPO are academic (see also Gering and Schmoch, 2003). Finally, a close scrutiny of PATVAL questionnaire data on EPO inventors, has revealed that many inventors of business-owned patents are indeed academic scientists (Crespi et al., 2006).
4. Whatever their rank, Italian professors both in public and private universities are tenured civil servants, recorded for all administrative purposes in the Ministry's list. However, the Ministry does not keep central records of PhD students nor of the numerous contract-based researchers and instructors who populate Italian universities. A comparison of the 2000 and 2004 lists reveal that the latter includes 8305 professors not present in the former, i.e. one third of the 2004 professors were not in the 2000 list. The large majority of these (7823) were indeed nominated after 1999, while 482 were nominated before then, and their absence from the 2000 list is explained by the fact that they were not on active service in 2000 for a number of reasons, such as leave of absence or reassignment to other civil services. The 2004 professors' list was kindly provided by Margherita Balconi.
5. For more methodological details, see Lissoni et al. (2006).
6. Figure 8.3b replicates a similar figure in Mowery and Sampat (2005), albeit with a slightly different classification. While the original data came with a USPTO classification, the KEINS database is based upon the International Patent Classification (IPC), typical of

EPO data. Figure 8.3a results from the application to IPC of the DT-7/OST re-classification scheme (OST, 2004). So, in order to obtain Figure 8.3b and make sure it was comparable to Figure 8.3a, we first applied to Mowery's and Sampat's original data, the USPTO-IPC concordance scheme produced by *IFI CLAIMS® Patent Services* (http://www.ificlaims.com/ifipitx/clsipc.htm), and then DT-7/OST re-aggregation. In the process, we were forced to drop 2422 observations out of 41 773, to which the concordance scheme did not apply.

7. Notice that, as a unique case in Sweden, Karolinska developed an explicit strategy to own patents since the early 1990s. As for Rome and Paris, the number of applications in their patent portfolio, far from being the result of a similar strategy, merely reflects their sheer size: Rome-La Sapienza is the prime example of Italian mega-universities. With a faculty of over 2700 tenured professors in the natural, medical, and engineering sciences, Paris 6 has the largest faculty, in the same disciplines, of all the universities located in the French capital.

8. To such loss of centrality it may have contributed, at least for Italy, the privatization of the formerly state-owned companies that occurred in the 1990s and deprived PROs of important research contracts (see Calderini et al., 2003). We gratefully acknowledge an anonymous referee for pointing out this interpretation of our results.

REFERENCES

Azagra-Caro, J. and P. Llerena (2003), 'Types of contractual funding and university patents: from analysis to a case study', paper prepared for the Knowledge and Economic and Social Change Conference, Manchester, 7–9 April.

Balconi M., S. Breschi and F. Lissoni (2004), 'Networks of inventors and the role of academia: an exploration of Italian patent data', *Research Policy*, 33 (1), 127–45.

Baldini, N., R. Grimaldi and M. Sobrero (2006), 'Institutional changes and the commercialization of academic knowledge: a study of Italian universities' patenting activities between 1965 and 2002', *Research Policy*, 35 (4), 518–32.

Ben-David, Joseph (1977), *Centers of Learning. Britain, France, Germany, United States*, New York: McGraw-Hill.

Bok, D.C. (2003), *Universities in the Marketplace*, Princeton, NJ: Princeton University Press.

Calderini M., P. Garrone and M. Sobrero (2003), *Corporate Governance, Market Structure and Innovation*, Cheltenham, UK and Northampton, MA, USA: Edward Elgar.

Clark, B.R. (ed.) (1993), *The Research Foundations of Graduate Education: Germany, Britain, France, United States, Japan*, Berkeley, CA: University of California Press.

Crespi, G., A. Geuna and B. Verspagen (2006), 'University IPRs and knowledge transfer. Is the IPR ownership model more efficient?', SPRU Electronic working paper no. 154, University of Sussex.

Dosi G., P. Llerena and P. Sylos-Labini (2006), 'The relationships between science, technologies and their industrial exploitation: an illustration through the myths and realities of the so-called "European Paradox"', *Research Policy*, 35 (10), 1450–64.

EC (1995), *The Green Paper on Innovation*, Commission of the European Communities, Luxembourg.

EC (2003), *Third European Report on Science and Technology Indicators*, European Commission, Luxembourg.

Fabrizio, K. and A. DiMinin (2005), 'Commercializing the laboratory: faculty patenting and the open science environment', Goizueta Business School paper series WP, GBS-OM-2005–004, Emory University.

Gallochat A. (2003), 'French technology transfer and IP policies', in OECD (2003), *Turning Science into Business. Patenting and Licensing at Public Research Organizations*, Paris: OECD.

Gering, T. and U. Schmoch (2003), 'Management of intellectual assets by German public research organisations', in OECD (2003), *Turning Science into Business. Patenting and Licensing at Public Research Organizations*, Paris: OECD.

Geuna, A. (1999), *The Economics of Knowledge Production*, Cheltenham, UK and Northampton, MA, USA: Edward Elgar.

Geuna, A. and L.J.J. Nesta (2006), 'University patenting and its effects on academic research: the emerging European evidence', *Research Policy*, **35** (6), 790–807.

Goldfarb, B. and M. Henrekson (2003), 'Bottom-up versus top-down policies towards the commercialization of university intellectual property', *Research Policy*, **32** (4), 639–58.

Henderson, R., A. Jaffe and M. Trajtenberg (1998), 'Universities as a source of commercial technology: a detailed analysis of university patenting 1965–1988', *Review of Economics and Statistics*, **80** (1), 119–27.

Iversen, E.J., M. Gulbrandsen and A. Klitkou (2007), 'A baseline for the impact of academic patenting legislation in Norway', *Scientometrics*, **70** (2), 393–414.

Lach, S. and M. Shankerman (2003), 'Incentives and invention in universities', NBER working paper no. 9727, National Bureau of Economic Research, Cambridge MA.

Lissoni, F., B. Sanditov and G. Tarasconi (2006), 'The KEINs database on academic inventors: methodology and contents', CESPRI working paper 181, Università Bocconi, Milano.

Meyer, M. (2003), 'Academic patents as an indicator of useful research? A new approach to measure academic inventiveness', *Research Evaluation*, **12** (1) 17–27.

Mowery, D.C. and B.N. Sampat (2001), 'Patenting and licensing university inventions: lessons from the history of the research corporation', *Industrial and corporate change*, **10** (2), 317–55.

Mowery, D.C. and B.N. Sampat (2005), 'The Bayh–Dole Act of 1980 and university–industry technology transfer: a model for other OECD governments?', *Journal of Technology Transfer*, **30** (1–2), 115–27.

Mowery, D.C., R.R. Nelson, B.N. Sampat and A. Ziedonis (2004), *Ivory Tower and Industrial Innovation: University–Industry Technology Transfer Before and After the Bayh–Dole Act in the United States*, Stanford, CA: Stanford Business Books.

OECD (2003), *Turning Science into Business. Patenting and Licensing at Public Research Organizations*, Paris: OECD.

OST (2004), *Indicateurs de sciences et de technologies*, Rapport de l'Observatoire des Sciences et des Techniques, Paris: Economica.

PVA-MV (2003), *Report on the Abolition of the German Professor's Privilege: Overview of Changes and Challenges*, Stockholm: Swedish Agency for Innovation Systems.

Saragossi, S., and B. van Pottelsberghe (2003), 'What patent data reveals about universities – the case of Belgium', *Journal of Technology Transfer*, **28** (1), 47–51.

Schmiemann, M. and J.N. Durvy (2003), 'New approaches to technology transfer from publicly funded research', *Journal of Technology Transfer*, **28** (1), 9–15.

218

Learning to compete in European universities

Thursby, J., A. Fuller and M. Thursby (2007), 'US faculty patenting: inside and outside the university', NBER working paper no. *13256*, National Bureau of Economic Research, Cambridge, MA.
Verspagen, B. (2006), 'University research, intellectual property rights and European innovation systems', *Journal of Economic Surveys*, **20** (4), 607–32.

9. The forgotten individuals: attitudes and skills in academic commercialization in Sweden

Mats Magnusson, Maureen McKelvey and Matteo Versiglioni

1. INTRODUCTION

During recent decades, the university as a societal institution has been under pressure to change, in ways relevant for their commercialization activities of starting up companies and patenting. One pressure for change has been that external actors like governments increasingly expect the university to play a central and important role for economic development. Studies have been made on the impact of university research and science on economic growth (for example Salter and Martin, 2001), and on the different mechanisms and channels for knowledge transfer, across different industries (for example, Cohen et al., 2002). Salter and Martin (2001) identify six major mechanisms for diffusion of university research to industry: increasing the stock of useful knowledge; educating skilled graduates; developing new scientific instrumentation/methodologies; shaping networks and stimulating social interaction; enhancing the capacity for scientific and technological problem-solving; and creating new firms. Similar lists can be found in other references. Cohen et al. (2002) show that the key channels for university research to impact on industry are publications, public conferences and meetings, consulting and informal information exchange. A second pressure for change has been the growing demands within the university to find new sources of income, beyond traditional ones of government block grants, student fees (where applicable), and competitive research grants (Powers and McDougall, 2005). Thus, topics such as the entrepreneurial university, university–industry relations and commercialization by universities and researchers have become hot topics, not only in university strategy and public policy but also in academic literature analysing these phenomena. However, much existing literature tends to view commercialization as a strategy and activity for the university as an organization, and one that will increase the economic impact of this soci-etal institution. As such, the literature as well as the practitioners' oriented university strategy documents and public policy initiatives often stress the necessity of building a large-scale support system, such as technology transfer offices, incubators, and the like.

Given this focus on the university level support structures, the individual researcher has mainly been conspicuous by his and her absence. This chapter therefore focuses on an issue which is just emerging in the literature, namely relating the skills and attitudes of the individual researcher to the overall outcome in terms of commercialization.

The question of how and why universities are suddenly pushing to 'become entrepreneurial' has generated much literature, mainly about the American situation but increasingly with insights also about Europe and Asia. According to Clark (1997), universities started to shift from a passive to an active mode regarding commercialization in the 1990s. They are thereby becoming an institution that explores and experiments with different reactions to internal and external demands. The trend at most uni-versities is that commercialization aspects of research are becoming an established part of their activities, and particularly in the biotech sector, university business development emerges as a fundamental component of the value creation chain (Campbell, 2005). One example of this shift is that many universities began to be involved in providing support structures to facilitate such activities, especially consultancy services, patents, licensing and start-up firms which are owned by faculty and previous students. This chapter focuses upon Sweden, partly due to the national institutional context, where Sweden ranks high in terms of R&D inputs (e.g. in the European Innovation Scoreboard 2007). However, the literature about Sweden is fairly divided as to whether the Swedish innovation is perform-ing fairly poorly or performing fairly well, in general and in terms of specific mechanisms (see reviews and differing opinions in Ejermo and Kander, 2006; Bitard et al., 2008; and Ljungberg and McKelvey, 2008).

Indeed, there are many ways and many levels at which to explain and analyse the societal benefits of public science, as developed below in section 2. Commercialization of research is a concept that has a meaning close to a variety of other concepts, especially academic entrepreneurship, technol-ogy transfer, externalities and knowledge spill-overs, and third-stream activities. In this chapter, the idea of transfer of technology refers to the process that permits academic research results to evolve in new processes and products, which can directly influence the development and the eco-nomic growth of society. The concept of commercialization is here limited to comprise patents and start-up companies. While there are other ways of commercializing academic research, these two approaches are the ones that so far have received most attention in commercialization research and practice, and they were therefore seen as the most important to investigate. The literature review provides an analytical framework of the important variables, which is then used to generate specific research questions. The analysis therefore uses a combination of factors at the individual, research group, university level and national institutional context.

This chapter focuses only on the commercialization of university-based science and technology, based on a survey in the Swedish innovation system, as further explained in section 3. The survey was sent to more than 1200 Swedish academics, working within six research fields of natural science and engineering, across different universities and colleges. For each field, at least one research group had received a competitive bidding, public policy research centre, which had the aim of promoting technology transfer as well as high quality science. The survey examines whether and how individual researchers are involved in commercialization, defined in terms of patents and start-up companies, linking the individual to the broader selection environment. The response rate was 24 per cent, with small variations between the different categories of researchers. Section 4 presents the results and analysis and section 5 the conclusions. Section 6 draws out the implications for university strategy and for public policy.

2. LITERATURE REVIEW

Much of the debate and research regarding commercialization has focused around patents and licensing, especially the effectiveness of specific mechanisms, and yet universities interact with society, and impact economic growth, in many other ways. Agrawal and Henderson (2002) found that only 6.6 per cent of knowledge transferred between the MIT departments of electrical engineering, mechanical engineering and computer science could be allocated to patents. The rest take a variety of other channels to communicate the results, including publications, consulting, informal meetings, recruiting, joint ventures, research contacts, and personnel exchanges. Other literature argues that technology transfer from universities is best facilitated by the active involvement of university inventors, and direct academic entrepreneurship is often seen as an effective means to facilitate technology transfer (Henrekson and Rosenberg, 2001; Slaughter and Leslie, 1997). The effectiveness of academic entrepreneurship can however also be disputed. Academic start-ups have been found to have lower performance than non-academic ones, in terms of cash flow and revenue growth (Ensley and Hmieleski, 2005), due to limited team heterogeneity, and then in particular a limited involvement of people with

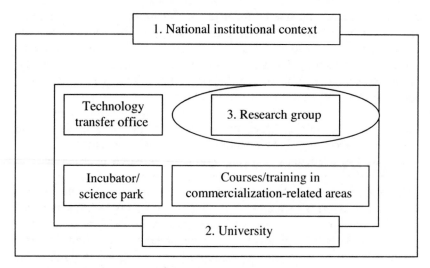

Figure 9.1   Conceptual model of the selection environment affecting
individual researchers

business skills. This ongoing debate about the relative effectiveness of these
different mechanisms for technology transfer is outside the context of our
research. Instead, our main focus here is to place the individual researcher,
within a broader organizational and institutional context. This chapter
therefore looks at the direct commercialization, and places Sweden in relation to literature about the USA and other European countries.

To structure the literature review and the survey, we conceptualize that
the individual researcher works within a specific selection environment.
That environment helps (or hinders) the individual by providing information which helps them to define incentives, mobilize resources, and realize
economic value. In other words, there is an interaction between the
individuals and their environment, which enables them to identify and act
upon innovative opportunities (Holmén et al., 2007). These individual
researchers must act in an entrepreneurial manner to identify, act upon,
and realize their ideas, also within a university context. Or, they may never
do so, because of a variety of 'blocking mechanisms' within their specific
selection environment.

Figure 9.1 illustrates the three main elements of the selection environment, namely the national institutional context, the university, and the
research group and subject within which the individual is active.

Therefore, this literature review is structured around four topics, namely
the influence of national innovation systems, the development of support

structures of universities, the impact of differing research fields, and the role of individual researchers.

2.1 National Innovation Systems, Including Institutions and Public Policy

The broadest level that we identify in the selection environment is the national institutional context. The national innovation system (NIS) literature stresses the need for learning and transfer of knowledge amongst actors involved in innovation. Since this idea can also be found in other theoretical traditions, theoretical linkages can be made about the role of the national institutional context, with the attitudes and actions of individuals. Within this tradition, the national institutional structures have been studied, including aspects such as financing, IPR, institutions, regulation, and public policy. Important issues include different mechanisms to stimulate interaction, learning environments, and the effects of specific policy measures on both interaction and on growth outcomes.

The American case has been widely used as a rationale to change national institutional context in other countries. One specific policy measure has been extensively commented upon, because it created an institutional change in the American system, namely Bayh–Dole. In general, it is seen as a key shift, but there have been debates about the impacts of the Bayh–Dole Act and its effects on university–industry interactions in terms patenting and licensing. The Bayh–Dole Act was passed in 1980 and made it possible for universities to patent federally funded research. Concurrently, the number of patents taken out by American universities and their licensing activities, started to grow and continued to grow sharply during the 1980s and 1990s. While the cause is often attributed to the Bayh–Dole, Mowery et al. (2001) found little evidence for this. Rather, they argue that changes were already under way prior to 1980, and that the sharp rise in patenting can also be attributed to the rise of the biomedical industry (where patents are a common form of IPR) and to the increased federal funding for this area. In addition, the patenting activities of universities were also stimulated in the USA by successful precedence (especially Stanford University and UCSF with the rDNA patent), by court rulings and by a broader shift in federal institutional framework that made it easier to patent research results in the biomedical field.

Without being the only reason for the increase of patents, most researchers agree that Bayh–Dole nevertheless likely hastened the entry into patenting and licensing by additional universities. According to Thursby and Thursby (2002), it increased the propensity and willingness to patent by administrators and faculty in particular. However, they argue that the institutional change did not necessarily lead to more research being commercialized. Rather than increasing the overall amount and distribution of commercially realizable research, the result was that more research results were patented, which led to a lower average quality per patent. This argument is supported by the empirical data which shows that only a very small share of all patents filed by universities make up the lion's share of all their revenues from patenting (Nelsen, 2004). Arguably, this would imply that instead of generating new income streams, many universities have either been spending money in technology transfer offices without substantial returns, or they may in some cases be dependent upon a low number of high-performing patents.

In Sweden, the national institutional context is different. One reason is that the individual researchers own the property rights of their research results, in what Europeans call the professor privilege. Hence, in contrast to the USA, the university does not own the IPR. The individual researcher can, however, choose to assign the rights to the university, in return for partial benefits. Henrekson and Rosenberg (2001) argue that Sweden has a general lack of favourable institutions and pertinent incentive structures that promote the emergence of an entrepreneurial culture. This, they argue is the major explanation for the modest role of academic entrepreneurship in Sweden. A number of other institutional problems that have been argued to influence the lack of academic entrepreneurship in Sweden are: under-developed private equity markets, heavy taxation of entrepreneurial income, and restrictive labour laws (see, for example, Goldfarb and Henrekson, 2001, 2003). Hence, the literature about the national innovation system in Sweden mainly stresses the negative sides of the national institutions.

The American case – and the need for economic growth – has stimulated much debate in Sweden, with the idea of following the American institutional model. Other European countries – notably Denmark in the Scandinavian context – have already done so. The different lines of argumentation in this debate go essentially as follows. On the one hand, removing the professor privilege clause should improve patenting and licensing, as it would increase universities' incentives to be involved in the processes. On the other hand, observers have pointed out that universities have neither the structures nor experience needed for handling this. As a response to this, the important public policy actor VINNOVA has implemented a programme to try to improve organizational capabilities for support structures.

Patenting and starting up companies are the direct and easily observable ways to identify how and when universities impact economic growth. These can also be seen as ways in which individual researchers act less like scientists, and more like businessmen, in terms of owning IPR and even running businesses.

However, this literature also suggests that the specific orientation and organization of the national innovation system will have a broader impact on how, and whether, universities and businesses are able to interact (Lundvall, 1992; Nelson, 1992). More recent work on these lines suggests that the more conducive the national environment and institutional structures are to collaboration, the greater will be the impact of university research on industry. Similarly, spill-overs and externalities are measured through certain proxies of collaboration and of indirect impacts through co-location. These proxies include the amount of co-publishing of university and industry researchers, references made to university research in articles published by industry researchers, and the number of citations to university research in patents. Measuring patent citations in one scientific field, Spencer (2001) found differences in citation rates between Japan and the USA, such that American patents tended to cite papers more often. She attributes these national differences to US policy-makers' intention throughout the postwar period to increase commercial relevance of university research. Also using patent citations, Narin et al. (1997) found that university research has become more salient in patents over time, possibly indicating effects of public policy stimulations to interactions. The results were, however, to some extent offset by changes in US patent reference policies.

In summary, the specific Swedish innovation system provides the individual with IPR, rather than the university, and the implications are that the university has little incentive or expected return to promote commercialization. Moreover, the implications of other research about Sweden suggest that we should observe a low level of commercialization, due to the lack of incentives and lack of entrepreneurial culture. Finally, the broader effects of the national innovation systems and of localized spill-overs are usually measured at the aggregate level, and they are quite difficult to capture at the level of the individual researcher. However, they do suggest that the actors need a positive attitude towards collaboration and technology transfer, before they engage in commercialization activities.

2.2 University Support Structures

The next relevant level in the selection environment is the university, and then in particular its support structures and the typical ways in which the universities interact with society.

This topic is clearly related to the previous one, because different institutional contexts appear to provide universities and colleges with different incentives, legal rights, and rationale to be active in building specific support structures. The question here becomes how and why the universities tend to end up with different structures and mechanisms for technology transfer. Etzkowitz (2003) argues that one important difference between Europe and the USA is that the entrepreneurial university emerged 'bottom up' in the USA in contrast to Europe, where the involvement in commercialization by academia is a recent 'top down' process. Establishing university policies that promote the commercialization of research has been the mainstream Swedish effort to assist academic entrepreneurship or other ways of technology transfer (Henrekson and Rosenberg, 2001). Swedish universities are said to be confronting several problems in the building up of such structures and policies. One view is that the Swedish government has invested lavishly in university research and enacted a set of policies to facilitate knowledge transfer, but it has failed to create a good incentive system for universities and academics to pursue the commercialization of ideas originating in academia (Goldfarb and Henrekson, 2003). Jacob et al. (2003) suggest that a considerable amount of tension still exists between those who see research as a public good and those who focus on the need to integrate university-based knowledge production with the rest of the economy: Hence, how increased commercialization and the new role of university inside the society should be harmonized with existing traditions in teaching and education is still a frequent issue. A clear example of this is that in 2003, the OECD reported that knowledge of patent policies at the university level was not well disseminated among faculty and researchers at public research organizations in Europe.

Moreover, the typical ways in which a specific university interacts with society, may be related to overall indicators of the quality of science on-going. For example, using citations of university research in patent application, studies have found highly cited American academic papers to be selectively cited by American patents (Hicks et al. 2001; Narin et al. 1997). Although patent data is influenced by reference policies set within national institutions, these indications have been confirmed in surveys. Mansfield (1995) showed that the research perceived as most important to industrial technology managers was often directly related to the quality of the university's faculty in the relevant department, and to the size of its R&D expenditures in relevant fields. However, while high quality of science seems to make the university more attractive as a collaborative partner for universities, this does not imply that marginal universities do not interact with industry. Mansfield (1995), in his survey, also found that the relationship between faculty rating and contribution to industrial innovation was so weak in several industries that it seems likely that many modestly-ranked departments play as big a role in this regard as some of the highest-ranked departments. Similar results are found in D'Este and Patel (2007) for the UK case.

Partly because so many other countries wish to imitate the overall American phenomenon, there has been an increasing in interest in how specific universities handle patenting and licensing. Consequently, much literature has come to focus on the role of university technology transfer offices (TTOs), as well as incubators and science parks.

Systematic data has become available for the American context, and increasingly for international actors through professional associations. The Association of University Technology Managers (AUTM) documents the commercialization of university research in the USA. In 2004, AUTM reported that 567 new commercial products were introduced to the marketplace based on licensed technologies from 137 universities and 462 new companies based on an academic discovery were formed in 2004 with an increase of 23.5 per cent with respect to the year 2003 (AUTM, 2004). One academic review of best practices in US universities' TTOs found that the existence of written policies relating to technology transfer practices provides a benefit to learning (Allan, 2001). Di Gregorio and Shane (2003) reached a similar conclusion when studying spin-off rates from US universities, and they also found that university policies of making investments in start-ups and maintaining a low inventor's share of royalties increase new firm formation.

Similar results have been found in the European context. In a survey to TTOs at 57 UK universities, Lockett et al. (2003) found that the more successful universities now have clearer strategies towards the spinning out of companies, and also use 'surrogate' entrepreneurs in this process. In addition, the more successful universities were found to possess a greater expertise and networks, and equity ownership was more widely distributed among the members of the spin-out company. Hence, the result of this line of research stresses that the presence of support structures at a university, such as TTOs and incubators, can increase the chances of successful commercialization and thereby the output of inventions (Powers and McDougall, 2005).

In summary, the national institutional context has been argued to differ in ways which impact on how universities actually build up their support structure. The US model is very much focused on creating incentives for universities to commercialize their research output, allowing them to experiment with the best ways to do that. In contrast, the Swedish model is very much an attempt by the government to directly create mechanisms to facilitate commercialization. The implication of this research would suggest that Swedish university faculty members have limited incentives for commercializing their research and consequently also ought to have less positive attitudes towards commercialization. Moreover, research in USA and Europe suggests that there are very similar, practical mechanisms like partial ownership, which seem to promote commitment and ultimate success. The implications are that the main support structures that individual researchers are likely to use are technology transfer offices and incubators (including various support and consultancy services associated with them). However, attending to the individual researcher level, and not only the university level, these mechanisms need to be complemented with courses in relevant areas like entrepreneurship and IPR, as these are clearly mechanisms that may promote positive attitudes and the learning of relevant commercialization skills.

2.3   Research Groups and Individual Researchers

The third relevant level is that of the research groups, set in relation to the activities of the individual researchers.

Many different characteristics could be analyzed, as relevant to commercialization, but the two main topics are quality and orientation of research. One important characteristic, long found in the debates, is the quality of the new knowledge. Quality of science is a difficult concept, but the indicators of scientific quality are usually quantified as publications, usually published within specific subsets of journals. This reflects a judgement about the output of individual researchers and research groups. At the overall level of the relation to university–industry interactions, most studies report a positive relationship between quality and industrial interactions. Di Gregorio and Shane (2003), for example, found that intellectual eminence (in terms of the overall academic rating score of graduate schools published in Gourman Reports) was related to the number of spin-offs from universities. Work by Zucker and Darby (1996) and Zucker et al. (1998) indicated that star scientists with relevant intellectual capital are more likely to start firms and move into commercial involvement than are marginal scientists, within the specific research area of biotechnology, and later in other areas. These star scientists should remain involved in commercialization, and not just transfer the knowledge to other companies, if companies are to grow quickly.

An issue related to quality and industrial interaction is the research area within which the individual and research group work, and existing literature shows a relationship between specific fields of research orientation and industry interaction. The research orientation is usually measured through groupings of scientific fields or to the extent that research is applied or basic in nature. These two approaches are partly overlapping. The results indicate only small differences in the extent of interaction, but the types of interaction vary depending on whether the university is more science-based or more applied in its approach. Using share of industry funding as a proxy for commercially oriented research, Di Gregorio and Shane (2003) found that higher shares did not increase the rate of spin-offs at least. The findings of Meyer-Krahmer and Schmoch (1998), though, suggests that there are differences in the preferred types of relationships where more applied research seems to call for more contract research. In their analysis of German universities, Meyer-Krahmer and Schmoch (1998) show that university departments within science-based fields, as defined by scientific citations within patents, focus on more basic research whereas university departments in less science-based fields tend to focus more on the solution of technical problems.

A topic that has received much less attention in relation to the commercialization of research is the attitudes and the commercialization skills of the individual researchers. It has even been argued that the academic inventors constitute a black box in theories on commercialization (Göktepe and Edquist, 2006), which needs to be better understood. As noted above, some literature about national institutions and university support structures do, however, make explicit predications about whether individual researchers should have incentives to engage in commercialization.

While the mentioned studies of 'star scientists' (Zucker and Darby, 1996; Zucker et al. 1998) indicate that the single researcher should be seen as a fundamental actor in initiating and enhancing the technology transfer process, there is still limited evidence for this idea on a more general level. This view is hardly surprising as the researchers' intellectual work constitutes the starting point for any resulting finding that may have the potential to be commercialized. Rather, it appears strange that some studies do not explicitly pay attention to the researchers' role in this process, apart from being seen as a detached source of transferable knowledge, something which is strongly questioned in more elaborate theories dealing with knowledge and learning. Based on the widely accepted notion that an important part of knowledge is tacit (Polanyi, 1966) and that knowledge cannot be expressed in its completeness in natural languages, it can thus not be converted to information and moved without the loss of this important tacit part. Hence, knowledge is to some extent contextualized in individuals and therefore has a certain 'stickiness' (Szulanski, 2000). The individual researcher's knowledge is however not isolated from the direct context in which he or she performs research activities, but is at least partly a result of the social interaction with colleagues.

Considering both social and individual types of knowledge (see, for example, Spender, 1996), it is clear that the research group's values, norms and ways of interacting influences the individual researchers knowledge that can be commercialized. The impact of the research group on university–industry interactions in general is often described in terms of quality and orientation of research on-going. Certain scientific and technical fields are more likely to engage in certain types of interaction with industry. More recent work is also beginning to stress the importance of individuals, because knowledge is contextualized within the individual.

The implications are that their actions in regards to patents and start-up companies will be conditioned by their attitude and competencies towards commercialization, as well as by the broader selection environment. Because the likely intensity and mechanisms for university–industry interaction can differ greatly by quality of science and research field, the implication is that the research design should focus on a population of individual researchers which are relatively homogeneous. Within that group, one can then investigate diversity. Moreover, we should expect that the more positive attitudes and more competencies in commercialization that the individual holds, the more likely they will be engaged in commercialization.

2.4 Research Questions

Figure 9.1 placed the individual researcher in relation to three elements of their selection environment, namely national institutions, their university support structure, and their research group. This literature review has gone through these variables in terms of their main findings, and drawn out the implications for what can be expected in the Swedish case. This is a new line of research, previously neglected in the literature, where this chapter explicitly relates the individual researchers' actions and attitudes, to their interpretation of the broader selection environment. In particular, the contribution of this chapter will therefore be to link the attitudes and skills of individual researchers to the commercialization of research findings.

Based on our analytical perspective, and the implications from existing literature, this chapter will therefore address the following three research questions:

- *RQ1*: How to characterize the commercialization activities of Swedish researchers, individually and at an aggregate level?
  - To what extent do they patent and start academic spin-off companies?
- *RQ2*: What are the researchers' attitudes and skills concerning commercialization and their university?
  - What are the researchers' attitudes towards patenting? Towards starting up new companies? Towards their own skills in commercialization?
- *RQ3*: What are the relationships between commercialization activities and the attitudes and skills of the researchers?

3. RESEARCH DESIGN

The research design has been based on our aims both to obtain systematic quantitative data about Sweden and to further develop concepts and theories relevant for understanding the process of commercialization of research results. In terms of developing concepts and theories, the main contribution is our shift to examining and explaining how and why individual researchers' attitudes and skills are related to the level of universities as organizations.

In order to answer the research questions specified above, we have carried out a survey of individual researchers in Sweden. The survey does not target all academic researchers in the country. Instead we have focused on six specific research areas in engineering and natural sciences, to decrease variance across the sample. All the fields are ones in which basic research is performed but where the results lead to specific technological solutions as well. These six chosen research areas have at least one Swedish university which set up a research centre (won through competitive bids) with the specific aims to promote university–industry interaction, commercialization, and more generally, economic growth. We then examined all universities and university colleges in Sweden with a research centre or department in that subject.

3.1 Methodology: Survey

The methodology consists of a web-based survey. The survey was designed after a thorough review of literature, and the aim was to elicit data that would increase our understanding of Swedish academic researchers' involvement in the commercialization of university research. Commercialization was defined as consisting of two activities, the generation of start-up firms, and the generation of patents that are licensed or sold out. In addition, the survey results should help us identify differences between researchers who have commercialized their findings and those researchers who have not been involved in such activities, as related to the three elements in the selection environment. Survey questions therefore asked questions about whether individuals were positive or negative towards different commercialization activities; about how the individuals perceived their attitudes as compared to their research group as a whole; about their knowledge and possible use of the university support structure; and about communication with industry and broader institutions. These questions were included because they represented possible explanations for differences between commercializers and non-commercializers that we identified in the literature review above.

The survey was sent to a little more than 1200 researchers employed at Swedish universities and university colleges, representing a number of personnel categories which can be assumed to engage at least to some extent in research. Six research areas of engineering and natural science were chosen, namely: fluid mechanics, inorganic chemistry, wood technology, computer science, biotechnology and automatic control. We chose them because these are all areas where at least one of the universities hosts a national competence centre. VINNOVA, the Swedish Agency for Innovation Systems, set up these VINNEX Centres, with the explicit aims 'to become an academic, multidisciplinary Centre of Excellence by actively involving a number of companies in joint research' and 'to promote the implementation of new technology and to strengthen the technical competence in Swedish industry'. All other universities or university colleges with centres and departments in the same research area were then identified and included in the sample. Hence, while only one of these universities has a specific VINN Excellence Centre in any given area, the research field per se has been identified as one of interest to companies and to Swedish industry.

Adding together the chosen VINNEX centres with the other major Swedish departments and centres found within the six mentioned research areas, a total of 50 research units were identified, distributed according to the list below. Note that each university may have more than one relevant centre or department in a specific research area. A survey was sent to all researchers of these different departments and centers. For a complete list of units included, see Appendix 9A.

1.   Fluid mechanics (5 departments at 4 different universities)
2.   Inorganic chemistry (6 departments at 5 different universities)
3.   Wood technology (7 departments at 6 different universities)
4.   Computer science (10 departments at 7 different universities)
5.   Automatic control (11 departments at 6 different universities)
6.   Biotechnology (11 departments at 6 different universities)

Before sending out the survey, we initially contacted the head of departments (or research leaders) for approval to conduct it. The survey was performed using a web-based questionnaire, with the initial query and reminders sent out during a period of three months. The data in the database was analysed using SPSS software.

3.2   Reliability

The population is quite large, to be inclusive of these six research areas, and hence the total population was composed of 1219 academic researchers.

Table 9.1   Responses from the different research areas

	Population	Sample (Responses)	Response rate (%)
Fluid mechanics	139	31	22.3
Wood technology	112	29	25.9
Biotechnology	327	80	24.5
Computer science	301	74	24.6
Automatic control	198	52	26.3
Inorganic chemistry	142	29	20.4
Total	1219	295	24.2

The response rate was 24.2 per cent, leaving us with usable responses from 295 researchers. The response rate is thus relatively low as compared to surveys on other topics conducted in Sweden, but about the same rate as surveys on university–industry relations conducted in other countries. Still, some reservations should be made for the comparably low response rate, which most certainly was influenced by the large number of questions in the web-based questionnaire. We therefore analysed for representativeness of the sample, as compared to the total population receiving the questionnaire.

To avoid bias of over- and under-representation of specific research areas, we also checked the response rate by research area (e.g. aggregated for all universities within a specific area).

Table 9.1 thus presents the population, sample and response rates per research area. On the whole, response rates were quite similar, although inorganic chemistry was slightly below the average and automatic control slightly above. Based on the limited variation in terms of response rates from the different research areas, we concluded that the sample was not biased towards any one research area, and decided to use the whole sample.

To avoid bias introduced by the over- and under-representation of specific types of personnel categories, we checked this in the response rate for the population and sample, as shown in Figure 9.2.

As seen in Figure 9.2, the sample is reasonably representative of the different types of jobs found in the population as a whole. The groups which are slightly over-represented are PhD students, postdocs and associate professors whereas the groups slightly under-represented are professors and research assistants. Nevertheless, the differences are small enough to allow us to regard the sample as representative for the whole population.

Obviously, the researchers in the sample, as well as the total population of researchers receiving the survey, work within only six specific science and engineering fields. Hence, care should be taken not to generalize from these

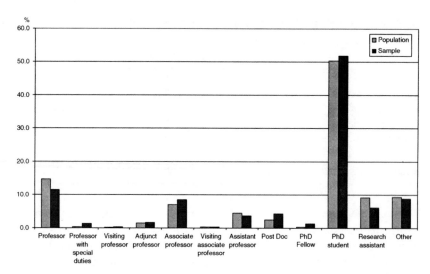

*Figure 9.2   Comparison of sample and population based on researcher
          categories*

fields to all other areas. Generalizations may most likely be possible
towards engineering fields, while it is more questionable whether the
findings presented here are valid also for science fields of a less applied
nature, such as for example, the more fundamental areas of physics.

4.   EMPIRICAL RESULTS AND ANALYSIS

This section consists of three parts. The first subsection answers the questions about how to characterize the commercialization of Swedish
researchers. The second subsection concentrates on the attitudes and skills
of the individual researcher. The final subsection addresses relationships
between commercialization activities and the skills and attitudes of the
individual researcher.

4.1   Commercialization Activities

This subsection addresses the first research question, namely how to characterize the commercialization activities of Swedish researchers, individually and at an aggregate level.

Taking into account all valid responses[1] a total of 23 researchers (8.6 per
cent) have tried to commercialize university research by creating and devel-

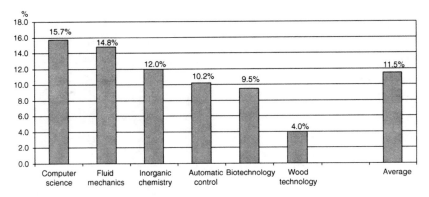

Figure 9.3 Commercialization frequency in different research fields

oping academic spin-offs. To this should be added that another 18 researchers (6.7 per cent) state that they have a stake in a spin-off started by someone else. Furthermore, 40 out of the researchers (14.4 per cent) had obtained patents. Out of these, 16 of the researchers (5.8 per cent) had also managed to sell the patent or license it out. As a number of researchers had used both ways to commercialize, a total of 52 researchers (19.3 per cent) had been engaged in patenting and/or the start-up of a spin-off company. If we only consider the start-up of firms and the patents that have so far been commercialized through sales or licensing, this figure drops to 11.5 per cent. Comparing the data from the different research fields, we note that the commercialization frequency in certain fields appear to be much higher than in others (see Figure 9.3). In the areas 'Computer Science' and 'Fluid Mechanics', as many as approximately 15 per cent of the researchers have commercialized some of their research findings, while the corresponding number for 'Wood Technology' researchers is 4 per cent.

Hence, this subsection has shown that a little more than 10 per cent of the researchers in the sample had directly commercialized their results, either through licensing out or selling patents they had generated, or by starting up a company based on their research findings. Extending the view of commercialization to also include patents that so far have not been sold or licensed out, almost 20 per cent of the researchers had been involved in commercialization. While there is only limited data available on the patenting of academic researchers, we can see that this is relatively well in line with the frequencies presented by Lissoni et al. (2007), which reveal a great variation between different fields of research, but smaller differences between researchers in different countries.

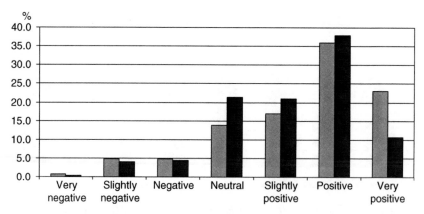

*Figure 9.4a   Attitude towards commercialization, for individual and
           research group*

4.2   Attitudes and Skills, in Relation to their University

This subsection addresses the second research question, namely what the researchers' attitudes and skills are concerning commercialization and how they perceive that commercialization is regarded by their university.

The results indicate that the respondents clearly have a positive opinion towards commercialization. Researchers were asked to respond on a 7-point Likert scale, about their personal opinion and about their perception of the predominant view in their research group. As shown in Figure 9.4a, they tend to give positive scores to commercialization of research results in general, with more respondents being 'very positive' than they perceive their research groups to be. A reasonable interpretation of the latter is that commercialization is not discussed that much and that some researchers may feel that they are more positive to this than they think is seen as positive by their peers.

Figures 9.4b and 9.4c show similar results towards, respectively, patenting and founding a company. From these results we can first of all conclude that more respondents are negative towards patenting than towards founding a company. Note also that a neutral attitude is more common towards these specific mechanisms, as opposed to commercialization in general, both for respondent's personal opinion and for the research group. This suggests that researchers are more positive to other mechanisms of technology transfer, which go beyond the narrow definition of commercialization used here.

Researchers were also asked if they had considered commercializing their research. Here the respondents were given several alternatives and

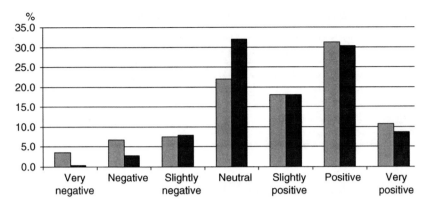

Figure 9.4b   Attitude towards patenting, for individual and research group

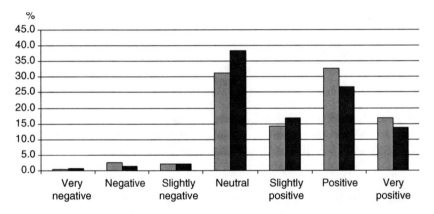

Figure 9.4c   Attitude towards founding a company, for individual and research group

could also provide answers besides these. The results of this are seen in Table 9.2 (percentages are given in relation to the full number of respondents, excluding those who have commercialized their research and the ones mentioning other reasons for not commercializing).

Based on the above, it is clear that many of the researchers have the ambition to sooner or later commercialize their research findings. Which may also actually become reality, given that a large number of the respondents are PhD students who in most cases have limited possibilities to combine studies with commercialization activities. However, we also see that as many as 21 per cent of them do not find that there is time for commercialization activities, and almost 14 per cent state that they do not know how

Table 9.2   Respondents' view on commercializing their own research

Have you considered commercializing your research?	%
No, I do not think that university research should be commercialized	3.4
No, my research does not have any application in industry	14.2
Yes, but I do not know how	13.9
Yes, but I do not have time	21.0
Yes, I am certainly going to	10.5

Table 9.3   Formal training in business and entrepreneurship and perceived ability to start a spin-off company

		Perceived ability to start a spin-off company		
		No	Yes	**Total**
Formal training in business	No	191	61	252
and entrepreneurship	Yes	12	31	43
	Total	203	92	295

they should commercialize it. Looking only at patents, the two most important reasons for not patenting are lack of personal time and resources for doing so, and a preference for publishing instead of patenting, underlining the results regarding attitudes above. The lack of commercialization knowledge and skills becomes even more striking if we look at the researchers' answers to the explicit question whether they actually feel that they have the necessary skills and knowledge to start their own spin-off company. A clear majority (69 per cent) then answered that they believe that at present they do not have sufficient skills to do so. Lockett et al. (2005) argue that knowledge gaps can occur at different levels of analysis, and that we need studies that address this. The results of this study clearly reveal one such knowledge gap, in terms of missing entrepreneurial and business skills.

What can also be seen from the statistics is that formal training in business and entrepreneurship, as well as work experience from outside the university, appear to reduce this problem. There is a significant difference (chi-square test) between individuals who have undertaken formal training and those who have not in terms of their perceived commercialization skills (see Table 9.3). However, formal training is of course only one way to improve individual skills in a practice-oriented discipline such as business and entrepreneurship. Another factor that definitely can make a difference for the perceived ability to start a company is work experience outside the

Table 9.4   Work experience from private firms and perceived ability to start a spin-off company

		Perceived ability to start a spin-off company		
		No	Yes	**Total**
Working experience from private firm	No	165	48	213
	Yes	38	44	82
	Total	203	92	295

university. Comparing researchers with work experience from private firms with the ones who do not have such experience, a significant difference in their perceived ability is seen (see Table 9.4).

Based on the above, we would argue that a substantial number of the researchers may actually refrain from commercializing their research due to their own perceived inability to do so, even if they in many cases have some research results that they consider to have a potential commercial value. It is in this context that the university support structure services are launched, of course, as a way to enable individual researchers to get around the problems of lack of skills and experience with commercialization. Instead of acquiring the skills needed themselves, researchers can to some extent rely on their university support structure for commercialization. This includes services such as technology transfer offices, access to patent attorneys, rent subsidies in incubators, consultancies for business plans and setting up companies, and the like. They help the individual researcher overcome blocking mechanisms within their national institutional context, something which appears logical given the researchers' responses. However, this is based on the possibility of separating the knowledge from the researcher who created it, and also that the specific piece of knowledge is of an explicit nature.

But do the individual researchers know that commercialization is part of the university strategy or that services are provided? Our results suggest that this awareness is limited. Despite the public debate in Sweden, our results indicate that universities may not have signalled their focus on commercialization internally well enough – or that the individual researchers were not listening, if they have signalled it. In as many as 35 per cent of the cases, the researchers were actually unaware of any commercialization focus in the university's strategy. Hence, despite the need for Swedish universities to increase the commercialization and the substantial efforts they put into this, the message does not seem to get through to all researchers. Moreover, many researchers did not feel that they receive support and encouragement from the university to patent or found an academic spin-off in order to develop their results commercially. This problem was also identified by Siegel et al. (2003), who found that the universities' stated strategies and goals in terms of research commercialization were not reflected in, for example, performance evaluations and reward structures. An important question here is thus to what extent it is actually beneficial for the single researcher's career development to spend substantial time on commercialization, as evaluations still have a very strong focus on research and teaching performance.

Summarizing the above, the survey has shown that the researchers in question are in general neutral or positive towards commercialization. Thus, the results show the opposite of what we would expect to see, based on the literature on the national institutional context, in which it is suggested that Swedish academics would be negative to commercialization, due to low entrepreneurial focus and lack of supporting institutions. This subsection also showed that 35 per cent of the respondents did not know about their university strategy for commercialization. While the attitude does not appear to constitute a problem, lack of skills and time definitely seem to be barriers for commercialization. This issue is however at least to some extent possible to tackle with formal training in business and entrepreneurship, or increased possibilities to go back-and-forth between positions in academia and industry.

4.3   Relationships between Commercialization Activities and Individual Skills and Attitudes

This subsection addresses the third research question, namely the relationships between commercialization activities and the researchers' attitudes and skills. Moving from the attitudes of the researchers to their knowledge and skills related to commercialization, we can distinguish two important sets of knowledge skills. On the one hand researchers need to be knowledgeable in their scientific field, and on the other hand they need skills to commercialize this knowledge. As a first step we turn to their scientific knowledge, here measured as number of scientific publications, to see if there is a difference regarding this between the individuals who commercialize and the ones who do not.

The results of the test indicate that there is a significant positive correlation between a researcher's number of publications and the act of commercializing research findings. Researchers who have commercialized their research have an average of 45.8 publications, while non-commercializing researchers on average have 15.4 publications. This seems logical, as the number of publications reflect the amount of research that is performed,

Table 9.5   *Interrelationship between training and commercialization of*
            research

		Has commercialized research		
		No	Yes	**Total**
Formal training in business and	No	181	18	199
entrepreneurship	Yes	25	9	34
	Total	206	27	233

and consequently also the potential for commercialization. However, a number of other factors that are positively correlated with the number of publications, such as for instance the age of the researchers, should be controlled for in order to be able to analyse this interrelationship in a more rigorous manner. What could also be argued against this result is that some publications can take place on behalf of, for example, patenting, and thus to some extent would limit commercialization. Nevertheless, this is in line with the empirical findings of O'Shea et al. (2005), pointing to the mutually reinforcing nature of excellent researchers and entrepreneurial activities at universities. This observation therefore once again points to the importance of the ideas about star scientists (Zucker and Darby, 1996) and indicates that we should regard commercialization as a complement to research, and not as a substitute for it (Etzkowitz, 2003). With more research being performed by skilled researchers, they are also more likely to generate new knowledge that can be commercialized.

A second issue is whether gaining skills through attending courses on commercialization not only influences the perceived commercialization skills, but also actually leads to more commercialization. We analysed attended courses on subjects related to commercialization to see if the use of these courses is correlated with the founding of an academic spin-off and/or licensing or selling of a patent. We conduct a chi-square test on two variables:

- Commercialization, whether an individual has tried to commercialize his/her research, either by licensing or selling a patent or by starting a new firm based on research findings.
- Attended courses in areas of direct relevance for research commercialization, such as for example, business, entrepreneurship and intellectual property rights.

Based on the results in Table 9.5, there appears to be a significant relationship ($p<0.01$) between the two investigated variables. Attending courses on

Table 9.6   Interrelationship between working experience and
commercialization of research

		Has commercialized research		
		No	Yes	**Total**
Working experience from private	No	179	60	239
firm	Yes	16	15	31
	Total	195	75	270

commercialization subject is directly linked with the creation of spin-offs and the selling or licensing of patents. The causal relationship behind this correlation is of course difficult to determine. Either it is the case that researchers who have taken courses related to commercialization are more likely to actually engage in such activities, or it may be that researchers who are considering the commercialization of some research findings, or are already involved in doing so, see a need to attend courses that can provide them with improved commercialization skills.

When comparing the frequency of commercialization between the group of researchers who have working experience from private firms outside academia and the ones who do not have such experience with a chi-square test, we see a similar pattern (see Table 9.6). The group with working experience has a significantly higher frequency of commercialization. This underlines the results from an earlier study by Dietz and Bozeman (2005), in which they found that even modest increases in industry experience influenced patenting rate significantly.

Comparing with the results concerning researchers' perceived commercialization ability, we can note that training and working experience do not only co-vary with a perceived improvement in the ability to commercialize research, but also with actual commercialization frequencies.

5.   CONCLUSION AND IMPLICATIONS

This chapter addresses the skills and attitudes of individual researchers, in relation to the commercialization of academic research.

The results and analysis above can be summarized as follows, thereby providing the answers to our three research questions. First of all, we note that a little more than 10 per cent of the respondents have actually commercialized their research, either in the form of starting a company or by generating patents that have been licensed or sold out. Taking into consideration also patents that so far have not come into commercial use, this figure rises to almost 20 per cent.

With regards the researchers' attitudes towards commercialization activities, it is seen that most researchers are positive to it and that only few of them are negative. It can be noted that they are more positive towards commercialization in general than towards patenting, implying that there are sometimes conflicting interests between publishing and patenting.

While attitudes towards commercialization were in general positive or very positive, and thus ought not to constitute a major issue, the perceived lack of commercialization skills is definitely a barrier to realizing the potential economic value of academic research results. The reasons for not commercializing that were brought forward were primarily lack of time and commercialization know-how. In particular, the lack of skills needed for starting spin-off firms appear to be a significant barrier to this kind of commercialization. Very few of the researchers felt that they had the necessary skills to start up a spin-off company on their own, which may explain part of the lack of commercialization actions. Another result that underscores this is that among researchers who had actually commercialized some of their findings, there was as significant over-representation of the ones who had taken courses in commercialization-related matters or had previous experience from working in firms outside the university.

What the causality behind these correlations looks like is difficult to say based on the data at hand. Either persons who are more interested in commercialization follow such courses, or people who get engaged in commercialization activities become aware of the need to improve their skills in this field. One thing that argues against the latter is that opinions about commercialization in general are positive among the researchers, and that the decision to commercialize thus ought to be more a matter of skills than attitude.

Based on the empirical observations, we fully agree with Lockett et al. (2005) that many researchers who are willing to commercialize their research are not capable of doing so, and that it is important to distinguish between the researchers who are willing to commercialize their research and the ones who are capable of doing it. However, apart from finding the ones with the appropriate skills, an even more important task is to make sure that more researchers who want to commercialize their research are also given the possibility to develop their business skills, for example through training programmes or periods in industry. As described by O'Shea et al. (2007), entrepreneurship development programmes at different levels are for instance, a fundamental part of the commercialization activities at MIT. This component is still missing at many universities, and this gap needs to be filled to enable other parts of the commercialization support system to work well. An alternative approach to deal with the problem of researchers lacking commercial skills is that they should more frequently take on a more technical role in their ventures and let more business-oriented individuals lead the spin-off (Lockett et al., 2005), possibly in combination with hiring more researchers with industrial experience, as suggested by Dietz and Bozeman (2005).

Furthermore, it was found that the knowledge among researchers about the universities' strategies and ambitions for commercialization is limited. A substantial number of the respondents did not know about their existence, which points to a need for more and clearer communication from university management regarding this aspect, and to assure that these strategies are reflected in actions. Just like Siegel et al. (2003), we see that one important way of facilitating commercialization of academic research is to align the performance evaluation systems at universities with the desire to commercialize more research, for example, by considering commercialization experience and skills in promotions and hiring. We can conclude that the strategies of many universities in their ambitions to commercialize more of the research findings put much emphasis on support structures that can facilitate commercialization initiatives once they have started, while they do not attend sufficiently to the genesis of research commercialization, which is more dependent on the attitudes and skills of individual researchers. This appears to be a particularly challenging issue in Sweden, where the professor privilege assigns the IPR of research findings to individual researchers and thus make it even more necessary that the individual researcher is both willing and able to take the first steps towards commercialization.

Our results can be put in context of the public debate, because we provide a very different focus. With the exception of a few vocal critics, our interpretation of the assumptions underlying the debates can be summarized as follows: Universities should commercialize more, so that society benefits more, and (the latter point has recently, at least to some extent, been questioned, give the observed costs and benefits of TTOs) universities generate new income streams. Often, the assumption has been that individual researchers choose not to, and are not good at, commercialization, and that universities and government agencies should focus on building university-specific support structures, especially for the handling of patents and intellectual property rights (IPR). While such structures play an important role in the process of commercializing research results, they are not always useful when the knowledge in question cannot be separated from the researchers who have created it. In accordance with O'Shea et al. (2007), we thus see a need for holistic approaches to research commercialization, looking at individuals, organizational features, culture and the external environment together to understand what can be fruitful ways forward, instead of focusing on emulating single aspects of well-known successful cases like MIT.

Our findings suggest that the impact of the university support structure may have been inflated. In contrast, other aspects of this process, and in particular the individual researchers being the holders of contextual and tacit knowledge and the genesis of innovations, have received too little attention. This highlights the possibilities of impacting on commercialization activities by influencing the attitudes and actions of individual researchers, through the use of various means.

Consequently, an increased focus on preparing researchers for these activities by providing training and increasing the possibilities of combining an academic career with work in companies stand out as two possible mechanisms to ameliorate the situation. A final implication is the need for universities to communicate their ambitions and strategies to commercialize research more extensively, something which actually by itself could raise the awareness and willingness to participate in commercialization activities.

ACKNOWLEDGEMENTS

The authors would like to thank Susanne Rudeke and Aliaksandr Stsefanin for their valuable assistance in designing the survey and analysing parts of the data, respectively.

The authors have been associated with the RIDE research network, financed by VINNOVA, during the work on this chapter.

NOTE

1. The percentage of researchers commercializing is not the sum of researchers patenting and of researchers starting spin-off companies, because some researchers have engaged in both activities.

REFERENCES

Agrawal, A. and R. Henderson (2002), 'Putting patents in context: exploring knowledge transfer from MIT', *Management Science*, **48** (1), 44–60.
Allan, M.F. (2001), 'A review of best practices in university technology licensing offices', *Journal of the Association of University Technology Managers*, **13**, 57–69.
Association of University Technology Managers (AUTM) (2004), 'AUTM U.S. Licensing Survey: FY 2004', accessed 11 August, 2006 at www.autm.net.
Bitard, P., C. Edquist, L. Hommen and A. Rickne (2008), 'Reconsidering the paradox of high R&D and low innovation: Sweden', in Charles Edquist and Leif

Hommen (eds), *Small Country Innovation Systems. Globalization, Change and Policy in Asia and Europe*, Cheltenham, UK and Northampton, MA, USA: Edward Elgar.

Campbell, A. F. (2005), 'The evolving concept of value add in university commercialization', *Journal of Commercial Biotechnology*, **11** (4), 337–45.

Clark, B. (1998), *Creating Entrepreneurial Universities: Organizational Pathways of Transformation*, Oxford: IAU Press and Pergamon.

Cohen, W. M., R.R. Nelson and J.P. Walsh (2002), 'Links and impacts: the influence of public research on industrial R&D', *Management Science*, **48** (1), 1–23.

D'Este, P. and P. Patel (2007), 'University–industry linkages in the UK: what are the factors underlying the variety of interactions with industry?', *Research Policy*, **36** (9), 1295–313.

Di Gregorio, D. and S. Shane (2003), 'Why do some universities generate more start-ups than others?', *Research Policy*, **32** (2), 209–27.

Dietz, J. S. and B. Bozeman (2005), 'Academic careers, patents, and productivity: industry experience as scientific and technical human capital', *Research Policy*, **34**, 349–67.

Ejermo, O. and A. Kander (2006), 'The Swedish paradox', CIRCLE electronic working paper series WP2006/1.

Ensley, M.D. and K.M. Hmieleski (2005), 'A comparative study of new venture top management team composition, dynamics and performance between university-based and independent start-ups', *Research Policy*, **34**, 1091–105.

Etzkowitz, H. (2003), 'Research groups as "quasi-firms": the invention of the entrepreneurial university', *Research Policy*, **32**, 109–21.

Göktepe, D. and C. Edquist (2006), 'A comparative study of university scientists' motivations for patenting: a typology of university inventors', paper presented at the SPRU 40th Anniversary Conference, 11–13 September 2006, University of Sussex.

Goldfarb, B. and M. Henrekson (2003), 'Bottom-up versus top-down policies towards the commercialization of university intellectual property', *Research Policy*, **32** (4), 639–58.

Goldfarb, B., M. Henrekson and N. Rosenberg (2001), 'Demand vs. supply driven innovations: US and Swedish experiences in academic entrepreneurship', Stanford Institute for Economic Policy Research discussion paper no. 00–35.

Henrekson, M. and N. Rosenberg (2001), 'Designing efficient institutions for science-based entrepreneurship: lessons from the US and Sweden', *Journal of Technology Transfer*, **26** (3), 207–31.

Hicks, D. (2007), 'University system research evaluation in Australia, the UK and US', Georgia Tech working paper series no. 27.

Hicks, D., T. Breitzman, D. Olivastro and K. Hamilton (2001), 'The changing composition of innovative activity in the US – a portrait based on patent analysis, Research Policy, 30(4), 681–703.

Holmén, M., M. Magnusson and M. McKelvey (2007), 'What are innovative opportunities?', *Industry and Innovation*, **14** (1), 27–45.

Jacob, M., M. Lundqvist and H. Hellsmark (2003), 'Entrepreneurial transformations in the Swedish University system: the case of Chalmers University of Technology', *Research Policy*, **32**, 1555–68.

Lissoni, F., P. Llerena, M. McKelvey and B. Sanditov (2007), 'Academic patenting in Europe: new evidence from the KEINs database', CESPRI working paper no. 202.

Ljungberg, D. (2008), 'Structural differences in competitive research funding and industry interaction', thesis for degree of licentiate, Chalmers University of Technology, Gothenburg, Sweden.

Lockett, A., M. Wright and S. Franklin (2003), 'Technology transfer and universities' spin-out strategies', *Small Business Economics*, **20** (2), 185–200.

Lockett, A., D. Siegel, M. Wright and M.D. Ensley (2005), 'The creation of spin-off firms at public research institutions: managerial and policy implications', *Research Policy*, **34**, 981–93.

Lundvall, B.-A. (1992), 'National systems of innovation–introduction', in Bengt-Åke Lundvall (ed.), *National Systems of Innovation: Towards a Theory of Innovation and Interactive Learning*, London: Pinter Publishers.

Mansfield, E. (1995), 'Academic research underlying industrial innovations: sources, characteristics, and financing', *Review of Economic Statistics*, **77** (1), 55–65.

Meyer-Krahmer, F. and U. Schmoch (1998), 'Science-based technologies: university–industry interaction in four fields', *Research Policy*, **27**, 835–851.

Mowery, D.C., R.R. Nelson, B.N. Sampat and A.A. Ziedonis (2001), 'The growth of patenting and licensing by U.S. universities: an assessment of the effects of the Bayh–Dole Act of 1980', *Research Policy*, **31**, 99–119.

Narin, F., K. Hamilton and D. Olivastro (1997), 'The increasing linkage between US technology and public science', *Research Policy*, **26**, 317–30.

Nelsen, L.L. (2004), 'A US Perspective on technology transfer: the changing role of the university', *Nature Review Molecular Cell Biology*, **5** (3), 243–7.

Nelson, R.R. (1992), 'National innovation systems: a retrospective on a study', *Industrial and Corporate Change*, **1** (2), 347–74.

O'Shea, R.P., T.J. Allen, A. Chevalier and F. Roche (2005), 'Entrepreneurial orientation, technology transfer and spinoff performance of U.S. universities', *Research Policy*, **34**, 994–1009.

O'Shea, R.P., T.J. Allen, K.P. Morse, C. O'Gorman and F. Roche (2007), 'Delineating the anatomy of an entrepreneurial university: the Massachusetts Institute of Technology experience', *R&D Management*, **37** (1), 1–16.

Polanyi, M. (1966), *The Tacit Dimension*, London: Routledge & Kegan Paul.

Powers, J.B. and P.P. McDougall (2005), 'University start-up formation and technology licensing with firms that go public: a resource-based view of academic entrepreneurship', *Journal of Business Venturing*, **20**, 291–311.

Salter, A.J. and B.R. Martin (2001), 'The economic benefits of publicly funded basic research: a critical review', *Research Policy*, **30**, 509–32.

Siegel, D.S., D. Waldman and A. Link (2003), 'Assessing the impact of organizational practices on the relative productivity of university technology transfer offices: an exploratory study', *Research Policy*, **32**, 27–48.

Slaughter, Sheila and Larry L. Leslie (1997), *Academic Capitalism: Politics, Policies, and the Entrepreneurial University*, Baltimore, MD and London: Johns Hopkins University Press.

Spencer, J.W. (2001), 'How relevant is university-based scientific research to private high-technology firms? A United States–Japan comparison', *Academy of Management Journal*, **44** (2), 432–40.

Spender, J.-C. (1996), 'Making knowledge the basis of a dynamic theory of the firm', *Strategic Management Journal*, **17**, 45–62.

Szulanski, G. (2000), 'The process of knowledge transfer: a diachronic analysis of stickiness', *Organizational Behavior and Human Decision Processes*, **82** (1), 9–27.

Thursby, J.G. and M.C. Thursby (2002), 'Who is selling the ivory tower? Sources of growth in university licensing', *Management Science*, **48** (1), 90–104.

Zucker, L.G. and M.R. Darby (1996), 'Star scientists and institutional transformation: patterns of invention and innovation in the formation of the biotechnology industry', *Proceedings of the National Academy of Science of the United States of America*, **93** (12 November), 709–16.

Zucker, L.G., M.R. Darby and M.B. Brewer (1998), 'Intellectual human capital and the birth of U.S. biotechnology enterprises', *American Economic Review*, **88** (1), 290–306.

APPENDIX 9A: DEPARTMENTS INCLUDED IN THE STUDY

1. Fluid Mechanics

Chalmers University of Technology (combustion and multiphase flow)
Royal Institute of Technology (internal combustion engines)
Lund University (combustion engines; continuum mechanics)
Luleå Technical University (energy technology)

2. Inorganic Chemistry

Chalmers University of Technology (SCI)
Royal Institute of Technology (materials process technology; physical metallurgy)
Luleå Technical University (materials science centre)
Stockholm University (inorganic chemistry)
Uppsala University (ångström materials chemistry)

3. Wood Technology

Chalmers University of Technology (forest products/chemical engineering)
Royal Institute of Technology (wood chemistry/pulp technology)
Swedish Agricultural University (wood science)
Växjö University (forest/wood technology)
Karlstad University (pulp technology, paper technology)
Luleå Technical University (wood technology)

4. Computer Science

Chalmers University of Technology (applied software; programming logic)
Royal Institute of Technology (software development)
Luleå Technical University (mobile networking/computing)
Uppsala University (computing science, computer systems)
Mälardalens University (Computer Engineering)
Lund University (LUCAS; Computer Science)
Linköping University (PELAB)

5. Automatic Control

Chalmers University of Technology (Automatic Control Group; Automation Research Group)

Royal Institute of Technology (Automatic Control)
Luleå Technical University (Control Engineering)
Uppsala University (Systems and Control)
Lund University (Automatic Control)
Linköping University (Control and Communication; Real-Time Systems; Theoretical Computer Systems; Vehicular Systems; Embedded Systems)

6. Biotechnology

Chalmers University of Technology (Chemical Reaction Engineering)
Royal Institute of Technology (Chemical Engineering; Energy Processes)
Luleå Technical University (Chemical Engineering)
Uppsala University (Biochemistry; Separation Technology)
Lund University (Biotechnology; Biochemistry; Applied Biochemistry; Chemical Engineering)
Linköping University (Biochemistry)

10. Elite European universities and the R&D subsidiaries of multinational enterprises

Anders Broström, Maureen McKelvey and Christian Sandström

1. INTRODUCTION

Open innovation, research and development activities (R&D) as well as science are recognized as very important prerequisites for many types of corporate innovations. As noted by Tidd et al. (2001), 'it would be hard to find anyone prepared to argue against the view that innovation is important and likely to be more so in the coming years'. Following both academic studies and the examples set by regional success stories such as Silicon Valley or the two Cambridges, many have argued that higher education and public research activities of a region also increase its attractiveness for private investments (Anselin et al., 1997; Davies and Meyer, 2004; Furman et al., 2005). Consequently public policy-makers are trying to find ways to encourage locally based cooperative relationships, often seeing the university sector as the engine for growth.[1] This chapter therefore addresses the workings and the benefits of university–industry interactions between global firms and leading research universities in Europe.

Specifically, this chapter will analyse firms which are R&D subsidiaries of MNEs. Our specific focus here is the role of elite universities within regions, which may be wishing to attract more foreign direct investment within R&D and multinational innovation activities, in order to compete. This study therefore draws upon results from two fairly separate bodies of literature addressing our topic, namely international business and innovation, as further discussed in section 2. Section 3 addresses research design and methodology. Of all firms located around a university, R&D-performing subsidiaries of multinational enterprises (MNEs) with substantial R&D activities seem particularly likely to benefit from the university's R&D capacity, as they have the resources necessary to exploit such opportunities (Cantwell and Piscitello, 2005). In fact, while academic knowledge production is attributed with an important role for economic growth in advanced economies, only a limited fraction of all firms regard direct contacts to universities a major factor for innovation (von Hippel, 1988). Empirically we examine 16 firms which collaborate with three European research universities. The firms are subsidiaries of multinational enterprises with headquarters located in a different country,[2] although some of the firms in our population have been acquired by foreign firms. These firms are located close to and have formal alliances with the following universities, respectively, Karolinska Institutet in Stockholm, Sweden; ETH Zurich in Switzerland; and Cambridge University in the United Kingdom.

Section 4 presents the results at an aggregate level, and section 5 presents the results in terms of four ideal types, and illustrative case studies, which are presented from the perspective of the firm. From this, section 6 discusses the role of European elite universities within the regions in order to outline some alternative strategies for policy-makers and university leaders interested in stimulating university–industry interaction.

2. R&D LOCALIZATION AND UNIVERSITY–INDUSTRY LINKAGES

This section considers relevant literature from international business and from innovation studies, including parts of economics.

2.1 R&D as Part of International Businesses

Within the international business literature, many studies explore topics such as the mechanisms behind the MNEs' choice to locate R&D, the reliance on R&D outside the boundaries of the firm, and increasingly the outsourcing and offshoring of R&D. The decisions of MNEs to locate R&D activities to a region outside their country of origin have been explained by the possibility of benefiting from localized flows of knowledge, with universities as a particularly important source (Dunning, 1994; Kuemmerle, 1999). Moreover literature has identified two trends in the reorganization of corporate R&D activities, namely (1) increasing globalization of R&D spending patterns and (2) increasing reliance upon external organizations, such as networks and outsourcing. While many studies have examined American university–industry interactions, a few have examined European ones, such as Davies and Meyer (2004).

These studies thus provide insight into why MNEs behave globally to access new knowledge and markets, and only occasionally provide particular focus on universities per se. Hence while studies of the localization of MNE R&D often state that 'access to knowledge infrastructure' of a certain region is a factor of locational advantage, the questions of how and why firms benefit from such access often remain unanswered. The specific role of research universities is also not explicitly studied to a large extent in this management-oriented literature. Furthermore our research question diverges from the dominant stream of literature, in that we study the immediate proximity (NUTS3-region) of three European renowned research universities. Other studies generally deal with differences between locations on a country level, or in large regions within a specific country (Heimann, 2005 and Cantwell and Piscitello, 2005, constitute notable exceptions from this observation).

The globalization of MNE R&D is accompanied by corresponding changes in corporate organization. In recent years, even larger firms have abandoned central R&D functions in favour of R&D tied to products or divisions or else they have imposed greater demands on central R&D functions coordinating their research agenda with division- and product managers (Gerybadze and Reger, 1999). As a consequence the room for 'blue sky' research from corporate budgets has shrunk significantly which makes the need for managed relations with universities and to academic research increasingly important.

The literature offers a rather large number of motives for why MNEs internationalize R&D. According to Chiesa (1996), a more dispersed corporate R&D structure is usually associated with a longer time horizon of research activities. Furthermore the structure also seems to depend on the degree of dispersion of (industry- and firm-specific) external sources of knowledge and the degree of dispersion of the key internal R&D resources. Gerybadze and Reger (1999) emphasize market characteristics of the foreign location, as for example regulatory designs and sophisticated customer demands that can provide impulses for 'global' innovation. Dunning (2000) claims that the OLI-framework which suggests that decisions about foreign direct investments are driven by factors of ownership, location and internalization can be generalized to R&D activities. In Dunning's framework, ownership-specific advantages let the firm exploit its assets whereas location-specific advantages enable the firm to exploit local capabilities and internalizing advantages are related to enhancing the knowledge base.

This literature strongly suggests that a region's attractiveness for R&D investments of MNEs is affected by (1) local market characteristics, (2) presence of scientific and educational infrastructure and (3) the presence of other R&D-performing firms (Cantwell and Piscitello, 2002, 2005). A number of studies highlight that a market's size and the business opportunities offered there may not be the only determinants of its attractiveness.

Gerybadze and Reger (1999) find that locational choices in some cases are affected by a need to work in 'lead markets' where impulses for innovation can be picked up and create advantages in other markets of the MNE. While earlier studies emphasized market factors (Ronstadt, 1978, Teece, 1976), more recent studies stress factors related to knowledge and knowledge flows. Narula and Zanfei (2005) related this development to two pressures. One is an increasing innovation pressure in the form of increasing cost and complexity of technological development and shorter product cycles and the other pressure is from public customers to locate R&D in their region.

Kuemmerle (1999) contributed to the analysis of MNE R&D location by differentiating between 'home-base augmenting' subsidiaries and 'home-base exploiting' subsidiaries. For the former type of subsidiaries whose purpose are related to the adaptation of existing assets to local prerequisites, output and input indicators of R&D and science are found to determine the attractiveness of a location (country). For the home-base exploiting type of subsidiaries the attractiveness of a country's market determines its attractiveness as R&D location. LeBas and Sierra (2002) offer a somewhat expanded taxonomy of four strategies explaining why a MNE locates R&D to a certain location. In addition to 'home-base exploiting' and 'market-seeking' (market access, etc.), the authors identify two types of strategies related to knowledge flows: 'home-base augmenting', which is complementary R&D to that done at the home-base, and 'technology-seeking' strategies which is R&D that the firm, given its technological level and that of its home-location, is not able to perform otherwise. In their empirical study, LeBas and Sierra find that technology-seeking strategies are not common in Europe.

Further evidence on the motives to locate foreign-owned R&D subsidiaries in Europe is presented by Criscuolo et al. (2005). They find that US MNEs in Europe do not have a tendency towards either one but strike a balance between both types of activities. The exception is the pharmaceutical industry, which is dominated by exploitation activities. Similarly European MNE subsidiaries in the USA are found to be dominated by exploitation for all five industries investigated. Simultaneous exploitation and augmentation in R&D subsidiaries is also reported by Kuemmerle (2002).

2.2 Role of Universities in Innovation

Within the innovation literature as well as parts of economics, we can find taxonomies for university–industry interaction per se as well as explanations of the linkages between knowledge spill-overs and regional growth.

University–industry relationships are the subject of a huge number of studies, especially focusing on commercialization as patents and start-up companies (Mowery and Sampat, 2005). Other studies address the mechanisms and rationale for university–industry relationships within different countries and sectors, the differential importance of applied and basic research within different industries, and the importance of universities within regional clusters (Feldman, 1994; Mansfield, 1998; Salter and Martin, 2001). These studies thus provide insight into how university–industry relationships work and the effects on regional growth, but only occasionally provide insight into corporate strategy.

R&D-investment decisions dominated by knowledge-seeking/asset augmenting motives are increasingly focused on very few locations described by Meyer-Krahmer and Reger (1999) as 'worldwide centers of excellence'. Such excellence is generally meant to be measured in the form of input factors such as skilled labour and R&D spending and output factors such as patents, publications, innovation-related exports etc. These factors are generally found to attract foreign investment (Chung and Alcácer, 2002). However it is interesting to note that Almeida and Phene (2004), in their analysis of subsidiaries of MNEs in the semi-conductor industry, do not find any proximity benefits on innovation from shear strength in innovation (as measured by a country's share of annually awarded patents) but do find that the diversity of a country's science base (as measured by a division of 20 patent classes) significantly contributes to proximity effects on innovation.

Adams (2002) and Arundel and Geuna (2004) both find that proximity is more important for the exploitation of academic R&D than industry R&D. Davies and Meyer (2004) investigate four aspects of local business environments and find that only the presence of scientific institutions has a consistent, positive effect on a region's attractiveness. A number of studies by Edwin Mansfield (Mansfield, 1991, 1995; Mansfield and Lee, 1996) find evidence supporting the importance of proximity in the transfer of knowledge between universities and firms. Hussler and Rondé (2007) trace university–industry linkages through patent application data and find that academic knowledge diffuses locally in particular when delimited to the kind of patents that the researchers classify as not possible to 'immediately apply'. We conclude that the empirical evidence points to possible albeit not automatic benefits from proximity to academic R&D for the R&D activities of MNEs (for a more extensive review of such evidence, see Varga, 2002).

Should we interpret these findings so that universities are somehow attracting the R&D investments of MNEs? Feinberg and Gupta (2004) clearly associate locational choices with discrimination with regard to locations on the behalf of MNEs. Supporting evidence is provided by Davies and Meyer (2004) who survey 950 R&D subsidiaries to investigate four aspects of locational advantage, and find that only the presence of scientific institutions has a consistent, positive effect on the incidence and level of subsidiary R&D. Hegde and Hicks (2008), who find that R&D subsidiaries of MNEs headquartered in the USA are strongly drawn towards countries with strong knowledge bases in science and engineering (S&E), are sceptical towards such an interpretation. They write: 'Global R&D is not initially attracted by scientific capability; rather we expect that market factors predominate in the early stages of international R&D. However, once an R&D . . . base has been established, growth of innovative global R&D requires indigenous world class scientific talent'.

Given that proximity effects exist, how should we understand the nature of such benefits? A popular interpretation has been to attribute these effects to the impact of cooperative relationships within a region. In fact most explanations for beneficial effects from proximity focuses on the value of direct, inter-personal contacts primarily in order to acquire tacit knowledge (von Hippel, 1987; Maskell and Malmberg, 1999; Siegel et al. 2003). However such interpretations of the positive effects of proximity are rarely backed by solid evidence. Some recent contributions question the importance of research linkages as a media for proximity benefits. Andersson, Gråsjö and Karlsson (2004), who analyse the location of industry R&D in Sweden and Faggian and McCann (2006) who undertake a similar analysis for Great Britain, find that while R&D location is partly determined by a region's access to students in higher education, the region's level of academic R&D is an insignificant factor.

In summary, our interpretation of these two literature streams is that although they provide convincing evidence that MNEs may gain advantages by locating R&D close to research universities, few studies have explicitly addressed the relationship between R&D subsidiaries and the geographically proximate university. It is therefore not clear to what extent the firms can identify and articulate rationale that supports arguments like localized learning and tacit knowledge, those of recruitment and labour mobility or other ones.

3. RESEARCH DESIGN AND METHODOLOGY

In order to make a reconceptualization of when and why firms may decide to interact with universities we have chosen an exploratory case study design. The case study firms are all engaged in formal collaboration, with one of three elite research universities of University of Cambridge (UK),

ETH Zurich (Switzerland), and Karolinska Institutet (Sweden). Sixteen R&D subsidiaries of MNEs with headquarters located in other countries have been selected as cases.

Our research methodology is hence based upon a grounded theory approach (Glaser and Strauss, 1967; Yin, 1989), but with an exploratory theoretical aim. More specifically our cases are used to strengthen and explain the theoretically derived propositions, rather than derive and create new theory directly from empirical work (Eisenhardt, 1989). The previous section defined how and why MNE subsidiaries could be expected to interact with research universities. We use these theories and the empirical case-based research as exploratory in the sense of being part of an iterative process to further strengthen and highlight important issues. These cases can thus be seen as the combination of our theoretically based propositions and initial exploratory findings.

One aim has hence been to develop and generate a more coherent and detailed set of categories of how and why firms actually interact with leading research universities. Based on this literature we decided to address four issues. These correspond to four variables which were identified and used to structure the interview guide and archival evidence: (1) the R&D activities of the subsidiary, (2) the rationale for cooperation with the university, (3) the perceived effects from that cooperation and (4) organizational forms of collaboration with the university. Based on the combination of literature and case study interpretation, we therefore set out to identify the intensity and organizational forms of collaboration, the perceived benefits, the main purposes of collaboration for each case, before moving on to examine whether these variables varied systematically.

3.1 Case Selection and Methodology

Two points of selection for the cases are important. The first is for the universities to define the total population of firms with whom they collaborate formally and the second choice is that of the firms working with those universities.

The first set of choices has to do with European regions and elite research universities. The seminal research on university–industry interaction has been on American universities (Mowery and Sampat, 2005; Thursby et al., 2007) and hence we chose to focus on Europe. To decrease the risk of producing results valid for only a specific region, we choose to study three different regions centred on three elite universities. The choice to concentrate our studies to 'elite' universities can be described as an 'extreme case sampling' (Patton, 1990). The underlying assumption behind this choice is that it will allow us to capture a greater variety of relationships.

The universities are similar in terms of rankings, but they differ in terms of research scope and in terms of country.

Three universities were selected from ranking lists produced by the British newspaper *The Times Higher Education Supplement*, based on 2005 year rankings.[3] The University of Cambridge repeatedly tops these lists, and thus is a natural choice. To avoid studying only British universities, which often top the European ranking lists, we selected Cambridge but left out Edinburgh, Imperial College, London School of Economics and Oxford. We also decided to concentrate on Switzerland and Sweden as two small but leading European economies where the regions surrounding the universities are much smaller and more defined than in other major metropolitan areas such as Paris or Barcelona. We therefore left out leading universities from other European countries and took the top from Switzerland and Sweden. ETH Zurich is constantly ranked among the top universities of Europe; in the THES 2005 lists, ETHZ is ranked fourth European university in science and third in technology. In the same list Karolinska Institutet was ranked fourth best biomedical university in the world surpassed only by Cambridge, Oxford and Harvard.

The three selected universities clearly have different profiles as well. We chose diversity here, as our purpose was to confirm and generate categories to define the different rationale and mechanisms for why firms collaborate with research universities. The University of Cambridge is active over almost the entire academic palette, the research efforts of ETHZ are heavily concentrated on science and engineering and Karolinska Institutet is devoted to medical research in combination with life-science research in biological and chemical sciences. Hence we are comparing one broad university with two specialized ones in, respectively, engineering and life sciences.

The second set of choices has to do with the selection of firms which make up the case studies. Section 2 explained why we focus on MNE subsidiaries with headquarters located in another country and doing R&D in formal collaboration with the university. We first made a list of all known such collaborative relationships, as known from the university. To identify the set of firms matching these criteria for each university and region we have used the assistance of university corporate liaison officers and regional enterprise officers. Extensive web searches and access to university registers on collaboration (for Cambridge and Karolinska Institutet) has also been used in the search process. This gave us the total population of known firms. More specifically we defined the population of firms matching the following criteria:

- C1: The firm is an R&D subsidiary of an MNE which is located in Stockholm County, the Canton of Zurich or Cambridgeshire.

Table 10.1   Firms interviewed, sorted by university

University, region, country	Firms (R&D subsidiary at that location)
Cambridge University, Cambridgeshire, United Kingdom	Intel, Hitachi, Kodak, Microsoft, Unilever
ETH Zurich, Canton of Zurich, Switzerland	Alcan, IBM, Google, Elan Microelectronics,
Karolinksa Institutet, Stockholm County, Sweden	Arla foods, AstraZeneca, Baxter, Linde Therapeutics, Merck, Pfizer, Wyeth

- *C2*: The firm belongs to an MNE group with more than 2000 employees, distributed over at least six countries, with its headquarter located in another country than that of the subsidiary.
- *C3*: The subsidiary has at least five employees designated to R&D activities.
- *C4*: The subsidiary has been involved in a formal agreement on collaboration (e.g. contract research, facility sharing and/or personnel sharing) with the local university at some point in the period 2003–06.[4]

These four criteria were used in discussion with the university and regional officers, to identify firms. All firms interviewed match the four criteria.

As a result of applying these criteria, we have identified 11 firms in Zurich, 12 firms in Stockholm and ten firms in Cambridgeshire. Hence, the total identified population was 33 firms. We contacted all of these firms and gathered published material about them, but some declined to participate in this study. We interviewed sixteen firms for the case studies, about half of the population. Table 10.1 specifies the firms interviewed.

We interviewed one to three representatives for the specified 16 MNE subsidiaries who are identified as cooperating with the universities of Cambridge, ETH Zurich and Karolinska Institutet respectively. Interviews were recorded and transcribed.

These interviews were performed in a semi-structured manner following an interview guide.[5] Four main topics were addressed, namely: (1) the R&D activities of the subsidiary, (2) the rationales for cooperation with the local university, (3) the effects from that cooperation and (4) on collaborative modes with the university organization and its researchers. Interviews were done on-site at the firm; each took one to two hours; they were noted and placed in the interview guide; and the data were matched to theoretical concepts through exercises in Excel sheets. Complementary information has been gathered through interviews with representatives of regional economic agencies and the three universities and from written or otherwise published material from firms and regions.

3.2 Description of the Universities

The description of the universities includes their most important features and presents the regional context in which they are operating.

Karolinska Institutet in Stockholm

Founded in 1810, Karolinska Institutet is today one of the largest medical universities in Europe. It is also Sweden's largest centre for medical training and research, accounting for 30 per cent of the medical training and 40 per cent of the medical academic research that is conducted in the country. Five scientists from Karolinska have received the Nobel Prize in physiology or medicine. In 2005, the university had a turnover of approximately US$520 million and employed about 3500 people.

The Science Park Novum was founded in 1984 and is located nearby the Karolinska Campus in Huddinge. Here university research is performed together with companies, mainly smaller firms but also some larger corporations such as Baxter have invested in research facilities here. Novum is currently expanding, Novum BioCity is an extension that aims to focus on basic research and attract more companies to the region.[6]

Cambridge University

Often described as Europe's leading research university, the University of Cambridge combines a commitment to fundamental research with an interest in commercializing its research. The 800-year-old university is surrounded by one of the strongest science park clusters in the world. The university had a turnover of US$1.3 billion in 2004 and teaching and research activities makes up about 80 percent of these expenditures. It employs around 8000 people.

The University of Cambridge has been cooperating with industry for a long time. For instance Rolls Royce, has located much of its jet engine research at the university during the last 50 years. More recently the university has become more aware of the importance of these links and therefore, they have sought to create a support structure for this. The university created a centralized Research Service Division (RSD) in 2000. A Corporate Liaison Office was founded in 2001, merging with the RSD in 2005. About 17 percent of the university's research income comes from companies. Interestingly most of these companies are multinational and have headquarters outside the UK.

ETH Zurich

ETH Zurich was founded in 1855 and has been a leading research university for a long time. Together with ETH Lausanne and four research institutes, ETH forms a federally directed institution committed to research, mainly in technical fields such as engineering sciences, mathematics, natural sciences and architecture. In total about 8200 people are employed by ETH Zurich and the university has a turnover of about US$800 million.

ETH has sought to be close to the economy, cooperating with many corporations in the region. The most renowned example is the relationship with IBM which has one of its largest research facilities located close to the university. ETH is taking a further step in this direction by creating the Science City. This initiative will improve the partnerships with business and society. Firms and donors can participate in the financing of the entire university. Start-up companies and established corporations will find not only office space in Science City but also services and international networks.

4.   COLLABORATION WITH EUROPEAN ELITE UNIVERSITIES

The first descriptive question is whether the intensity and rationale for collaboration is similar for all the firms or whether it differs.

The first theme discussed in our interviews was to establish how intensively the R&D subsidiaries work with the universities. We interpret the statements of the respondents as fitting into either of two rough categories. Five firms perceive that they have what was referred to in an interview as 'occasional' or what we call 'on-demand' collaboration, whereas the remaining 11 firms maintained what was perceived as continuous relationships. Continuous relationships between firm and university are the most common which we interpret as a high intensity of relationships, or what could be expected to be a dense set of linkages in the network. Many of these R&D subsidiaries of MNEs do interact intensely with the local university.

However the five firms that have specified their relationship as 'on-demand' collaboration are also quite interesting. These firms only interact when they need a specific kind of research. Among these five respondents several stated that the university which has geographical proximity is not a very relevant partner for R&D. Two refer to mismatches between the research profile of the specific local university and that of the firm subsidiary. Moreover four of these managers do not see universities as a particularly important type of R&D collaborator. Hence, despite being organizations with clear 'absorptive capacity', these firms do not necessarily think that universities have something specific to offer.

Table 10.2   Responses of the 11 firms stating continuous relationship with university, rationale given

Category of answers	Number of firms
Getting access to international networks	10/11
Continuous recruitment	8/11
Getting access to local networks	7/11
Possibilities to strengthen brand of firm and/or products	7/11
Continuous need for consultation	3/11
Affecting the university research agenda	3/11

Let us look more closely at the 11 firms which identified a continuous relationship with the elite university in their region. Table 10.2 specifies the number of firms mentioning any of the following rationale for collaboration.[7]

As shown in Table 10.2, 10 of the 11 firms expressed in interviews that an important rationale was the need to obtain access to scientific networks, in particular international contacts, and seven of 11 mentioned access to local networks. Other key areas were recruitment (8/11) and possibilities to strengthen the brand of the firm and/or product (7/11). Note that only three of the 11 firms mentioned the continuous need for consultation or the desire to affect the overall agenda of research at the university.

Access to people and networks are thus important. In the interviews, several R&D managers perceived the close geographical proximity university as gateways to a wider academic community. Through these nodes the R&D subsidiary felt it could obtain access to a community of researchers that could be relevant to them. It is particularly noteworthy that these managers stressed the unique nature of collaboration with the specific university and research team. They underlined the particular nature of that collaboration, and stated that it is unique for the firm, in terms of form, intensity and scope. In other words they go to one elite university to fulfil this function of access to international networks.

The second descriptive question is what organizational forms of collaboration are visible in the cases. Formal relationships between universities and firms can be organized in different ways, reflecting different purposes of the collaboration and different funding arrangements (Tidd et al., 2001). As with the previous question, existing literature suggests a number of organizational forms, which were used in the interview guide in combination with open-ended questions. Table 10.3 shows the results.

The most common forms for the R&D subsidiaries are joint venture research (12/16), consulting (12/16) and joint staffing (11/16). Our inter-

Table 10.3 Organizational forms for collaboration

Form of collaboration	Number of firms
Joint venture research	12/16
Consulting	12/16
Joint staffing (e.g. industry financed PhD students)	11/16
Commissioned research and development	8/16
Research sponsoring	6/16
Licensing/purchase of patents	5/16
Hiring equipment/renting facilities	3/16
Jointly-owned centres	3/16

pretation is that the most common organizational forms include types which involve very direct and long-term collaboration (joint venture, joint staffing) as well as types which mainly involve arm's-length relations in the market (consulting, commissioned R&D).

The least common organizational forms for collaborative R&D are quite interesting, given the current emphasis in public policy and in the literature. Only 5/16 emphasize patents and only 3/16 mention jointly owned centres.[8] Note that we expected more patents, given that policy stresses changing institutional patterns to facilitate IPR and given that patents are the main measurement of university impact on society (McKelvey et al., 2008). We also expected more centre-form collaboration because this has been a key policy instrument of the innovation policy agencies of both Sweden and Switzerland (Arnold et al., 2004). At least for this set of R&D subsidiaries of MNEs our results indicate that intellectual property and jointly-owned centres are not that common.

The most common organizational forms seem to involve primarily either people and networks (joint venture research, joint staffing) or specific problem-solving on scientific and technical issues (consulting, commissioned).

We also wanted to use the interviews to more specifically identify the effects and benefits for the firm, in their own words. Hence respondents at the subsidiaries were asked to evaluate and describe the effects of its collaborative relations to their geographically proximate university. We have classified these statements in six categories, which were later discussed with the respondents, and these are presented in Table 10.4.

To us some of the benefits from collaboration were expected, as they have been identified in previous literature. Freeman (1994) suggests that universities keep open options for the future. Of the studied firms, 11/16 found benefits in 'helping the firm to identify opportunities for innovation'. Other

Table 10.4   Managers' view on relative importance and types of benefits for collaboration

Collaboration with the local university. . .	Not at all / only to some extent	Beneficial / very beneficial effects
Gives the firm valuable orientation and outside-in views of its technology	4	12
Has important branding and/or marketing benefits for a product or the firm	4	12
Enables further valuable contacts (networks)	5	11
Helps the firm identify opportunities for innovation	6	10
Helps the firm realise innovation opportunities identified by the firm	9	7
Is important for recruitment	13	3

benefits were unexpected, and generated by the case studies. In particular, we did not expect that so many (13/16) would state that collaboration has important branding and/or marketing benefits for the firm. In contrast to the university–industry literature which assumes universities to be the primary motor of regional development, this result is more in line with international business literature which emphasizes that R&D may be adapted to local markets (LeBas and Sierra, 2002).

In summary, this section has examined the 16 R&D subsidiaries of MNEs by answering two questions. The first one was whether the intensity and rationale for collaboration is similar for all the firms or whether it differs, and the second one was the mechanisms and organizational forms for R&D. Our results are valid for a very small but important subset of firms – namely R&D subsidiaries of MNEs with headquarters elsewhere and with formal collaboration with elite European universities. The results are in line with existing literature, but they also generated new insights, especially two dichotomies of firm behaviour when formally collaborating with elite universities. The first dichotomy is the type of university knowledge asset most relevant for the R&D subsidiary. Here, the aggregate empirical results suggest that they may be primarily interested in science and technology or else in market, customers and branding. The other dichotomy lies in whether collaboration with the university is a primary mechanism to reach company goals, or a complementary one.

5. FOUR IDEAL TYPES OF FIRM STRATEGIES

The two dichotomies outlined above, which were generated through our reading of the literature and the aggregate empirical results, suggest that firms may follow four ideal types of strategy, when collaborating with elite universities. Firms involved in running clinical trials are primarily interested in market, customers and branding, but see collaboration as a primary mechanism to reach a firm goal. Firms involved with universities as solution demanders are also primarily interested in market, customers and branding, but see collaboration as a complementary mechanism. Firms involved with universities as competent buddies are primarily interested in science and technology, but see collaboration as a complementary mechanism. Firms involved with universities as seamless network are also primarily interested in science and technology, and see collaboration as a primary mechanism to achieve their goal. Hence, these four ideal types are described below, namely 'Running Clinical Trials', 'Solution Demanders', 'Competent Buddies' and 'Seamless Networks'.

5.1 Running Clinical Trials

The first ideal type is the 'Running Clinical Trials' or R&D subsidiaries with an orientation towards clinical activities. The firms categorized as such are Wyeth (Stockholm) and Merck (Stockholm). The illustrative case is of Wyeth in Stockholm.

Clinical trials of firms in the pharmaceutical sector constitute something of a 'special case' in terms of U–I relations. Clinical activities of pharmaceutical firms are almost totally dependent on the access to the clinical expertise and patients of university hospitals and thus generally maintain continuous contacts with universities. However this is a separate category because firms that seek to perform clinical trials are not necessarily drawing on university research capacity.

Wyeth in Stockholm provides an illustrative example. The company is primarily in Stockholm in order to run clinical trials, in order to test new drugs in accordance with regulations. The firm is interested in drug approval for Sweden and Europe, and relevant clinical trials are easily organized in this population. According to Göran Skoglund, the R&D manager in Stockholm, the subsidiary otherwise only collaborates with a few professors, whom are approached when special consultation is needed.

In summary, clinical trial firms can be found collaborating with Karolinska Institutet. These firms are looking for a type of long-term contacts with clinical doctors, in order to run large-scale clinical trials for pharmaceuticals. This is the only ideal type which is specifically restricted to one industrial sector, namely pharmaceuticals which is subject to extensive regulation.

5.2   Solution Demanders: R&D Subsidiaries with an Agenda Dominated by Development

The second ideal type is the 'Solution Demanders' or R&D subsidiaries with an agenda dominated by development. The firms categorized as such are Arla Foods (Stockholm), Pfizer (Stockholm), Google (Zurich), Elan Microelectronics (Zurich), and Alcan (Zurich). The illustrative case is of Alcan in Zurich.

The firms in this ideal type have more loosely organized collaboration with the geographically close university, with limited numbers of organizational forms and lower intensity of contacts. Moreover the linkages to the university tend to be related to applied development rather than basic research. They also often focus upon existing R&D projects within the firm and consultations rather than exploratory activities. Some of these firms collaborate with universities in order to get access to equipment and facilities that they do not have.

In the interviews, the R&D managers were asked why they did not have more interactions with the universities. We interpreted the responses from these five firms as falling within three themes: limited funds on behalf of the firm, limited need for external expertise and mismatches between the R&D needs of the subsidiary and the current research expertise and interests of that university.

One illustrative case is Alcan which is a global corporation headquartered in Canada. Following the acquisition of AluSuisse in 2000, the corporation has restructured its R&D. The corporation today runs research laboratory and engineering centres in Canada, Switzerland, France and the USA. The research laboratory in Neuhausen, just north of Zurich, and the Engineering centres of Zurich are among the largest R&D facilities of the group. The lab has two emphases: aluminium fabrication and packaging. The engineering centre is responsible for development for the mass transportation industry within the group.

From a central perspective, Alcan's Director of Innovation Management, Dr Ernst Lutz states that the firm does not have much contact with the ETH. The respondent argues that the distance between the continuous improvement R&D of the firm and the research-oriented university generally is too great for regular collaborations to be set up. The firm has much stronger relations to less well-known academic institutions throughout Switzerland. However, the respondent is also responsible for a new initiative called Future Options, which is set up to run R&D projects meant to provide the firms with new impulses and an 'early warning system' for technological changes that may disrupt the firm's current markets or open up new business opportunities. The respondent plans to fund 'leading professors and places', demanding regular consultancy and discussions to guide the firm's R&D but not imposing demands that the academics using the firm's funding follow specific research agendas. However Dr Gerald Rebizter, who is responsible for Life Cycle Management within Alcan, reports different experiences. He works with academics all over the world but has a particularly strong relationship with a group at ETH. Apart from informal contacts, Alcan provide some sponsorship money for conferences and seminars within the area (networking and brand benefits for the firm).

To conclude, the formal relationship between the firm and the ETH is restricted to a few organizational forms (only some sponsorship contracts confirmed in interviews). While a few individual R&D employees such as Dr Rebitzer may work with the ETH on a regular basis, this is an issue of informal contacts and networking. The contact we identified is restricted to a narrow field (life cycle analysis). Dr Lutz describes the relationship in general as weak/not intense.

In summary solution demander firms can be found collaborating with ETH Zurich and Karolinska Institutet. These firms are looking for a type of problem-solving activities, related to specific areas of expertise of the university and in this case they do not give a preferred position to the geographically proximate university.

5.3 Competent Buddies: R&D Subsidiaries with Research-intensive Agendas

The third ideal type is the 'Competent Buddies' or R&D subsidiaries with research-intensive agendas. The firms categorized as such are Kodak (Cambridge), Linde Therapeutics (Stockholm), AstraZeneca (Stockholm) and IBM (Zurich). The illustrative case is of the IBM lab in Zurich.

These R&D subsidiaries differ in organizational characteristics from those found in the solution demanders type, in that they are significantly larger, more complex organizations. As compared to the seamless network firms discussed below, these competent buddies are slightly less oriented towards research and somewhat more towards product development. At the same time, they tend to be major centres of R&D expertise within the MNE globally. Here the interaction with the specific elite university which is geographically proximate is considered a more unique knowledge asset to the firm than in the ones discussed above.

For competent buddies, they see themselves as competent within the field of science and technology within they are collaborating, and likely have complementary knowledge to that of the university. The geographically proximate university and its researchers are a natural partner with whom both formal collaboration and informal networking can be practised. The creation of network contacts and access to people is facilitated by the continuity of relations and significant recruitment. The university close to the subsidiary is presented as a preferred partner in the subsidiary's often extensive academic network. While the subsidiary may recruit extensively from the local university, however, there is generally no room in R&D budgets to set up collaborations focused primarily upon recruitment and support of the local knowledge base at the research level; instead, these factors are seen as an outcome, and a long-term added-value of local collaboration.

Note that these firms likely interact with many universities and the geographically proximate university is only one of many. In the words of one interviewee: 'We are allergic to "regional" initiatives and do not want to establish special relationships to universities: we want to pick the best available university researcher for each and every need that we may have rather than staying with some kind of preferred "local supplier"'.

One illustrative example of the competent buddy strategy is IBM's research lab in Zurich; a classic example of a large, R&D-oriented MNE subsidiary fostering strong linkages to the local university environment. Among the most notable forms of current collaboration are a commonly owned research centre (ZISC) and a programme for utilization of IBM technological assets in academic research (CASE).

The ZISC and CASE initiatives represent the two most structured forms of collaboration between ETH researchers and IBM, an opinion supported by both respondents and by IBM's local public relations manager. ZISC is a research centre that is jointly funded by IBM and other partner companies associated with ETH. CASE is a programme for utilization of IBM technological assets in academic research.

The lab was established in 1955 as IBM's first R&D initiative outside the USA. Today, the Zurich lab is one of eight IBM corporate research labs in an organization that the corporation describes as 'the largest industrial research organization in the world' (IBM, 2008). The lab has a strong position within the IBM research organization and hosts the full range of R&D activities; from research to product development. In recent years, the focus has shifted from internal R&D to collaboration in teams of researchers, developers and marketing managers in client-related projects. However, in contrast to the corporation's R&D labs in China, Japan and Israel, the Swiss lab is perceived as serving the needs of the IBM corporation in general more than serving a 'local' market (Schär, 2006). ZISC coordinator Günter Karjoth describes the rationale for establishing a centre as follows:

We already had some collaboration with ETH in the area of information security, but it was not different from the relations that we have with other universities, where we follow research work and attend talks. But we realised that we had two world-class research teams sitting close to each other without talking very much to each other. We wanted the two teams to learn about the works of each other, in particular we wanted the PhD students at ETH to learn about our work. Where we have students interested in our topics, we see an opportunity to influence their research agenda by cooperating on particular topics.

Besides these benefits from collaboration, the ZISC coordinator describes a need 'to look ahead, not to get insights in new technologies, but to prepare the avenue for new technologies.'

Both collaborative initiatives are described as 'interaction between peers', which can be interpreted as a confirmation of the high level of the research done at IBM. However, while ZISC represents an initiative oriented towards 'basic' research, the second initiative discussed here has a focus on IBM technology.

In 2001, IBM launched a new collaborative programme called CASE for the design of novel high-frequency analogue circuits for the advance of wired and wireless communication technologies. Initially IBM sponsored the centre with about one million Swiss francs and then close to half a million annually in the following years. While the CASE programme is not exclusively associated with ETH, the proximity allows ETH researchers who work on issues that are relevant for IBM to participate very actively. The director of CASE explains:

IBM has a very strong technological base in certain technological areas, such as transistor design. Our basic idea with CASE was that in order to educate key people in using our state-of-the-art technology, we need to enable access to it. Obviously we also wanted to make use of any important research results that come out of this initiative.

CASE offers a mix of limited direct funding and more indirect values. The chairman of the board, states that this is 'an exemplary of the type of collaboration IBM seeks with academia', mainly since it is done in a technical area of increasing importance for IBM.

The collaboration requires powerful computer systems and therefore IBM has donated six workstations that will be part of the computer infrastructure used. While IBM gets access to skilled researchers and a pool of talented students, ETH obtains knowledge and equipment that they can't host on their own. IBM funds doctoral students and masters students that are involved in the projects undertaken and IBM researchers lecture at ETH regularly. The firm has also, through the lab, participated in recent ETH fundraising initiatives.

In summary, competent buddies firms can be found collaborating with ETH Zurich, Cambridge University, and Karolinska Institutet. These firms are looking for a type of interaction, which is quite close and depends upon specific competencies in both partners.

5.4 Seamless Networks: Integrated Research Units

The fourth ideal type is the 'Seamless Networks' or integrated research units. The firms categorized as such are Intel (Cambridge), Unilever (Cambridge), Hitachi (Cambridge), Baxter (Stockholm), Microsoft (Cambridge). The Hitachi Cambridge Laboratory located close to Cambridge University will here be used as an illustrative example.

Five firms are thus cases where corporate R&D resources are closely integrated – often even physically embedded and integrated through people – in university environments.[9] These R&D subsidiaries have a high intensity and variety of organizational forms for collaboration with their specific elite university. They engage over a longer period of time in recruitment, access to university researchers, staff sharing as well as formal and informal collaborative arrangements.

Four of the five subsidiaries with a seamless network strategy are fairly young, having existed about 5–10 years. Hitachi is the notable exception having had an embedded laboratory in Cambridge since 1989. This unit of Hitachi is oriented towards basic research and performs it together with the Microelectronics Research Centre in Cambridge. The laboratory specializes in advanced measurement and characterization techniques, and the university department specializes in nanofabrication techniques. At the intersection of these fields, Hitachi seeks to increase its knowledge about semiconductor physics for future electronic and optical devices.

The director of the laboratory, Dr David Williams, states that this form of close collaboration makes it possible for Hitachi to get access to the university's researchers on a daily basis. By collocating to such an extent, a firm like Hitachi can get access to more researchers than they are paying for themselves. Conversely, the university gets access to about 25 researchers in the Hitachi Cambridge Laboratory.

Several firms of this seamless network type describe their collaboration as a way of obtaining the 'blue sky' research that they are usually not willing or able to perform themselves. In the interviews and also theoretically, one main rationale for these R&D subsidiaries is linked to aspects of 'listening posts' or 'preparing for future disruptive innovations'. To do so the R&D managers stress the need to engage in, access results, equipment and networks concerning the latest basic research findings.

Another rationale appears to be the attempt to achieve a critical mass of research staff and equipment, where partial payment from each actor helps to create an organizational form where both parties benefit. The MNE can leverage its internal research investment with public resources and the university can augment and develop specific lines of research.

In summary, four of the five seamless network firms are collaborating with Cambridge University, and the fifth with Karolinska Institutet. These firms are looking for a type of continuous, multidimensional interaction with the university, where they access networks and people in relation to scientific and engineering knowledge.

6. CAN ELITE EUROPEAN RESEARCH UNIVERSITIES ATTRACT THE KNOWLEDGE ECONOMY INTO THEIR REGION?

The chapter has so far focused on the organizational forms and benefits that R&D subsidiaries of MNEs perceive, when collaborating with one of three elite European universities in their respective region. This section asks how the results from three universities, which are all considered leading in their fields, should be interpreted, relative to public policy goals to attract the knowledge economy into their region.

Our interviews suggest that the R&D subsidiaries are located close to these elite European research universities for very different reasons. Moreover, though, these differences across variables are systematic in a manner that has enabled us to propose four ideal types for firm strategies for collaboration with universities. In one ideal type, that of seamless network, the interview results suggest that these elite research universities can exert a clear attracting force on R&D investments that are embodied as R&D subsidiaries. Similarly firms acting as competent buddies also find a lower level but still multifaceted rationale for being geographically proximate to their university. However for solution demanders and running clinical trials these firms identified only minor direct benefits of proximity to the research university. These results thus suggest that only some types of MNEs will be attracted to elite European research universities for activities that require intense collaboration, multiple organizational forms, and long-term 'windows' into scientific results and networks.

With the exception of the category of clinical trials for pharmaceuticals, this classification extends beyond commonly used sectoral divisions. This may be surprising, as the heterogeneity of needs for collaboration between industries is a stylized fact of previous literature on U–I relations (Meyer-Krahmer and Schmoch, 1998; Nelson, 1986) and the differences between sectors is documented in the literature on R&D-localization of MNEs (Hegde and Hicks, 2005). However, we have been able to identify these three ideal types of firm strategy, which transcend industry-specific factors, as well as one ideal type which is specific to the pharmaceutical industry.

Our results thus suggest that firms go to elite research universities to access particular types of international scientific knowledge, which have a high value to the firm. Only a few universities can offer this even amongst the elite ones. Firms access these universities because they find it more beneficial than to develop all these competencies in-house and firms appear to be located close to the respective universities for similar reasons. In each case the R&D managers were clearly reflecting upon what they get out of any specific university or collaboration. Depending upon the answer to that, they developed different strategies, goals, and outcomes of the university–industry interactions. From the firm's perspective, they are clearly placing their R&D investments in a specific region, as a part of the strategy of a global company.

A related issue is the overall importance of the being close to elite universities. The results raise questions about our current understanding of the value of 'knowledge flows' as a driver for collocation, as emphasized in the literature about localized knowledge spill-overs. Direct and strong flows of knowledge between university research and corporate R&D activities are only found to be relevant for the understanding of one of our four identified ideal types, namely seamless networks. In fact, our tentative conclusion that seamless network subsidiaries are mainly found in the vicinity of only one of our three elite universities, Cambridge University, suggests that even the academic excellence of a university in itself does not guarantee R&D investments from foreign MNEs.

This empirical result has implications for public policy and for university leaders. Our results suggest that universities are not 'magnets' for foreign direct investment (FDI) in general, but only for specific reasons which are set in relation to the global corporate strategy. Depending upon the firm's rationale, it may be looking for very different ways and benefits of collaboration. Moreover, if not even the top ranked and well-renowned universities Karolinska Institutet and ETH Zürich can attract subsidiary R&D by direct power of research excellence, then opportunities for other universities to do so seem dire. It is also interesting that global firms can go to a leading university like Karolinska in order to run clinical trials, although they also have other types of formal collaboration.

Therefore, policy-makers and university leaders must have a more nuanced understanding of firm's differing rationale for collaboration. One aspect involves contracts, access and specific agreements. Special arrangements in terms of facilities and legal contracts may need to be arranged for seamless network firms, whereas solution demanders may be handled with more traditional technology transfer instruments. All in all, elite research and teaching universities may be very important to help develop the region as a whole, but in taking strategic decisions about R&D location, firms will differ in their assessments of the value of opportunities to local academic collaboration.

ACKNOWLEDGEMENTS

This book chapter has been financed through SISTER research institute and RIDE research network at IMIT, in a collaborative research project involving three universities. Many thanks to organizers and participants of special sessions, where earlier versions of this chapter were presented, at the 2007 Uddevalla symposium and the 2007 Academy of Management, in Philadelphia.

NOTES

1. Public policy-makers have also been encouraged to interact with MNEs, because R&D subsidiaries not only create attractive jobs, but also form networks and act as customers which can potentially improve the business climate of a region (Ylinenpää and Lundgren 1998).
2. This work addresses issues relevant to a very specific type of firm, because for the great majority of firms, regardless of sector of activity, universities are not regarded as the main source for innovation but rather as a complementary activity (von Hippel, 1988).
3. These universities are also high for European universities on the other major rankings.
4. An alternative criteria would be to include only firms in particular sectors, which are assumed to be working in areas known to exist at the university. However, we do not feel that either the NACE-code system nor the Frascati manual provide sufficient grounds upon which to match the R&D needs of particular industrial sectors with research. Moreover, by making this assumption, we would have missed any 'unexpected' collaboration, in other areas, such as suggested in literature on technology search.
5. Details of the interview guide are presented in Broström (2007).
6. http://www.novum.se/ and http://ki.se/content
7. Based on previous literature, the interview guide provided some examples but respondents were also free to answer in their own words. We then grouped their answers. The following is therefore partly based on theoretically-derived categories and partly on empirically-derived ones, found as a result of the interviews.
8. We do not know the reason, but we could speculate that it may be related to the foreign ownership status of our firms, as funding agencies that set up such centres might possibly favour firms perceived as 'national' or 'regional'. Another rationale might be that the university researchers tend to find national and regional partners, due to asymmetric information and search.
9. All the subsidiaries in this category except Microsoft are in fact integrated research units. The Microsoft Research Laboratory is located in a different building, next to the Computer Science Laboratory in Cambridge.

REFERENCES

Adams, J.D. (2002), 'Comparative localization of academic and industrial spillovers', *Journal of Economic Geography*, **2**, 253–78.

Almeida, P. and A. Phene (2004), 'Subsidiaries and knowledge creation: the influence of the MNC and host country on innovation', *Strategic Management Journal*, **25**, 847–64.

Andersson, M., U. Gråsjö and C. Karlsson (2004), 'Industry R&D location – the role of accessibility to university R&D and institutions of higher education', CESIS working paper series no. 68.

Anselin, L., A. Varga and Z. Acs (1997), 'Local geographic spillovers between university research and high technology innovations', *Journal of Urban Economics*, **42**, 422–48.

Arnold, E., J. Clark and S. Bussillet (2004), 'Impacts of the Swedish Competence Centres Programme 1995–2003', summary report to VINNOVA, the Swedish Agency for Innovation Systems.

Arundel, A. and A. Geuna (2004), 'Proximity and the use of public science by innovative European firms', *Economics of Innovation and New Technology*, **13** (6), 559–80.

Audretsch, D.B. and M.P. Feldman (1996), 'R&D spillovers and the geography of innovation and production', *American Economic Review*, **86** (3), 630–40.

Audretch D.B and E.E. Lehmann (2006), 'Do locational spillovers pay? Empirical evidence from German IPO data', *Economics of Innovation and New Technology*, **15** (1), 71–81.

Blanc, H. and C. Sierra (1999), 'The internationalisation of R&D by multinationals: a trade-off between external and internal proximity', *Cambridge Journal of Economics*, **23**, 187–206.

Bolon, D. and J. Cheng (1993), 'The management of multinational R&D: a neglected topic in international business research', *Journal of International Business Studies*, **24**, 1–18.

Bramwell, A. and D.A. Wolfe (2005), 'Universities and regional economic development: the entrepreneurial university of Waterloo', Paper presented at Canadian Political Science Associations annual conference, 2–4 June 2005.

Breschi, S. and F. Lissoni (2001), 'Knowledge spillovers and local innovation systems: a critical survey', *Liuc Papers n. 84 Serie Economica e Impresa*, 27 March.

Broström, A. (2007), 'Appendix II: guide for interviews with firms, in Collaboration for Competitiveness', *Appendices*, accessed 12 February, 2008 at www.ab.lst.se/upload/Projektwebbar/Innovation.

Cantwell, J. and L. Piscitello (2002), 'The location of technological activities of MNCs in European regions: the role of spillovers and local competencies', *Journal of International Management*, **8**, 69–96.

Cantwell, J. and L. Piscitello (2005), 'Recent location of foreign-owned research and development activities by large multinational corporations in the European regions: the role of spillovers and externalities', *Regional Studies*, **39** (1), 1–16.

Chiesa, V. (1996), 'Managing the internationalization of R&D activities', *Engineering Management*, **43** (1), 7–23.

Chung, W. and J. Alcácer (2002), 'Knowledge seeking and location choice of foreign direct investment in the United States', *Management Science*, **48** (12), 1534–54.

Criscuolo, P., R. Narula and B. Verspagen (2005), 'Role of home and host country innovation systems in R&D internationalisation: a patent citation analysis', *Economics of Innovation and New Technology*, **14** (5), 417–33.

Davies, L.N. and K.E. Meyer (2004), 'Subsidiary research and development, and the local environment', *International Business Review*, **13** (2), 359–82.

Dunning, J. H. (1994), 'Re-evaluating the benefits of foreign direct investment', *Transnational Corporations*, **3** (1), 27–51.

Dunning, J. (2000), 'The eclectic paradigm as an envelope for economic and business theories of MNE activity', *International Business Review*, **9**, 163–90.

Eisenhardt, K.M. (1989), 'Making fast strategic decisions in high-velocity environments', *Academy of Management Journal*, **32** (3), 543–76.

Fagerberg, J., David C. Mowery and Richard R. Nelson (eds) (2005), *Handbook of Innovation*, New York: Oxford University Press.

Faggian, A. and P. McCann (2006), 'Human capital flows and regional knowledge assets: a simultaneous equation approach', *Oxford Economic Papers*, 2006, **58** (3), 475–500.

Feinberg, S.E. and A.K. Gupta (2004), 'Knowledge spillovers and the assignment of R&D responsibilities to foreign subsidiaries', *Strategic Management Journal*, **25**, 823–45.

Feldman, Maryann P. (1994), *The Geography of Innovation*, Dordrecht, the Netherlands: Kluwer

Freeman, C. (1994), 'Critical survey: the economics of technical change', *Cambridge Journal of Economics.* **18**, 463–514.

Furman, J.L., M.K. Kyle, I. Cockburn and R.M. Henderson (2005), 'Public and private spillovers, location and the productivity of pharmacautical research', NBER working paper series no. 12509.

Gerybadze, A. and G. Reger (1999), 'Globalization of R&D: recent changes in the management of innovation in transnational corporations', *Research Policy*, **28**, 251–74.

Glaser, Barney G. and Anselm L. Strauss (1967), *The Discovery of Grounded Theory: Strategies for Qualitative Research*, Chicago, IL: Aldine Transaction.

Hegde, D. and D. Hicks (2008), 'The maturation of global corporate R&D: evidence from the activity of U.S. foreign subsidiaries', *Research Policy*, **37** (3), 390–406.

Heimann, P. (2005), 'Foreign-owned R&D facilities in China, England, Germany, and Sweden – an analysis of regional entry and integration behaviour', dissertation at University of Augsburg, urn:nbn:de:bvb:384-opus-1326.

Hussler, C. and P. Rondé (2007), 'The impact of cognitive communities on the diffusion of academic knowledge: evidence from the networks of inventors of a French university', *Research Policy*, **36**, 288–302.

Jaruzelski, B., K. Dehoff and R. Bordia (2005), 'Money isn't everything', *Strategy and Business*, 41, Winter.

Kuemmerle W. (1999), 'Foreign direct investment in industrial research in the pharmaceutical and electronics industries – results from a survey of multinational firms', *Research Policy*, **28** (2), 179–93.

Kuemmerle, W. (2002), 'Home base and knowledge management in international ventures', *Journal of Business Venturing*, **17** (2), 99–122.

LeBas, C. and C. Sierra (2002), 'Location versus home country advantages in R&D activities: some further results on multinationals' locational strategies', *Research Policy*, **31**, 589–609.

Mansfield, E. (1991), 'Academic research and industrial innovation', *Research Policy*, **20**, 1–12.

Mansfield, E. (1995), 'Academic research underlying industrial innovations: sources, characteristics, and financing', *Review of Economics and Statistics*, **77**, 55–65.

Mansfield, E. (1998), 'Academic research and industrial innovation: an update of empirical findings', *Research Policy*, **26**, 673–95.

Mansfield, E. and J. Lee (1996), 'Intellectual property and foreign direct investment', *Review of Economics and Statistics*, **77**, 55–65.

Maskell, P. and A. Malmberg (1999), 'Localised learning and industrial competitiveness', *Cambridge Journal of Economics*, **23**, 167–85.

McKelvey, M., M. Magnusson, M. Wallin and D. Ljungberg (2008), 'Var ligger problemet? Synen på sambandet mellan forskning och kommersialisering i Sverige', in Mats Benner and Sverker Sörlin (eds), *Universitet som framtidens kunskapsmiljö*. Stockholm: SNS förlaget.

Meyer-Krahmer, F. and G. Reger (1999), 'New perspectives on the innovation strategies of multinational enterprises: lessons for technology policy in Europe', *Research Policy*, **28**, 751–76.

Meyer-Krahmer, F. and U. Schmoch (1998), 'Science-based technologies: university–industry interactions in four fields', *Research Policy*, **27**, 835–51.

Mowery, D. and B.N. Sampat (2005), 'Universities in national innovation systems', in Jan Fagerberg, David C. Mowery and Richard R. Nelson (eds), *Handbook of Innovation*, Oxford University Press, pp. 209–39.

Narula, R. and A. Zanfei (2005), 'Globalisation of innovation: the role of multinational enterprises', in J. Fagerberg, D. Mowery and R. Nelson (eds), *Handbook of Innovation*, Oxford: Oxford University Press, pp. 318–46.

Nelson, R. (1959), 'The simple economics of basic scientific research', *Journal of Political Economy*, **67**, 297–306.

Nelson, R. (1986), 'Institutions supporting technical advance in industry', *American Economic Review*, **76** (2), 186–9.

Patton, M.Q. (1990), *Qualitative Evaluation and Research Methods*, 2nd edn, Newbury Park, CA: Sage Publications.

Pearce R. (1994), 'The internationalisation of research and development by multinational enterprises and the transfer sciences', *Empirica*, **21** (3), 297–311.

Ronstadt, R.C. (1978), 'International R&D: the establishment and evolution of research and development abroad by seven US multinationals', *Journal of International Business Studies*, **9**, 7–24.

Salter, A.J. and B.R. Martin (2001), 'The economic benefits of publicly funded basic research: a critical review,' *Research Policy*, **30** (3), 509–32.

Schär, P. (2006), 'Die Internationalisierung von F&E am Beispiel des IBM Forschungslaboraorium Rüschlikon', master thesis, University of Zurich, Institut für Empirische Wirtschaftsforschung.

Siegel, D., D.A. Waldman, L.E. Atwater and A.N. Link (2003), 'Commercial knowledge transfers from universities to firms: improving the effectiveness of university–industry collaboration', *Journal of High Technology Management Research*, **14**, 111–33.

Teece, David J. (1976), *The Multinational Corporation cost of International Technology Transfer*, Cambridge, MA: Ballinger.

Thursby, M., J. Thursby and S. Gupta-Mukherjee (2007), 'Are there real effects of licensing on academic research? A life cycle view', *Journal of Economic Behavior and Organization*, **63** (4), 577–98.

Tidd, Joe, John Bessant and Keith Pavitt (2001), *Managing Innovation – Integrating Technological, Market and Organizational Change*, Chichester: Wiley.
United Nations (2005), *World Investment Report 2005*, New York and Geneva: United Nations.
Varga, A. (2002), 'Knowledge transfers from universities and the regional economy: a review of the literature', in A. Varga and L. Szerb (eds) *Innovation, Entrepreneurship, Regions and Economic Development: International Experiences and Hungarian Challenges*, Pécs, Hungary: University of Pécs.
von Hippel, E. (1987), 'Cooperation between rivals: informal know-how trading', *Research Policy*, **16**, 291–302.
von Hippel, Eric (1988), *The Sources of Innovation*, New York: Oxford University Press.
Yin, Robert K. (1989), *Case Study Research – Design and Methods*, Thousand Oaks, CA: Sage Publications.
Ylinenpää, H. and N.-G. Lundgren (1998), 'Regional dynamics – A comparison of two Nordic regions', paper presented at the conference 'SMEs and districts', LIUC, Castellanza, Italy, November.
von Zedtwitz, M. and O. Gasssman (2002), 'Market versus technology drive in R&D internationalization: four different patterns of managing research and development', *Research Policy*, **31**, 569–88.
Zucker L.G., M.R. Darby and J. Armstrong (1998), 'Geographically localized knowledge spillovers or markets?', *Economic Inquiry*, **1**, 65–86.

Web references

Annual Report of Karolinska Institutet:
accessed 11 November 2006 at http://ki.se/content/1/c4/04/13/KI_Year 05. pdf.
accessed 11 November 2006 at The Novum website, www.novum.se.
accessed 20 November 2006 at The University of Cambridge, www.cam.ac.uk.
accessed 19 November 2006 at ETH Zürich, Wnlaut www.ethz.ch/index_EN.
accessed 19 November 2006 at Hitachi, www.hitachi-eu.com/r&d/rdcentres/cambridge.htm.

11. Running the marathon

William B. Cowan, Robin Cowan and Patrick Llerena

Universities are delicate organizations, and can be destroyed. Elaine Scarry
It's all very well for you to say that: you have tenure. A junior colleague

INTRODUCTION

Universities, private and public alike, indubitably compete, and in many ways. But over which spoils? There is general agreement that the markets in which they compete are not normal ones: almost no contemporary university pursues profit-maximization as its ultimate goal (Bok, 2003; Kirp, 2003). What, then, is the goal? It's easy to compile a long list of circumstances in which competition is observed: undergraduate and graduate student recruitment, professorial hiring, fund-raising, gaining support for research, and so on.[1] In each case it is possible to identify a scarce resource, such as top students or prominent professors. Yet, the competition, usually against other universities, to gain the lion's share of the resource is clearly instrumental.

Acquiring good students or prominent professors or ample funding is not the goal of the university; they merely contribute to achieving a superordinate goal. What is that goal?

A standard justification for the public support of the university, or any other institution, is that it provides some public good. If the products of a university could be privately owned and were easily appropriable, it would be difficult to justify public funding. Industrial firms could fund the research output, internalizing the results in their own products. Equally they could fund training, benefiting from the increased human capital of their workers. For example, universities of the middle ages, creatures of the church, provided training that increased the human capital of church functionaries. Scholarly activities were concentrated on the production of goods consumed internally, such as copied and original manuscripts. Alternatively, students could fund the training themselves from higher future earnings, a model common in the professional schools of North America.[2] Consequently, one way to seek the superordinate goal of universities is to ask what public goods they can provide, which cannot be provided in other ways.

There are many possible answers to this question, which have received varying emphasis at different times. We follow the historical arguments of Readings (1996) and Cowan (2006) to see how the answer changed during the twentieth century, only to discover that misconceptions about the unique strengths of the university thrusts into types of competition that could easily be ruinous.

Universities in North America and Europe have, by and large, followed the model of the nineteenth century German university, the model which Bill Readings calls the 'university of culture'. Readings argues that Humboldt and the German idealists, who shaped the university of culture, saw universities as primary repositories of a nation's culture. In the university of culture, scholarly activity spread into new disciplines, such as literature, which studied, preserved, extended and even created the national culture.

In this model the university creates a unique public good. Fostering the nation's culture, it defines a national identity in which all citizens participate. Educated within the university of culture, future leaders of the nation acquire a common view of the nation, which makes it possible for them to work easily together. The graduates of the Grandes Ecoles in France embody this benefit at its apogee. Their common education creates a distinct social class, the members of which move effortlessly among the leading roles in political, business and intellectual culture. The value of a common culture in facilitating a cohesive nation cannot be overestimated. Specially able students from outlying provinces, where culture is more varied, are drawn toward Paris by the lure of the Grandes Ecoles so as to participate more fully in the common culture of the nation.[3]

The university of culture well describes most of the world's universities into the first half of the twentieth century, and provided a strong reason for central governments to fund them and to coordinate what they taught. Subsequently, however, universities themselves participated in, and sometimes initiated, changes that undercut the university of culture. The rapid growth of science and technology created within the university a large and influential group of scientists, the allegiances of which were, and continue to be, transnational; graduates of newly founded professional schools of business spread corporations across national boundaries, weakening the monopoly governments had previously held over the culture of their citizens. Finally, the commercialization of culture made it no more or less than any other commodity, to be selected and consumed at will.[4]

Deprived of their role as the repository of a nation's culture, public universities cast about for a new one, and found the support of innovation as their new model, which we call the 'university of innovation'. The foundation for this shift was an analysis of the incentives of scientists, which are to be open and to communicate findings publicly; and of the nature of scientists' output: fundamental, widely applicable, and inappropriable knowledge. These ideas combine to guarantee the under-provision of basic science by the private sector, in terms of both funding and outputs. In the middle of the twentieth century, basic research was to be the main activity of the university, and it would be funded to a great extent publicly. After several decades, however, governments seemed to have become disappointed with the results produced by this model: papers in scientific journals or conferences did not translate quickly into product innovation. Thus, a second stone was added to the foundation, which ushered in a more intense era for the university of innovation. This was the idea that laboratory benches of universities were littered with innovations, provided by public funding, which could invigorate innovation in the private sector. The policy problem now became how to get the knowledge or innovations more rapidly and directly out of the university and into industry.

In most cases, the cure was seen to be more private participation in the funding of university research, which implied that the measure of university output should be broadened from 'scholarly publication' to include measures of ownable research, such as patents.[5] The result was a further shortening of the time span on which research was expected to produce concrete (aka pecuniary) results. Almost unnoticed in this process was a shift in the proposed mission. In the early years of the university of innovation, universities seem to have planned that they would evolve from repositories of a nation's *social* culture to repositories of the world's *scientific* culture. But as time passed the governments that fund them wished the product of the university, research and innovation, to be appropriable by the nation, and thus tried to tie them closer to the industrial innovation process of the nation.

We should note a certain irony, when this is seen in the European context. An ongoing concern of the European Union is 'social cohesion', a target that is written into many of its research programmes. In order to submit applications to the Framework programmes for example, it is often an explicit requirement (and certainly an implicit one) that the consortium submitting should include partners from all regions of Europe. In the latter part of the twentieth century, when social cohesion was again a concern of policy-makers, European universities could have been recruited to play a modern (European) version of the role that they had played historically at the national level. But partly in response to pressure from the EU itself, universities abandoned this role to take up their new role in innovation. And one is left to wonder where the European social cohesion will come from.

This chapter argues that this unfortunate evolution of the university's role during the last half century is a result of misunderstanding the process of innovation, and of mistaking the purpose of research done within universities. This misunderstanding, shared between university administrations and the governments that fund them, induced universities to compete inappropriately both with vocational schools and with industrial laboratories, which engage in activities that occur on much shorter timescales than those of the university of culture. We argue that universities ought to be competing in a very different race than public policy now encourages. Our conclusion is not that competition is antithetical to universities – indeed, it is deeply rooted in university culture (Cornford, 1908) – but that the unique role universities should occupy is subverted when the university is expected to compete in the direct provision of industrial innovation or vocational education. The following anecdotal description of the reactions of universities to a recent survey of their relative standing well illustrates two important points about how universities compete most naturally.

Much of the day-to-day work of a university consists of marking and ranking. Thus, universities feel strongly when they themselves are marked and ranked with respect to one another. Their schizophrenic responses to these rankings tell us much about how universities see themselves.

The recent Shanghai survey (Liu and Cheng, 2005) shows typical university responses to being ranked. Most of the universities that ranked below their self-evaluations (or perhaps self-image) rejected the survey, at least in their explicit reactions, criticizing the metrics and the algorithm combining them into an overall ranking, sometimes even rejecting the possibility that ranking universities is possible, even in principle. Yet their actions belied their words: favourable interpretations of their rankings were placed prominently in their promotional literature, and the hunt was on for Nobel prize winners who would accept an additional position, since adding Nobel laureates to one's faculty was the easiest and fastest way to rise in rank. Thus, in their actions, universities indicated a willingness to compete, even as they derided the competition as futile and not even in good taste, and when the rules of the competition were regarded as mistaken.

The critics of such surveys are wrong: competition is not, in itself, bad. Universities should desire to be better, and being judged better by one's peers in Shanghai is quite appropriate. But the process has perverse features. The source of the judgement should not, we all agree, be personal opinion: it should be formed from a collection of objective metrics, so that it has the coercive nature observed to be characteristic of scholarly argument by Nozick (1981, pp. 4–5). But, just as the ranking stands proxy for the quality of the university, the metrics stand proxy for the ranking. As Goodhart (1984) points out, once targets, which are proxies for actual objectives, are known, competitors immediately find ways of satisfying the targets without achieving the objectives.[6] The process is most invidious when the targets are rankings (Hirsch, 1976) because only one university can be number one. Currently, the stated goal of many universities in Europe is to be a 'top European institute', and as one waggish colleague pointed out: 'It is going to be pretty crowded up there at the top.' In a competition for ranking, because the rewards are not commensurate with the effort expended, universities overcommit resources to enhancing their rankings, to the detriment of other, more directly useful, activities. An extreme reaction to the Shanghai survey occurred in France, where the Grandes Ecoles fared less well, compared to the public universities, than managers in the tertiary education system would have expected. The response was extreme. Because the metrics were objectively measured they could only be rejected as inappropriate. Surely enough, l'Ecole des Mines, one of the Grandes Ecoles, provided a new survey using metrics said to be more suited to French educational objectives (Ecole des Mines de Paris, 2007). Naturally, the Grandes Ecoles had pride of place, even on the world stage. Laughable, perhaps, if you are outside France, but it demonstrates something fundamental about the nature of competition among universities. Suppose, for example, the Shanghai survey had ranked the University of Waterloo and l'Université Louis Pasteur in the top ten of the world, while ranking Stanford, Harvard, Oxford, and Cambridge below two hundred. Despite the objectivity of the metrics, the reaction of the academic world would not have been, 'What an interesting surprise!' And yet this was exactly the reaction of the financial world when the market capitalization of Google surpassed all firms except Exxon and General Electric. In contrast to the way this sort of news is received in the financial world, had the Shanghai survey reported such a sudden change in status, its results would have been ignored as obviously incorrect, and rightly so. This draws attention to one of the key differences between the world of industry and the world of the university.

Sudden drastic changes in the stature of economic entities, such as firms, is normal because the time constants of the tastes and technologies that determine economic success are short. But similar changes in the relative status of universities is not normal. To be sure, ill-advised policies can destroy the status of universities within as little time as a generation, such as occurred with the university system in Argentina after the 'glorious' era of the 1960s. There, uncoordinated policies, political interference and under funding managed to seriously weaken a previously robust system.[7] But climbing the ladder takes several generations, so that the sudden appearance of an outsider at the top of a university ranking undercuts the authority of the ranking more than it elevates the status of the newcomer.

We take two lessons from this example. First, competition for status, the most natural way in which universities compete, easily goes wrong because the yardstick can be mistaken for the quality it imperfectly measures. Status is highly subjective, while the dominance of natural science within the modern public university demands the veneer of objectivity. Second, changes in status occur on a timescale of generations. In contrast to firms, universities are slow-moving institutions. This has to do, fundamentally, with differences in the ultimate motivation of the two institutions: in the first case it is profits, and the search for profitable activities; in the second it is truth, its discovery, elucidation and dissemination. By their very nature, profitable activities change rapidly (especially in a competitive economy) whereas what we believe to be true changes slowly. Institutions must be designed to operate and expected to compete on the same timescale as their core activities, which for universities is very long.

THE UNIVERSITY OF INNOVATION

Readings (1996) suggests that the university of culture is succeeded by the university of excellence. He noticed both the vacuity of 'excellence' and its prominence in the 'zombielike rhetoric'[8] that fills university promotional literature. Readings was writing early in the evolution of the university's role. We suggest that, were he writing today, he would observe the frequency with which 'innovation' is paired with 'excellence' in describing the strengths of universities.[9]

'Innovation' *tout court* is, of course, as vacuous as 'excellence', but increasingly it is used to describe the university as a player in the nation's system of innovation. This model of the university we call the 'university of innovation'. We argue that the role assigned the university in this system has two faults, that it misunderstands both the process of innovation and the strengths of the university, and that it thrusts the university into competition that undermines it as a public institution. The argument rests largely on the linear model of innovation and its reorganization by Cowan (2006).

Innovation has often been considered a linear process, summarized in 'the linear model'. In the linear model, basic research creates the knowledge on which applied research is founded, and applied research is the basis for innovation in product development. Innovation is a good diffused to consumers in the form of improved products. The innovation process is linear and uni-directional, with one stage feeding the next.[10] In this model, it is relatively easy to identify the actors: universities provide the basic research; development laboratories of industry supply the applied research; and industry manufactures the products. Proponents of this model identify the various products of basic research as public goods (Arrow, 1962; Nelson,

1959) that are insufficiently supplied by firms acting on their own owing to problems of appropriability. Thus, basic research, the most widely applicable of all types of knowledge, is severely under-supplied by the market, and must be provided publicly. Presumably it is supported by taxes on consumers who, after all, eventually benefit from better and cheaper products as a result of the innovations based on this research. Universities argue that they are uniquely suited to providing basic research: casting themselves as an ultimate foundation on which innovation is based, and justifying public funding for their activities. Industry, by contrast, is further downstream in the innovation process: the benefits of its research are appropriable in the form of patents or trade secrecy, reducing the necessity for public subsidy.

The linear model provides a clear framework in which the university of innovation competes: to provide as much basic research input to the nation's innovation stream as possible. Getting basic research across the finishing line is the goal, and measures of success are easy to find, papers published and research prizes received, which are gratifyingly similar to the criteria that scholars freely use to evaluate one another. Equally, the reward for competing successfully is clear, increased public funds to support research.

All is not so smooth, however: many public agencies have been dissatisfied with the difficulty of documenting university-initiated innovation, and industry has complained about its slow pace. Together they have introduced additional goals for the competition, such as patents and explicit collaboration in applied research. In response, universities have encouraged researchers to work more closely with industry and to engage in more targeted research, complete with milestones and deliverables. As a result, university research has moved downstream in the innovation process, where the results of research are more appropriable. This movement coincided with funding shortages, and universities were expected to fund more of their activities by marketing the innovations created in their research laboratories, or by receiving contributions from industry collaborators with whom they share their results.[11] These pressures brought universities a new, and conflicted, collection of competitors, the applied research laboratories of innovative firms, with whom they were simultaneously expected to collaborate. The university of innovation has evolved from providing a foundation for downstream activities that take place in industry, to hosting downstream activities within the university itself.

These changes undermine the university's claim to special status. Research that is patentable is, by definition, appropriable and not a public good. If it is worth doing, the value of the patent will certainly exceed the cost of doing it. If the university contribution to an applied research collaboration is worth what it costs, the firm, which appropriates the results, will surely be willing to cover fully the university's costs. Furthermore, there exist a host of consultants offering services very similar to the collaborative services supplied by the university, so that the market puts a clear value on what the university offers.

These arguments feel comfortable if we take the university for a firm: they appear because the university of innovation provides value as a supplier of wealth, justifies itself by claiming that the wealth it creates exceeds the public funds it consumes. Implicit in this claim is the ability to value the contribution of the university, which is done by allocating to it a share of the private good created by innovation in which it participates. But, if this allocation is possible in practice, then this share of the wealth can be provided directly to the university through the market by the consumers of the products to which it contributes. The argument for public funding vanishes, which is not surprising given that the university of innovation eschews any unique role, such as that possessed by the university of culture.

The university of innovation has, however, another output, its students, once they have graduated. Without them, neither applied research nor product development is possible. As supplier of cannon fodder for private innovation, the university competes with vocational colleges and trade schools. Is there an argument that justifies the higher cost of a university education? And is there an argument that explains why the full cost should not be paid by the students who receive the benefit, or possibly the firms that employ them, but should instead be covered by public funds? To answer such questions we must look more closely at the university's contribution to innovation.

THE UNIVERSITY OF REFLECTION

Not surprisingly, the linear model and the early stages of the university of innovation go well together: basic research is the central activity of the university; the source of research ideas lies within the internal dynamics of the scientific disciplines; universities compete only with each other, on the familiar grounds of refereed papers, citations and scientific prizes; and the goals of competition are the reputations and the self-perpetuation of universities. This is a conservative model of the university, which would be instantly recognizable to Ernest Rutherford or G.H. Hardy. A single added feature makes it modern: consumers, in the form of applied research laboratories in industry, take the ideas created by basic research and turn them into product innovation. The happy result is an economic justification for public funding of the university, and the academic legitimacy of the professor-entrepreneur, who combines the life of the mind with the wealth of a successful businessman.

The previous section suggested one problem with this picture of academic life. As it meets the reality of the market for innovation and evolves towards the later stages of the university of innovation, it is corroded by profit seeking. This section pursues a second problem: the observation of Cowan (2006), Rosenberg, (1982), von Hippel (2005) and others that it simply doesn't fit the facts of innovation. First, the firm is not a passive recipient of ideas generated within the university: as a client in the market of ideas it attempts to pull the basic research it requires out of the university.[12] And second, while basic research may be determined on short timescales by the internal dynamics of its discipline, on long timescales it is determined by unexplained, but seemingly explicable phenomena. Sometimes these phenomena follow the picture book story of the scientist sitting on a hillside wondering why the sky is blue or why a rainbow is curved. More often the phenomena to be explained are the result of technology. That is, basic research is the result, not the cause of technology. For example, in ancient astronomy the observation that patterns in the sky provided reliable cues for agriculture or navigation seems to have come first, with the creation of models to explain the regularities later. Or, more recently, thermodynamics followed high pressure technology in order to, among other things, explain regularities observed in steam tables.

Cowan suggests that the linear model requires two amendments in order to fit these facts. It must be made circular, with the innovation activities of firms, and their customers (von Hippel, 2005), providing an important, even dominant, input to the basic research of universities. Also, the output from the university to the firm must be re-examined: it is not ideas encoded in papers, patents or prototypes, but ideas encoded as the human capital of its graduates. Within a round of innovation, users lead, industry follows, and basic research brings up the rear, systematizing, codifying and understanding what the others have been doing. But for the next round of innovation, universities lead: teaching the basic research of the last round's innovations to their students, who, on graduation, become the innovators of the next round. Thus, the university is indeed an essential component of any system of innovation, not by supplying the ideas on which applied research and then innovation is based, but by supplying an understanding of past innovations to the personnel in whose minds innovation occurs.

How large software systems are developed illustrates this point.[13] Software projects begin with what is known: knowledge that their designers gained through education or experience. On this basis a more or less predictable implementation plan is created. At the beginning the work done by implementers simply follows this plan and is routine. Inevitably, however, misconceptions in the plan are uncovered and parts of it are found to be unimplementable with existing techniques. In addition new or modified features, not easily accommodated in the original plan, are added. These problems are solved one by one, not by a complete reworking of the plan, but by ad hoc expedients.[14] This is true innovation and it occurs by trial and error, not by doing research.[15] The result of these innovations, which accommodate changes in the plan, is an increase in the complexity of the software, not matched by an increase in understanding on the part of the implementers because it accrued through one ad hoc change after another. As complexity increases the difficulty of implementation increases, and at a certain point the project stops: an improvement in one place makes, by an interaction no one understands, a problem in another. Usually, features are subtracted from the plan until it is possible to declare that the product is complete, at which point it is released, often with the promise of an imminent upgrade or service pack that will fix outstanding problems. In the software industry there are many methodologies, such as frequent refactoring, that are supposed to remedy such problems. But the real solution is what universities do well, undirected rethinking, in other words, reflection.

That is, the best solution is to think deeply about the particular troublesome software, and software in general: examining existing ad hoc solutions to differentiate aspects that are fundamental to providing the functionality from those that are adventitious, discovering commonalities of function among modules, and creating a controlled incorporation of the functionality within a modified design. This is what university research, professor and graduate student working together under minimal pressure, does best. When the student graduates he or she has the understanding needed to proceed in a controlled way to the next version of the software, which will subsequently be pushed into a similar state of uncontrolled complexity, and require another passage through the university.

Unfortunately, this cycle is too slow for industry in the twentieth century. Cowan (2006) describes a senior manager responsible for university–firm interaction at a major North American computer firm. The manager was clear that he invited professors into his firm, not to solve his current technical problems, but to interest them in his firm's probable future problems. Most likely, he was looking for faster ways of pushing problems that his firm would need to understand into the university and receiving back graduated students with the expertise to solve them. He may, however, have been pushing on a string, because separating the enduring from the transient, which is an important goal of reflection, cannot be hurried.

Cowan's, seemingly minor, changes to the linear model have profound consequences for the superordinate goal of the university, for the timescales on which universities change, and for the markets in which universities can compete. To understand this let us look closely at how universities transform the input they receive from innovating firms. The relational database is a typical example. In the 1960s, E.F. Codd, working for IBM, developed a new type of database, the relational database, which remedied many problems of earlier navigational, or codasyl[16], databases. This was the first database design sufficiently formal to draw significant interest from researchers in universities, which were then in the process of forming departments of computer science. Unwilling to cannibalize an existing, market-dominating product, IBM moved slowly in developing a relational database management system (DBMS),[17] so that during the mid-1970s IBM and its rivals, including Oracle and Sybase, brought relational DBMSs to market. Academic research developed in parallel, the first regularly-scheduled database conferences starting in the mid to late 1970s, a decade after Codd's work. University research did not, however, feed ideas to industry where programmers were struggling to implement DBMSs, which were arguably the biggest and most complex software artifacts of their time. Instead,[18] professors made themselves familiar with the relational model, by proving theorems, generalizing algorithms, extending the relational model, teaching database courses and writing textbooks. By the mid-1980s, database courses based on the relational model were in the final year of most computer science curricula. The result was a flood of graduates. They provided the configuration and end-user programming expertise needed to configure DBMSs; they were the programmers implementing, and debugging, DBMS implementations, and they were the applied scientists adding novel features to DBMSs. These graduates are the primary input from universities to the innovation process, the critical input that universities provide to innovating industry and its customers. This is a typical example of universities supporting innovation, but not by creating innovations that are then pulled out into the world by industry (or pushed out by technology transfer offices), as the university of innovation would have it. Instead, universities *reflected* on an innovation produced elsewhere,[19] understood it and pushed that understanding into the world in the human capital of their graduates.

Reflection covers many scholarly activities. It centres on understanding by rethinking: scholars create simple causal models through which they understand phenomena; they do experiments to test and refine their models; they create metaphors and analogies that allow them to communicate their understanding to others, first to colleagues through seminars, then to graduate students through research collaboration, and finally to undergraduate students through lectures.

It is possible to observe how the university of reflection interacts with industry to further innovation at different stages. An early stage example is reputation systems. Less than a decade ago e-Bay, in an attempt to induce cheating traders to leave its community, created an ad hoc online reputation system: participants in transactions were asked to rate other participants, and the aggregate ratings were publicly visible. Interested by the contrast between face-to-face and online communities, scholars became curious about online reputation, and began to ask themselves questions: What is reputation? How is reputation enhanced or spoiled? Can online interaction produce the complex interactions that subserve face-to-face reputation? Can we by experiment show that e-Bay's reputation system works?

Currently this research is embryonic: precious little understanding has so far been created from the dozen or so investigations by graduate students and professors. But two important lessons are clear. First, most of this research is truly basic. It is not competing with e-Bay to patent the killer reputation system, because its goal is understanding. And second, no one knows at present whether online reputation is a fundamental concept or a passing fad. The long view of universities, passing online reputation from research to graduate teaching to the undergraduate curriculum, takes time. It can be, and will be, aborted if its central concepts turn out to be neither fundamental nor fruitful.

A final example shows the innovation–understanding–innovation cycle occurring twice. A recent paper by Talbot (2003) argues that Renaissance artists probably discovered perspective by noticing the illusion of depth in patterns used to compose pictures on the image plane. This innovation in artistic practice, developed by trial and error, produced a revolution in realistic depiction. Alberti and Brunelleschi, reflecting on these practices, then found analogies that gave simple explanations of how they worked. These models were not for the benefit of their contemporaries who had already mastered drawing the illusion of depth. They were for teaching non-artists and future artists. And indeed, they are used in first-year drawing classes. During four centuries the models were also formalized and elaborated by university mathematicians into a highly abstract subject: projective geometry (Coxeter, 1987).

Then, in the 1970s, scientists, mostly in government and industry laboratories, put projective geometry to work as the mathematical foundation of the computational geometry required by three-dimensional computer graphics. The source of this innovation was the mathematics courses they had taken in university, which enabled them to create algorithms to do geometry. The algorithms have subsequently been reworked within the university and are now part of the undergraduate curriculum in computer science. Graduates of these programmes are, mostly in industry laboratories, creating innovations that flow back into universities in the games played by incoming students.

Notice that competition occurred twice, when artists competed to acquire more prosperous patrons through innovation, and when firms competed to bring three-dimensional computer graphics to the market. Within the *reflective* component of this cycle, market competition did not occur. To be sure, Alberti and Brunelleschi competed for readers and future reputation, just as professors compete for publication and recognition, but this competition bears little relationship to the competition in which the university of innovation gets stuck (Kirp, 2003, p. 2).

Considering this final example, we note that the second round of innovation was not initiated by professors of projective geometry. They did not feel any urge to push projective geometry out of the university into innovative products. Yet, without the algebra they created in their quest for understanding, and without the courses they taught, the quick development of three-dimensional computer graphics would have been impossible. To be sure, once innovation had taken place, professors of mathematics tried to jump on the bandwagon, offering software packages and textbooks taking advantage of the formal simplicity of their subject. However, the conceptual clarity sought in basic research turned out to be quite different than the efficiency and quick results necessary for innovation.

The above examples show that the university of reflection values basic research differently than the linear model and the university of innovation. In it, basic research follows innovation and the domestication of innovation by basic research is essential not for the innovation of today, but for the innovation of tomorrow. Innovation is not the direct application of basic research, but the indirect result of graduates applying basic research stimulated by previous rounds of innovation.

With basic research a part of scholarship, which is subordinated to education, universities of reflection compete only with each other, and on the grounds of reputation: reputation for the quality of the environment they provide to professors and students, and reputation for the public goods they supply as they work together to increase understanding. This competition is highly subjective: its results are found in the collective opinions of professors and students. Attempts to make the competition objective are both self-defeating and distorting. Competition with entities that have different goals and different timescales, such as firms that create innovative products, simply makes no sense.

SCHOLARSHIP AS A PUBLIC GOOD

The sections above identify the modern university's superordinate objective as support of innovation, which is appropriate for a society that values economic growth highly[20] and that identifies innovation as the source of growth. They argue that the university of innovation, which is currently the most popular model of the university's role, and which has been used to justify expansion of the university's basic research during the last half century, is based on a misunderstanding of the nature of innovation, and of the university's role in it, and the university of reflection better describes the important role of the university in innovation. Probably the most important practical difference between the two models of the university is how they compete in the marketplace for innovation.

The university of innovation competes in a market of product-relevant ideas with other sources of innovation, most of which are private firms. The university's claim on society is determined by its success at producing marketable ideas. The success of this model creates pressure on the entire university to live within a market for ideas. Literature departments, for example, which were central in the university of culture, market courses in technical writing. And to justify their placement in a university, as opposed to a vocational school, technical writing must be a 'fast-moving field', taught by professors who have research programmes in technical communication. These departments are, *ipso facto*, undermining their claim to any activity that has no immediate value in the market.

Similarly, philosophy departments offer courses on the ethics of business. These courses, which teach prospective businessmen how to reason about ethics, are an indubitable social good. But they force philosophers to compete in a market that includes management consultants and motivational speakers. The clients, executives and budding executives, choose whom they will patronize. All too often the clients' interest in ethics is purely instrumental: how ethics contributes to the success of their businesses.[21] When philosophers succeed in such a market they contradict the intuition that philosophers are a better source of ethical guidance because their advice is disinterested. Even worse, the necessity of competing successfully with management consultants corrupts philosophy itself. Why?

Truth is a core value of philosophy: statements uttered without regard to their truth or falsity do not belong to philosophy. In a market for ethical advice, clients are the masters, they have market power to demand whatever advice they wish. Philosophers can compete successfully in this market only if they let the clients' demands take priority over other values, including truth. To be sure, what truth is, as opposed to what is true, can be a matter of contention. Many philosophers (e.g., Rorty, 1979) think it is more complex than the simple Platonism of most natural scientists. But all members of the university regard truth as an indispensable value: it is even worth arguing over the truth of theories of what truth is. In the university of reflection, 'It doesn't matter whether what I write and teach is true or untrue, as long as it gets me tenure,' is simply unacceptable, and rightly so.

Truth both trumps all, and is inappropriable. When firms fall into dispute with universities the appropriability of truth is usually the key issue, and when firms succeed in appropriating truth the result is unfortunate for the university. Cowan (2006) reviews two cases in which satisfying its clients in a highly competitive market brought universities into conflict with their own fundamental values. These cases are unique only in being unusually well documented. A host of editorials in biomedical journals testifies that the problem is widespread. It should not be a surprise to find universities subverting their own values in competing to supply ideas to industry: clients expect to dictate the nature of the product they receive.[22]

One might ask why it is important at all to have some institution worried about truth. Whether or not it is important in some objective sense, in any society it is possible to find some institution that sees 'taking care of truth' as its role. Astrologers, priests, witchdoctors, gurus of various types, and scientists, have all played that role in some time or place. If no institution is charged with this task, it does create a vacuum that will be filled in some way. In the west, the university has been given this role over the past several centuries, and one could argue that it has coincided with tremendous progress, not only in science, but also in humanism. One must ask in response, if the universities are denied this role, are we willing to live with the consequences of it being taken up by we know not whom? This is not an idle question. It is the nature of teaching that causes the university to value truth. Universities and vocational schools offer different sides of the commitment each generation makes to the next, the university promising, 'We will teach you what is true,' and the vocational school promising, 'We will teach you what is useful',[23] the university fulfils its promise by expecting every professor to pursue truth in scholarship, which is the traditional activity of the university. It is a more encompassing concept than research, including all the activities that integrate new truths with old, separate deep central truths from evanescent details, and make truth systematic and teachable.

How scholarship responds to revolutionary ideas in science, the most extreme form of innovation, demonstrates in sharp relief the moulding of innovation in the hands of scholarship. Episodes of true scientific revolution (Kuhn, 1980) occur rarely. The ideas they generate are, almost by definition, inaccessible to the community in which they arise. Yet within a few generations they spread within the research community and become the subject of normal science. How does this occur? Scientists teach the new ideas first to themselves, then to their research students. In doing so they rework formalisms, simplify models, add features and do experiments that test their work, all aspects of basic research within normal science. And the process does not stop there. In subsequent generations, the once revolutionary ideas continue to be reworked again and again, simplified as adventitious aspects are shed, systematized as commonalities are noticed with other ideas. This reworking tames the ideas as it makes them teachable: they move progressively earlier in the education of a student.

The differential calculus is probably the canonical example. What took Newton and Leibniz two lifetimes to 'learn' can now be taught in fewer than a hundred hours to many 18-year-olds. Three centuries of scholarship, including both basic research, which created simple proofs and notations and that extended greatly the original theory, and also pedagogy, which developed texts, curricula and teaching strategies, made this possible. Knowledge of calculus among scientists and engineers is now responsible for most of the technology that pervades all aspects of modern life. This extraordinary achievement is a triumph of the university as an institution: hundreds or thousands of researchers and teachers systematized knowledge, building in small increments on each others' work to make possible more effective pedagogical practices. It only occurs in the university of reflection. This is normal science, not well-rewarded in the university of innovation, but at home in the university of reflection and as essential as the initial discovery. Furthermore, the process is never complete.[24] Calculus is currently moving from early tertiary to advanced secondary curricula, and the search continues for better ways of codifying it. Throughout this activity the tension between simplicity and truth, which cannot be compromised, is typical, as in all scholarly activity.

Revolutionary science can occur anywhere: Newton, to be sure, was a professor, but Leibniz was a courtier. At the same time, Boyle worked in his country house, and Hooke in the Royal Society. And lest it be thought that this dispersion is obsolete, consider the twentieth century: relativity was discovered in a patent office, quantum mechanics in universities, the transistor in an industrial research laboratory, and the computer in government laboratories.[25] In all cases, however, it was scholarship within the university that took revolutionary concepts, available to few, and created from them simple causal models teachable to many. When considering the public contribution of the university systematizing the revolutionary outweighs all. The long timescales and the openness of science, where each scientist contributes a little, make these contributions inappropriable.

Systematizing calculus took several centuries. All timescales are not so long. The revolutionary ideas on which first-year chemistry is based are only one or two centuries old, and even younger ideas, such as plate tectonics, are taught in other first-year science courses. These timescales suggest that smaller and smaller innovations might enter the undergraduate curriculum after shorter and shorter delays. But there is a lower limit: university graduates are expected to benefit from their education for their half-century working lives. The specific skills with which they graduate are likely to become obsolete quickly, but their foundation knowledge and analytical skills should endure. This sets a lower limit on timescales for the university of reflection: patient reworking of innovation within the university should concentrate on concepts and principles that are likely still to be important half a century later, a timescale that is reinforced by the style of normal science: a host of small advances that eventually cumulate to a significant whole.

Essential to the continuation of scholarship is the requirement that every faculty member should perform research, as the handmaiden of teaching, and not as an end in itself, as it is in most contemporary universities. Normal scientific research[26] forces faculty to know current innovation well enough to shepherd its transition to the curricula of graduate courses. That is, we should not expect university scientists to do research because it provides ideas from which firms innovate, but because it contributes to teaching based on the essence of previous innovation.

The long timescale of this process makes it a public good, which will be supplied inadequately by the market. Furthermore, even if firms would pay for the creation of teachability, it is bad for society if the resulting understanding is appropriable. Presumably, the unpatentability of knowledge per se recognizes the undesirability of private appropriation of understanding.

Finally, remember that successful reworking of scientific truth produces expertise in differentiating the essence from the accidental. Firms must follow the tastes of their clients, which vary on a timescale of years, and must be nimble. But universities supply education to students who will use it for half a century. Neither individuals nor firms have discount rates low enough to consume the right amount of a good having such a long lifetime: only nations do. Thus, nations must supply as a public good the university, which uses the long timescales of scholarship to select what is enduring. The providers of education, not the clients, have the knowledge necessary to judge what is in the best interest of those to be educated. This consideration, combined with the disinterestedness that makes philosophers better suppliers of ethical education, demonstrates that universities focused on scholarship rather than research supply a genuine public good, one that is better for innovation as well as better for the long run interests of the nation.

UNIVERSITIES COMPETING NATURALLY

Having established the superordinate goal of the university of reflection we are ready to think about competition. The product of the university is scholarship, an openly-conducted activity of normal science that works and reworks revolutionary science, which includes innovation,[27] into systematic and simple models that are easily teachable. Teaching is, of course, part of scholarship, and for two reasons: first, success and failure can be judged only by teaching, and second, scholarship is the opposite of solipsistic: its very purpose is diffusion of knowledge. Scholarship is a unique human activity, depending on continuous growth over centuries: old ideas being revived and reworked.

Who benefits from scholarship? Directly, the students who receive its results; indirectly, firms that employ these students to create products that are ever more suffused with knowledge, and societies that benefit from long-term secular growth through innovation. Nation by nation we see a strong correlation between innovation-related productivity growth and scholarship-related growth in the productivity of teaching, which manifests itself not as an increase in students graduated per scholar-hour, but as an increase in depth of understanding, per student per scholar-hour.

Of course, such a claim is easier to make than to substantiate: how do we measure, for example, 'depth of understanding', when Goodhart's law tells us that any 'objective' proxy will be immediately subverted. The best answer we can give is discouraging: reputation. The superordinate goal of the university of reflection is scholarship, and scholars, who are by nature competitive (Cornford, 1908), continuously generate a collective reputational ranking. That is, universities provide scholarship as a public good, as doctors collectively provide public health. And just as doctors themselves judge the health they produce, scholars judge each other's scholarship, usually harshly.

A natural competitor to the university would seem to be the vocational school, but they serve qualitatively different constituencies. Universities try to provide their students with knowledge that will remain useful for half a century.[28] Expecting their graduates to inhabit a changing world, they stress principles over specific skills. Vocational schools also take the long view, but in a different way. Many goods and services are the product of technologies that are truly mature. Their processes and procedures evolve slowly over decades. Vocational schools equip their graduates with the skill to carry them out, which they expect to last a working lifetime. Thus, universities and vocational schools occupy not competing, but complementary, roles. They do, however, have one commonality: they both compete, not with each other but within themselves, on reputation.

It is rightly argued that reputation lags ten to twenty years behind the current state of a university. Fortunately, what reputation measures changes even more slowly: it takes forty years to turn over completely the faculty of a university and there is a strong correlation between the quality of new faculty hired and a university's reputation.[29] It is natural that universities compete, and the natural measure on which they compete is reputation, which changes slowly. In athletic terms, the university runs the marathon against other universities, with the end not in sight. But the athletic metaphor is surely too strenuous: the natural competition for universities is more like birdwatchers out for a stroll in the forest, competing to fill out their life lists.

Competition that is so slow and unintensive is exclusive to the university. Successful nations comprise a variety of institutions that operate on different timescales: firms producing fashion-oriented consumer goods are nimble, changing direction in weeks or months; firms producing basic materials make investments that pay off over a decade; firms supplying the base infrastructure that shapes settlement patterns must plan with a time horizon of several decades. Let us make two observations about this uncontroversial fact: first, that as the timescale increases, the coordinating authority moves to a higher political level, and second, that competition is only natural between institutions operating on similar timescales. The university of reflection competes on even longer timescales, as it works and reworks the core ideas of science. Here we see most clearly the failure of the university of innovation: requiring the university to enter the market for innovation pushes the university into a timescale, six months to three years, that is already over-populated, and in doing so it both undermines the unique role the university plays in society, vitiates its claim for public funding as the provider of a public good, and leaves unoccupied its important niche of retaining truths that change very slowly. Very few institutions take such a long view: we may think of political institutions, but only when they operate at their best, and religious ones. Society cannot afford to undermine the long-term foundation that supports the activities of faster changing institutions.

The position that the university vacates is one for which it is uniquely suited: preserver and arbiter of the enduring in a world that is increasingly changeable. The willingness to think once, and then think again, which is characteristic of scholarship, is a fatal weakness in the context of competition on short timescales: the intuition that the university plays against its own strengths when pushed into the rapidly changing market for innovation is certainly true.

Finally, the long timescale of the university makes it one of the few institutions that explicitly value reflection. Sometimes it is best to act without thinking, which society delegates to institutions that abjure history for nimbleness. Sometimes it is best to think without acting, where the right response is, 'Wait. Is it really true? Let's think about it.' We do this best in the university.

ACKNOWLEDGEMENT

Sincere thanks to Elodie Fourquet for innumerable critical readings of draft versions, and for enlightening observations about the French educational system.

NOTES

1. All three authors have, on request, participated in these activities.
2. Beneath the surface, professional schools also have an unexpected commonality with education in the Middle Ages, growing, as they did, from the apprenticeships that educated surgeons, solicitors and engineers. As then, the greatest pecuniary benefit of education seems to be membership in an exclusive guild, for which students are willing to pay dearly.
3. In this respect it is tempting to view the displacement of ENA to Strasbourg as spreading the common culture of the French elite across the European Community. In another age and with similar goals, Great Britain brought the leading students of its colonies to Oxford and Cambridge via Rhodes scholarships in order to spread a common English national culture across its empire.
4. Toward the end of the twentieth century, the survivors of the university of culture in the English-speaking world struggled against these changes, most visibly in the 'culture wars': public, and commonly violent, arguments about which culture should be studied, or the cultural content of courses. Important contributors to these arguments were new departments of cultural studies, a sure signal that culture was no longer the glue holding together the university and the nation that funds it, but a discipline like any other. The culture wars, of course, were neither won nor lost, but merely faded into the background noise from other tables at the faculty club.
5. Indeed, in Denmark today, this is taken so seriously that the level of a university's funding depends in part on how many patents it owns. In France the Loi Organique relative aux Lois de Finance of 2001, states that patent applications and licences are to be used as indicators for the success of public funding in higher education and research. And naturally, French patent statistics show the effects of Goodhart's law. Innovation in the CNRS and universities sky-rocketed starting after that law was fully implemented in 2006. Sky-rocketed that is, as measured by patent data!
6. This observation, profound enough to seem obvious, is sometimes called Goodhart's law.
7. Thanks to Ezequiel Tacsir for this comment.
8. We are indebted to David DeVidi for this evocative phrase.
9. A very recent example, (Anonymous, 2007) shows that excellence may be losing ground. In an advertising supplement describing research in German universities, 'excellent' and its cognates occur only 187 times in 57 pages.
10. Intuitively, there should be positive feedback through which some good potentially available by the consumer returns to fuel the early stages of this engine of innovation. This feedback, however natural it seems, is rarely included explicitly in the linear model.
11. As a concrete contribution governments provided universities with the intellectual property generated by government-funded research. How valuable is it? One university, UC Berkeley, which we would expect to be well positioned to benefit financially, seems to have concluded that this property is more beneficially employed increasing reputation than earning money (Butler, 2007).
12. The last statement is a true oxymoron. Properly phrased it would say that the consumers of basic research don't want basic research at all, but something different, which they call 'research', probably because tax credits encourage them to do so. It is, in fact, not uncommon to hear university researchers say about the industrial collaborators, 'They don't

even know what basic research is.' This is a serious problem, but not for the industrial collaborators.

13. The story told here is schematic, but in the abstract describes many specific cases. Brooks (1995) gives a well-known example.

14. Operating system kernels really do have in their code comments like, 'This seems to work, but I don't know why.'

15. Industry scientists often encourage management to solve such problems by research, but the timescales are wrong: research is too slow compared to trial and error. In an extreme case (Mack et al. 1983) the research was not completed until after the product had been introduced, marketed and discontinued.

16. 'Codasyl' refers to an industry consortium, the 'Conference on Data Systems Languages', whose members were largely data processing organizations. Its initial aim was to guide the development and creation of a standardized programming language. It gave its name to a specific type of flat database.

17. DBMS – database management system. The relational model is formally clean, so databases are no longer custom-built each time they were needed. Instead, databases are created by configuring standard DBMSs to the business rules of a firm.

18. With one exception, the INGRES project at UC Berkeley.

19. For which reason we call this model of the university the 'university of reflection'.

20. Possibly even above all other values. So much the worse for society!

21. Google's slogan, 'Do no evil,' where 'evil' is defined situationally, is an example of this tendency.

22. In compromising their unswerving allegiance to truth universities are, as a marketing student would tell them, in danger of diluting their brand. Well-advertised adherence to 'truth above all' is the best reason for industry to collaborate with universities. Saleable items as different as clinical trials and encryption algorithms have their value enhanced when given the imprimatur of a university known for its dedication to truth. Thus, universities, allying themselves with industry in the competition to innovate, require careful brand management to retain their value as partners. This discussion contradicts our intuition of what a university is (but, see Kirp, 2003).

23. This is not to say that everything taught in a university is true, any more than everything taught in a vocational school is useful, only that, as institutions they strive to fulfil these commitments to the best of their ability.

24. Ask any student studying calculus if today's pedagogy can be improved.

25. One could even argue that the main contribution of universities to revolutionary science is the provision of an undemanding job that allow ample time for undirected thought. However, as the examples in this paragraph show, there is stiff competition for this role, and there are few university presidents who would seek government funding on the basis of providing undemanding jobs for professors.

26. It is important not to be misled by the claims of tenure and promotion statements or of grant applications, in which all research is revolutionary. Few scientific revolutions happen each century, so we can be certain that all the scientists in the world, except one or two, are doing normal science at any time. Like it or not we are all normal. We claim that this activity is justified because its result is that the truly revolutionary scientific developments are sufficiently reworked that many can learn and understand.

27. Why is innovation included with revolutionary science? They are end-points of a range of results that has in common unpredictability and unexpectedness. Furthermore when they occur almost no one understands them. For this reason both are inputs to the university of reflection, where socially distributed understanding is generated from new ideas.

28. Universities that promote life-long learning merely admit that they don't do the job properly in the first place.

29. Newly-hired faculty say that reputation and academic environment are the two most important factors determining which job offer they choose. Economic considerations, like salary, are less important, reinforcing the non-market aspects of most universities noted by Kirp (2003).

BIBLIOGRAPHY

Anonymous (2007), 'Spotlight on Germany', (advertising supplement), *Nature* **450** (7168), 452–3, Naturejobs 1–Naturejobs 55.

Arrow, K. J. (1962), 'Economic welfare and the allocation of resources for innovation', in Richard R. Nelson (ed.), *The Rate and Direction of Technical Change*, New York: National Bureau of Economic Research.

Bok, Derek (2003), *Universities in the Marketplace*, Princeton, NJ: Princeton University Press.

Brooks, F. P. (1995) *The Mythical Man-Month*, Reading: Addison-Wesley.

Butler, D. (2007) 'Lost in translation', *Nature*, **449**, 158–9.

Cornford, J. F. (1908), *Microcosmographia Academica*, Oxford: Oxford University Press.

Cowan, R. (2006) 'Universities and the knowledge economy', in Brian Kahin and Dominique Foray (eds), *Advancing Knowledge and the Knowledge Economy*, Cambridge, MA: MIT Press.

Coxeter, H.S.M. (1987), *Projective Geometry*, 2nd edn, New York: Springer-Verlag.

Ecole des Mines de Paris (2007) 'Professional ranking of the world's universities', accessed 11 February, 2008 at www.ensmp.fr/ Actualites/PR/EMP-ranking.html.

Goodhart, C. (1984), *Monetary Theory and Practice: The U.K. Experience*, London: Macmillan.

Hirsch, F. (1976), *The Social Limits to Growth*, Cambridge, MA: Harvard University Press.

Kirp, D. L. (2003), *Shakespeare, Einstein and the Bottom Line*, Cambridge: Harvard University Press.

Kuhn, T. S. (1980), *The Structure of Scientific Revolutions*, 2nd enlarged edn, Chicago, IL: University of Chicago Press.

Liu, N.C. and Y. Cheng (2005), 'The academic ranking of world universities', *Higher Education in Europe*, **30**, 127–37.

Mack, R.L., C.H. Lewis and J.M. Carroll (1983), 'Learning to use word processors: problems and prospects', *ACM Transactions on Information Systems*, **1**, 254–71.

Nelson, R. (1959), 'The simple economics of basic research', *Journal of Political Economy*, **67**, 297–306.

Nozick, R. (1981), *Philosophical Explanations*, Cambridge, MA: Belknap Press of Harvard University Press.

Readings, B. (1996), *The University in Ruins*, Cambridge, MA: Harvard University Press.

Rorty, R. (1979), *Philosophy and the Mirror of Nature*, Princeton, NJ: Princeton University Press.

Rosenberg, Nathan (1982), *Inside the Black Box: Technology and Economics*, Cambridge MA: Cambridge University Press.

Talbot, R. (2003), 'Speculations on the origins of linear perspective', *Nexus Network Journal*, **5**, 64–98.

von Hippel, Eric (2005), *Democratizing Innovation*, Cambridge, MA: MIT Press.

12. What does it mean conceptually that universities compete?

Enrico Deiaco, Magnus Holmén and Maureen McKelvey

1. INTRODUCTION

This book addresses the issue of how and why European universities are learning to compete, in a situation where the national institutional context and sectoral conditions are undergoing transformation. This view is quite a long way from traditional views of the nature of academia. Academics are to some extent localized to the specific university that pays their wages, and yet they also share a world of beliefs, value and experiences with academics located around the world. Robert Merton (1973) articulated a world in which scientists evaluated knowledge based on an ethos of universalism, organized scepticism, disinterestedness, and communism.[1] In Merton's writings, communism refers to the community, and hence that scientists openly share their work with their community for the common good. The Humboltian ideal of the university from Germany was very influential for the 'research universities' and similarly defines a particular type of mission to society and way of organizing. This view projected a university based on three formative principles: unity of research and teaching, freedom of teaching, and academic self-governance (Shils, 1997).

However, as outlined in Chapter 1 and as detailed in subsequent chapters, the contemporary environment of researchers, teachers and students seems to be moving far from these ideals. One can see that these new competitive regimes for national universities within Europe are related to factors such as: (a) Increasing globalization of students, resources and faculty; (b) Changes in national public policy for education, science and innovation; and (c) Changes in business R&D strategies. Underlying these changes are the increased recognition and importance of the role of knowledge in creating economic wealth of nations and individuals as well as firm profits. This means that universities in some respects are becoming more central and more integrated to nations and firms' economic activities than previously. The reason is that their mission to create, renew and transfer knowledge has become a prized asset and commodity in the modern economy. Therefore, as universities are becoming more of a core organization to society in this sense, then more foci should be put upon critically observing their activities and the broader transformations ongoing.

Because of these broader changes, European universities – from top leaders, faculties, research groups and individual employees – are increasingly forced to explain to many stakeholders about how, whether, and why their scientific knowledge and educational programmes are relevant to society or not. For example, if universities are not contributing to public and private goods, why should society continue providing resources? Why should students pay for education, if the individual returns are too low? Why should companies and private foundations pay for research, if the results are not directly relevant to their goals? How can the efficiency and productivity of the university be improved – and which metrics can be used to demonstrate that those goals have been met? What are the dilemmas and trade-offs that this new competitive regime imposes on the functioning of universities and of society? These are the types of questions currently raised within universities in Continental Europe and Nordic countries, and ones that university leaders, faculty and staff will have to answer. Or else they should raise new types of questions and perspectives about the role of the university in society.

Despite – or perhaps because of – their new roles, these organizations face significant economic and political challenges, which arise due to ongoing massification and internationalization of research and education as well as demands on higher quality, 'measurable' outcomes, and explicit economic benefits. Universities in Continental and Nordic countries are thus now moving to a new competitive regime, where universities are becoming 'knowledge businesses' in trying to become more similar to firms in how they conceptualize their 'business', develop strategy, act to renew their service offerings and exploit their existing resources (staff and infrastructure) and capabilities. However, this means that universities struggle to find their particular solution to balancing their traditional roles of research, teaching with immediate demands of societal usefulness. Traditionally, many universities focused on the long-term, which was discussed in Chapter 11, 'Running the Marathon'. Usefulness in the past could be defined in terms of developing new areas of knowledge through research for use in future decades – and of widening the societal base of new knowledge through teaching and diffusion of students. However, universities now face clear demands of producing knowledge that is *immediately* useful to students, businesses and society (enhanced by, amongst other things, the Bologna process). The pressures on the university to quickly respond to societal and industrial demands have thus been more forcefully articulated in recent years.

If these organizations wish to retain the traditional values of scholarship, they will need to do so, in parallel with understanding – and changing – their selection environment in the future. Hence, here, we focus upon the competition aspect from a Schumpeterian view, in order to draw out the logical conclusions but we do not focus upon whether those outcomes are desirable or negative. We choose this focus because we know that universities play major roles in the knowledge society, and current debates within the EU indicate that we will see additional major changes in the national institutional context and global markets. Yet this book only makes some initial steps towards understanding how European universities are changing, as well as whether and how well European universities and colleges are learning to compete, in comparison with their global competitors and collaborators. For future analysis, we will need more precision in whether competition exists in the university system, especially what competition means, and how metrics and feedback loops affect the distribution of winners from losers, the latter which is called selection mechanisms in the evolutionary literature.

This chapter therefore turns to more abstract questions, such as whether competition exists amongst universities and if so, what are the major trends and future outcomes of this shift from a social institution to a knowledge business as discussed in Chapter 13. Thus, do universities really compete? And if so, how do they compete? And over what?

2.   DOES COMPETITION EXIST IN THE UNIVERSITY SECTOR?

Park (1998, p. 347) points out that competition is a pivotal concept in economics, so different interpretations of the concept are worth detailing here. Students 'learn of perfect competition as a particular market structure that consists of a large number of perfectly knowledgeable buyers and sellers who are individually too small to affect the market price and who engage in the exchange of a homogeneous good'. It is also often assumed that increased competition pushes GDP upwards but does not affect the shape of the long-run GDP-development although the new growth theory certainly challenges this view (Romer, 1994) showing amongst other things, the existence of increasing returns to scale. This simple view on perfect competition is sometimes associated with negative connotations such as struggle, rivalry and extinction of socially productive actors, values and behaviour. This simple textbook mode of describing perfect competition has been developed and made more realistic by incorporating a much more sophisticated description on how various actors economize on information (Stiglitz, 1993). Thus, the textbook model of perfect competition requires the absence of strategic interaction – for example, firms do not take into account the possible responses of other firms to their own actions' which is a poor description of the competitive process.

This book sees competition from a modern Schumpeterian perspective in theories of innovation and entrepreneurship, where successfully competing means that an actor is able to innovate, interact with the environment, and respond to changes. Many evolutionary inspired social scientists have taken a broader view on the role of competition viewing it as mainly a process of discovery and experimentation (Schumpeter, 1942; Dahmén, 1950; Eliasson, 1990). In order to satisfy customers a producer is forced to constantly modify or create new products or services mainly by innovating. It has to produce the same products to a lower price or introduce new products that have a better price and performance ratio. This process is viewed as a discovery and experimental process where new knowledge is invented or where new knowledge is combined with older knowledge to introduce new products and services. Only a test on the market will show which experiment will be successful. In practice, this view of the competitive process means that competition will coexist with co-operation, that entry of new firms will coexist with firm exit and that expansion is as common as closures. In the broader perspective, this joint interactive process will result in dynamics that generate positive and long-term GDP growth.

When we started working on this book, questions arose about whether universities compete or not, whether there were positive or negative implications, and so forth. Many colleagues from Continental Europe and Nordic countries argued that European universities do not compete, at least not in the sense companies do nor in a way that the economic and static model of perfect competition suggest (see, for example, Engwall, 2007). For many, universities represent social institutions and bastions of learning for future generations where the universities, colleges and the like are deeply entrenched societal institutions, as a place for critical, independent debate. So, the response was that any competition that arose would not be of the economic type, but it would instead be around values, prestige and reputation. Various arguments and assumptions were brought forth, about the special nature of universities and the obvious lack of competition.

In contrast, colleagues from North American, Australian and British institutional contexts clearly knew that competition existed – mainly because they had lived within a science and R&D system, driven by specific metrics and management techniques. They were only too aware that competition did exist, and many of them were wary of the long-term and unintended consequences.[2]

These divergent opinions had a positive effect, in that it stimulated us to start thinking more deeply about theoretical and empirical implications of a Schumpeterian, innovation and evolutionary perspective. When we then started looking more closely at the empirical material about European universities, we felt that many of these arguments against the whole notion that universities compete became weaker. This strengthened our conviction that universities will increasingly have to act like innovative firms – even though we know little about how these changes may have long-term effects. More should be done, to discuss whether the long-term effects are positive or disastrous and whether they may preserve core values or change them completely. Let us address some of these arguments against the whole notion of competition in this sector directly:

First, European universities are not competing because they are regulated
It is correct that the higher educational sector is very regulated and dependent upon government financing. But the same is true for the pharmaceutical industry, but no one would argue that pharmaceuticals do not constitute an industry, competing on a global scale. Moreover, the pharmaceutical industry is certainly characterized by sales of products of high upfront but low marginal costs, but this is not that different from much university teaching and research which are services of a high upfront cost but low marginal cost kind. This implies that a change in the regulation of universities could lead to a similar change of the university sector as the pharmaceutical sector underwent, such as mergers but also a division of labour where large actors govern the complementary assets whereas new actors focus upon discovery and development.

Indeed, higher education is being deregulated around the world. Deregulation in the higher education sector takes many forms. Examples include the current debate for more autonomy of universities, the emphasis on research excellence as a mechanism for distribution public funding, and current GATS negotiations on liberalizing services, including education services. A better analogy to the ongoing transformation may therefore be the deregulation of telecommunications and PTT in Europe. These were national champions and great bastions of technology, communicative resources and the like. Yet they have been deregulated and now fight on the global – and on very limited local – markets. Hence, an important issue is what strategies, niches and outcomes are possible as research and higher education become deregulated.

Second, government funding is allocated in a non-competitive manner
Clearly, in the past, many European national governments allocated financing to HEIs in a non-competitive manner, but this is changing (Frölich, 2008). Traditionally, governments provided fixed funding and budgets, based on allocations from previous years. However, public policy

in Europe is increasingly moving towards internal competitive mechanisms to allocate financial resources to education and research. Public funding is given, based on metrics for outcome goals such as publications to measure research excellence, number of active professors per student to measure the science in teaching, and number of PhD degrees granted to measure higher-level training. These types of funding schemes introduce more competitive and outcome-related selection environment, in the sense that organizations change their organizational and incentive structure to realize those performance measures. The most elaborate system is the UK research assessment exercise (RAE), which has been conducted five times since 1986. Although the data measuring the effects of RAE on performance is rather evidentiary and flimsy, several studies suggest that the exercise has strengthened research performance of universities in the UK and Australia (Butler, 2003; Hicks, 2007). Many discussions are now underway as to whether, and what system should come after the 2008 RAE in the UK, as well as how to implement similar mechanisms in other countries.

Our interpretation of these trends suggests that European government funding is increasingly based on a type of competition, and universities will have differential positions, where rankings and performance measures will affect resource allocation. Rationales for changing these mechanisms may differ, such as to raise quality and to diffuse education to groups normally not taking advanced degrees. This implies that the government no longer just hands out financial resources, where future budgets will simply reflect previous years. Instead, the universities increasingly have to demonstrate results, as an outcome of the financial resources which society invests. So, de facto, HEIs will have to perform and to compete increasingly in national institutional contexts, based on specific criteria for selection to allocate resources.

Third, there are not any markets, and therefore there cannot be competition
This assumption is to some extent based on a traditional neoclassical view of competition, where a particular type of market can be assumed to exist and play a central role as a coordinating mechanism. We agree that this type of market mechanism does not dominate higher education and research in most of the countries we studied.

However, more modern economic theory and other theoretical perspectives have studied a number of diverse forms of markets and also how market 'mechanisms' may be at work, even without a 'pure market'. The questions then become quite different, such as what is the equivalent of the market, and what is being traded, at what price?

Education clearly is – or is becoming – a knowledge-based service, for sale at a price. That price is often differentiated based on home country (or other geographical aspect) of the student as well as by characteristics of the provider. In the USA, for example, one can clearly see that different 'quality' and mission of educational services command different prices. Countries differ in how far education has become a knowledge-based service as opposed to a public good. This is not surprising as research shows that the transformation from a national, social institution to a market actor takes time regardless of sector. Still, the UK in recent decades shows how quickly a national institutional context can move from the idea of free education in the 1970s to a pay-as-you-go system today. In other countries like in Sweden, the idea of taking fees from students still meets strong resistance, but discussions are underway to introduce fees – but only for international students outside the European Union. Moreover, many countries like Italy and Spain now allow parallel private and public systems. In comparison with education, it is perhaps less clear whether, and how, research is a knowledge-based service for sale, to the same extent as education. In some cases, university–industry interaction does provide direct funding for research, where firms purchase a type of service, albeit usually one difficult to define. A 'market' may be developed in other dimensions, such that the UK labour market pays quite a premium for highly cited academics publishing in top journals – even for part-time or post-retirement affiliation.[3]

Fourth, the majority of funding is from government agencies, not firms
This statement is similar to the above two, but focuses more upon the source of funding. In fact, the validity of this statement varies greatly, depending both on the discipline analysed and the national context (Bonaccorsi and Daraio, 2007). Some aggregate trends also indicate changes. OECD statistics indicate that between 1981 and 2003, the percentage of government-funded academic research has decreased by 10 percent, and the share of the business sector in the financing of higher education R&D has doubled and reached 6 percent in 2003 (Vincent-Lancrin, 2006). This business financing is unevenly spread across fields but also across universities. Case study type of evidence from specific HEIs indicates that many are working to position themselves to compete from additional industrial funding. Budget autonomy is part of the push towards deregulation, as well. These changes will have implications for the future. If money and budget autonomy is correlated with good research performance as new research seems to indicate (Aghion et al., 2007), then we would expect the universities and HEIs to have even more diverse income streams in the future.

Slaughter and Leslie (1997) identify and analyse an important phenomenon in these changes. They discuss 'academic capitalism' which they define as the market or market-like efforts to secure external monies. External monies from new sources such as alumni are of great significance within some national institutional contexts. For example, in 2007, the leading ten universities in the USA all managed to raise funds over $300 million while Harvard alone in 2006 had an endowment of well over $25 billion (CAE, 2007). Of course, the ability to raise funds and to rely upon income from endowments is highly skewed among universities. Therefore, this is one major reason for the differences in what an individual university can do and what it can accomplish.

However, the increasing reliance on external funding is only part of the story of how universities in many countries are changing their behaviour. Thus in contrast to Slaughter and Leslie (1997), our approach to understanding universities as competing is somewhat broader as we intend to capture changes across the three roles of the university; research, education and third mission.

Fifth, universities do not act like firms

University leaders talk about strategy and competition but do not know what they are talking about. These statements are impossible to validate or reject, and similar statements could be made about strategy in firms. Still, there are reasons to discuss similarities and differences. Engwall (2007) argues that even if universities today are increasingly adopting management methods and rhetoric, they still cannot be labelled corporations since they remain professional organizations with unclear ownership structure and aiming for reputation and prestige rather than profit. However, the boundaries do certainly change, and effects are similar to competition amongst firms. Empirical studies show that universities have emergent strategies (rather than deliberate ones), which can be defined and measured as positioning in the multidimensional output space (Bonaccorsi and Daraio, 2007; Chapters 6 and 7, this volume). The very same studies show that universities try to differentiate themselves by taking specific strategic positions such as specializing in certain fields. Moreover, this differentiation does lead to observed and large benefits for those that act strategically. This process of differentiation is however limited in Europe by various institutional constraints at the national level. An example of one such constraint would be the lack of autonomy of many European universities because they are government agencies. Perhaps the greatest difference between firms and universities is the highly decentralized power structure of universities and the limited or even negligible power of the vice-chancellors. This stands in quite a contrast to the power of CEOs to, for example, hire and fire staff. This does not mean university strategy does not exist. Instead, strategic actions take place on different levels within the organization. Still, some changes towards very large research centres and integrated masters programmes seem to favour that strategic decisions are taken at the top level, as demonstrated in Chapter 3 (this volume). Concepts of strategy and competition are often fuzzy, and difficult to capture precisely, and certainly university leaders at many levels are trying to incorporate this type of thinking into their decisions and resource allocation.

3.   WHAT MIGHT LEARNING TO COMPETE MEAN IN THE UNIVERSITY SECTOR?

One of the aims of this book is to further conceptualize what it means that universities are competing. Buzzwords like strategy, quality, global player and competitive edge have become de rigueur for university managers and for policy-makers within Europe. This occurs at the same time as the European conception of the 'usefulness' and 'value-added' of the university, college and technical institute is slowly changing. It is changing from a primarily national institution serving the public good to a population of diverse actors trying to attract resources and competencies in order to grow and survive. To understand the changes, we propose using evolutionary-inspired theories of the role of knowledge, uncertainty and opportunities for transformation in the sector and for the pressures placed upon the organization. This paradigm stresses transformation as an intrinsic feature of the economy and the importance of knowledge and of positioning the organization to identify, act upon and realize innovative opportunities. To do so, we must understand universities as strategic actors, especially as we can empirically observe that the top organizational leaders and also research groups are developing competencies and responding to pressures for change (for example, Slaughter and Leslie, 1997; Shattock, 2003; Slaughter and Rhoades, 2004). This section therefore answers a series of questions, of what learning to compete might mean in the university sector.

> *1.   Does existing literature already cover the issues of competition, learning and strategic actors?*

Universities have been the subject of much research (for example Birnbaum, 1990; Bauer et al., 1999; Fuller, 2000) within many different traditions such as economic geography, innovation studies, science and innovation policy, triple helix, innovation systems, technology transfer, and economics of science. Each of these address different issues. Key existing university literature has addressed their role in constructing regional advantage and clusters and more broadly how universities act as vital institutions within the innovation system (Etzkowitz and Leydesdorff, 1997; Cooke and Piccaluga, 2004; Asheim et al., 2006; Braunerhjelm and

Feldman 2006). Economics of science focuses on the justification of public basic research, the connection between science and technology, the individual scientist's incentives for conducting research and research productivity, funding regimes and scientific labour markets (see, for example, Dasgupta and David, 1994; David, 1994; McKelvey, 1996; Stephan, 1996; Salter and Martin, 2001).

A vast amount of literature has been written specifically on university–industry interactions. Topics include relationships between science and technology on university patenting; on academic entrepreneurship and start-up companies; and on the functioning of technology transfer offices and university support structures (Mansfield and Lee, 1996; Ziman, 2000; Salter and Martin, 2001; Mowery et al., 2001; Shane, 2004; also Nowotny et al., 2001). A number of pieces examine the 'entrepreneurial university', with an emphasis on technology transfer and related issues (Etzkowitz, 2003). Each tradition has its own set of ideas and results.

With a few exceptions, the existing literature generally does not address universities as strategic and competing actors in the way done in this book. Still, if one wishes to re-interpret those existing results within our conceptual framework, then that literature does provide many detailed empirical insights about single cases as well as background information about specific national institutional contexts. Given the overall lack of attention to the topic, this implies that such a re-analysis as well as more empirical work and theoretical explanations are needed specifically about the changes in how universities and research groups compete for scarce resources, react to institutional changes, and develop competencies.

2. What do we mean by the transformation from social institution to knowledge business?

In an earlier book, *Flexibility and Stability in the Innovating Economy*, McKelvey and Holmén (2006) stressed that transformation of the economy involves an inherently dynamic and complex system, consisting of diverse components and elements, which are interacting and changing in different ways over time. Economic transformation therefore refers to a non-reversible process, referring to quantitative and qualitative changes in components and connections, and often driven by opportunities, defined in a broad sense. These processes may be driven by processes of complexity and self-organization, as well as processes of adaptation and co-evolution.

Hence, the starting point for this book is that the European universities are trying to survive – and change – due to internal factors and pressures as well as external ones in ongoing processes of transformation. To understand that, we need to analyse emergent strategies and competition, the impact of national context and global trends, as well as rethink 'accepted wisdom' about the roles and mechanisms available for universities to compete. Actors must position themselves, and chose to learn, react or exit niches.

By this idea of 'transformation from a social institution to a knowledge business', we wish to capture the notion that universities are increasingly competing against each other, as places where knowledge is reproduced, transferred, developed and applied to specific problems. The universities are *in* the knowledge business. Therefore, universities must compete for financial and intellectual resources to cover costs for students and staff, and in an increasingly performance-driven European context. They must also compete in the provision of intangible service outputs like quality of education, research impact, and societal relevance. This implies that we need further conceptual understanding of scarce resources, uncertainty, and the necessity of using competencies and resources in order to deliver knowledge-based services through core organizational activities. How they do so is another matter, since acting like a firm may not be the answer. Indeed, it is certainly plausible that later research might find that the traditional values, missions and organizational forms of the research universities enabled them to 'compete' in the way defined here, under specific historical institutions. Still, what we need to better understand is what the modern competition and competitive regimes may mean for the future of European universities.

3.   What do we mean by competition, in general?

If we look more closely, there are at least three different conceptualizations of competition. These can be found, respectively, in the neoclassical economics literature, the Schumpeterian and evolutionary economics literature, and the modern value creation and knowledge-based literature (Slywotsky, 1996; Park, 1998; Saviotti and Krafft, 2004). The first conceptualization views competition from a resource allocation and efficiency perspective (Park 1998). The economic system is coordinated by the market mechanism. Much analysis within this paradigm views competition either on price competition between producers or consumers on a market or the competition among firms producing the same economic good (Park, 1998; Saviotti and Krafft, 2004). This view assumes that if one wants to understand competition within the economy, then one should either focus on market mechanisms and/or upon a population of firms that are within the same sector because they are selling substitutable products.

The second conceptualization of competition comes from Schumpeterian views of the economy as a dynamic process of rivalry amongst firms in which only the fittest survive and thrive (for example Metcalfe, 2006). In this view what separates the successful from the unsuccessful competitors is the ability to create, invent and innovate (Park 1998). The third view is similar to the second but comes from management literature. Here, there is even more focus on the strategies, business models and resources and capabilities of individual actors. Relevant underlying paradigms can be found within business economics and related fields such as strategic management, which also have other dimensions of differences between definitions of competing and competition (Penrose, 1959; Slywotsky, 1996).

Our view combines the second and third perspectives on competition.[4] One starting aspect is the overall system. From an economist's viewpoint, Saviotti and Krafft (2004) develop a definition of competition, which they claim combines the first and second theoretical perspectives. In their view, competition is based on three aspects: competition as interaction (amongst firms), competition as involving qualitative change, and competition as an ongoing process. Krafft (2000) and Saviotti and Krafft (2004) define competition to involve rival firms, industries, markets, as well as the techniques of production. 'Competition is a process of rivalry between firms which takes the form of contests within existing markets (intra-industry competition), and the form of potential entry into new areas (inter-industry competition). Competition includes rivalry in terms of price, but also in terms of altered or improved techniques of production or products, and in terms of the provision of information to consumers about products' (Saviotti and Krafft, 2004, p. 2). Thus, one central aspect of competition is that when two actors compete, their relative success depends on the views of some other, third party. Normally this party is a paying customer or by some social representative, such as the state. In our interpretation, they have added a dynamic element to a traditional definition of competition, but retained the focus upon overall system and exchange of resources within the market system.

This implies that by combining the second and third perspectives, we can propose a new direction for understanding universities learning to compete. In contrast to the first perspective and some evolutionary approaches, universities are seen not as some kind of calculating machine that simply adapts to signals and changes in its environment. Therefore, an important aspect in this book is the opportunities in the environment and the competencies developed by strategic actors, as further discussed below.

4. How to understand competition in universities, by combining a Schumpeterian and competence-based view of the firm.

Universities are here seen to be actors which respond to signals in the environment but also actively affect their selection environment, and in doing so, they also have diverse and sometimes unique competencies, resources and strategies. Universities are constituted not only by visible leaders like vice-chancellors, presidents and deans but also by research groups and faculties, student bodies, and individual researchers. People within universities work to shape their internal processes as well as their environments, and these decisions and actions represent active 'pushes' to change things as well as more passive 'responces' to internal as well as external pressures.

From a dynamic perspective, competition is the process in which actors (individuals, firms or other organizations) act to improve their access to scarce resources that can fulfil their wants or needs. Access can refer to the existence of a resource as well as to the ability of an actor to get hold or create such a resource. Core to competition is that it is not enough to do something but to do it so effectively or efficiently compared to its competitors that it can 'afford' to continue to operate.[5]

In part explained by external events, competition is dynamic and is never at rest. Just as important are the endogenous processes of consumption, production, institutional changes, and innovations (Foster and Potts, 2006). As these processes are connected, in any actor system, the actions of one affect actions of others (e.g. March 1996). Such ongoing processes internal to any economic system create uncertainty in terms of what the scarce resources are, and consequently what actors compete over and how they compete (Lane and Maxfield, 2005; Metcalfe, 2006). Thus, time, perception and actions must be an explicit element of the conceptualization of competition (e.g. Hayek, 1937).

To compete then means that an actor undertakes actions to advance its situation under uncertainty but where these actions themselves create uncertainty. Consumption and production affect scarce resources differentially as these processes transform, destroy or even increase the availability of resources. Innovation and institutional changes affect the scarcity of resources as they hinder or steer consumption and production towards some but not other resources. Innovation affects the range of offerings that are made to customers but also how these offerings are created and distributed.

Therefore, when studying industries and firms, our theoretical perspective of combining Schumpeterian economics and competence-based theory of the firm leads us to stress the role of opportunities in creating new activities and enterprises in relation to changes in investment (Schumpeter, 1942; Hanusch and Pyka, 2007). A first insight has to do with opportunities for change. Empirically it has been demonstrated that over time different technologies and research are consistently characterized by different levels of opportunities, i.e. the likelihood of coming up with some novelty differ greatly depending on the nature of the technology or the problem (e.g.

Klevorick et al., 1995). Another theoretical insight links to opportunities related to capabilities. The innovation management literature deals with how individual actors such as entrepreneurs perceive, identify, act or construct opportunities (Shane, 2004; Holmén et al., 2007). This is greatly affected by the resources and the capabilities available to the organizations as they construct what they can and should do (e.g. Penrose, 1959). As organizations 'add' or terminate capabilities over time, they also continuously leverage their accumulated capabilities, meaning that they are both path-dependent and path-breaking. The end result of this process is differentation among various universities and therefore (changes in the) division of labour.

5. Who is competing in the university sector?

The question remains of who is competing in the university sector. Given the top-down style of many recent strategic initiatives in European universities, strategy and competition have been increasingly seen as something for the 'university as a whole'. In reality and in the chapters in this book address competition across levels of analysis, and generally include interactions across at least two of these six layers. Figure 12.1 visualizes the layers, internally, and theses layers were also used in Chapter 1 to provide an overview of the chapters in this book.

The first four layers represent ways of representing the inside of the university and HEIs. The last two layers are not included in Figure 12.1, but represent the broader external environment, which is affecting the four internal layers.

1. Individuals
2. Research environments
3. Departments
4. University as an organization
5. National science and education system, including public policy
6. Global university sectoral innovation system.

The first three layers relate to individuals, research environments and departments. Many years of research has demonstrated the importance of key individuals for science, and yet the research environment is also key, to enable collaboration and stimulate new endeavours. Departments refer to the organizational unit, which provides administrative support, organizes undergraduate education and usually retains many control functions. These three layers are crucial for understanding what goes on within universities and colleges, given the distributed nature of this type of knowledge work.

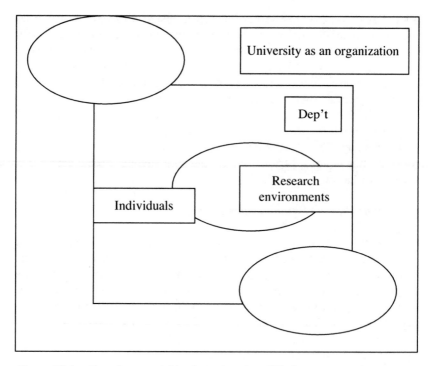

Figure 12.1   Four layers within the university: Who's competing?

The fourth layer is the university as an organization. Here, one can analyse the university acting as a more or less coherent and cohesive organization, similar to how one discusses 'the firm' or 'the government agency'. Competition is affected by how the people leading the organization have defined some goals and direction, so that analysis may focus on the top offices (vice-chancellor, rector, president) as well as on leadership roles such as faculties, deans, and committees. This layer is also affected by the organizational actions and outcomes at an aggregate level, such as recruitment policy, the total number of students educated, and whether more research is being published in top journals, within a time period.

The last two layers are the external ones of national science and education policy system and the global sectoral innovation system. These refer to the broader innovation systems, and as such, these are more the arenas within which specific universities and colleges can choose to compete. At the national context, one can analyse the 'university sector' as a population of actors or one can analyse national institutional variations, such as the existence of specialized research institutes in comparison to universities and the specific policies and institutions governing higher education. The global sectoral innovation system has been less studied than the other levels (except the sector for management education see, for example, Sahlin-Andersson and Engwall, 2002), but may be increasing in importance, due to internationalization, including the new global competitors and trends amongst students and researchers.

We argue that university competition does take place at different layers, and for different 'customers' and stakeholders. Thus being clear about these layers is useful for designing future empirical work on how, why and whether universities are learning to compete. The most interesting ideas about strategy and competition likely centre around how several layers interact in specific processes.

6. What are the service products for sale?

At the most extreme, we could think of universities and colleges as a type of knowledge factory, delivering knowledge-intensive services. Even manufacturing companies making traditional industrial products have moved towards adding value through services, so this conceptualization is in line with much research on companies (Prencipe et al., 2003) The question remains, what are universities and colleges 'selling'?

We suggest that universities and colleges are involved in three key areas of knowledge-intensive services which are 'education', 'research' and 'societal interactions' especially commercialization.

Gallouj (2002) provides a review of literature about innovation in services, including the specificity of services as being consumed as they are produced, as involving some degree of customer participation; and as exhibiting extreme diversity. In a study of knowledge-intensive business services, Tether and Hipp (2002) review the literature to find the following specific characteristics of knowledge-intensive services: close interaction between production and consumption; the intangible nature of service outputs; the key role of human resources in service provision; the critical role of organizational factors in firms' performance; and the weakness of intellectual property rights in services.

This implies that the boundaries of the university will be rather 'fuzzy' when services involve consumption and production as well as that human resources and organizational factors will have large impacts on the successful delivery of these three knowledge-intensive services. Figure 12.2 shows that individuals and research groups are organized within departments at the university, in relation to the three knowledge-intensive services on offer.

Much of the provision of the three knowledge-intensive services will directly involve those individuals, but also occur at the boundaries between the employees of the organization and other groups. To take an

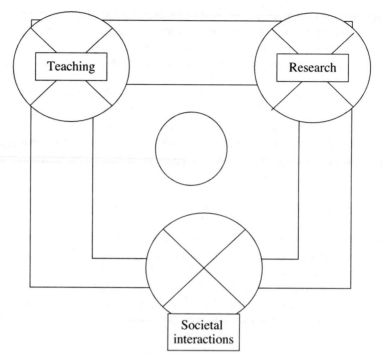

Figure 12.2   Knowledge-intensive services creating open boundaries in the university

obvious example, students are an integral part of what makes a university, and often 'consume' their education on-site, and yet they are not employees.

Figure 12.2 thus demonstrates how the delivery of the three types of knowledge-intensive services opens up the organization towards multiple stakeholders, while at the same time often requiring the involvement of multiple layers within the organization.

4.   SELECTION MECHANISMS AND METRICS

This section uses some of the previous concepts, in order to characterize how universities compete from the point of view of selection, that is how outside actors chose among existing or expected offers from different universities.[6] So what is it that universities offer, if we go beyond the characteristics outlined above? From a more abstract perspective, universities are specialized organizations whose motivation for existence is the fact that knowledge is a scarce resource in society. Universities are a particular organizational form that is set up (almost) solely to alleviate the scarce knowledge problem in society. This is not a minor task as evidenced by the discussion of the 'knowledge society' where knowledge should be the most important asset for economic competitiveness, especially for firms and other organizations. This scarcity can occur in society, in two main ways, either as being poorly disseminated among actors or simply as genuine ignorance or lack of knowledge across the entire population.[7] The remedies for the problem of poorly disseminated knowledge as provided by the universities tend to come in the shape of education but also third mission activities while the problem of lack of knowledge tend to come in the form of university research.

We have outlined the three types of knowledge-intensive services that most universities offer individuals, firms or society, and the idea of scarcity helps us see why the universities compete. Education is a knowledge-intensive service in the sense that universities provide students with new insights and skills by drawing upon the existing skills and competencies of its staff. Research is a knowledge-intensive service in the sense that the university is to discover, analyse, synthesize or test new knowledge and then disseminate its findings in society. It may do so by publication and teaching but also by setting up new companies that exploit the new knowledge, allowing society to purchase its findings. These are three ways in which the university as an organization provides its knowledge-based services. All three are knowledge-based services in the sense of being intangible offerings, often requiring a combination of producer and user interaction, as discussed in the previous section.

Universities can provide these knowledge-intensive services because someone is willing to pay for (or purchase) them, through public or private funding. The nature of the scarcity depends on the constituency, that is for whom the organization exists (e.g. Morris, 2005). For example, an undergraduate student is likely to be more interested in what and how a university teaches than its research or the university's commercial outreach or societal impact. At the same time, the interest of society and firms tend to be broader but also more indirect than the interests of individuals as they may be interested in the number and general quality of graduates rather than what these students know individually. Still, all constituents of universities have some interests in all types of university outputs, as they influence each other directly and indirectly. Nonetheless, this leaves us with the question of what the relation looks like between the services universities provide and the different wants and needs of its constituents – or 'customers'.

One broad answer can be found in the extensive bodies of literature that deal with how universities interact with their environment and on the overall role of science and of universities in society (e.g. Bush, 1945; Arrow, 1962; Etzkowitz, 2003). Importantly, from a knowledge-based perspective, there is ample empirical analysis of the unique contribution of basic science and how society benefits from scientific research and university activities. Thus, there is a long tradition of research which has tried to specify the contributions of basic science and of universities per se to society (Mansfield, 1991, 1995; Salter and Martin 2001; Geuna and Nesta 2006). These studies conclusively show that different types of public research as well as universities per se contribute to public and national objectives for society. While this literature generally focuses upon the contributions of research, it is sufficiently general to show a broader contextual understanding of what universities do for whom.

A literature review of the economic benefits of publicly funded research identifies seven channels for the economic benefits of publicly funded research (Salter and Martin 2001; Martin and Tang 2007). These are (1) Increase in the stock of useful knowledge; (2) Supply of skilled graduates and researchers; (3) Creation of new scientific instrumentation and methodologies; (4) Development of networks and stimulation of social interaction; (5) Enhancement of problem-solving capacity; (6) Creation of new firms; and (7) Provision of social knowledge, such as policy-relevant knowledge.

Hence, in this section, we wish to link these seven mechanisms by which universities interact with society towards different types of 'customers', stakeholders or others whom are willing to pay and consume these intangible services. Table 12.1 therefore specifies the differing perspectives of three main groups of constituents – students, firms, and governments (or society).

Let us then explain how Table 12.1 links the type of knowledge-intensive service to the benefits expected from different types of customers in terms of these seven mechanisms.

Clearly, there are differences in that students are directly interested in the skills, knowledge and aptitudes they acquire while firms and government are more concerned with the general increase and dissemination of useful knowledge via supply of skilled graduates and researchers. The provision of the three knowledge-intensive services may be interlinked across customers and services. The interests of firms are more specific than governments, so that firms demand competent employees while governments are more concerned about creation of socially useful capabilities. Research as such is rarely directly useful to students but it can have many indirect effects, especially by making education more up-to-date. Firms can also find research to be relevant as it creates new problem-solving abilities or instruments that may solve many of their business problems or provide them with

Table 12.1   *University services and beneficiaries: benefit to different types of customers*

Type of knowledge-intensive service	Students	Firms	Government
Education	Training to create skills and knowledge	Creation of competent employees Alleviation of scarce human capital	Alleviation of scarce human capital Creation of societal capabilities
Research	Better 'proven' knowledge	New or proven knowledge Business opportunities	Trained professionals New knowledge
Third mission	Firm, business and societal connections Entrepreneurial opportunities	Access to specific problem-solving skills Mentoring Diffusion of scarce knowledge	New firms Diffusion of scarce knowledge about societal problems Identification analysis of the nature of societal problems

new business opportunities. Finally, universities also 'sell' a whole range of third mission activities. While this is not the primary concern of students, they do tend to be interested in making connections with companies for future careers or starting up firms.

Table 12.1 above also has some distinct strategic and competitive implications for universities. A shift towards a new competitive regime where the selection of output determine which universities will become 'winners' and 'losers' could then be found in terms of various metrics that represent Table 12.1. Ways of quantifying the outputs of the universities and HEIs are 'metrics' such as number of publications and citations, and these can be seen as signals to potential consumers, who compare different universities. When comparability across organizations becomes more important, then metrics in terms of outputs matter more. This is similar to the role of the price mechanism in more traditional market situations. The metrics used within a specific national context or region is clearly related to public policy decisions, such as whether to count publications, company start-ups or patents.

Table 12.2 *Example of metrics used by different customers in the university sector.**

Type of offerings	Students	Firms	Government
Education	Type of courses; employability; expected employment and salary; reputation, prestige and university/ educational ranking	Number of graduates with relevant profiles	Number and type of students and graduates, deflation of unemployment numbers
Research	Prestige and university ranking	New proven exploitable knowledge (patents) PhDs with relevant profiles	New proven knowledge No. of PhDs Prestige research (mass media coverage, university rankings)
Third mission	Employability Prestige	Employability Problem-solving skills and advice Spinoffs Meeting places	Employability National and regional prestige and development Guidance of societal concerns and debates Spinoffs Meeting places

Note: * Many of the listed metrics are already in use. For example 'New proven knowledge' can be assessed in the number of publications, paper citations and the number of patents. There are many examples of 'university/educational ranking' such as the *Financial Times* list of rankings of MBA (Master of Business Administration) programmes around the world.

Note that the exact nature of the metrics does not need to be straightforward, or rather, they are often mitigated by other forces. In industry, firms do not just compete only by offering homogeneous products for a price but also in terms of other aspects like branding, reputation, and consumer loyalty. The same should hold true for universities.

Based on Table 12.1, a list of suggested metrics is shown in Table 12.2.[8] These should all reflect outputs of the interests of the different constituents along the three different university services. As student interests of education is in terms of its training, metrics corresponding to the output could be expected to be what type of courses they have had, whether they are likely to get a job and their (expected) future salary. An indirect output is also the prestige of their educational profile and their university as reflected by the perceived quality of other graduates. Firms are more likely to focus on the number of 'good enough' graduates that can be usefully employed, while the government should also be concerned with keeping unemployment figures down.[9]

In terms of research, students should be concerned with the prestige they can draw as reflected in research announcements, while firms would both be concerned with the creation of potential highly skilled employees (PhDs) and access to exploitable knowledge. In addition, governments would find demonstrated knowledge relevant but also more prestige related issues such as the number of leading universities or research groups as compared to other nations.

Finally, students are likely to look for employability and prestige as a reflection of the outcome of third mission activities. Firms would view third mission activities to increase the likelihood of employability of students, but would also be interested in the existence and size of meeting places or the number of spin-offs in a region from a university. In addition, governments would likely care about national or regional prestige stemming from third mission activities as well as being able to identify perceived experts that can be enrolled whenever some nationally strategic question arises.

In conclusion, there are strategic implications for how universities will act based on the metrics-based selection logic outlined above. Metrics form a type of selection mechanism, where there are feedback loops so that strong performers on one or several important metrics are rewarded for what they have accomplished, while poorly performing universities are punished.

We argue that this means that over time (most) universities will try to act strategically to improve their standing on important metrics – or else try to change the metrics by which they are judged. To begin with, European universities are already working to improve their standing on important metrics, and to do so, they are using internal and external review panels, based upon specific criteria and lists of acceptable journals. However, there are different constituents, and some but not all metrics may be difficult to combine in the same organization. Consequently some universities will focus only upon a few, where they seem to be more likely to be successful. This means that different universities will attempt and learn to specialize to score high on very specific metrics. Thus, positive and/or negative feedback based on relative performance on metrics will reinforce specialization. Moreover, some universities will still perform poorly on existing metrics, regardless of the constituency. Or, they may wish to retain their reputation, by being involved in all three types of knowledge-intensive services. These considerations matter greatly in a world characterized by scarce resources and where the relative performance in terms of outputs is correlated to the amount of resources the universities can get hold of. Consequently, poorly performing universities need to do something to stay in the game, and not only competing for market shares (e.g. expansion of students). These universities can do so by trying to change the rules of the competitive game, in order to improve their standing. One way is to create additional and new metrics, that can be thought of as tailor-made metrics that should fit their particular profile. Another alternative is to point out that existing measurements and indicators are inherently biased (or even downright erroneous).[10]

This idea about metrics and feedback mechanisms can be used to assess the relative degree of how far countries have advanced along shifting their university sector more towards the new competitive regime. The reason is straightforward. The more a nation has shifted towards the new competitive regime, the greater explanatory power that we can find in the universities' 'market share' in terms of research funding, amount of high paying or highly talented students, the amount of spin-offs, etc. This can provide one way to scrutinize the relative amount of 'university competition' rhetorics compared to whether the actual performance really results in, for example, larger market share of research funding for good performers. It can also provide insight into how specific organizations – or the national context – provides ways 'around' the new competitive regime, allowing for business as usual (!) for the universities.

5. DISCUSSION

This chapter has addressed what competition may mean for the universities. While we recognize the validity of many arguments about the specific nature and context of universities, colleges and HEIs, one of the points of this chapter is to see how far that we can push the argument that universities do compete, and that the way they compete is changing. We have done this to explore where and how universities can be analysed using tools traditionally reserved for industries and firms.

We find them sufficiently similar to firms and competition to push the argument further. From the above discussion, we propose that:

1. The question about the extent to which universities are similar or different from firms is an empirical, not an ideological, question.
2. Nonetheless, universities and colleges may have missions and ideals that are poorly represented within the new competitive regimes developing within Europe.

3. Universities compete within a higher educational sector in that there is a population of competing organizations, which have differential assets and competencies.
4. Like firms, some universities primarily compete locally or nationally whereas others compete internationally.
5. Individual universities can decide to try to strategically assess their competencies and capabilities, in order to position themselves to compete in the future. They do so in relation to three knowledge-intensive services and their relative importance is determined by different constituencies (market segments).
6. Universities have to develop knowledge assets, which may be developed internally or which may be sourced externally through mechanisms such as collaboration. These are key to providing the goods and services demanded within the higher education sector.
7. Selection mechanisms based on metrics (indicators) are usually related to different customers, and a specific university will have difficulties in maximizing all of the metrics (the term de-harvardization was coined to describe that even Harvard is unable to supply all subjects).
8. The correlation and causation between how universities perform on different metrics and various forms of market shares can be analysed to capture how far nations have gone towards a new competitive regime as compared to the regimes of social institutions, financed by public monies to produce public goods.

From the perspective of the university, these knowledge-intensive services are all activities in which individuals, groups, departments, and the organization as a whole participate and shape. Clearly, as this process proceeds, conflicts do arise between activities and between different parts of the university. Trying to deliver upon these different domains of activities usually involves difficult choices, involving trade-offs between different sets of metrics, priorities and desired effects. Moreover, providing knowledge-intensive services can be carried out by separate parts of the organization, or else the same people can be involved within all types of activities. This implies that rather than treating the university as one entity, future research needs to further define and refine how, why, and what levels these changes are occurring – as well as identifying what is being lost in the new competitive regimes. This chapter has suggested some ways in which the individual organizations and the sector can be analysed, understood, and managed as providing knowledge-intensive services to different customers, and under different forms of selection mechanisms.

European academia do seem to be transforming by facing new internal and external pressures to change and conform to a competitive regime, within the university sector. They face deregulation at national level of education and less direct funding. Many governments want teaching factories, rather than elitist organizations – although quality research also has high prestige. Goals are often conflicting, between different knowledge-based services. In some national institutional settings, research is still clearly financed by the state and in other national settings, researchers must find external funding, sometimes accompanied by an assumption that external monies certify high quality of research. This implies that the conceptualization of what a university is, how it works, and what benefits it provides to society are changing, but may also be quite different in different European countries. Despite that diversity, all the European universities seem to be struggling with renewal of education and research, with maintaining traditions as well as incorporating new tasks. Given our broader view of competition as a dynamic process, requiring innovation and specialization, we could predict and identify attempts by HEIs to consolidate position and to compete through knowledge-based services. The question of strategy and how to compete then arises, as do their attempts to change the national institutional setting and selection environment, to fit their own profile and goals.

NOTES

1. Universalism means that the personal and social attributes of the researcher should not affect the perceived validity of the conclusions. Disinterestedness means that the beliefs should not be biased by authority, and communism refers to open communication and common ownership of knowledge.
2. The present authors found this debate to be extremely interesting, and it stimulated the book project.
3. The output of HEIs has traditionally been handled as a merit good, that is a commodity that should be distributed to an individual or society by other means than consumer preferences (Musgrave, 1987). And it is assumed that merit good are under consumed or under produced because they create positive externalities which arise from the consumption or production of the good or services. As individuals are myopic they might not take into account the long-term benefits of consuming a merit good. Education has often been taken as an example of this. Clearly, a merit good does not have to be provided by government as is shown by recent development in primary education and management education. For instance, US experience with charter schools have shown how dynamic competitive elements can be introduced in the provision of education.
4. Based upon previous work, we have decided to differentiate on whether the definitions are primarily static or dynamic; whether they are primarily concerned with the overall system or focus upon actors; and whether the focus is upon exchange of resources within the market system or upon the accumulation of resources within the organization (McKelvey and Holmén 2006; Holmén et al., 2007).
5. Competition is often indirect as modern economies are characterized by a high division of labour (e.g. Knight, 1921). This means that an actor competes over resources in one area to improve its standing in another. Often the rewards are financial but other means for satisfying wants and needs are also important.

6   One way actors compete is how they construct their business model. The business model can be viewed as the 'script' or 'logic' by which economic value is extracted from resources in association with one or several business opportunities. Central to the business model is how value is created for the customer and how the innovating firm appropriates economic value. From a dynamic and forward-looking aspect the firms attempts to create value and appropriate returns from its investments. Value is a subjective notion that relates to the perceived wants or needs of a user and is thus here defined from the user(s) perspective (Menger [1871](1981); Lepak et al., 2007). A business model includes the activities from making something to reaching customers, distributing the products, designing the revenue model and so on (Amit and Zott, 2001; Chesbrough and Rosenbloom, 2002; Magretta, 2002; Markides and Charitou, 2004; Morris et al., 2005). Therefore, the business model refers to the customer segments that are being defined and served and the customer offering, which activities should be and are performed in-house and which should be outsourced, how the firm configures its resources, what the position is/should be in the value network, how the firm sells and distributes its offering and what value is created for the customer and by what means a profitable and sustainable part of that value is appropriated through its revenue model. The activities of the firm is thus to participate in forward-looking value-creation activities under uncertainty, and to appropriate and capture a part of the forthcoming value.

7.   There is also a third aspect, retention or remembrance in the sense that universities can be thought of as consisting as a specialized collective memory.

8.   Of course, these metrics can be converted to quantitative measures and/or be assessed by indicators.

9.   As the goals of having low unemployment but also high quality in education may be incommensurable, this may be an example of different metrics being incommensurable.

10. The universities that are likely to be winners are the ones that can align their knowledge base with their services while reaping increasing returns. With this combination in place, they will receive positive feedback compared to other universities allowing them to use their advantage to invest in new knowledge assets. The winners here are the ones that do more by knowing less. That means to specialize so as to reuse knowledge in some domain(s) time and time again in order to improve their scoring on the particular metrics that matter. When the selection mechanism in terms of comparability becomes more important, the metrics in terms of outputs matter more. This argument is closely connected with the above point as 'losers' in one metric over time may need to shift their emphasis to other domains.

REFERENCES

Aghion, Ph., M. Dewatripont, C. Hoxby, A. Mas-Colell and A. Sapir (2007), 'Why reform Europe's universities?', *Bruegel Policybrief*, issue 2007/04.

Amit, R. and C. Zott (2001), 'Value creation in e-business', *Strategic Management Journal*, **22**, 493–520.

Arrow, K.J. (1962), 'The economic implication of learning by doing', *Review of Economic Studies*, **29** (3), 155–73.

Asheim, B., P. Benneworth, L. Coenen and J. Moodysson (2006), 'Co-evolution in constructing regional advantage: multiple roles of Lund University in strengthening the Scania regional innovation system', LIEE / NTUA, Athens, December 2006, accessed 17 January, 2008 at http://dime-liee.ntua.gr.

Bauer, M., B. Askling, S.G. Marton and F. Marton (1999), *Transforming Universities. Changing Patterns of Governance, Structure and Learning in Swedish Higher Education*, London: Jessica Kingsley.

Birnbaum, Robert (1990), *How Colleges Work. The Cybernetics of Academic Organization and Leadership*, San Francisco, CA, and Oxford: Jossey-Bass.

Bonaccorsi, Andrea amd Cinzia Daraio (eds) (2007), *Universities and Strategic Knowledge Creation – Specialization and Performance in Europe*, Cheltenham, UK and Northampton, MA, USA: Edward Elgar Publishing.

Braunerhjelm, Pontus and Maryann P. Feldman (2006), *Cluster Genesis: Technology-based Industrial Development*, Oxford: Oxford University Press.

Bush, V. (1945), *Science and the Endless Frontier*, Washington, DC: National Science Foundation.

Butler, L. (2003), 'Explaining Australia's increased share of ISI publications – the effects of funding formula based on publication counts', *Research Policy*, **32** (1), 143–55.

CAE (2007), Contributions to Colleges and Universities, Council for Aid to Education, accessed 14 February, 2008, at www.cae.org.

Chesbrough, H. and R. Rosenbloom (2002), 'The role of the business model in capturing value from innovation: evidence from Xerox Corporation's technology spin-off companies', *Industrial and Corporate Change*, **11** (3), 529–55.

Cooke, Philip and Andrea Piccaluga (eds) (2004), *Regional Economies as Knowledge Laboratories*, Cheltenham, UK and Northampton, MA, USA: Edward Elgar.

Dahmén, E. (1950) *Svensk industriell företagsverksamhet. Kausalanalys av den industriella utvecklingen 1919–1939*, Stockholm: IUI.

Dasgupta, P. and P.A. David (1994), 'Toward a new economics of science', *Research Policy*, **23** (5), 487–521.

David, P.A. (1994), 'Positive feedbacks and research productivity in science: reopening another black box', in Ove Granstrand (ed.), *Economics of Technology*, Amsterdam, North Holland, and London: Elsevier.

Eliasson, G. (1990), 'The firm as a competent team', *Journal of Economic Behaviour and Organization*, **13**, 275–98.

Engwall, L. (2007), 'The university: a multinational corporation?', paper for the Academia Europea and Wennergren Foundations Conference The University in the Market Place, Stockholm, 1–3 November 2007.

Etzkowitz, H. (2003), 'Research groups as 'quasi-firm': the invention of the entrepreneurial university', *Research Policy*, **32**, 109–21.

Etzkowitz, Henry and Loet Leydesdorff (1997), *Universities and the Global Knowledge Economy: A Triple Helix of University–Industry–Government Relations*, London: Cassell.

Foster, John and Jason Potts (2006), 'Complexity, evolution, and the structure of demand', in M. McKelvey and M. Holmén (eds), *Flexibility and Stability in the Innovating Economy*, Oxford: Oxford University Press.

Frølich, N. (2008), 'The politics of steering by numbers – debating performance-based funding in Europe', NIFU STEP rapport 3/2008.

Fuller, Steve (2000), *The Governance of Science, Ideology and the Future of the Open Society*, Milton Keynes: Open University Press.

Gallouj, Faïz (2002), *Innovation in the Service Economy: The New Wealth of Nations*, Cheltenham, UK and Northampton, MA, US: Edward Elgar.

Geuna, A. and L.J.J. Nesta (2006), 'University patenting and its effects on academic research: the emerging European evidence', *Research Policy*, **35** (6), 790–807.

Hanusch, Horst and Andreas Pyka (eds) (2007), *Elgar Companion to Neo-Schumpeterian Economics*, Cheltenham, UK and Northampton, MA, USA: Edward Elgar.

Hayek, F. A. (1937), 'Economics and knowledge', *Economica*, **4** (13), 33–54.
Hicks, D. (2007), 'University system research evaluation in Australia, the UK and US', Georgia Tech working paper series no. 27.
Holmén, M., M. Magnusson and M. McKelvey (2007), 'What are innovative opportunities?', *Industry and Innovation*, **14** (1), 27–45.
Klevorick, A.K., R.C. Levin, R.R. Nelson and S.G. Winter (1995), 'On the sources and significance of inter-industry differences in technological opportunities', *Research Policy*, **24**, 185–205.
Knight, Frank H. (1921), *Risk, Uncertainty and Profit*, New York: Harper.
Krafft, J. (2000), *The Process of Competition*, Cheltenham, UK and Northampton, MA, US, Edward Elgar, pp. 1–10.
Lane, D.A. and R.R. Maxfield (2005), 'Ontological uncertainty and innovation', *Journal of Evolutionary Economics*, **15**, 3–50.
Lepak, D.P., K.G. Smith and M.S. Taylor (2007), 'Value creation and value capture: a multilevel perspective', *Academy of Management Review*, **32** (1), 180–94.
Magretta, J. (2002), 'Why business models matter', *Harvard Business Review*, May, 3–8.
Mansfield, E. (1991), 'Acadamic research and industrial innovation', *Research Policy*, **20**, 1–12.
Mansfield, E. (1995), *Innovation, Technology and the Economy: The Selected Essays of Edwin Mansfield*, Vols I and II, Cheltenham, UK and Brookfield, VT, USA: Edward Elgar.
Mansfield, E. and J.Y. Lee (1996), 'The modern university: contributor to industrial innovation and recipient of industrial R&D support', *Research Policy*, 25, 1047–58.
March, J.G. (1996), 'Continuity and change in theories of organizational action', *Administrative Science Quarterly*, **41** (2) 278–87.
Markides, C. and C. Charitou (2004), 'Competing with dual business models: a contingency approach', *Academy of Management Executive*, **18** (3), 22–36.
Martin, B.R. and P. Tang (2007), 'The benefits from publicly funded research', SPRU electronic working paper series no. 161.
McKelvey, Maureen (1996), *Evolutionary Innovations: The Business of Biotechnology*, Oxford: Oxford University Press.
McKelvey, Maureen and Magnus Holmén (eds) (2006), *Flexibility and Stability in the Innovating Economy*, Oxford: Oxford University Press.
Menger, Carl (1871), *Grundsätze der Volkswirtschaftslehre*, translation published as, *Principles of Economics*, 1981, New York: New York University Press.
Merton, Robert K. (1973), *The Sociology of Science: Theoretical and Empirical Investigations*, Chicago: Chicago University Press.
Metcalfe, J.S. (2006), *Evolutionary Economics and Creative Destruction The Graz Schumpeter Lecture*, New York: Routledge.
Morris, M., M. Schindehutte and J. Allen (2005), 'The entrepreneur's business model: towards a unified perspective', *Journal of Business Research*, **58**, 726–35 .
Mowery, D., R.R. Nelson, S. Sampat and A. Ziedonis (2001), 'The growth of patenting and licensing by U.S. universities: an assessment of the effects of the Bayh–Dole Act of 1980', *Research Policy*, **30**, 99–119.
Musgrave, R.A. (1987) 'Merit goods', in J. Eatwell, M. Milgate, and P. Newman (eds), *The New Palgrave: A Dictionary of Economics*, London: Macmillan.

Nelson, Richard R. (1996), *The Sources of Economic Growth*, Cambridge, MA: Harvard University Press.

Nelson, Richard R. and Sidney Winter (1982), *An Evolutionary Theory of Economic Change*, Cambridge, MA: Harvard University Press.

Nowotny, H., P. Scott and M. Gibbons (2001), *Re-Thinking Science: Knowledge and the Public in an Age of Uncertainty*, Cambridge: Polity Press.

Park, D. (1998), 'The meaning of competition: a graphical exposition', *Journal of Economic Education*, **29** (4), 347–57.

Penrose, Edith. T. (1959), *The Theory of the Growth of the Firm*, Oxford: Blackwell.

Prencipe, A., A. Davies and M. Hobday (2003), *The Business of Systems Integration*, New York: Oxford University Press.

Romer, P.M. (1994), 'The origins of endogenous growth', *Journal of Economic Perspectives*, **8**, (1) (Winter) 3–22.

Sahlin-Andersson, K. and L. Engwall (eds) (2002), *The Expansion of Management Knowledge: Carriers, Flows and Sources*, Stanford, CA: Stanford Business Books.

Salter, A.J. and B.R. Martin (2001), 'The economic benefits of publicly funded basic research: a critical review', *Research Policy*, **30**, 509–32.

Saviotti, P.P. and J. Krafft (2004), 'Towards a generalized theory of competition', presentation to the DRUID Conference, Elsinore, Denmark.

Schumpeter, Joseph A. (1942), *Capitalism, Socialism, and Democracy*, New York and London: Harper.

Shane, Scott (2004), *Academic Entrepreneurship: University Spinoffs and Wealth Creation*, Cheltenham, UK and Northampton, MA, USA: Edward Elgar.

Shattock, Michael (2003), *Managing Successful Universities*, Buckingham: Open University Press.

Shils, Edward A. (1997), *The Calling of Education: 'The Academic Ethic' and Other Essays on Higher Education*, Chicago, IL: University of Chicago Press.

Slaughter, Sheila and Larry L. Leslie (1997), *Academic Capitalism: Politics, Policies, and the Entrepreneurial University*, Baltimore, MD and London: Johns Hopkins University Press.

Slaughter, Sheila and Gary Rhoades (2004), *Academic Capitalism and the New Economy*, Baltimore, MD and London: Johns Hopkins University Press.

Slywotsky, Adrian J. (1996), *Value Migration. How to Think Several Moves ahead of the Competition*, Boston, MA: Harvard Business School Press.

Stephan, P. (1996), 'The economics of science', *Journal of Economic Literature*, **34** (3), 1199–235.

Stiglitz, J.E. (1991), *Welfare Economics with Imperfect and Asymmetric Information*, New York: Oxford University Press.

Tether, B.S. and C. Hipp (2002), 'Knowledge intensive, technical and other services: patterns of competitiveness and innovation compared', *Technology Analysis and Strategic Management*, **14** (2), 163–82.

Vincent-Lancrin, S. (2006), 'What is changing in academic research? Trends and future scenarios', *European Journal of Education*, **41** (2), 169–202.

Ziman, John M. (2000), *Real Science: What It Is, and What It Means*, Cambridge: Cambridge University Press.

13. From social institution to knowledge business

Enrico Deiaco, Magnus Holmén and Maureen McKelvey

1. INTRODUCTION

This book, *Learning to Compete in European Universities*, addresses the challenges facing modern universities and colleges. The main issue is how universities and colleges transform from social institutions into knowledge businesses. The previous chapters provide analysis, which frames the debates and provides some insights into this new situation. This is a necessary debate, because European universities are moving from a nationally focused and secure environment into a global and regional, uncertain future, where the selection rules and environment are more difficult to predict. So how and why do European universities see their role and their environments changing? And how are environments changing, within national institutional contexts and within the global context of science, technology, R&D and education? What alternative strategies are available?

The need for debate can be illustrated by the rhetorics of the concept competition. One current trend is that many European university leaders are claiming to be for 'strategy', 'focus', 'specialization' and the like – as demonstrated by metres of bookshelves full of university documents. Yet, we feel that too few are seriously considering the negative and positive implications of this transformation for what the specific university does as well as the implications for the role of societal institutions within society. The hypothesis put forth here is that there is a new competitive regime, or a new 'competitive game', with new winners and with rules of the game that the actors are only beginning to understand. From our Schumpeterian-inspired theoretical perspective, we can extrapolate that innovation, flexibility, strategy and responding to new opportunities are necessary for European universities to face this future. So learning is necessary.

Chapter 1 presented the idea that European universities are transforming to fulfil old and new tasks, within a new context. The book has provided evidence that European universities are now working within the context of the increasingly internationalized knowledge economy. In doing so, we must begin to understand how and why the researchers and universities are now more explicitly competing with each other – where competing to achieve competitive advantage can include strategies such as mergers and cooperation with select partners. The ongoing transformation of the university per se and of the overall system are placing pressures on the specific university as an organization.

Thus, there are internal and external pressures upon the university, whereby the specific university must learn to develop capabilities to adapt and maintain their lead competencies, within a dynamic environment. Internal pressures for change are articulated through shifts in university leadership, development of new core competencies, and attempts to develop relative specialization. External pressures also exist, such as shifts in government science policy, decisions of multinational companies to relocate R&D, and international flows of students and faculty.

Hence, this concluding chapter focuses upon the future. The reason is that our argument is thus: the future will look quite different from the past and that is why European universities are learning to compete. In doing so, however, this book challenges the 'accepted wisdom' on Europe and raises concerns about the direction and ultimate impacts of these longer-term developments.

Our theoretical and empirical results can be summarized in the following six propositions:

1. *European universities will be pushed to behave more like firms.*

The reason is that universities have to transform as a consequence of internal and external pressures by both delivering more socially relevant knowledge in a more cost-efficient manner. This implies internal changes, for example, towards more top-down management styles, more financial control, better use of resources and organizational innovations. Externally, the organizations will be pushed towards specialization in terms of delivering knowledge-based services, an increasing emphasis upon rankings as well as the recognition of the role of the national context and specific HEIs in the global value chain.

2. *The universities and HEIs which are able to react more flexibly to the changing national institutional contexts as well as to the international movement in people and resources will do better in the current period.*

Flexibility is a current priority, and will affect the transformation, and it includes reactive and proactive responses to changes in the selection environment. Those HEIs which are able to react more flexibly to the changing national institutional contexts as well as to the international movement in people and resources will do better in the current period. The more flexible ones are already bringing in more resources and developing new areas of education and research, relevant to society. It is likely that this will be linked to top-down and bottom-up attempts to act more strategically, develop internal competencies and engage in relevant collaborations. However, in the long run, it is unclear whether the less flexible ones will 'lose out' or whether those upholding traditional values of the university will be proven right in having other values for teaching and scholarship.

3. *The universities that can create a sufficient resource base which, over time, they recombine to reach and leverage new research and educational opportunities will become the future winners.*

Despite the need for more flexible action, the environmental shifts should not be too major or too unpredictable, if the goal is to promote quality. The same argument holds true for university strategy; an approach to research and education that is too opportunistic is likely to be punished. Building competencies takes time. Researchers (individual and groups) have clear difficulties in acting flexibly, if the movement of resources swings too rapidly. With dependency upon a type of short-term and rapid capitalism within academia, they have to be focused upon immediate returns, and have difficulties in building up long-term knowledge and learning capabilities. Such short-term academic capitalism will also lead to reactive responses such as 'it was better before' and 'we are losing academic freedom', which could block future changes.

4. *The university sector as a whole will become more dynamic.*

This will be visible in that entry and exit of research groups, master and bachelor programmers and courses will become similar to the patterns that have become so visible within studies of industrial dynamics and sectoral systems of innovation. Some areas will expand and others contract, as will the balance between different knowledge-intensive services that are provided. These changes might have huge implications for how universities recruit staff and what to deal with in-house and what areas that can be outsourced.

5. *The university structure in Europe will remain, and possibly intensify, a diverse institutional context, with diverse populations of universities, colleges and HEIs.*

The new competitive regime will not lead to greater homogeneity, but can work as a strong force pushing universities towards greater specialization in Europe in the future, not just among the universities but also among nations. Clearly, timing of the changes to national institutional contexts will matter too, as universities in national contexts like the UK have moved much earlier to competitive regimes than those in other national contexts like the Continental and Nordic countries. An interesting issue to follow is whether there are first mover advantages, or whether other combinations of resources such as integrated research–teaching strategies are possible.

6.   *National contexts may mitigate the severity of these outcomes, even if pan-European trends push towards broader 'rules of the game' and 'level playing fields' for all organizations.*

The actions of an individual university cannot be understood without considering its relationship to its national and global environments. Hence, the universities including its leaders and research groups are trying to interpret their national science and education policy in order to react to, and influence, the broader public policy arena. Particularly in Europe, where the majority of funding tends to come from the government, the degrees of freedom for the university to access resources and appropriate depend upon the broader public policy arena. The global competitors and trends are becoming an increasingly important level of analysis for European universities. So far, we do not expect European governments to allow 'bankruptcy' of whole organizations, but it is likely that they will change incentive structures and resource flows as well as push for collaboration, mergers, alliances and a general rethinking of the organizational agenda, as necessary changes for survival.

These six propositions are developed in more detail in the concluding section. What this book and these concluding propositions do indicate is a new type of future, which we expect will be part of the transformation of European research and education to a more competitive regime where competition is fiercer and qualitatively different from a decade ago. The larger issue at stake is whether we want competition in the European university sector that is increasingly similar to firm competition, and if the answer is affirmative, what are the implications of changing from social institutions to knowledge businesses?

2.   EUROPEAN UNIVERSITIES ARE LEARNING

The book title – *Learning to Compete in European Universities* – stresses that universities are only now beginning to experiment with competition, and learning how to compete due to the ongoing transformation of the university sector into a new competitive regime. To capture this notion, the chapters have been grouped within four themes, which represent broader, horizontal issues of relevance and importance to the debates introduced above. They are 'Emergent Strategy', 'Differentiation and Specialization', 'Rethinking University–Industry Relations' and 'Reflections'. This section reassesses what we have learnt within each theme.

2.1   Emergent Strategy

The first theme is 'emergent strategy', as pursued by European universities. Strategy is concerned with the effective management of key organizational attributes that cannot be altered quickly, without cost and/or being irreversible. The concept covers many aspects such as developing capabilities, developing an internal strategic process, protecting reputations (with customers, employees, suppliers, rivals, regulators), keeping key personnel, and acting on observation of the effects of choices in terms of scale and scope of education and research. Strategizing is the opposite of drifting, 'firefighting' and similar myopic approaches. The emergent strategy of the specific universities refers to their choices over time, including aspects of 'winning' and whether they learn to survive and excel (or not) in their selection environment.

The three chapters of this theme describe strategy as an emergent process, which results from decisions that are made at many levels within a university. Moreover, there is usually an ongoing interaction between universities on the one hand, with the national institutional contexts on the other hand. Although the focus here is upon the universities per se, their choices are set in terms of national and regional institutional contexts, which provide incentives, institutions, resource flows and the like. Competition is therefore also often implicit and resulting from the differential ability of universities to access resources and to provide knowledge-based services. It is a dynamic process requiring innovation and specialization on behalf of the universities in order to be competitive.

Chapter 2 shows an increasing use of alliances and collaboration as strategic devices. It seems that alliances are responses to a hardened competitive climate such as external pressures for change. The motives behind alliances vary, but a common theme is preparation for or implementation of an adjustment to new international approach that emphasizes critical mass, renewal, profiling and branding of research and educational offering, and competition for internationally mobile students and companies. The picture suggests that the traditional rationalization benefits are probably limited, and that an alliance has sometimes been used as an end in itself rather than as a mean of achieving the organization's objectives. Rather, the opportunities offered by an alliance involve increased interfaces between the universities at all levels. The case studies do seem to indicate a considerable flow of resources, money and people in building and managing the alliances and that many of the alliances have been attractive to external financing organizations and secured more corporate funding. Thus, management of university alliances (and mergers) is a process that requires delicate planning, considerable management attention and strong mutual trust. Hence, pursuing this strategy means that management is subject to the same risks and rewards as in any other business.

Chapter 3 demonstrates a clear example of the transformation of two institutions in a merger, through top-down management techniques. In the United Kingdom and other Anglo-Saxon countries, the universities have more radically and quickly responded to the new competitive regimes. This chapter stands in stark contrast to the traditional way European universities change. They have had a kind of genteel competition for prestige rather than finances. Strategy has traditionally been a bottom-up process, resulting from decisions taken by individuals and by the research group or departments. This chapter demonstrates something else all together, where now the strategy processes are increasingly top-down, driven by the upper management of the university. They also introduce explicit goals and performance measures, where, for example, the university explicitly decide to gain its market share in terms of its share of publication in prestige journals. This example clearly demonstrates how universities can increasingly act like firms, working towards specific goals, hiring in attractive (and lucrative) fields and individuals, firing others, and the like. This is often linked to changes to include new behavior and performance incentives, such as wage bonuses for publications in specific journals. Writing papers is no longer assumed a 'natural part of science' but instead an output to be rewarded. At the same time, the chapter also hints at the problems of becoming a winner, while the metrics have improved, the finances have deteriorated. Finally, this case shows how the interaction between the market, the environment and the organizational competences are changed, to maximize the outcomes within the specific national context. Manchester University wants to compete 'in the big league', to use an analogy from sports.

Chapter 4 is about emergent strategy in that it examines shifts in the way that research groups which are dependent upon large-scale laboratories (facilities) interact. As such, this case represents a study at the micro-level of the historical shift identified above. These researchers and groups are dependent upon a complex set of instruments and technology – as well as human capital to use the physical infrastructure – in order to do research at all. Not everyone involved in this type of research will have a big lab, and so instead, one university usually takes a leading role, and others are allowed to interact, based on some set of rules. This chapter tells a story of an increasing 'marketification' of access to that scientific infrastructure, which is necessary to conduct national and international projects. Initially, access was run on a very informal base, with ideas of the collective effort, fair returns, national asset, and the like. Above all, teams located at other universities could trade their competencies and time to develop specific solutions for access. In more recent years, however, the governing mechanisms of this 'big science' have become more explicitly market driven. Money buys time. Money allows groups whom were previously outside of this national 'collective effort' to enter, wherever they are located on the globe. On the flip side, those groups without financial resources may still be able to trade extra effort for access, but only on the margin. Hence, research groups in resource-strong environments in Sweden and internationally increase their competitive ability to do this type of research – while incumbents with poor resources are squeezed out. This, the authors argue, also reflects a shift within the Swedish science policy system. We place no value judgement on the two systems, but simply point out that the selection mechanisms for being 'insider' or 'outsider' differs tremendously in these two different situations.

Hence, this first theme of 'emergent strategy' provides insights into a number of ongoing trends. We suggest that the three chapters show signs of an emergent historical shift in Europe. They reflect a situation where actors not only in the UK but also in Nordic and Continental countries move towards more formal organizational forms and towards specific management tools to achieve goals related to the provision of their specific knowledge-based services. Whether those chosen tools are indeed appropriate to reach the goals of a university is an unanswered question – instead, the point here is that the organizations are responding to the new competitive regimes by acting more like firms do.

Two of these chapters examine new organizational forms at the university level – namely collaborations, alliances and mergers. The sceptical reader might argue that these are in fact counter-evidence to our idea of competition. However, in the business strategy literature, collaborations, alliances and mergers have been clearly identified as ways to maximize the resources and opportunities of an organization (Grant, 2005; Tidd et al., 2005). As such, these examples are very similar to what we see going on within business, with a relevant example being the pharmaceutical industry. There, we can observe both major mergers into enormous firms as well as extensive collaboration and outsourcing of R&D to small firms. Universities appear to be engaged in them for the same reasons. Their intention with experimenting with new organizational forms is to increase their capabilities and resources, as well as put existing resources to more productive uses.

2.2 Differentiation and Specialization

The second theme is 'differentiation and specialization', across different populations of European universities. These chapters describe the process of how and why market-based mechanisms and other types of competitive forces are increasingly differentiating the population of universities. While perhaps news to the HEIs, theoretically, this should not come as a surprise since the level of specialization increases with the size of market as Stigler has already shown (Stigler 1951), and the market for research and education has greatly expanded since World War II.

Chapter 5 addresses differentiation, relative to the size of market and institutional structures. By examining PhD education specifically across European countries, the results show that countries respond differently. Four specific paths for responding to the need to revise PhD education are identified: inertia (Spain, Italy); dynamic renewal (Netherlands); abundance for all (Finland) and consolidated differences across organizations (UK). Specialization becomes more visible within the UK system, as well as across different European countries. The chapter demonstrates a strong relationship between universities having a differential outcome or not and the degree to which the nations have moved into the competitive regime. In particular, the Netherlands seems to foster very different types and some very fast-moving universities, especially in contrast to the more stagnant landscape of Spain and Italy.

Chapter 6 examines the total population of universities and colleges within Sweden, in order to identify specific sub-groups in terms of education, research, and access to resources from companies. The empirical analysis shows how the organizations end up in clearly different niches. Interestingly enough, the specialization shown is not in terms of education versus research, as might be expected from the American case. Instead, in the Swedish case, the colleges tend to have relatively few students. The universities with the highest research density and productivity tend also to have the most students. The latter category includes the old and broad all-encompassing universities as well as specialists in engineering, medicine and business. This latter category is thus relatively more dependent upon external resources for research than the colleges, and yet in total number, they educate many times more students.

Hence, this second theme is 'differentiation and specialization', where the chapters show that these processes of diversification and specialization clearly exist, and they are driven by a combination of internal choices and of new external competitive regimes. These chapters show that within different national institutional contexts, the individual university may be driven to make larger, or smaller, changes over time in order to position itself. These changes are due to the specifics of institutional context including incentives and allocation of resources. This type of analysis thus shows the relative position and strategies of the organizations, which calls into question some of the rhetorics of strategy and 'competition'. Over time, these changes in the institutional structure push universities providing apparently similar outputs into occupying very different niches.

2.3   Rethinking University–Industry Relations

The third theme is 'rethinking university–industry relations', including American and European data. These chapters question accepted wisdom within one incredibly popular topic of debate and public policy, namely the relationships of science and universities with businesses. We totally agree with the need for a broader perspective, which demonstrates theoretically and empirically that science and research have a variety of indirect and long-term impacts on society. These are highly important for understanding the role of universities as social institutions. However, our focus here is only on direct contacts, because even there, a focus upon the rationale for public policy and the ways of interacting needs serious rethinking, in general and in the European case.

Chapter 7 examines technology transfer in the USA, and thereby illustrates some of the dilemmas and inherent trade-offs of the new competitive regime and of universities acting like companies. One example is that universities increasingly do spin off new companies to satisfy the expectation that they are to be engaged in local economic development. Still, the metrics that measure the universities' performance focus only on a small range of performance parameters; the contributions of universities to their local environment go well beyond technology transfer per se. The chapter raises the issue that there may be a huge mismatch between what is measured and assessed in comparison with what matters the most (read: education and new ideas).

Chapter 8 goes to the core of the accepted wisdom about the European paradox. This chapter questions the general understanding of the low level of commercialization in some countries in Europe (Italy, France and Sweden) using patent statistics. Because of the teachers' privilege, one has to examine academic patents at the level of individuals (that is, individual inventors) rather than the level of organizations (that is, universities). By doing so, you get a completely different view of patenting in these three countries. The three countries have about the same proportion of academic patents as a percentage of total patents as the USA. Moreover, they patent in the same areas. This implies that this mechanism for technology transfer is working in Europe but in a different way compared to the USA. Ownership differs across the countries, but firms play an important role in owning the patents, and thereby assumedly also in using those patents to produce goods and services.

Chapter 9 addresses a similar question, but in a somewhat different way. Much research and public debate has suggested that key problems in Europe are the lack of 'entrepreneurial spirit' and a negative attitude towards commercialization, within the universities. This chapter examines these assumptions, and finds that 11 per cent of researchers within applied engineering fields have been involved in academic patents, in start-up companies, or in both patents and start-up firms. Hence, the population of surveyed researchers have actively commercialized research results, which questions the often loose references to lack of 'entrepreneurial spirit' in the Nordic context. Moreover, this survey focused upon the attitudes of the individuals, their research groups and their universities. For the different mechanisms for commercialization, the respondents were predominately positive and sometimes neutral. Interestingly enough, the survey did pick up that many interested in commercialization had little ideas about the overall university strategy towards commercialization, the technology transfer office and the like. This supports the idea that by imitating the American model of a separate technology transfer office, Sweden and Europe will likely introduce a parallel system, cut off from the core knowledge-based services of education and teaching. If universities want to commercialize more, they need to find new ways to engage their key asset, namely researchers and teachers, if they are to centralize these types of functions.

Chapter 10 examines how and why R&D subsidiaries of multinational enterprises have formal collaboration with three elite universities. This chapter clearly demonstrates that university–industry relations cannot be understood only from the university's perspective, but must instead be placed in relation to the strategy of the firms. The firms interviewed used a variety of mechanisms and identified a variety of rationales for interacting with university, in a manner confirming previous research on the American and British contexts. This chapter was then able to match mechanisms and rationale, in order to generate four distinct ideal types. These types can be used to identify how and why firms interact with universities. Some of the implications are that university strategy to commercialize and interact with society will need different portfolios of management tools and segmented behaviour, in order to match very different demands from different firms. Many wanted 'problem-solving' of very specific issues, and they were not interested in the broader implications of university research. Moreover, from this very small sample, an interesting observation raises issues. Only one of the three, Cambridge University, was able to attract firms to interact with scientists about leading edge research. They were there to find out about the path-breaking research, in a number of fields, including ones not normally classified as 'basic'.

Hence, this theme 'rethinking university–industry relations' demonstrates that even if we focus upon the direct contacts with multinational companies as well as start-up firms, we need to rethink accepted wisdom and arguments about how and why policy should intervene. Much of the debate in the European Union, in European countries and at individual universities assumes that Europe is way behind the USA in terms of commercializing university knowledge. In short, the analysis put forth for Europe is that the basic science is good but the commercialization is bad, and therefore more ought to be done to push commercialization. Hence, the 'European paradox' and 'Swedish paradox' have become policy buzzwords, to push changes in policy and institutional framework. Dosi et al. (2006) question this, especially the assumption of linear effects from science to industrial competitiveness. This book goes further, in that the results show that many of the accepted wisdoms do not hold up under empirical scrutiny. Many critical issues are raised about why and when companies interact with universities, as well as the implications for both research and industry.

2.4 Reflections

The fourth theme is 'reflections,' in relation to what competition might mean and unintended consequences of introducing a competitive-based paradigm for universities within Europe. These chapters are intended to stimulate debate and raise questions about how the identified competition and transformation is fundamentally changing the behaviour and goals of universities.

Chapter 11 addresses the long-term roles and perspectives of the university, especially the research-based university. In doing so, the chapter asks how universities compete, and how the measurement of specific variables (such as patents and papers) affects their outcome. This chapter thus answers affirmatively that universities do indeed compete but that it seems that the nature of *how and with whom* universities should compete has been misunderstood by university administrators and governments. The role of 'real' universities is not to compete with organizations that work on a much shorter timescale, such as vocational schools and industrial laboratories. The chapter thus questions the shift towards firm-like behaviour as various metrics miss the point of the 'true' goal of universities. A range of unintended consequences will arise from this misunderstanding. Chapter 12 proposes a theoretical understanding for what competition may mean, conceptually, within the higher educational sector. The chapter reviews different views on competition and what has been said about competition in the university sector. It finds that apart from talking about competition in terms of competition over reputation and so on, not much has been done. Consequently, this chapter proposes a specific analytical framework, developed for this context, using a Schumpeterian economics view. Chapter 13 is the current one, and brings together reflections about the chapters and the horizontal themes, in terms of what we have learnt and what the implications are for the future.

In concluding, the results of our research clearly show that the ongoing European transformation is placing great demands on the individual universities as organizations, as well as on the national educational, R&D and science systems within specific countries. External changes in national science and educational systems provide new incentives and resource flows, often based upon performance-linked measurements for teaching and education. The chapters in this book also show that European universities and colleges are changing substantially and trying to become more flexible, not only adapting to changing environments but also actively trying to develop new opportunities. The empirical contributions show that European universities are exhibiting new ways of competing, and that they are increasingly trying to act like knowledge-intensive firms, as they manage, analyse, innovate and act. They are competing with each other over resources, faculty and students as well as visibility, attention and resources from companies and financiers. Note, however, that also within the same organization, different individuals and groups may have conflicting competencies and goals, because some want to maximize teaching, while others focus on research, etc. Clearly then, this transformation is having unintended consequences, as well as changes in a social institution, as the universities deliver their knowledge-intensive services.

3.   A NEW COMPETITIVE REGIME

This section concludes the book, by moving to the implications of this new competitive regime for the future, in terms of the overall sector and in terms of strategy.

3.1   Restructuring the University Sector Through Opportunities and Pressures

Restructuring the university sector is related to opportunities and pressures, as felt at the organizational level. The reason is that the ability to change depends on perceived opportunities, available resources, incentives and the organizational capabilities to manage the process. Hence, in order to understand how the university sector will restructure in the future, one has to place universities (as well as firms) in a wider system of market and non-market institutions. Innovation-based competition is driven by opportunities, differentiation and selection across these dimensions.

As stated in the first pages of this book, the European university sector is in a process of change. As put so well by *The Economist* (February 26, 2005, 63): 'There used to be three near-certainties about higher education [in Europe]. It was supplied on a national basis, mostly to local students. It was government-regulated. And competition and profit were almost unknown concepts.. . .How that has changed'. This set of concluding remarks therefore addresses this ongoing transformation and restructuring of the European university sector, set in relation to opportunities and pressures.

Clearly, the selection environment of European universities has changed radically. Gone is the splendid but lone national policy actor that determined the role of universities. In its stead, in line with the expansion in the range of responsibilities of universities and in line with the expanded amount of metrics that the university is measured against, the university is dependent on a range of actors. The two principal forms of selection in the future will therefore be competition with other organizations – including universities and the entry of new organizations – as well as competition based upon using and developing new internal resources and ways of doing things (and the demise of those activities that no longer pass the test of economic viability).

Nowadays, the university is driven by external forces. We can imagine three arrows run from the external demands to change research, education and commercialization, towards the university and HEI.

The arrows from research and from education exemplify the pressures and forces for restructuring the sector, where the selection mechanisms each include the national institutional context and the globalized university sector. One example is the recent set of national institutional reforms in the Nordic countries of Norway, Denmark, Finland and Sweden, which are to implement performance-based measures to allocate research monies for 'fixed' government funding. In Norway and Denmark, this is linked to a reduction in the number of organizations. In contrast, in Sweden the official rhetoric for years have been to suggest voluntary co-operation between institutions and universities but so far only moderate progress can be seen. The discussion of performance-based measures for Nordic and for the post-RAE (research assessment exercise) in the UK include proposals to measure quality as citations and publication in high-impact journals (either as measured by Thompson/ISI Web of Science or national list). Higher education is also increasingly subject to reviews and evaluations, in order to create comparisons across organizations. Examples are the increasingly common rankings, accreditation and certification processes. The purposes of these exercises are to create more 'market-like conditions', where the MBA is an example of standardization of education (Hedmo et al. 2006). Another example of standardization of education is the attempt to create pan-European educational learning objectives promoted by the Bologna process. This should also increase student mobility, after each degree (or 'cycle' of education).

The arrow from commercialization to the university relates to selection mechanisms where the university is involved in technology transfer and university–industry interactions. The vast literature on university–industry relationships shows the role of informal networks. These informal networks help link entrepreneurial start-ups to the universities (often combined with some transfer of resources) as well as helping to explain why some multi-national enterprises continue working with geographically proximate HEIs. An interesting question at the moment is whether such informal networks will remain important to access company interactions and monies in the future, given the push within MNEs to use more formalized measurement techniques and to develop international centres of R&D excellence. It is likely many of the issues of commercialization and of university–industry interactions will be increasingly driven by the business logic of the companies, instead of by government policy.

For the future, then, our theoretical perspective suggests that the universities will change due to new opportunities and pressure (or forces) from a changing selection environment. This includes new negative and positive feedback mechanisms but also the possibility of universities creating and exploiting new opportunities. There are many ways to compete, in the sense developed in this book. Competition can include collaboration (such as alliances and larger projects) as well as specialization and cooperation to ensure a special division of labour. Learning and positioning are also a key part of the notion of competition developed here. These transformation pressures are underway, and lead to a restructuring into specialized providers. This means a very different university and college in the future.

The question here is, given this new situation, what types of changes do we expect to see in the future? In what direction may restructuring head?

One aspect of restructuring the sector has to do with the dynamics between the size of the market and the behaviour of specific organizations (or 'knowledge businesses'). The size of the market for research and education has been, and still is, expanding rapidly, as a higher proportion of European youths take higher degrees. The degree of specialization increases with the size of the market (Young 1928; Stigler 1951). Hence, we expect more differentiation and specialization across competing and collaborating organizations in the university sector (which may be analysed within specific countries or across different countries). American universities are definitely expanding into the global market. As an example, Doha in Qatar has an 'Education City', where five American schools have started degree programmes on the huge campus. The five universities active in 2008 provide education in areas in which they excel, such as Cornell Medical School and Texas A&M petroleum engineering.

In a more abstract sense, these ideas about increasing future differentiation and specialization are important concepts for the actors, within Schumpeterian-inspired economics, because there is no equilibrium around which the average will converge. Learning, innovating, building competencies and reallocating existing resources to new ventures are therefore keys to the process of differentiation and specialization in the future. Hence, it makes 'sense' for Texas A&M to export petroleum engineering education to Doha, because they have highly specialized equipment, research and education about oil related issues, based on years of experience in Texas. This has implications for the future. Despite the broad mandate of many universities, the HEIs will have to develop internal capabilities and obtain external resources, which the organization can then use to develop new combinations of offerings.[1] Previous chapters have already shown some of the ongoing experimentation and specialization patterns that have evolved over the last decade in Europe.

A related, second aspect is how the organization will develop a 'business logic' or 'business model'. One type of business logic is to focus upon large, integrated units which can develop a 'critical mass' of researchers and teachers to compete internationally. Many of the large universities have become highly vertically integrated over the past several decades, and they are basically controlling many aspects of learning. German universities regularly teach more than 800 undergraduates taking the same class. More recently, the aspect that has demanded most attention within the EU is the scale of technological inputs such as the quest for a European Institute of Technology. In some circles, the push then is to lift that idea of large-scale, vertically-integrated organizations from the national to the European level. As with industrial policy of the past, we interpret these pushes as a 'European national champion' for higher education.

However, we feel that scale is only a small part of the quest for excellence, also forcefully documented in Bonaccorsi and Daraio (2007). Given the amount of uncertainty in the future and given the innovativeness of others in the game, it is not a viable strategy just to react to external pressures and opportunities through a vertically-integrated strategy and by only taking strong decisive actions at top management level. So, the third aspect is to develop a more flexible business logic and model. We argue that a different, more appropriate business logic is to consider how the organization can use scope in both inputs and outputs, to cope with a world of such rapid and profound change. We would argue that if the competitive logic of a knowledge-based firm is a relevant model also for universities, then scale is of less importance compared to scope in both inputs and outputs. A more realistic approach is to explore possible futures of the university as seen through a process of learning, experimentation and discovery. Not so surprisingly given the results from management and strategic literature, under a new, more competitive regime, university management will also have to ask how to capitalize on their strength and what to outsource. This implies a more flexible business logic, where core assets are used productively as well as external alliances to promote change needed to respond to external opportunities and pressures.

We have already seen that there are emerging webs of alliances and mergers, where the Manchester merger is one of the more spectacular. And evidence from different international mergers seems to suggest that university mergers, international offices and foreign-based units are becoming quite common management techniques. We can see a number of foreign campus locations, even by the Ivy League universities. For instance, MIT put up a new logistics institute in Zaragoza and various universities in Australia (Monash, Curtin and RMIT). The University of Nottingham has gone transnational setting up branch campuses. There were 82 branch campuses in the world in 2006 compared to 24 in 2002 (OBHE, 2006). The focus of these new locations are mostly in providing undergraduate education and the motives, at least the rhetoric, seem to see these investments as natural continuation of their internationalization strategies. However, universities have run into legal and financial problems as a consequence of their attempt to create campuses offshore and other modes of internationalization. Nonetheless, we expect these processes to continue, we also expect more international alliances and units as well as hostile takeovers in the future. As Duderstadt (2000) concludes, the evolution of world culture could even lead to the establishment of several world universities as the focal point for some specific topics of international order.

A related but different outcome from this push towards capitalizing on large-scale internal capabilities and outsourcing with partners is to develop small niche organizations. One example may be the specialized suppliers of business education, which only provide the education, often through alliances with international partners to grant the actual degree. Hence, in contrast to the above trends towards concentration, the move away from a vertically integrated university would of course see entry, exit, and the movement of existing actors into new markets. This implies a future with the entry of new differentiated competitors as well as untraditional alliances say between universities and various companies specialized in packaging and delivering content. Clearly, we can imagine a world where universities might be superior at producing superior research and educational content but they could let others package and deliver the services to a much more sophisticated and picky customer than a decade ago. There are of course many other university activities that can be outsourced. This can happen in the future, although university managers and techniques as well as incentive structures inside the university are often rather conservative, and seem to instead push for keeping as much in-house as possible. Thus, there will be counter-trends towards an out-sourced, networked type of organization.

Therefore, a fourth aspect for the future is how and where to allow for experimentation, both internally and in collaborations. This implies that the university and college must allow experimentation, ideas or paradigms to change, and that how they experiment will affect future positions. The transformation of Michigan as described by Duderstadt (2000) shows how experimentation can be allowed at a large university. They first followed a traditional approach to planning and change involving a formal strategic process. But during this process and when their understanding about the fundamental driving forces increased they realized how profound and rapid the changes were and they came to the conclusion 'that the most realistic near-term approach was to explore possible futures of the university through experimentation and discovery' (Duderstadt, 2000, p. 277).

The consequences of experimentation will be visible in the variety of changes, across the organization. It may be changes in the things (products/services) which an organization offers, changes in the ways in which they are created and delivered, changes in the context in which the products/services are introduced and changes in the underlying mental and business models which frame what the university does. Australian universities, for example, have led the way in educating international (especially Asian) students, through combinations of changes at the Australian campus and through degree programmes delivered in other countries.

An important question is then how experimentation will be playing out within European universities and colleges. We feel that Europe is struggling with the massification of education – accompanied by demands for excellence of research – without a clear vision of how to achieve those goals. The conflicting modes of operation and goals can be found in this shift from an elite social institution supported by public policy to a knowledge business dependent upon many 'customers'. Public policy has clearly pushed a new type of organization in recent decades. European governments have shifted their attention from first class research per se paired with elitist education towards mass education (Trow, 1974). At the same time, the governments across Europe are deregulating which gives universities the opportunity to be less dependent upon government and upon local and national students for earning their income. Thus, universities have dramatically expanded and increased in absolute numbers during the last decades, and have been taking in a higher proportion of international students. Unfortunately, as the European universities tend to do many things, we expect that their systems are poorly prepared to accept students in increasing number and with greater variance in background and skills. They need new solutions for the future.

The fifth aspect is how far European universities and HEIs are prepared to become specialist suppliers of knowledge. The fifth aspect is thus specialization. Theoretically, it is possible to become specialized in only one of the knowledge-intensive services or by creating and filling new types of niches across the services. As to the first point, clearly in the USA some organizations like University of Phoenix already primarily focus upon education, replicated across the country, whereas others like Stanford are primarily known for their research, combined with educational and commercialization services. As to niches, business schools in Europe can use a specialist 'quality' niche to compete on the mass market for education such as MBAs where INSEAD has used American alliances to compete globally or by combining business education with very specific fields of engineering knowledge for an application, such as risk and environmental management. Of course, rather than specializing, the organizations can continue on the business logic of the large-scale, integrated organization. Hence, instead of specializing, the other alternative is to come up with ways that the university can satisfy all of its roles at the same time, although even the large American research universities such as Harvard have difficulties providing all three services. Still, the small regional colleges can use specialized research to innovate in undergraduate education as has been done by Mälardalen Research and Technology Centre at the University College of Mälardalen (Geschwind and Johansson, 2008).

This sixth aspect is thus that the future outcomes in terms of specialization (or not) will partly depend upon the national context. European countries differ in terms of the relative specialization of universities, where in some countries like Germany, universities co-exist with the Max Planck (for basic research) and Fraunhouf Institutes (for applied research) whereas in countries with very different innovation systems – like Sweden – universities and colleges juggle most of these roles. The future outcomes will also depend on what happens when one organization (or ideal type of organization) does start 'winning' at the apparent expense of others. An example is when those universities which are able to mobilize internally and be goal-directed towards calls for large-scale research centres like the Germany initiative for excellence, gain access larger amounts of financing. The question is whether there is a tendency for financiers to 'evenly and fairly' distribute resources across organizations in the next round. Future outcomes also depend upon internal politics and power games. As an example, top management at elite European organizations like Bocconi are pushing for 'centres of excellence', but powerful university departments then react, and push to recreate themselves as a 'centre', whether or not they fulfil the so-called objective criteria for 'excellence'. In contrast, in the UK context, universities have had few qualms about firing more than half the staff in some areas like the Imperial College business school (before it became the Tanaka Business School) – if deemed necessary to reach excellence.

Hence, clearly the decisions of both the leaders of universities and those of national actors like research councils and ministries of education will affect whether Europe really does go along this path towards a harsher competitive regime, which will demand a much higher degree of differentiation and specialization. Many of the reactions listed above would put the selection mechanisms out of play, allowing many actors to not become excellent within narrow fields of specialization.

Finally, the overall deregulation of the university and HEI sector will promote the differing possible paths of restructuring which have been identified above. The point here is that we believe that changes in markets, technologies and competitors will trigger similar restructuring as one can witness in sectors that were deregulated. From other examples like the deregulation of the public telecommunications sector and the so-called PTTs (Post, Telecommunications and Telegraph) public telecom sector in Europe, one can learn two things. One is that the deregulation and decreasing government control of economic sectors that once were dominated by public control will lead to massive transformation. Deregulation leads to changes within many domains, including organizational, institutional and technological. Another is that a successful adjustment unleashed by market forces will need intelligent re-regulation of a more independent sector in order to avoid many of the negative consequences faced in deregulated manufacturing sectors. At the moment, many European universities and colleges seem to be growing in all directions, and in all three of their roles related to knowledge-intensive services. This will cause them difficulties in the future, especially if they are reactive instead of innovative.

3.2 Creating Change through Strategy and Competencies

Strategy is the main process that binds cognition, control and coordination together for the organization. Mintzberg and Waters (1985) differentiated between deliberate, emergent and unrealized strategy and also identified many ideal types, where the intended plan did not work out as assumed. In this book, we view strategy as an emergent process, which must be tested against the external selection environment, and so a priori, we assume more experimentation than one would assume if the university were run by one centralized decision-maker. In order to know whether universities are 'competitive' and what makes a university 'competitive', we believe that more work needs to be done on analysing strategy and understanding the factors driving and inhibiting the search for 'competitive advantage' in the provision of their knowledge-based services, within a global knowledge economy. Specifically, how does a broad view of innovation as including both new technologies and new ways of doing things relate to core internal organizational problems of cognition coordination and control? Clearly, what specific HEIs can do in terms of their actions, strategies and perceptions of competition is related to the restructuring of the university sector, as discussed above, including the clear importance of national institutional contexts and global innovation systems. Continental and Nordic national contexts are (so far) not as driven by market-based mechanisms as Anglo-Saxon ones – but the reforms underway are clearly pushing many national contexts towards competitive funding regimes, for both education and research.

Moreover, many organizations must now decide whether they choose to really compete globally or whether they choose to compete in a much defined and very local or regional niche. Those aiming to be 'world leading' need one set of strategy and management tools to push international standards and mobility of resources and people but those intent upon being 'best in their municipalities' need a very different set. So what does this mean, for creating change through strategy and competencies?

We can now imagine internal pressures for change, such that there are arrows running from the university and HEI, out to research, education and commercialization. They run from the organization and out, because of the role of strategy and competencies, so that the organization can not only respond to external environmental pressures, but also attempt to change their selection environment.

Hence, these arrows should represent how the organization can change itself – and attempt to change the external environment. In terms of research, the UK example under the RAE clearly demonstrated the 'market value' of particular staff, able to publish and of organizing teams into larger groups to bid for very large grants. In terms of education, most of Europe has been offering new educational programmes in terms of areas and degrees, as well as attempting to change the pedagogical ambitions to match financing and ambition. The Bologna process is being used to try to standardize and replicate, in a situation of much experimentation. In terms of commercialization, the HEIs are trying to position themselves both through networks (who you know) as well as showing that 'best' in a particular field (what they know). These are examples of how HEIs are changing their strategies and competencies.

Indeed, strategy and strategic discussions are by now a rather common vocabulary among university boardrooms and university management. Hence, an interesting result from this book is to question what strategy means in higher education institutes. The results can be interpreted in terms of the debates within strategic management about implicit versus explicit and about bottom-up versus top-down strategies. Today, most European universities are declaring their explicit (macro) strategies.

However, often, as analysed in sections 2 and 3.1 of this chapter, this book demonstrates that European universities often have very implicit (micro) strategies, from the bottom-up, which result from a broad set of decisions and ways of working. These are strategies, even though the actors have not conceptualized it that way. One could even go so far as to say that sometimes, they only discovered after a while that they have a 'strategy' or 'are competing'. For example, they discover that competition is ongoing de facto when their educational programmes attract many (or high quality) students or that their research agenda in an area holds world class and thereby brings in external resources.

A first aspect is experimentation with strategy. Given that European universities face a new situation, we can ask, what are the strategies identified in this book, as to how universities compete? The chapters analysed in section 2 indicate that the following strategies are already being tried in Europe:

- Specialization (differentiation) is being used, and should help to improve performance, within specific national institutional contexts.
- Collaboration and alliances as an alternative to 'going it alone'.
- Mergers are possible but require much top management.
- Larger universities get more resources.
- Specific labs are changing, and turning the research process into a more organized, strategic process by using market-based mechanisms.
- Some researchers are able to take out patents and start companies, as well as write scientific papers and get grants. However, many feel they lack the necessary skills.
- European universities have some patents, but much of the IPR is held at individual level (not assigned to university).
- Firms have very different rationale, and mechanisms, for interacting with universities. This requires more nuanced interactions at the research group and university levels.

- It is possible to develop multiple mechanisms for tech transfer, within specific national contexts, and it is also necessary to assess negative side-effects.
- Competition may not be the only alternative, given the long history of the university in defending other societal values.

The interesting question is how these developments in strategy and building competencies will affect the future. By now a large innovation literature suggests that variation between innovation and performance depends on three major factors (Tidd 2006): (1) Management – differences in cognition, co-ordination and control (learning); (2) Scale – of technological inputs – critical mass, and market value of commercial outputs – complementary assets; and (3) Opportunity – spill over within sectors and between firms. In our view, these factors do influence the positioning and organizations of universities as well but, and as usual, one has to take account of various sector specificities. It is the interplay between environmental changes, innovation and deliberate strategic actions that will determine the consequences of the new competitive paradigm for the future.

A second aspect is what the 'knowledge business' means for the traditional views of the university. For many, the comparison with a knowledge-based company may be at first sight incompatible with the key roles and values that must be protected and preserved during the period of transformation such as education of the young and preservation of culture or academic freedom as a rational spirit of enquiry and commitment to shared governance. Clearly these are values that have to be protected (by some universities). But our knowledge of how new knowledge-based firms are governed show both similarities and differences but also a potential for learning.

Hence, a third aspect is whether these new strategies will work 'better' than the old. As a result of these shifts in strategy and management, the universities and colleges will change fundamentally, including many unintended consequences and a push to maximize the quantifiable performance measures, at the loss of other activities and values. This will raise many very interesting issues about whether this explicit and top-down process of strategy works (in general) better over the longer term, within knowledge-intensive services. In the short run, specific outcomes can be maximized, and that in itself will lead to positive feedbacks within national institutional systems with quantifiable and specific measures for allocating resources.

The longer run is different. Research indicates that knowledge-based services depend upon a more complex set of commitments to continue to excel. One aspect of knowledge-intensive services is the dependency upon individuals and creative groups, and so a key issue is whether they will remain committed to this new system. Individual researchers and research groups must be included because, in many ways, universities act as a hotel for a series of more or less motivated and driven individuals (Gibbons et al., 1994). Individuals and research groups often work like small businesses, in that they demand degrees of autonomy in return for actively leading activities to develop the 'business'. Their business includes activities such as designing and winning research grants, developing strategies to publish papers and improving the quality of teaching to attract future talented students into their field. These activities thereby contribute to the 'knowledge-based services' offered by the university – but the activities can be run in many ways, from very loosely to very tightly controlled by management. Many people work at universities, as an alternative to working at companies – so why stay if the control and coordination systems are similar but the pay is worse? Hence, we expect increasing pay for talented people, as has happened in the UK.

A fourth, related aspect is the need for diversity, which will continue to be a prerequisite for the organizations since science, research and commercialization are genuinely uncertain activities. To balance the need for strict control and diversity, we expect that experimentation with new organizational forms like centres and networks will continue and even accelerate. Hence, we feel that even though universities must do more to identify and manage their niche, they must also find new ways to manage complex knowledge-intensive services, which are dependent both upon key top individuals as well as larger groups.

A fifth aspect goes beyond the current attempt to capture control from the top-down. The new push is likely to be how to move from financial management techniques, to ones which enable innovation and synergies within knowledge-intensive services. A quote from the strategy process at University College of London highlights the stakes involved in meeting future challenges: 'I believe the time is right for a fundamental review of this great institution, not from a perspective of financial stringency (though we are in exceptionally uncertain times financially), but from a sense of making the most of our opportunities for the next 10 years' (Malcolm Grant, Provost and President, University College London UCL*).*

From this perspective we see that the most critical challenge is to develop the capacity to change and remove the constraints that prevent them from responding to the needs of a rapidly changing environment. This adaptation will depend on the universities' (at all layers) collective ability to learn and to improve products and processes. Thus the universities will likely try to run themselves as business – even at the risk of losing talented people. We expect that many universities will have to tighten their strategic processes considerably. First, they have to search the environment for technical and economic opportunities to guide the process of change. Then they have to ensure a good match/fit between the strategy and the proposed change – without a knee-jerk response to a competitor. They will have to recognize the limitation of their competence base and connect to external sources of knowledge, information and equipment. In short, universities need to learn, become more competent. And increased learning will lead to structural change in the university sector.

The sixth aspect is therefore strategy and building competences, from a dynamic, innovation perspective. Companies achieve competitive advantage through acts of innovation. They approach innovation in its broadest sense including both new technologies and new ways of doing things. And when the premium for innovation increases it has to be actively managed. This means exploiting change as an opportunity for a different business and service. It is capable of being presented as a discipline, capable of being learned, capable of being practised. This is also increasingly the environment universities face. When value is created through innovation in positions and paradigms it has to be co-ordinated and controlled in a much more sophisticated fashion. Our guess (or hope?) is that simple approaches to top-down management style will soon be replaced by more sophisticated management tools and techniques, used within other knowledge-intensive sectors like consultancies and professional societies.

A related, seventh aspect is costs and how to choose amongst alternative 'customers'. In line with the overall growth of universities during recent decades, their costs have increased greatly, and this is creating problems at the core. Although public policy has been demanding increasing access to higher education, at the same time European governments are becoming increasingly reluctant to fund the increased costs of university research and education, especially when universities are unable to show the relevance of output. Universities and colleges become more open to other influences, and in parallel, other actors have become more explicitly interested in what universities do and how well they do it. Entering the market is the picky student who has a tremendous set of education options to choose from. Just as important, firms are interested in what universities do, even more so than in the past as Swedish data seem to suggest (Broström and Deiaco, 2007). In the future, these multiple dependencies upon different types of 'customers' will then create tensions in terms of what the university and college is doing or should be doing. Each of these services may rely upon different income streams and sets of resources in order to deliver a portfolio of specified knowledge-based services. Universities compete with some others in order to attract appropriate income streams and resources, as well as to deliver the desirable quality of services. In most countries, different types of higher education as well as institutes compete in different niches –

to obtain research grants, students, other sources of money, faculty, rankings, contacts, etc.

4. CONCLUDING REMARKS

Deciding upon the boundaries of what will be 'inside' and what will be 'outside' the university of the future will depend upon which knowledge-intensive services, and in what areas, that they are concentrating.

European universities and their context are changing as explained in the initial propositions to this chapter. Of course, selection in these terms is a tough game. An interesting issue then is how governments will act, and particularly to what extent European governments will allow selection mechanisms to push out the 'losers' and prioritize the 'winners'. We may expect a push to avoid a harsher competitive regime in the national and European contexts, but future research needs more detailed understanding of how Asia is now also competing with Europe to develop top-ranking institutions. That is one reason for the choice of buildings on the cover of this book. There, these industrial dynamics are being applied to the whole sector, and we can see many examples of new HEIs being started (or existing ones rapidly expanding) in Asia and these newcomers are quickly developing and finding profitable niches.

This book provides many examples of how strategy and management are moving from implicit to explicit action, and from a bottom-up to a top-down process. As compared to traditional academic governance, Europe is starting to experience explicit top-down strategy and management styles, with explicit performance-related goals. The shift now is towards much more explicit statements of strategy, linked to new goals, micro related organizational changes, and management tools. As part of this shift, universities themselves are then acting more like firms do. For example, they are changing organizational forms and institutions. They are beginning to conceptualize education, research, and 'societal usefulness' (including commercialization) as knowledge-intensive services, and try to reorganize internal processes to deliver those services. Our view is that top management will therefore do more in the future to obtain power, and try to direct faculty and students towards quantifiable goals.

For universities, their knowledge-based services are linked to their three core activities of research, education and societal interaction – but how, why, and when do they gain advantage either from specializing in one or two as opposed to diversifying across all three to gain synergies? The traditional view is that research–education cross-fertilize each other, but if they are becoming more standardized – as argued above – then at least the lower levels of education and the more 'normal science' part of research would not necessarily require much cross-fertilization. This means that the entire sector may deverticalize compared to today. This allows organizations to occupy more specialized niches, within the larger university sector. American community colleges, for example, focus upon providing teaching to certain types of students, whereas the famous American research universities specialize in cutting-edge research as well as advanced teaching (usually to a low number of students).

A main shift affecting the universities is the balance between elite-mass education and between unique service and standardized ones. Standardization of knowledge-intensive services in the sense detailed above enables comparisons of what is being 'measured' or 'provided' by different HEIs. However, standardization is only one side of the story. As is well established in management and strategy literature from business and industry studies, much of competition is about differentiating and offering unique products and services – rather than about competing over mass market and commodity products and services. The reason is that unique products and services generally compete on more abstract aspects like quality, experience and reputation whereas the mass market and commodity products and services compete primarily upon price.

Therefore, immediate decisions about whether to prioritize existing competencies or develop new ones will have long-term effects on the overall specialization of the organization. Specializations – what they are good at and whether others recognize and provide resources – directly affects the ability of universities and specific research groups to compete. We mean that although some major areas like 'economics' or 'physics' would not be allowed to disappear, some universities and research groups can still be so starved for resources that they do disappear, migrate abroad and/or find alternative income streams. Therefore, prioritizing between historical specializations and new ones has large effects on future competitiveness. However, these 'decisions' are made not only or even not primarily by university vice-chancellors but by them in combination with research groups. Hence, this is a game in an evolutionary sense where there are no possible optimal outcomes. Instead, a variety of outcomes are possible, and cycles of learning and building competencies in particular fields affect the delivery of research and education.

Clearly, the new competitive paradigm implies that there is variation on which selection can do its work. The current push to qualify and measure the output of universities has had consequences. With the use of different metrics, selection processes for resources will reward those that perform in relation to them. But are we left with a dilemma? On the one hand universities need internal stability, security and continuity, and on the other hand, selection in a world of multiple pressures, the internal mode of organization has to fit with the demands of the external environment. We do not have an answer to this. However, one thing seems clear. European universities will provide more value for their money if they face a greater extent of competition in the sense that depending upon what they sow, they will reap. This does not mean that an extreme, winner takes all approach is the 'best' in any sense.

NOTE

1. Or, put in other words, this organizational ability to use internal resources to provide offerings in a specific selection environment will determine the competitive advantage of the specific organization in the future, within a larger population.

REFERENCES

Bonaccorsi, A. and C. Daraio (2007), *Universities and Strategic Knowledge Creation: Specialization and Performance in Europe*, Cheltenham, UK and Northampton, MA, USA: Edward Elgar.

Broström, A. and E. Deiaco (2007), 'Räcker det med Forskning i Världsklass?: Nya Perspektiv på Teknikföretagens Samarbete med Offentligt Finansierade Forskningsmiljöer', ['Is world leading research enough?']. SISTER Arbetsrapport 2007:73.

Dosi, G., P. Llerena and M. Sylos Labini (2006), 'The relationship between science, technologies, and their industrial exploitation: an illustration through the myths and realities of the so-called 'European Paradox', *Research Policy*, 35 (10), 1450–64.

Duderstadt, James J. (2000), *A University for the 21st Century*, Ann Arbor, MI: University of Michigan Press.

The Economist (2005), 'Special report on universities', 26 February, p. 63.

Geschwind, L. and M. Johansson (2008), 'Utbildningsanknytning i praktiken – En fallstudie av KK-stiftelsens profilsatningar vid fyra unga lärosäten', SISTER Arbets rapport 2008: 86.

Gibbons, M., C. Limoges, H. Nowotony, S. Schwartzman, P. Scott and M. Trow (1994), *The New Production of Knowledge: The Dynamics of Science and Research in Contemporary Society*, London: Sage.

Grant, Robert M. (2005), *Contemporary Strategy Analysis*, 5th edn, Malden, MA: Blackwell Publishing.

Hedmo, T., K. Sahlin-Andersson and L.Wedlin (2006), 'Is a global organizational field of higher education emerging? Management education as an early example', in G. Krücken, A. Kosmützky and M. Torka (eds), Towards a Multiversity? Universities between Global Trends and National Traditions, Bielefeld, Germany: transcript-Verlag.

Mintzberg, H. and J.A. Waters (1985), 'Of strategies, deliberate and emergent', *Strategic Management Journal*, 6 (3), 257–72.

Stigler, G.J. (1951), 'The division of labour is limited by the extent of the market', *Journal of Political Economy*, **59** (June), 185–93.

Tidd, Joe (2006), *From Knowledge Management to Strategic Competences.* 2nd edn, London: Imperial College Press.

Tidd, Joe, John Bessant and Keith Pavitt (2005), *Managing Innovation: Integrating Technological, Market and Organizational Change*, 3rd edn, New York: John Wiley & Sons.

Trow, M. (1974), 'Problems in the transition from elite to mass higher education', in 'Policies for Higher Education', from the *General Report on the Conference on Future Structures of Post-Secondary Education*, Paris: Organisation for Economic Co-operation and Development, pp. 55–101.

Verbik, L. and C. Merkley (2006), 'The international branch campus – models and trends', The Observatory on Borderless Higher Education', accessed 5 August 2008 at www.obhe.ac.uk/products/reports/.

Young, A.A. (1928), 'Increasing returns and economic progress', *Economic Journal*, **38**, 527–42.

Index

SOLD TO:

PROFESSOR ROGER KING
MBS Gratis Account
* * * *
* * * *

Original

MARST

Distribution, fulfilment and

GB787
Marston Book Servi
160 Milton Park, Abingdon, Oxford
Tel: (01235) 465500 Fax: (

64453000   64453000 AA;3461259   IB1929712 OHI

Pick Batch				Batch/Doc	Transact
HSS 30962			CSG 0810	47811/097	Gratis

Pub Code	Edition Binding	Standard Book No.	Author/Title		
			GRATIS INVOICE		
			These title(s) are being sent with the comp		
EE					
EE	1P	9781849804349	Dues Released, Our Document Ref B0610704 2		
			MCKELVEY\LEARN TO COMPETE IN EURO UNI'S		

E & OE

TOTAL
DUES

0.6

Registered Office: 160 Milton Park, Abingdon, OX14

SHIP TO:

PROFESSOR ROGER KING
TELHAM LODGE
TELHAM LANE
BATTLE
EAST SUSSEX
TN33 0SN

ON
print solutions

4454 78
es Ltd.
hire, OX14 4SD, U.K.
1235) 465555   (001)

n Type	Account No	Date/Tax Point	Payment Terms	Document No.	Page
nvoice	64453000	16-AUG-10	Terms: 30 Days	IB1929712	1

Customer Reference	QTY	Retail Price	Net *	Discount	Value	VAT	VAT Amount
iments of The Publisher							
-MAY-10							
KIN/BAT	1	29.95	*				

Total Quantity	1

VAT Codes	

SUB TOTAL	
CARRIAGE	
TOTAL VAT	
TOTAL TO PAY	

4SD. Registered in England No: 1186721